D1356419

INVESTMENT TREATIES
AND THE RULE OF LAW PROMISE

Investment treaties are said to improve the rule of law in the states which enter into them. Fearing claims, governments will internalise international investment obligations into their decision-making processes, resulting in positive spillover effects on the rule of law. Such arguments have never been backed by empirical research. This book presents an analytical framework for thinking about the internalisation of international commitments in governmental decision making that takes account of the complexities of governance. In so doing, it provides a typology of processes whereby international treaty obligations may be internalised by governments and identifies factors that may affect whether and to what extent international commitments are internalised in governmental decision making. This framework serves as the background for the main body of the book in which empirical case studies address whether and how a select group of governments in Asia internalise international investment treaty obligations in their decision making.

N. JANSEN CALAMITA is Head of Investment Law and Policy, Centre for International Law; Research Associate Professor (CIL), Faculty of Law, National University of Singapore.

AYELET BERMAN is Lead of Global Health Law and Governance, and Senior Research Fellow, Centre for International Law; Adjunct Assistant Professor, Faculty of Law, National University of Singapore.

INVESTMENT TREATIES AND THE RULE OF LAW PROMISE

The Internalisation of International Commitments in Asia

Edited by

N. JANSEN CALAMITA
National University of Singapore

AYELET BERMAN
National University of Singapore

CAMBRIDGE
UNIVERSITY PRESS

CAMBRIDGE
UNIVERSITY PRESS

University Printing House, Cambridge CB2 8BS, United Kingdom

One Liberty Plaza, 20th Floor, New York, NY 10006, USA

477 Williamstown Road, Port Melbourne, VIC 3207, Australia

314–321, 3rd Floor, Plot 3, Splendor Forum, Jasola District Centre,
New Delhi – 110025, India

103 Penang Road, #05–06/07, Visioncrest Commercial, Singapore 238467

Cambridge University Press is part of the University of Cambridge.

It furthers the University's mission by disseminating knowledge in the pursuit of
education, learning, and research at the highest international levels of excellence.

www.cambridge.org
Information on this title: www.cambridge.org/9781009153010
DOI: 10.1017/9781009152990

© Cambridge University Press 2022

First published 2022

A catalogue record for this publication is available from the British Library.

Library of Congress Cataloging-in-Publication Data
Names: Calamita, N. Jansen, editor. | Berman, Ayelet, editor.
Title: Investment treaties and the rule of law promise : the internalisation of
international commitments in Asia / edited by N. Jansen Calamita, National University of
Singapore; Ayelet Berman, National University of Singapore.
Description: Cambridge, United Kingdom ; New York, NY : Cambridge University Press,
2022. | Includes bibliographical references and index.
Identifiers: LCCN 2022016942 | ISBN 9781009153010 (hardback) | ISBN
9781009152990 (ebook)
Subjects: LCSH: Investments, Foreign – Law and legislation – Asia. | Investments, Foreign
(International law) | Rule of law.
Classification: LCC KNC747 .I588 2022 | DDC 346/.5092–dc23/eng/20220628
LC record available at https://lccn.loc.gov/2022016942

ISBN 978-1-009-15301-0 Hardback

For Alyda and Frank and Nancy and Johann
JANSEN

For Michel and Viki and Asaf and Ella and Imri and Itai
AYELET

CONTENTS

vii

NOTES ON CONTRIBUTORS

DAFINA ATANASOVA is a lecturer at the Geneva LLM in international dispute settlement (MIDS), a joint program of the Graduate Institute of International and Development Studies (IHEID) and the University of Geneva. She teaches international commercial and investment arbitration and carries out research in the field of international economic law. She holds a PhD from the University of Geneva (summa cum laude). Prior to joining the MIDS, Dafina was a postdoctoral research fellow at the Centre for International Law, National University of Singapore. She worked as a legal consultant at UNCTAD, a research assistant at the University of Geneva and an associate at Dokovska, Atanassov and Partners LLP (Sofia, Bulgaria).

AYELET BERMAN is Lead of the Global Health Law and Governance Program and Senior Research Fellow at the Centre for International Law and Adjunct Assistant Professor at the Faculty of Law, National University of Singapore. She is Co-Chair of the American Society of International Law International Organizations Interest Group. Her research focuses on global governance and regulation. She has published in peer-reviewed journals, including the *American Journal of International Law (Unbound)* and the *European Journal of International Law*. She is the co-editor of the book *Rethinking Participation in Global Governance* (Oxford University Press, 2022). She holds a PhD (summa cum laude) and DEA from the Graduate Institute in Geneva and an LLB (magna cum laude) from the Hebrew University.

JONATHAN BONNITCHA is a senior lecturer in the Faculty of Law and Justice at the University of New South Wales. His primary area of research interest is international economic governance, with a particular interest in investment treaties. He is the author of two books – *The Political Economy of the Investment Treaty Regime* (Oxford University Press, 2017) and *Substantive Protection under Investment Treaties: A Legal and Economic*

Analysis (Cambridge University Press, 2014) – as well as many academic articles. He holds degrees of DPhil, MPhil and BCL (Bachelor of Civil Law) from the University of Oxford and degrees of LLB and BEc (Soc. Sci.) from the University of Sydney. Jonathan lived in Myanmar from 2013 to 2016, where he worked as an advisor to the Myanmar Government on investment governance.

N. JANSEN CALAMITA is Head of Investment Law and Policy at the Centre for International Law and Research Associate Professor (CIL) at the Faculty of Law, National University of Singapore. He is the author of *ASEAN and the Reform of Investor-State Dispute Settlement* (Edward Elgar, 2022) as well as many academic articles on issues related to international investment law and international dispute resolution. Prior to entering academia, he served in the Office of the Legal Adviser in the US Department of State and as a member of the UNCITRAL Secretariat. Jansen is a series co-editor (with Loretta Malintoppi) of *International Litigation in Practice* (Brill) and a member of the editorial board of the *Yearbook on International Law and Policy* (Oxford University Press). He holds a BCL from the University of Oxford and a JD (Doctor of Jurisprudence) (magna cum laude) from Boston University School of Law. He continues to advise governments and international organisations on matters relating to international investment law and dispute resolution.

SACHINTHA DIAS is State Counsel for the Attorney-General's Department of Sri Lanka. He is a DPhil candidate in international law at the Faculty of Law, University of Oxford, supported by the Faculty of Law Graduate Scholarship and the Firth Senior Scholarship. His research focuses on international organisations and their jurisdictional immunities before domestic courts. He holds an MPhil in international law and a BCL with distinction from the University of Oxford and an LLB with first class honours from the University of Colombo. He was the winner of the Honoré Scholarship awarded by the Oxford Law Faculty and The Queen's College for the BCL and the university-wide Tilak Hettiarachchi award for academic excellence from the University of Colombo for his LLB.

YOUNSIK KIM is an associate professor of constitutional law at Sungshin Women's University in Korea. Previously, he was a senior researcher at the Korean Constitutional Research Institute at the Constitutional Court of Korea. He has written several publications on international and constitutional law, with articles published in a number of journals and reviews. Younsik holds a PhD in law from the University of Edinburgh, where his thesis focused on the relationship between investor–state arbitration and national constitutional law. He holds an LLM from the University of Chicago and an LLM and LLB from Korea University. His research interests cover constitutional law and administrative law, legal theory and international investment law.

JOHN LUMBANTOBING is Vice Dean at the Faculty of Law, Parahyangan Catholic University. His main research interests and publications are in the fields of arbitration, international investment law and the domestic application of international law. Some of his previous works have been published in the *Oxford Reports on International Law* and as part of an edited volume by Oxford University Press and Cambridge University Press. He obtained his law degrees from Parahyangan Catholic University and the University of Cambridge (Hughes Hall). John is also the current chair of the Chartered Institute of Arbitrators YMG Committee for Indonesia.

PRABHASH RANJAN is Professor and Vice Dean (Continuing Education) at the Jindal Global Law School, O.P. Jindal Global University, India. Prabhash holds a PhD in law from King's College London. He studied at the School of Oriental and African Studies for an LLM on a British Chevening Scholarship. He is the author of the book *India and Bilateral Investment Treaties: Refusal, Acceptance, Backlash* (Oxford University Press, 2019). His work has also appeared in leading international journals like the *Netherlands International Law Review, ICSID Review, Journal of World Trade, Asian Journal of International Law, Cambridge International Law Journal* and *Northwestern Journal of International Law and Business.* He regularly contributes opinion editorials in India's leading national newspapers like the *Hindustan Times, The Hindu* and *The Indian Express.*

TRAN VIET DUNG is Associate Professor and Dean of the International Law Faculty at Ho Chi Minh City University of Law. He is a member of the Governing Board of the Foundation for the Development of International Law in Asia (since 2016) and a member of the editorial boards of the *Vietnamese Journal of Legal Science* (since 2019), the *ASEAN Journal of Legal Studies* and the *Asian Year Book of International Law* (both 2018). He is also a senior research fellow at the Law Department in Tallinn University of Technology. Tran combines academic knowledge with practical experience as an international lawyer. He has practised law at the top-tier law firms of Singapore for six years, and later with Victory LLC, a premier law firm based in Ho Chi Minh City, and undertaken many consultancies for multinational corporations with respect to their foreign investments in Viet Nam and in the region.

TEERAWAT WONGKAEW is a diplomat at the Ministry of Foreign Affairs of Thailand. In the ministry, he has served in the Department of Treaties and Legal Affairs in a wide range of practices, including international investment law, international humanitarian law and the laws of international organisations. He was previously at the Department of International Economic Affairs, involved with the negotiations of bilateral and regional investment treaties as well as free trade agreements. He earned LLB and LLM degrees from University College London and a PhD in international law at the Graduate Institute of International and Development Studies (IHEID) (2016). He is the author of a number of articles in the area of international investment law and international humanitarian law. His latest publication is *Protection of Legitimate Expectations in Investment Treaty Arbitration: A Theory of Detrimental Reliance* (Cambridge University Press, 2019).

ACKNOWLEDGEMENTS

This book was developed through a collaborative and iterative process. Each of the contributors participated in workshops organised by the editors at the Centre for International Law at the National University of Singapore in 2017 and 2019. Earlier drafts of various chapters of this book were presented at annual meetings of the Asian Law Institute and the Asian Society of International Law, as well as at meetings of the American Society of International Law Research Forum and the Oxford University Public International Law Discussion Group. Draft papers were also presented at Asia School of Business, MIT Sloan School of Management; Ho Chi Minh City University of Law; University of Geneva; and Panthéon-Assas University Paris 2.

We are grateful to our contributors for their dedication and commitment to this project over the past several years. We are also grateful to the great many people who offered comments on the analytical framework presented in Chapters 1 and 10. They include Anthony Angie, Dafina Atanasova, Jonathan Bonnitcha, Julien Chaisse, Sachintha Dias, Younsik Kim, John Lumbantobing, Naazima Kamardeen, Josef Ostřanský, Mahdev Mohan, Facundo Pérez Aznar, Lauge Poulsen, Prabhash Ranjan, Mavluda Sattorova, Ashley Schram, Wenny Setiawati, Tran Viet Dung, Trinh Hai Yen, Zoe P. Williams, Teerawat Wongkaew, and four anonymous reviewers.

Finally, we are grateful for the support provided by colleagues at the Centre for International Law and Faculty of Law at the National University of Singapore, including Bryan Jun Qing Chia, Daniel Ang Wei En, Charalampos Giannakopoulos, Eugenio Gomez-Chico, Neha Mishra, Nilufer Oral, Lucy Reed, and J. Christopher Thomas.

TABLE OF AUTHORITIES

I Treaties

Full title	Abbreviation	Page(s)
Agreement on Investment under the Framework Agreement on Comprehensive Economic Cooperation between the Association of Southeast Asian Nations and the Republic of India, *signed 12 November 2014; not yet in force*	ASEAN–India Investment Agreement (2014)	70 n. 15, 271 n. 33
Agreement among the Governments of Brunei Darussalam, the Republic of Indonesia, Malaysia, the Republic of the Philippines, the Republic of Singapore, and the Kingdom of Thailand, for the Promotion and Protection of Investments, *signed 15 December 1987; entered into force 2 August 1988; amended 1996; terminated 29 March 2012*	ASEAN Investment Guarantee Agreement (1987)	270 n. 25
Framework Agreement on the ASEAN Investment Area, *signed 7 October 1998*	ASEAN Investment Area Framework Agreement (1998)	270 n. 24
Agreement on Comprehensive Economic Partnership among Japan and Member States of the Association of Southeast Asian Nations, *signed 28 March 2008; entered into force 1 December 2008*	ASEAN–Japan EPA (2008)	70 n. 15, 271 n. 33
Agreement on Investment under the Framework Agreement on Comprehensive Economic Cooperation among the Governments of the Member Countries of the Association of Southeast Asian Nations and the Republic of Korea, *signed 2 June 2009; entered into force 1 September 2009*	ASEAN–Korea Investment Agreement (2009)	70 n. 15. 235 n. 3, 271 n. 33
Regional Comprehensive Economic Partnership Agreement, *signed 15 November 2020; entered into force 1 January 2022*	Regional Comprehensive Economic Partnership (RCEP) (2020)	70 n. 16, 99 n. 7, 172 n. 28, 235 n. 4, 262, 265, 271 n. 32, 272 n. 37, 279

II   Cases (by Jurisdiction)

England

Germany

India

Indonesia

Singapore

IV   Other International Proceedings

The Internalisation of Investment Treaties and the Rule of Law Promise

N. JANSEN CALAMITA AND AYELET BERMAN

1.1 Introduction

Over the past thirty years, international treaties for the promotion and protection of investment have proliferated, with over 3,000 such treaties concluded. The bulk of these treaties were concluded in the 1990s and 2000s, largely between developed and developing states.

In general structure, investment treaties provide special protections to foreign investors in host states, such as protections against discrimination, arbitrary treatment and uncompensated expropriation, as well as guarantees of fair and equitable treatment. The scope of coverage of these protections is broad. Generally speaking, the disciplines imposed by these treaties are applicable in respect of any measure attributable to the state in respect of a covered investment or investor, regardless of the subject matter of the measure (e.g. environment, public health, energy policy, etc.), regardless of the responsible organ of government and regardless of the sector of the investment. In addition, investment treaties establish specialised dispute settlement mechanisms. Under the treaties, foreign investors may bring claims for breach of the treaty against the host state before an international arbitration tribunal, generally without having to go first through the host state's domestic courts.

Traditionally, two theories have been advanced for how host states might benefit from entering into investment treaties. The first theory is that – by offering special protections to foreign investors – investment treaties help developing states attract foreign investment.[1]

---

[1] For an early statement of the justification, see Earl Snyder, 'Protection of Private Foreign Investment: Examination and Appraisal' (1961) 10 *International and Comparative Law Quarterly* 469, 92 (quoting Hartley Shawcross, one of the originators of the ill-fated Organisation for Economic Co-operation and Development [OECD] Draft Convention on the Protection of Foreign Property: 'The *quid pro quo* for the States' undertaking is, in fact, in the English vernacular, the provision of the quids, that the capital importing countries, in

The second theory is that – by way of additional effect – investment treaties have positive effects on national governance in the host state. On this latter theory, because of a desire to avoid liability for breaches of investment treaties, developing states will internalise consideration of their international legal obligations into their governmental decision making, reform their decision-making processes, and thereby, over time, improve the rule of law not just for foreign investors but also for all those within their territories.[2] As Roberto Echandi has put it, the fear of arbitration by foreign investors should act as 'a deterrent mechanism' against short-term policy reversals and 'assist developing countries in promoting greater effectiveness of the rule of law at the domestic level'.[3] Or, as Stephan Schill has asserted, '[d]amages as a remedy sufficiently pressure States into complying with and incorporating the normative guidelines of investment treaties into their domestic legal order'.[4]

Such claims have not been based upon empirical evidence regarding the actual effects of investment treaties on state governance. Rather,

return for agreeing to abide by the generally recognized procedures of international law, will receive more private investment and with the capital, the benefits of the technical and commercial skills which go with them than would otherwise be the case'). See also Jeswald W. Salacuse, *The Law of Investment Treaties* (2nd ed., Oxford University Press, 2015), ch. 4.4(b); Jonathan Bonnitcha, Lauge N. S. Poulsen and Michael Waibel, *The Political Economy of the Investment Treaty Regime* (Oxford University Press, 2017), 207; Beth A. Simmons, 'Bargaining over BITs, Arbitrating Awards: The Regime for Protection and Promotion of International Investment' (2010) 66 *World Politics* 12; Zachary Elkins, Andrew T. Guzman and Beth A. Simmons, 'Competing for Capital: The Diffusion of Bilateral Investment Treaties, 1960–2000', in Geoffrey Garrett, Beth A. Simmons and Frank Dobbin (eds.), *The Global Diffusion of Markets and Democracy* (Cambridge University Press, 2008), 220; Alan O. Sykes, 'Public versus Private Enforcement of International Economic Law: Standing and Remedy' (2005) 34 *Journal of Legal Studies* 631, 644. See generally, on credible commitment theory, Beth A. Simmons, 'Treaty Compliance and Violation' (2010) 13 *Annual Review of Political Science* 273, 276.

[2] See, for example, Salacuse, *The Law of Investment Treaties*, 113–14; Stephan W. Schill, 'International Investment Law and the Rule of Law', in Jeffrey Jowell, J. Christopher Thomas and Jan van Zyl Smit (eds.), *The Importance of the Rule of Law in Promoting Development* (Singapore Academy of Law, 2015) 81, 87–93; Rudolf Dolzer, 'The Impact of International Investment Treaties on Domestic Administrative Law' (2005) 37 *New York University Journal of International Law and Policy* 972; Susan D. Franck, 'Foreign Direct Investment, Investment Treaty Arbitration, and the Rule of Law' (2006) 19 *Pacific McGeorge Global Business and Development Law Journal* 337.

[3] Roberto Echandi, 'What Do Developing Countries Expect from the International Investment Regime?', in Jose E. Alvarez and Karl P. Sauvant (eds.), *The Evolving International Investment Regime: Expectations, Realities, Options* (Oxford University Press, 2011), 13.

[4] Stephan W. Schill, *The Multilateralization of International Investment Law* (Cambridge University Press, 2009), 377.

proponents of this theory have based their views upon the content of the obligations in investment treaties and assumptions about state behaviour. Kingsbury and Schill, for example, have argued that the obligation to provide fair and equitable treatment – found in almost all investment treaties – 'ought to prompt States to adapt their domestic legal orders to standards that are internationally accepted as conforming to the rule of law'.[5] Thus, they predict that the obligations contained in investment treaties will 'have effects over time on specific law and administrative practices within states', and that these improvements in governance will not only inure to the benefit of foreign investors but also 'indeed to others under national law'.[6] In other words, as a result of incorporating their investment treaty obligations into their dealings with foreign investors, host states can be expected to experience positive 'rule of law' spillover effects with regard to governance in the host state generally, such that improvements to the rule of law will be felt by all within the host state, not only covered foreign investors.[7] We refer, henceforth, to this theory of the possible effects of investment treaties on national governance as the 'rule of law thesis'.[8]

---

[5] Benedict Kingsbury and Stephan W. Schill, 'Investor-State Arbitration as Governance: Fair and Equitable Treatment, Proportionality and the Emerging Global Administrative Law' (2009) *NYU School of Law Public Law Research Paper No. 09–46.*

[6] *Ibid.* For a similar view, see also Thomas Schultz and Cédric Dupont, 'Investment Arbitration: Promoting the Rule of Law or Over-Empowering Investors? A Quantitative Empirical Study' (2015) 25 *European Journal of International Law* 1147, 1161.

[7] See also Michael Reisman and Robert D. Sloane, 'Indirect Expropriation and Its Valuation in the BIT Generation' (2004) 75 *British Yearbook of International Law* 115, 117 (arguing that investment treaties will compel states with weak regulatory capacity to develop 'an effective normative framework' which includes, *inter alia,* 'impartial courts, an efficient and legally restrained bureaucracy, and the measure of transparency in decision'); Celine Tan, 'Reviving the Emperor's Old Clothes: The Good Governance Agenda, Development and International Investment Law', in Stephan W. Schill et al. (eds.), *International Investment Law and Development: Bridging the Gap* (Edward Elgar, 2015), 147, 158–61 (saying, *inter alia,* that 'the language of good governance, its associated rule of law narrative and their relationship to development outcomes have been used to justify the normative and institutional evolution of law and policy in [the area of international investment law]'). José Alvarez, 'Are Corporations "Subjects" of International Law?' (2011) 9 *Santa Clara Journal of International Law* 15–16 (providing an overview of the argument underlying the rule of law thesis).

[8] The scholarship advancing the 'rule of law' thesis uses the term without definition, although, as noted in the text, some have stressed notions of due process, effectiveness, transparency, non-arbitrariness and accountability. The general literature on the rule of law is vast. For an overview of different definitional approaches to the rule of law, see, for example, Rachel Kleinfeld, 'Competing Definitions of the Rule of Law', in Thomas Carothers (ed.), *Promoting the Rule of Law Abroad: In Search of Knowledge* (Brookings Institution Press, 2010), 31; Kevin E. Davis and Michael J. Trebilcock, 'The Relationship between Law and

Over the past fifteen years, there has been a significant amount of empirical research on the impact of investment treaties on foreign direct investment (the findings of which have yielded little consensus).[9] In contrast, we still know little about the effects of investment treaties on governance. Despite the rule of law thesis implicitly underlying much of the investment treaty discourse, and despite anecdotal indications that 'the signature of international investment agreements by states was generally not followed by regulatory or institutional changes at the domestic level to enable states to meet their newly acquired commitments',[10] empirical studies examining the veracity of this claim have been rare. Mavluda

---

Development: Optimists versus Skeptics' (2008) 56 *American Journal of Comparative Law* 895; Brian Z. Tamanaha, *On the Rule of Law: History, Politics, Theory* (Cambridge University Press, 2004). See also United Nations, 'Delivering Justice: Programme of Action to Strengthen the Rule of Law at the National and International Levels, Report of the Secretary General', UN Doc A/66/749 (16 March 2012), at para 2:

> [T]he rule of law [i]s a principle of governance in which all persons, institutions and entities, public and private, including the State itself, are accountable to laws that are publicly promulgated, equally enforced and independently adjudicated, and which are consistent with international human rights norms and standards. It requires, as well, measures to ensure adherence to the principles of supremacy of law, equality before the law, accountability to the law, fairness in the application of the law, separation of powers, participation in decision making, legal certainty, avoidance of arbitrariness and procedural and legal transparency.

[9] See, for example, Josef C. Brada, Zdenek Drabek and Ichiro Iwasaki, 'Does Investor Protection Increase Foreign Direct Investment? A Meta-Analysis' (2020) *Journal of Economic Surveys* 34; Lauge N. S. Poulsen, 'The Importance of BITs for Foreign Direct Investment and Political Risk Insurance: Revisiting the Evidence' (2010) *Yearbook on International Investment Law and Policy* 539; UNCTAD, The Impact of International Investment Agreements on Foreign Direct Investment: An Overview of Empirical Studies 1998–2014 (2014) *UNCTAD IIA Issue Note*; Simmons, 'Bargaining over BITS, Arbitrating Awards: The Regime for Protection and Promotion of International Investment', 12 and 29–30; Todd L. Allee and Clint Peinhardt, 'Delegating Differences: Bilateral Investment Treaties and Bargaining over Dispute Resolution Provisions' (2010) 54 *International Studies Quarterly* 1; Peter Eger and Valeria Merlo, 'The Impact of Bilateral Investment Treaties on FDI Dynamics' (2007) 30 *World Economy* 1536; Andrew Kerner, 'Why Should I Believe You? The Costs and Consequences of Bilateral Investment Treaties' (2009) 53 *International Studies Quarterly* 73; Eric Neumayer and Laura Spess, 'Do Bilateral Investment Treaties Increase Foreign Direct Investment to Developing Countries?' (2004) 33 *World Development* 1567; Jason W. Yackee, 'Do Investment Treaties Work – In the Land of Smiles?', in Julien Chaisse and Luke Nottage (eds.), *International Investment Treaties and Arbitration Across Asia* (Brill, 2017), 83.

[10] Andrea Saldarriaga and Kendra Magraw, 'UNCTAD's Effort to Foster the Relationship between International Investment Law and Sustainable Development', in Stephan W. Schill et al. (eds.), *International Investment Law and Development: Bridging the Gap* (Edward Elgar, 2015), 132.

Sattorova's work on the impact of investment treaties on host state governance is a notable exception.[11] The purpose of this book is to contribute towards filling this gap.

Three assumptions about state behaviour underlie the rule of law thesis. The first assumption is that states make policy choices to seek to comply with their international treaty obligations. The second assumption is that – out of this desire to comply – states internalise their international investment obligations and that these obligations are taken into account in governmental decision making. The third assumption is that this desire to comply with investment treaty obligations ultimately will become operationalised in the host state's general dealings with all addressees of its legal and regulatory system.

The rule of law thesis, moreover, is rooted in a traditional view about the way in which the international legal order functions. On this view, states affirmatively seek to comply with their international treaty obligations[12] either because it is in their self-interest to do so (they would not have consented to the treaty otherwise)[13] or because they benefit from the reciprocity of compliance.[14] Further, when states are tempted not to comply, the argument goes, they face the threat of sanctions, which in

---

[11] Mavluda Sattorova, *The Impact of Investment Treaty Law on Host States* (Hart, 2018). See also Christine Coté, 'Is It Chilly Out There? International Investment Agreements and Government Regulatory Autonomy' (2014) 16 *AIB Insights* 14; Jason W. Yackee, 'Do Investment Promotion Agencies Promote Bilateral Investment Treaties?' (2013) *Yearbook on International Investment Law and Policy* 529 (examining the awareness of investment treaties among national providers of political risk insurance); Tom Ginsburg, 'International Substitutes for Domestic Institutions: Bilateral Investment Treaties and Governance' (2005) 25 *International Review of Law & Economics* 107, 108 (carrying out a quantitative empirical analysis as to the impact of BITs on domestic governance); Josef Ostřanský and Facundo Pérez Aznar, 'Investment Treaties and National Governance in India: Rearrangements, Empowerment, and Discipline' (2021) 34 *Leiden Journal of International Law* 373.

[12] As Louis Henkin famously put it: 'almost all nations observe almost all principles of international law and almost all of their obligations almost all of the time'. Louis Henkin, *How Nations Behave* (Columbia University Press, 1979), 47. See, for example, Harold H. Koh, 'Why Do Nations Obey International Law?' (1996) 106 *Yale Law Journal* 2599.

[13] Abram Chayes and Antonia H. Chayes, 'On Compliance' (1993) 47 *International Organization* 175, 179–84; Kal Raustiala and David G. Victor, 'The Regime Complex for Plant Genetic Resources' (2004) 58 *International Organization* 277 (arguing that compliance is a sign that states join agreements with which they know they can comply).

[14] Robert O. Keohane, 'After Hegemony: Cooperation and Discord in the World Political Economy' (1984) 61 *International Affairs* 290; Simmons, 'Treaty Compliance and Violation', 275; Harold K. Jacobson and Edith Brown Weiss, 'A Framework for Analysis', in Edith Brown Weiss and Harold K. Jacobson (eds.), *Engaging Countries: Strengthening Compliance with International Environmental Accords* (MIT Press, 1998), 1, 2.

turn provides a coercive incentive to comply and deters violations in the future.[15] International relations literature explains this traditional international law approach through a 'rational choice' theory of the state. Rational choice theory considers the state to be rational, which is understood to mean that when setting policies and taking decisions, the state undertakes a cost–benefit analysis of alternative actions and their consequences, and that it chooses the action which maximises its preferences.[16] Given the benefits of compliance and the costs of violation alluded to above, a rational choice model predicts that states, on balance, gain more from compliance, and as such, expects them, for the most part, to internalise their obligations and comply with them.[17]

There are good reasons to be sceptical of the assumptions underlying the rule of law thesis. First, the rational choice theory on which it is based simply does not reflect the complexities of governance. Indeed, empirical studies on compliance with international law carried out in recent years illustrate how inconsistent compliance is and highlight the many domestic and international factors that can impede it.[18] Such impediments are amplified in developing countries, where, as established in the law and development literature, low regulatory capacity, and/or the absence of a well-developed regulatory governance model, serve as a further hindrance to the internalisation of international obligations into governmental decision making.[19]

Second, internalising international investment obligations into the myriad processes of government is markedly demanding. The pervasive presence of foreign investment throughout national economies is such that a wide range of entities and persons for whom the state is internationally responsible may take measures of one kind or another with respect to a foreign investment or investor. This wide range of entities and persons is reflected in the wide range of actors that have taken measures giving rise to investment treaty arbitrations. According to a study of investor–state

---

[15] Jacobson and Brown Weiss, 'A Framework for Analysis', 2.

[16] Duncan Snidal, 'Rational Choice and International Relations', in Walter Carlsnaes, Thomas Risse and Beth A. Simmons (eds.), *Handbook of International Relations* (SAGE Publications, 2013), 85.

[17] Andrew Guzman, *How International Law Works: A Rational Choice Theory* (Oxford University Press, 2008); Robert O. Keohane, 'Rational Choice Theory and International Law: Insights and Limitations' (2002) 31 *Journal of Legal Studies* 307.

[18] See, for example, Oona A. Hathaway, 'Between Power and Principle: An Integrated Theory of International Law' (2005) 72 *University of Chicago Law Review* 469.

[19] Michael J. Trebilcock and Mariana M. Prado, *Advanced Introduction to Law and Development* (Edward Elgar, 2014).

treaty disputes by Zoe Williams, examining 584 arbitration cases from 1990 to 2014, 61 per cent of cases were triggered primarily by administrative measures; 26 per cent were triggered by legislative measures alone; and 11 per cent were related to judicial decisions.[20] Moreover, the economic sectors of the underlying investments in these disputes ranged across all aspects of the host economies, from investments in extractive industries to banking to construction to agriculture to the provision of public services (energy, water services, etc.) to manufacturing, transport and telecommunications.[21]

In this introductory chapter, we develop a framework for thinking about the internalisation of international treaty obligations in governmental decision making that attempts to take account of the complexities of governance. In so doing, we lay out a typology of processes whereby international investment treaty obligations may be internalised and identify factors that may affect whether and to what extent international investment law is internalised by the state. This framework serves as the background for the main body of the book in which we present case studies addressing whether and how a select group of governments in Asia internalise international investment treaty obligations in their decision-making processes: India, Indonesia, Myanmar, Republic of Korea, Singapore, Sri Lanka, Thailand and Viet Nam.[22] These case studies serve as a foundation for testing our theoretical framework by empirically examining whether and to what extent these governments take investment treaty obligations into account in their governmental decision-making processes and whether such internalisation has had spillover effects on governance in the state more generally.

The organisation of this introduction is as follows. Section 1.2 begins by setting out the principal research questions with which we are concerned

---

[20] Zoe P. Williams, 'Risky Business or Risky Politics: What Explains Investor State Disputes?', unpublished dissertation, Hertie School of Governance (2016), 42.

[21] *Ibid.*, at 40–41. Using the World Bank sectoral classification system, Williams noted disputes across at least fifteen different sectors: oil, gas and mining (25%); electric power and other energy (14%); construction (7%); banking and finance (6%); manufacturing (6%); agricultural, forest and fisheries (6%); telecommunications (6%); transportation (5%); water and waste management (4%); food and beverage (3%); other services (3%); real estate (3%); hospitality/tourism (3%); healthcare and pharmaceuticals (2%); media (2%); other (3%); and unknown (2%).

[22] The authors of these country-specific case studies are Dafina Atanasova (Singapore), Jonathan Bonnitcha (Myanmar), Sachinta Dias (Sri Lanka), Younsik Kim (South Korea), John Lumbantobing (Indonesia), Prabhash Ranjan (India), Tran Viet Dung (Viet Nam) and Teerawat Wongkaew (Thailand).

in order to clarify the scope of our inquiry. We additionally set forth a definition of 'internalisation' in the context of our thinking about the role of investment treaties in governmental decision making. Section 1.3 situates the project in the existing theoretical and empirical literature on the role of international law in state behaviour. Section 1.4 builds on the literature to set out a framework for exploring the internalisation of international investment treaties by governments. In Section 1.4, we operationalise the concept of internalisation and offer a typology of the kinds of internalisation processes that states may adopt. In Section 1.5, we consider factors that may impact the internalisation of investment treaty obligations and the extent to which governments take those obligations into account in their decision making. Section 1.6 provides an introduction to the case studies that make up the core of this volume, addressing the issues of case selection and methodology.

1.2   Definitions, Research Questions and Scope

For investment treaties to improve governmental administration, the obligations contained within them must have an effect on the decision-making processes of government. They must be 'internalised' into the domestic regulatory system. Such internalisation is a foundational assumption to the claim of the rule of law thesis that investment treaties will improve domestic governance. Yet, as mentioned earlier, there are reasons to be sceptical about the degree of internalisation actually present in government and the role of international obligations in governmental decision making.

We define 'internalisation' as referring to the formal and informal processes by which the state's international legal obligations are taken into account in governmental decision making. Our focus, within government, is on the executive, the public bureaucracy and the legislature. In setting this definition, we note two main decision-making situations in which governments may take international law into account. The first situation is when the government implements international law as a domestic law or regulation. In this situation, the government naturally considers international law because the international obligation forms the subject matter of the governmental measure. The second situation is when the government adopts a measure on a matter of domestic law or regulation, which is itself not directly related to international law. In this circumstance, while the government may take into consideration whether the adopted measure is in line or in tension with its international legal obligations, such consideration is in a sense 'elective' as the international obligation does not form the subject matter of the measure. Our study focuses on this second situation. That is, we are interested in the question of whether governments take international investment obligations into account when they are considering an original domestic measure (e.g., considering whether to issue or revoke a license, adopt a new financial regulation, etc.).

It is important to note how our understanding of 'internalisation' differs from the related concepts of 'implementation' and 'compliance'. In our understanding, compliance refers to the level of agreement or conformity between a state's behaviour and the requirements of an international obligation. Asking about compliance asks a question about an end result and whether a state has *actually adhered to* the international obligation.[23] Internalisation, in contrast, and as we use it, refers to the processes whereby the government considers its existing international legal obligations in its decision-making processes. Importantly, our definition of internalisation does not suppose that the state will always decide matters in accordance with its apparent international investment treaty obligations. To adopt such a definition of internalisation would be to conflate the concept with a kind of compliance. Moreover, while it may be true that the internalisation of international legal obligations increases the likelihood that the government will act in conformity with its obligations, this is by no means always the case. As discussed further below, an international obligation may be one of a number of (political, economic, organisational, etc.) considerations in the decision-making process, and governments may ultimately – in the 'battle of the norms' – decide in line with other competing norms or interests.[24] Internalisation, thus, may be a factor that influences compliance but is conceptually distinct.[25]

We also distinguish our conception of internalisation from 'implementation'. Implementation is typically understood as the adoption of international law into domestic law, its purpose being to give domestic legal effect to international law, making it enforceable before domestic courts by citizens.[26] Implementation is also understood as carrying

---

[23] Jacobson and Brown Weiss, 'A Framework for Analysis', 4.

[24] See Julia Black, 'New Institutionalism and Naturalism in Socio-Legal Analysis: Institutionalist Approaches to Regulatory Decision Making' (1991) 19 *Law and Policy* 51.

[25] States may have high levels of compliance with an international obligation which are unrelated to internalisation if the state's behaviour is already treaty-compliant.

[26] Beth A. Simmons, *Mobilizing for Human Rights: International Law in Domestic Politics* (Cambridge University Press, 2009), 131.

out obligations under the treaty and undertaking positive enactments required by the treaty.[27] After the adoption and ratification of a treaty, implementation represents the stage when international obligations are integrated into domestic law through enactment of domestic legislation or regulation.[28] Not only is implementation conceptually different from our conception of internalisation, it is also a poor fit for an inquiry regarding investment treaties. Whereas certain treaties require or imply the need to take domestic regulatory or legal action under their terms,[29] in the case of investment treaties similar action is not required. Governments rather are expected to refrain from certain actions in order to implement and comply with their obligations.

In adopting this conception of internalisation, we position our research as an attempt to identify specific processes for the operation of investment treaties on governmental decision making in a complex regulatory environment (in which states may be taking a variety of steps in order to make their economies attractive to investment). Our research thus attempts to isolate in this environment the impact of investment treaty obligations on the processes of governmental decision making. By way of distinction, this research is interested in the institutional effects of investment treaties, the institutional processes. We do not, therefore, consider questions regarding the subjective awareness of investment treaty obligations by individual decision makers, nor the psychological internalisation of investment treaty commitments. Similarly, the research we pursue is not interested in questions of 'socialisation' but, rather, internalisation as an institutional matter.

---

[27] See Gerald Staberock, 'Human Rights, Domestic Implementation', in Rüdiger Wolfrum (ed.), *Max Planck Encyclopedia of Public International Law* (Oxford University Press, 2011). We acknowledge that broad approaches to the term implementation, commonly found in the public policy literature, would consider implementation as covering any activity for realising a policy and would share much in common or would be almost identical to our concept of internalisation. However, the common use of the term in international law is much more limited and, as noted, is limited to the act of giving domestic legal effect to an international obligation.

[28] Depending on the local legal system, to be enforceable in domestic courts, treaties can either be automatically internalised into the domestic legal system or must be adopted through domestic law or regulations. Implementation covers the latter case, that is, when certain domestic laws or regulations must be adopted.

[29] By way of example, the Framework Convention on Tobacco Control requires states to undertake certain implementing measures that will reduce demand for tobacco through legislation, regulation or policies. See WHO Framework Convention on Tobacco Control (2003), 2302 UNTS 166, Art. 7.

To this end, our research addresses three main questions:

- First, *descriptive*: whether and if so in what ways do governments internalise investment treaty obligations into their decision-making processes?
- Second, *explanatory*: what are the factors that affect whether governments internalise international investment obligations in their decision making?
- Third, *inferential*: to the extent that there is evidence that states have internalised international investment treaty obligations into governmental decision making, is there evidence that this has led to improvements in regulatory practices more generally, that is, the positive spillovers suggested by the rule of law thesis?

1.3   Internalisation in the International Legal Literature

We conceptualise our understanding of internalisation against a background of existing legal literature: (1) the liberal international school, which blurs the distinction between the international and the national and opens up the black box of the state; (2) the law and development literature, which addresses the role of law in bringing about good governance and development in low- and middle-income countries; and (3) the empirical legal scholarship, which examines the impact of international law through empirical investigations.

Traditional international law has devoted little attention to the question of how or whether international legal obligations are internalised or considered in the decision-making processes of governments. With respect to the question of how international law impacts domestic law, most scholarship has explored questions of 'compliance' or 'implementation', proceeding on the underlying yet unspoken assumption that governments internalise their international legal obligations and take them into account in their decision making (even though there may ultimately be forces or reasons which result in non-compliance).

Classic international law treats the state as a unitary actor, without delving into internal state dynamics. The classical literature has argued that states comply with international obligations because it is in their self-interest to do so (they would not have consented to the treaty otherwise)[30]

---

[30] Chayes and Chayes, 'On Compliance', 179–84; Raustiala and Victor, 'The Regime Complex for Plant Genetic Resources' (arguing that compliance is a sign that states join agreements with which they know they can comply).

or because they benefit from the reciprocity of compliance.[31] Further, classical realist theory asserts that when states are tempted not to comply, the threat of sanctions provides a coercive incentive to comply, and deter violations in the future.[32]

The classical approach, to which the rule of law thesis seems to owe much, rests on a 'rational choice' theory of the state. The rational choice theory considers the state to be rational, which is understood to mean that in making decisions, the state undertakes a cost–benefit analysis of alternative actions and their consequences, and that it chooses the action, which maximises its preferences.[33] Given the benefits of compliance and the costs of violation, a rational choice model predicts that states, on balance, will gain more from compliance, and as such, assumes that, for the most part, states will take their international obligations into account and comply with them.[34]

Moving away from classical, realist paradigms, liberal international legal theory exposes the fiction of the unitary state model and opens up the 'black box' of the state.[35] The work of scholars such as Harold Koh and Gregory Shaffer examines the impact of *domestic preferences and dynamics* on the international behaviour of a state.[36] Rather than seeing the state as a unitary actor with one unified interest (as realist theories of the state have), liberal theory emphasises that the state is 'disaggregated' into different, and at times competing, actors and interests.[37] This literature recognises

---

[31] Keohane, 'After Hegemony'; Simmons, 'Treaty Compliance and Violation', 275; Jacobson and Brown Weiss, 'A Framework for Analysis', 2.

[32] George W. Downs, David M. Rocke and Peter N. Barsoom, 'Is the Good News about Compliance Good News about Cooperation?' (1996) 50 *International Organization* 379, 386.

[33] Snidal, 'Rational Choice and International Relations'.

[34] Beth A. Simmons, 'International Law', in Walter Carlsnaes, Thomas Risse and Beth A. Simmons (eds.), *Handbook of International Relations* (SAGE Publications, 2013), 352.

[35] Andrew Moravcsik, 'Taking Preferences Seriously: Liberalism and International Relations Theory' (1997) 51 *International Organization* 513; Peter Gourevitch, 'The Second Image Reversed: The International Sources of Domestic Politics' (1978) 32 *International Organization* 881; Jeffrey T. Checkel, 'Norms, Institutions and National Identity in Contemporary Europe' (1999) 43 *International Studies Quarterly* 83; Jeffrey W. Legro, 'Which Norms Matter? Revisiting the "Failure" of Internationalism' (1997) 51 *International Organization* 31; Kenneth Schultz, 'Domestic Politics and International Relations', in Walter Carlsnaes, Thomas Risse and Beth A. Simmons (eds.), *Handbook of International Relations* (SAGE Publications, 2013), 478.

[36] Harold H. Koh, 'Transnational Legal Process' (1996) 75 *Nebraska Law Review* 181; Gregory C. Shaffer, *Transnational Legal Ordering and State Change* (Cambridge University Press, 2012).

[37] Moravcsik, 'Taking Preferences Seriously'; Anne-Marie Slaughter Burley, 'International Law and International Relations Theory: A Dual Agenda' (1993) 87 *American Journal of International Law* 205; Robert D. Putnam, 'Diplomacy and Domestic Politics: The Logic of Two-Level Games' (1988) 42 *International Organization* 427.

the important impact of domestic factors, structures and actors – such as surrounding social and political discourses or behavioural factors – on the manner or extent by which international obligations become internalised within the state by the government as well as within society.

Within this realm, Koh's work on the *transnational legal process* defines the transnational legal process as 'the theory and practice of how public and private actors – nation states, international organisations, multinational enterprises, non-governmental organisations, and private individuals – interact in a variety of public and private, domestic and international fora to make, interpret, enforce and ultimately, internalise rules of transnational law'.[38] Through this transnational legal process, states internalise international law not only into their domestic *legal* system but also more broadly into their domestic practices, values or processes. In other words, the internalisation process is not limited to legal means but may also be of a social or political nature.[39] It is also not only limited to state actors, but both (domestic and transnational) state and non-state actors have a role in the internalisation process.[40]

Shaffer's work on 'transnational legal orders' and 'state change'[41] follows a similar logic, which emphasises the role of domestic factors on state behaviour. In Shaffer's view, domestic dynamics are the most important factors in understanding the impact of international rules on the state: 'Arguably, the most important determinant of state change is the affinity of the transnational legal reform efforts with the demands and discursive frames of

---

[38] See Koh, 'Transnational Legal Process', 183–84.

[39] Koh, 'Why Do Nations Obey International Law?', 2656–67 (saying that 'Political internalisation would include, for example, acceptance and adoption of the norms by the political elite, and social internalisation, exists when a norm acquires so much public legitimacy that there is widespread general obedience to it'. See also Jean Frédéric Morin and Edward R. Gold, 'An Integrated Model of Legal Transplantation: The Diffusion of Intellectual Property Law in Developing Countries' (2014) 58 *International Studies Quarterly* 781, 783 (discussing the role of 'socialisation', i.e. the process of internalisation of principles, beliefs, and norms by which international or foreign rules are adopted within a state).

[40] Examples of studies that have followed this approach: Amichai Cohen, 'Bureaucratic Internalization: Domestic Governmental Agencies and the Legitimization of International Law' (2005) 36 *Georgetown Journal of International Law* 1079, 1081 (examining internalisation in bureaucracies); Galit A. Sarfaty, *Values in Translation: Human Rights and the Culture of the World Bank* (Stanford University Press, 2012) (demonstrating the role of internal dynamics within the World Bank and domestic legal and political constraints on the internalisation of World Bank policies in borrowing countries). See also David Bach and Andrew Newman, 'Transgovernmental Networks and Domestic Policy Convergence' (2010) 64 *International Organization* 505 (discussing the diffusion of ideas within the state).

[41] Shaffer, *Transnational Legal Ordering and State Change*.

domestic constituencies and elites in light of domestic configurations of power and the extent of change at stake'.[42] Thus, domestic demands, domestic power struggles and domestic culture 'shape how transnational legal norms are received and implemented in practice', and '[s]ometimes they lead to the rejection of transnational law'.[43] Goodman and Jinks take a constructivist approach, arguing that the internalisation of international law into national behaviour is a result of 'patterns of acculturation', or a process of socialisation of social pressures on the state.[44] Jacobson and Weiss similarly observe that: 'The social, cultural, political, and economic characteristics of the countries clearly influence implementation and compliance'.[45] In the international investment regime specifically, Williams likewise argues that domestic factors are the main reason for investor–state disputes.[46]

The global administrative law literature similarly moves away from sharp distinctions between international and national law. One of global administrative law's main insights is that many legal and normative activities take place in a global administrative space, which blurs the distinction between the international and national.[47] The acts of national government officials or regulatory agencies in dealing with the state's international obligations,[48] and questions about the impact of

---

[42] Gregory C. Shaffer, 'The Dimensions and Determinants of State Change', in Gregory C. Shaffer (ed.), *Transnational Legal Ordering and State Change* (Cambridge University Press, 2012), 37, 43.

[43] *Ibid.*

[44] Ryan Goodman and Derek Jinks, 'How to Influence States: Socialization and International Human Rights Law' (2004) 54 *Duke Law Journal* 621.

[45] Jacobson and Brown Weiss, 'A Framework for Analysis', 7.

[46] Williams, 'Risky Business or Risky Politics'. See also N. Jansen Calamita, 'Are Investments in Water Different? Sectoral Economics, Investment Treaty Architecture, and the Role of Governance', in Julien Chaisse (ed.), *Governance of the Global Sanitation and Water Services Market* (Cambridge University Press, 2016), 27 (observing the role of domestic regulatory capture in disputes involving water privatisation concessions); Alison E. Post, *Foreign and Domestic Investment in Argentina: The Politics of Privatized Infrastructure* (Cambridge University Press, 2014) (observing the role of domestic constituents in the developments of disputes with foreign investors during Argentina's financial crisis); Cédric Dupont, Thomas Schultz and Merih Angin, 'Political Risk and Investment Arbitration: An Empirical Study' (2016) 7 *Journal of International Dispute Settlement* 136.

[47] Benedict Kingsbury, Nico Krisch and Richard B. Stewart, 'The Emergence of Global Administrative Law' (2005) 68 *Law and Contemporary Problems* 15, 37.

[48] Benedict Kingsbury and Megan Donaldson, 'Global Administrative Law' in Rüdiger Wolfrum (ed.), *Max Planck Encyclopedia of Public International Law* (Oxford University Press, 2011) (explaining that global administrative law is concerned with situations in which 'domestic regulatory agencies or officials may be charged by treaties and other international governance arrangements to take regulatory decisions in pursuance of an internationally agreed objective').

international law on domestic governance,[49] thus fall within this global administrative scope.

Within the law and development literature, there is a strong current of opinion arguing that law is a tool for promoting development in low- and middle-income countries, and that the rule of law and good governance are preconditions for such development.[50] While this premise has served to underlie much international development policy,[51] other accounts in the law and development literature note that a central 'uncertainty' remains 'about the validity of basic assumptions underlying efforts to promote legal reform', and that 'given what is at stake for inhabitants of developing countries', this uncertainty is 'unsettling'.[52] Trebilcock, Davis and others give reason to be sceptical of optimistic claims as to the power of law to trigger reform, most notably due to the challenges posed by economic,

---

[49] Examples of global administrative law literature examining the impact of international law on domestic governance include Richard B. Stewart, 'The Global Regulatory Challenge to US Administrative Law' (2005) 37 *New York University Journal of International Law and Politics* 695; Daphne Barak-Erez and Oren Perez, 'Whose Administrative Law Is It Anyway? How Global Norms Reshape the Administrative State' (2013) 46 *Cornell International Law Journal* 455; Andrew Edgar and Rayner Thwaites, 'Implementing Treaties in Domestic Law: Translation, Enforcement and Administrative Law' (2018) 19 *Melbourne Journal of International Law* 24; Joel P. Trachtman, 'International Legal Control of Domestic Administrative Action' (2014) 17 *Journal of International Economic Law* 753. Notable examples of recent work examining the intersection of international law and the public administration in particular include, Paul Mertenskötter and Richard B. Stewart, 'Remote Control: Treaty Requirements for Regulatory Procedures' (2018) 104 *Cornell Law Review* 165 (demonstrating how recent trade agreements prescribe specific procedures for domestic administrative decision making); Jon S. T. Quah, *The Role of the Public Bureaucracy in Policy Implementation in Five ASEAN Countries* (Cambridge University Press, 2016) (examining the role of the public bureaucracy in policy implementation, including the implementation of ASEAN treaties); Hao Duy Phan, 'The Effects of ASEAN Treaties in Domestic Legal Orders: Evidence from Viet Nam' (2019) 17 *International Journal of Constitutional Law* 205 (illustrating the effects of ASEAN treaties on administrative procedures for the implementation of ASEAN treaty obligations in Viet Nam).

[50] See, for example, Thomas Carothers, *Promoting the Rule of Law Abroad: In Search of Knowledge* (Brookings Institution Press, 2010); Kenneth W. Dam, *The Law-Growth Nexus: The Rule of Law and Economic Development* (Brookings Institution Press, 2006). For an overview of the history of the study of law and development, see Davis and Trebilcock, 'The Relationship between Law and Development', 4. See also Stephan W. Schill, Christian J. Tams and Rainer Hofmann, 'International Investment Law and Development: Friends or Foes?', in Stephan W. Schill et al. (eds.), *International Investment Law and Development: Bridging the Gap* (Edward Elgar, 2015), 19–20; Trebilcock and Prado, *Advanced Introduction to Law and Development*.

[51] Tan, 'Reviving the Emperor's Old Clothes', 150–1.

[52] Davis and Trebilcock, 'The Relationship between Law and Development', 4, 6.

political and/or cultural obstacles.[53] This study seeks to contribute to this scholarship by empirically investigating (1) whether there is evidence that governments in a select group of countries in Asia have internalised investment treaty obligations into their decision-making processes; (2) what factors have affected whether these governments have internalised international investment obligations in their decision making; and (3) whether there is evidence in these case studies that treaty internalisation has led to governance reforms more generally, that is, the positive spillovers suggested by the rule of law thesis.

In the past decade, international legal scholarship has taken what Shaffer and Ginsburg identify as an 'empirical turn'.[54] Empirical studies now focus on the effects and effectiveness of international law and aim to explain variations. Empiricism has emerged in diverse fields of international law, including human rights (e.g. Simmons' empirical study on the effects of international human rights law on domestic politics),[55] international humanitarian law,[56] international trade law[57] and international environmental law.[58] In international investment law, empirical work has focused largely on the *economic* impact of investment treaties. Notable studies on the impact of investment treaties on FDI flows to host countries include, among others, work by Yackee,[59] Neumayer and Spess,[60] and Sauvant and

---

[53] *Ibid.* See also Trebilcock and Prado, *Advanced Introduction to Law and Development*, 45–62; Alvaro Santos, 'The World Bank's Uses of the "Rule of Law" Promise in Economic Development', in David M. Trubek and Alvaro Santos (eds.), *The New Law and Economic Development: A Critical Appraisal* (Cambridge University Press, 2006), 253; Michael J. Trebilcock and Ronald J. Daniels, *Rule of Law Reform and Development: Charting the Fragile Path of Progress* (Edward Elgar, 2008).

[54] Gregory C. Shaffer and Tom Ginsburg, 'The Empirical Turn in International Legal Scholarship' (2012) 106 *American Journal of International Law* 1.

[55] Simmons, *Mobilizing for Human Rights*.

[56] See, for example, James D. Morrow, 'When do States Follow the Laws of War?' (2007) 101 *American Political Science Review* 559, 566.

[57] See, for example, Andrew Guzman and Beth A. Simmons, 'To Settle or Empanel? An Empirical Analysis of Litigation and Settlement at the World Trade Organization' (2002) 31 *Journal of Legal Studies* 205; Chad P. Brown, 'Participation in WTO Dispute Settlement: Complaints, Interested Parties and Free Riders' (2005) 19 *World Bank Economic Review* 287; Gregory C. Shaffer, 'The Challenges of WTO Law: Strategies for Developing Country Adaptation' (2006) 5 *World Trade Review* 177; Judith Goldstein, Douglas Rivers and Michael Tomz, 'Institutions in International Relations: Understanding the Effects of the GATT and the WTO on World Trade' (2007) 61 *International Organization* 37.

[58] See, for example, Helmut Breitmeier, Oran R. Young and Michael Zürn, *Analyzing International Environmental Regimes: From Case Study to Database* (MIT Press, 2006).

[59] Yackee, 'Do Bilateral Investment Treaties Promote Foreign Direct Investment?'

[60] Neumayer and Spess, 'Do Bilateral Investment Treaties Increase Foreign Direct Investment to Developing Countries?'

Sachs.[61] Bonnitcha, Poulsen and Waibel review existing studies.[62] Others have examined whether an increase in FDI actually promotes growth in host states,[63] or whether investment treaties are more effective at attracting FDI in certain sectors (such as work by Busse and others on the extractive sector,[64] work by Colen and Guariso,[65] and Danzman).[66]

Compared to the work on the economic impact of investment treaties, empirical research on the impact of investment treaties on national governance is sparse. Scholars such as Bonnitcha[67] and Calamita[68] have flagged this absence. That said, a notable exception is the recent important work by Sattorova, who has developed an empirical argument with respect to investment treaties and national governance.[69] Further work

---

[61] Karl P. Sauvant and Lisa E. Sachs, *The Effect of Treaties on Foreign Direct Investment: Bilateral Investment Treaties, Double Taxation Treaties and Investment Flows* (Oxford University Press, 2009).

[62] Bonnitcha, Poulsen and Waibel, *The Political Economy of the Investment Treaty Regime*, 155–66 See also Poulsen, 'The Importance of BITs for Foreign Direct Investment and Political Risk Insurance'; Jonathan Bonnitcha, 'Foreign Investment, Development and Governance: What International Investment Law Can Learn from the Empirical Literature on Investment' (2012) 7 *Journal of International Dispute Settlement* 31.

[63] Laura Alfaro, Areendam Chanda, Sebnem Kalemi-Ozcan and Selin Sayek, 'Does Foreign Investment Promote Growth? Exploring the Role of Financial Markets on Linkages' (2010) 91 *Journal of Development Economics* 242; Eduardo Borensztein, José R de Gregorio and Jongwha Lee, 'How Does Foreign Investment Affect Economic Growth?' (1998) 45 *Journal of International Economics* 115; Frederick van der Ploeg, 'Natural Resources: Curse or Blessing?' (2011) 49 *Journal of Economic Literature* 366.

[64] Matthias Busse, Jens Königer and Peter Nunnenkamp, 'FDI Promotion through Bilateral Investment Treaties: More than a BIT?' (2010) 146 *Review of World Economics* 147.

[65] Lisabeth Colen and Andrea Guariso, 'What Type of FDI Is Attracted by BITs?', in Johan F. M. Swinnen, Jan Wouters and Olivier De Schutter (eds.), *Foreign Direct Investment and Human Development: The Law and Economics of International Investment Agreements* (Routledge, 2012), 138; Lisabeth Colen, Damian Persyn and Andrea Guariso, 'Bilateral Investment Treaties and FDI: Does the Sector Matter?' (2016) 83 *World Development* 193.

[66] Sarah B. Danzman, 'Contracting with Whom? The Differential Effects of Investment Treaties on FDI' (2016) 42 *International Interactions: Empirical and Theoretical Research in International Relations* 452.

[67] Jonathan Bonnitcha, 'Assessing the Impacts of Investment Treaties: Overview of the Evidence' (IISD Report 2017).

[68] N. Jansen Calamita, 'The Rule of Law, Investment Treaties, and Economic Growth: Mapping Normative and Empirical Questions', in Jeffrey Jowell, J Christopher Thomas and Jan van Zyl Smit (eds.), *The Importance of the Rule of Law in Promoting Development* (Singapore Academy of Law, 2015), 103.

[69] Sattorova, *The Impact of Investment Treaty Law on Host States*. See also Ginsburg, 'International Substitutes for Domestic Institutions', 119–20; Côté, 'Is It Chilly Out There?'; Christine Côté, 'A Chilling Effect? The Impact of International Investment Agreements on National Regulatory Autonomy in the Areas of Health, Safety and the Environment', unpublished PhD Thesis, London School of Economics and Political Science (2014).

in this vein includes Ginsburg's 2005 article on 'Bilateral Investment Treaties and Governance'.[70]

Finally, while some recent empirical work has begun to address the intersection of international law and public administration, there has been little work addressing how, if at all, government officials internalise international law when they take decisions regarding original, domestic measures. Exceptions in this regard include work on decision making in the executive branch in the United States[71] and in New Zealand.[72] We are not aware of any similar studies involving Asian or developing states.

1.4   A Typology of Internalisation Processes and Mechanisms

How does a government attempt to internalise its international obligations in its decision-making processes? What are the processes through which this happens?[73] An empirical inquiry into the abstract notion of internalisation is impossible without clear indicators which operationalise the term. To that end, we distinguish between three broad types of institutional processes of internalisation: informational, monitoring and remedial (Figure 1.1). We would expect to observe at least one of these processes in a state that seeks to internalise its international obligations. Although the focus of our present inquiry is on international investment law, the typology we set out below may be of value to inquiries regarding the internalisation of international law in any field.

Given our interest in the processes of governmental decision making, we take a governance rather than a black letter law approach. In our view, a narrow, black letter law approach would hardly capture the reality of

---

[70] Ginsburg, 'International Substitutes for Domestic Institutions' 119–20.
[71] See, for example, Neomi Rao, 'Public Choice and International Law Compliance: The Executive Branch Is a "They", Not an "It"' (2011) 96 *Minnesota Law Review* 194; Rebecca Ingber, 'Interpretation Catalysts and Executive Branch Legal Decisionmaking' (2013) 38 *Yale Journal of International Law* 359; Kevin L. Cope, 'Congress's International Legal Response' (2015) 113 *Michigan Law Review* 1115; Daphna Renan, 'The Law Presidents Make' (2017) 103 *Virginia Law Review* 805; James P. Pfiffner, 'Decision Making in the Obama White House' (2011) 41 *Presidential Studies Quarterly* 244.
[72] Dan Moore, 'Engagement with Human Rights by Administrative Decision-Makers: A Transformative Opportunity to Build a More Grassroots Human Rights Culture' (2017) 49 *Ottawa Law Review* 131; Arla Marie Kerr, 'Untapped Potential: Administrative Law and International Environmental Obligations' (2008) 6 *New Zealand Journal of Public and International Law* 81.
[73] See Peter J. May, 'Policy Design and Implementation', in B. Guy Peters and Jon Pierre (eds.), *The SAGE Handbook of Public Administration* (SAGE Publishing, 2012), 279 (addressing the role of policy design in carrying out and implementing policies).

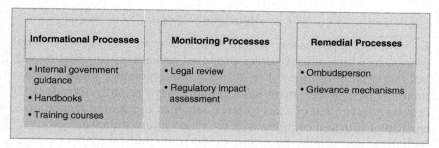

Figure 1.1   Examples of informational, monitoring and remedial internalisation processes and mechanisms

how governments run their affairs and would provide very few insights regarding the possible effects of investment treaties on national governance. We are thus interested not only in formal, legally binding laws and rules but also informal (legally non-binding) norms, practices and processes, through which the government manages its affairs.[74]

We set out our typology in the following subsections.

1.4.1   Informational Processes

By 'informational processes', we refer to processes that diffuse information and communicate the state's international legal obligations to relevant domestic actors.[75] For example, higher executive or administrative bodies might issue internal guidance, policies or instructions to guide officials as to the application of international obligations. Such processes might include a handbook or a manual, or a training course that informs government officials of the existence and content of the international obligations and seeks to improve knowledge within ministries, agencies or local authorities.[76] Informational processes attempt to internalise the state's international obligations *ex ante* – before or during the process of decision making.

---

[74] See Thomas G. Weiss and Rorden Wilkinson, *International Organization and Global Governance* (Taylor & Francis, 2013).

[75] See, for example, OECD, *Policy Framework for Investment* (OECD Publishing, 2015), 35. The OECD sets out a checklist on effective compliance with investment treaties, which includes the following point: 'What efforts are made to communicate to government agencies the implications of IIAs for their areas of responsibility (e.g., implementation guides)?'.

[76] See, for example, Government of Colombia, Ministerio de Comercio, Industria y Turismo, *Conozca los Compromisos y Obligaciones en Materia de Inversion de Colombia* (2009); Government of Colombia, Ministerio de Comercio, Industria y Turismo, *ABC de los*

1.4.2   Monitoring Processes

By 'monitoring processes', we refer to processes such as a governmental process by which officials screen proposed policies for consistency with international obligations. For example, the regulatory impact assessments (RIAs), which many OECD states have recently introduced,[77] require government officials to assess whether a proposed regulation is consistent with and complies with the state's international obligations,[78] including, specifically, its international trade and investment obligations.[79] Another example might be a requirement to consult relevant governmental legal experts regarding the compliance of proposed measures with international obligations,[80] or any *ex ante* (legal) review of

---

Acuerdos Internacionales de Inversion (undated); Government of Peru, Ministerio de Economia y Finanzas, *Guía de Compromisos en los Acuerdos Internacionales de Inversión y Prevención de Controversias Internacionales de Inversión en Perú* (2013). See generally N. Jansen Calamita, 'Investment Treaties and Governance Project Concept Paper: An Investment Treaty Handbook for APEC Economies', *NUS Centre for International Law Working Paper* 19/04 (February 2019) (surveying handbooks and other materials used by governments to disseminate information about investment treaty obligations within government). See also Melissa A. Poole, 'International Instruments in Administrative Decisions: Mainstreaming International Law' (1999) 30 *Victoria University Wellington Law Review* 91; Jürgen Friedrich and Eva J. Lohse, 'Revisiting the Junctures of International and Domestic Administration in Times of New Forms of Governance: Modes of Implementing Standards for Sustainable Development and Their Legitimacy Challenges' (2008) 2 *European Journal of Legal Studies* 49, 54–55 (describing how the Brazilian Secretary for Agriculture and Fisheries enacted an internal administrative directive which determines that the development of fisheries and aquaculture should follow the international code of conduct for responsible fisheries).

[77] See OECD, *Introductory Handbook for Undertaking Regulatory Impact Analysis* (OECD Publishing, 2008); OECD, *Regulatory Impact Assessment*, OECD Best Practice Principles for Regulatory Policy (OECD Publishing, 2020).

[78] Government of Canada, Treasury Board of Canada Secretariat, *Guidelines on International Regulatory Cooperation and Cooperation* (2007).

[79] Robert Basedow and Céline Kauffmann, 'International Trade and Good Regulatory Practices Assessing the Trade Impacts of Regulation', *OECD Regulatory Policy Working Papers*, vol. 4 (OECD Publishing, 2016). The European Union's 'Better Regulation Toolbox' requires the government officials in charge of a proposed regulation to screen it against the EU's international trade and investment obligations and to assess its compatibility. See European Commission, *Better Regulation Toolbox*, https://ec.europa.eu/info/sites/info/files/better-regulation-toolbox_2.pdf. See also OECD, *Policy Framework for Investment* (OECD Publishing, 2015), 116.

[80] That is the case, for example, in Canada. See Government of Canada, *Guidelines on International Regulatory Cooperation and Cooperation* in Section 3.1. See also Basedow and Kauffmann, 'International Trade and Good Regulatory Practices', 26 (providing the example of Germany where, if a proposed regulation has an impact on international trade obligations, the government official in charge of the proposed regulation must involve the Ministry of Foreign Affairs and Trade).

decisions or actions within the government for conformity with international obligations.[81]

1.4.3   Remedial Processes

Remedial processes are designed to correct or defend the state's compliance with its international obligations.[82] For example, states might create an ombudsperson that reviews a final administrative regulation for consistency with international obligations or resolves problems with foreign investors before they become formalised disputes.[83] Alternatively, states might adopt an early warning system to address investment grievances and consider the state's position under its international obligations.[84] Such processes are *ex post* – after a decision has already been made.

1.4.4   Cross-Cutting Characteristics of Internalisation Measures and Processes

Within the typology of measures that we have identified, further refinements are possible regarding processes of internalisation. In the following subsections, we highlight four main cross-cutting characteristics (Figure 1.2). We distinguish between them for analytical purposes, though in practice they may overlap.

1.4.4.1   Specific versus Adapted Processes of Internalisation

Conceptually, a particular measure or process of internalisation may have been designed specifically for investment treaty obligations or it may

---

[81] See Government of Canada, *International Trade Agreements and Local Government: A Guide for Canadian Municipalities*, www.international.gc.ca/trade-agreements-accords-commerciaux/ressources/fcm/complete-guide-complet.aspx?lang=eng. See also Koh, 'Why Do Nations Obey International Law?', 2656 (defining legal internalisation as occurring when 'an international norm is internalised into the domestic legal system through executive action, judicial interpretation, legislative action or some combination of the three ... Legislative internalisation occurs when domestic lobbying embeds international law norms into binding domestic legislation or even constitutional law .... ').

[82] See, for example, OECD, *Policy Framework for Investment* (OECD Publishing, 2015), 116; OECD, *Best Practice Principles in Regulatory Policy: Regulatory Enforcement and Inspections* (OECD Publishing, 2014).

[83] OECD, *Best Practice Principles in Regulatory Policy*, 28.

[84] For example, Peru's *Sistema de Coordinación y Respuesta del Estado en Controversias Internacionales de Inversión* (SICRECI), established by Ley No. 28933 (2006) (and modified by Ley No. 29213 (2010)) and the Dominican Republic's *División de Prevención, Solución de Controversias e Inversión*, established by Resolución del 22 de Agosto de 2012.

Cross-cutting Characteristics	Informational Processes	Monitoring Processes	Remedial Processes
Specific	Training course for government officials on investment treaties.	Legal review for consistency of decision, policy or law with the state's investment treaty obligations.	Grievance mechanism designed to address complaints by foreign investors.
Adapted	Training course for government officials on public international law, including on investment treaties.	Legal review for consistency of decision, policy or law with the state's international legal obligations, including its investment treaty commitments.	Grievance mechanism generally available for complaints by the public against the administration.
Ad Hoc	Training course held periodically, or when the opportunity or need arises.	Legal review carried out on a case-by-case basis, or when the need or opportunity arises.	Decision to set up a committee to review a grievance when a particular complaint is raised.
Consistent	Training course held regularly for government officials.	Legal review carried out on all draft decisions, policies or laws.	A standing ombudsperson institution.
Formal	A government guidance document or policy setting out binding directions.	Legal review is part of the regular institutional process within the government.	A law or policy establishing a grievance mechanism.
Informal	Materials to promote awareness of state's investment treaty commitments.	'Corridor discussions' with the legal advisor when the need arises.	Internal government discussions or negotiations regarding investor's concerns.

Figure 1.2   Examples of cross-cutting characteristics of internalisation measures

have been originally designed for a different purpose and later have been adapted for use with regard to investment treaty obligations. An example of a specific process would be the creation of informational handbook on investment obligations, or the creation of an early warning system or process for regulating intra-government coordination in the event of a foreign investor grievance.

In contrast to specific processes, adapted processes are designed for a different purpose but are then applied to investment treaty commitments; for example, a process by which government legal advisors review prospective measures for general legality (which comes to include review for compatibility with investment treaty commitments, alongside other legal commitments). Likewise, RIAs, which monitor for *any* impacts of proposed measures, also assess the impact of the proposed regulation on investment law obligations (alongside other international and domestic legal obligations). Such processes are created or available for the review of adherence with a different (sometimes broader) category of norms than investment treaty obligations.

1.4.4.2 Ad Hoc versus Consistent Processes of Internalisation

The consistency of a process of internalisation may vary from one country to another or within a particular country as among different internalisation measures. An example of an *ad hoc* process of internalisation might be a short-term informational campaign on investment treaty obligations for government officials or an episodic training programme, which does not occur on a consistently recurring basis. Examples of consistent processes, by contrast, can be found in well-established processes for the internal assessment of the compatibility of new legislation or new regulation with investment treaty obligations, or in regularised training programmes within government.

1.4.4.3 Formal versus Informal Processes

As observed earlier, we think that a narrow, black letter law approach to internalisation would hardly capture the reality of how governments run their affairs, and would provide few insights regarding the effect of investment treaties on national governance, and how international obligations are considered. When conceptualising processes of internalisation, therefore, we seek to capture the range of both informal (legally non-binding) and formal (legally binding) rules, norms and practices, through which the government manages its affairs.

Informal processes may manifest themselves as processes that are undertaken without a legal obligation to do so. Such informal processes may become institutionalised over time, such as when a process becomes a matter of government convention or custom that is not dependent upon individual actors or groups of actors, for example established, informal channels of communication among agencies.[85] Informal measures might also include handbooks, education, training, etc., which, although serving as an informational resource for officials about the state's obligations, are informal inasmuch as the materials do not prescribe binding practices or processes. Formal processes, on the other hand, are established through legally binding norms, such as a regulation establishing procedures for coordinating the exchange of information within government regarding potential investment treaty claim[86] or a requirement that an RIA be conducted with respect to prospective government measures.

1.4.4.4 Principle versus Practice

Finally, in observing processes for internalisation, it warrants noting that evidence of the existence of a formal process does not mean that it is followed in practice. A state may adopt formal processes of internalisation, which are not used, whether as a result of bureaucratic intransigence, lack of awareness or lack of capacity. Similarly, informal processes, such as governmental conventions, may be recognised in principle but fail in practice to operate in whole or in part. While the existence of a process is a necessary condition for its possible effect on decision making, its existence in itself does not indicate the actual effect that it will have in practice.

1.4.5 Locating Internalisation in Governmental Decision Making

In the preceding section, we have set out a typology of measures and processes which framework operationalises the concept of internalisation as

---

[85] As highlighted in the law and development literature, while Western legal models assume the centrality of law, in some developing countries, law plays a less central role, with most governmental and social interaction and control being informal. Such informal processes appear to be particularly significant in certain Asian countries. See Tom Ginsburg, 'Does Law Matter for Economic Development? Evidence from East Asia' (2000) 34 *Law and Society Review* 829.

[86] For example, Peru's 'early warning' system for addressing potential investor–state disputes is established and operates by virtue of Ley No. 28933 (2006) (and modified by Ley No. 29213 (2010)). The systems in the Dominican Republic and Colombia are similarly established by formal legal instrument. See Dominican Republic, Resolución del 22 de Agosto de 2012 (establishing the *División de Prevención, Solución de Controversias e Inversión*).

an observable phenomenon of government. In this section, we consider where within government the internalisation of international obligations is likely to be observed.

Looking at the issue from a governance perspective, we see that decision making occurs across the entire state network of government, often at identifiable nodes. Decisions may be taken within different branches of government (executive, legislative and judicial), at different levels of government (central, regional/state and local) and sometimes across branches and across levels. In addition, within each branch of government, there may be nodes along the hierarchy: for example, between central and local levels of government, between ministries and the public administration (bureaucracy), between high-level and mid-level bureaucrats within administrative authorities or agencies, and, in federal states, between the federal and state governments.

Considering the issue from the perspective of international law, as noted earlier, international legal doctrine treats the 'state' as a unified entity such that the acts or omissions of all the state's organs, as personified in its officials, are regarded as acts or omissions of the state for the purposes of international responsibility.[87] States thus incur international responsibility for actions taken by every branch of government, at every level of government, whether national or sub-national,[88] as well as by non-state actors exercising governmental authority[89] or acting under governmental direction or control.[90]

The wide range of entities and persons capable of taking measures for which the state is internationally responsible is amplified by the nature of investment treaties and foreign investment. The pervasive presence of foreign investment throughout national economies is such that a wide range of entities and persons may take decisions of one kind or another with respect to or impacting upon a foreign investment or investor. Moreover, the broad scope of investment treaty obligations means that virtually all aspects of the host's economy and regulatory system will be subject to the investment treaty's disciplines, regardless of sector of investment and regardless of the type of government measure. As a result, for states with investment treaty portfolios, virtually all decisions across government branches and levels with respect to a

---

[87] International Law Commission, 'Articles on the Responsibility of States for Internationally Wrongful Acts, with Commentaries' (2001) Art. 4, comment (5).
[88] *Ibid.*, Art. 4 and comment (1).
[89] *Ibid.*, Art. 5.
[90] *Ibid.*, Art. 8.

foreign investor or investment are likely to be of a kind for which the host state may be legally responsible.

That said, it does not follow that all governmental decision makers are equally likely to take decisions that implicate obligations under an investment treaty. As noted previously, according to a study of investor–state treaty disputes by Williams, examining 584 arbitration cases from 1990 to 2014, 61 per cent of cases were triggered primarily by administrative measures, whether taken at the level of central, regional or local government; 26 per cent were triggered by legislative measures alone; and 11 per cent were related to judicial decisions.[91] Moreover, the economic sectors of the underlying investments in these disputes ranged across all aspects for the host economies, from investments in extractive industries to banking to construction to agriculture to the provision of public services (energy, water services, etc.) to manufacturing, transport and telecommunications.[92]

Building upon this evidence, and the role of administrative or executive decision making in the governance of the modern state, our emphasis in this study is largely focused on the executive and the public administration (although the legislature and the judiciary are also considered in the case studies). To the extent that states may be observed to have internalised their investment treaty obligations, we would expect those processes of internalisation to be found most likely with respect to decision making by the government actors whose decisions are most likely to affect foreign investors and their investments and who are most likely to have direct contact with them – the executive branch of government and its administration.

[91] Williams, 'Risky Business or Risky Politics', 42. These findings are similar to those developed in an earlier, smaller scale study by Jensen and Caddel. Looking at the distribution of investment treaty disputes as of September 2013, Jensen and Caddel found that 48 per cent of investor claims had been based upon measures originating in the executive branch of central government. An additional 38 per cent of claims had been based on measures originating at the sub-national level, by state-owned or controlled entities or by other agencies. The balance of claims was based upon measures taken by the legislative and judicial branches. See Jeremy Caddel and Nathan M. Jensen, *Columbia FDI Perspectives*, No. 120 (28 April 2014).

[92] Williams, 'Risky Business or Risky Politics', 40. Using the World Bank sectoral classification system, Williams noted disputes across at least fifteen different sectors: oil, gas and mining (25%); electric power and other energy (14%); construction (7%); banking and finance (6%); manufacturing (6%); agricultural, forest and fisheries (6%); telecommunications (6%); transportation (5%); water and waste management (4%); food and beverage (3%); other services (3%); real estate (3%); hospitality/tourism (3%); healthcare and pharmaceuticals (2%); media (2%); other (3%); and unknown (2%). *Ibid.*, 41.

We note, however, that like the state itself, the executive is not a unified decision maker but rather comprised of a wide variety of decision-making nodes and that variations in internalisation among those nodes are likely. Thus, for example, while the ministry charged with negotiating free trade agreements for the government can be expected to evidence a high awareness of the obligations contained in the investment treaties it is charged with negotiating, and to consider them in its decision making, the situation is likely to be different in other ministries or at sub-national levels of government.

1.5   Factors Impacting Internalisation

Inasmuch as international legal theory has opened up the 'black box' of the *state*, it has not accounted for the specific factors and dynamics influencing the work of the executive and the bureaucracy. This is an important omission. Bureaucracies are complex organisations that seldom function in a regular and predictable manner, with many factors influencing bureaucratic effectiveness.[93] This is even more so in host developing states that lack developed regulatory infrastructures, and must deal with significant political, economic and cultural challenges.[94]

Traditional theories of international law, as noted previously, have assumed that the state will internalise international law. The public administration and public policy literature, antithetically, elaborates on the complexity of the regulatory process and the many factors that influence its success or failure.[95] Moreover, the law and development literature highlights the daunting challenges that developing countries must overcome in adopting legal or regulatory reform. Davis and Trebilcock thus stress that our 'expectations about the impact of such reforms should be modest'.[96]

In what follows, we set out a framework for understanding the factors that may affect the internalisation process or the adoption of internalisation measures, drawing on insights from the public policy, international relations, and law and development literature. This model is designed to collect sometimes disparate strands of scholarship and to provide a roadmap for the empirical inquiry carried out in the case studies. While much of this literature is focused on implementation or compliance, its

---

[93] Søren C. Winter, 'Implementation', in B. Guy Peters and Jon Pierre (eds.), *The SAGE Handbook of Public Administration* (SAGE Publications, 2012), 255.
[94] Davis and Trebilcock, 'The Relationship between Law and Development'.
[95] Winter, 'Implementation'.
[96] Davis and Trebilcock, 'The Relationship between Law and Development', 6.

insights are equally instructive for the question of internalisation. To this end, while we take a generous approach, addressing many of the factors mentioned in the literature, we do not take an *a priori* position regarding the relative importance of any factor. Moreover, depending on the case, factors may overlap or weigh differently in their relative importance. This categorisation serves analytical purposes.

We organise our thinking about the factors that may affect internalisation into three main categories.[97] The first category encompasses elements with respect to the context of public administration in the state. The second category subsumes elements related to the state's broader national context. The third category concerns the international context, namely the state's investment treaty commitments and the presence of claims thereunder. We outline these categories and elements in Figure 1.3.

1.5.1   Public Administration Context

1.5.1.1   Internalisation Strategy?

The public policy literature stresses the importance of a policy design, or policy strategy, that is, a clearly planned set of measures or processes – be they instruments, designated actors or allocation of resources – for achieving the policy goal.[98] In operationalising our conception of internalisation above, we outlined our distinction among broad types of processes of internalisation: informational, monitoring and remedial. We recall that typology here because the presence or absence, as well as the character and operation, of such processes will obviously bear upon the internalisation of the state's investment treaty commitments.

1.5.1.2   Bureaucratic Culture

While the liberal international legal scholarship has opened up the 'black box' of the state, it still treats the government and bureaucracy as a 'black box', assuming that it translates international law inputs into outputs.[99] Yet, as James Wilson asserts in his seminal work on bureaucracy, 'organisation

---

[97] Most of the literature we draw upon focuses on compliance. Although compliance goes further than internalisation as it refers to whether a state actually has adhered to the international obligation, see Jacobson and Brown Weiss, 'A Framework for Analysis', 4, this work provides insight into factors that influence state behaviour, and as such is relevant for the question of internalisation.

[98] May, 'Policy Design and Implementation', 279.

[99] James Q. Wilson, *Bureaucracy: What Government Agencies Do and Why They Do It* (Basic Books, 1989), 23.

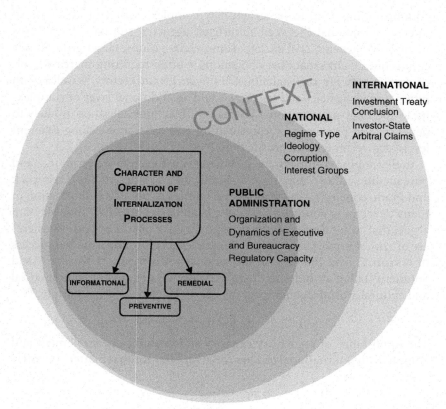

Figure 1.3   Model of factors impacting internalisation

matters'![100] The dynamics of *organisational* and *inter-organisational pro-cesses* are very important[101] and may impact internalisation. For example, according to the public policy theory on 'complexity of joint action', imple-mentation is negatively related to the number of actors, the diversity of their interests, and the number of decision and veto points.[102] Contemporary

[100]   *Ibid.*, 14–28.
[101]   Laurence J. O'Toole, 'Interorganizational Relations and Policy Implementation', in B. Guy Peters and Jon Pierre (eds.), *The SAGE Handbook of Public Administration* (SAGE Publications, 2012), 292.
[102]   Winter, 'Implementation', 259; Jeffrey L. Pressman and Aaron B. Wildavsky, *Implementation: How Great Expectations in Washington Are Dashed in Oakland; Or, Why It's Amazing That Federal Programs Work at All, This Being a Saga of the Economic Development Administration as Told by Two Sympathetic Observers Who Seek to Build Morals* (University of California Press, 1974).

administrations tend to be structurally complex, with a proliferation of inter-organisational (between ministries, agencies, sub-national governments and agencies, civil society, commercial groups, target groups, etc.) connections.[103] International obligations – often requiring increased collaboration between national ministries, agencies and sectors, as well as with international agencies and partners – add an additional layer of complexity to the inter-organisational process.[104] Thus, internalisation is likely to depend upon processes for coordination and coherence among different levels of government and jurisdictions.[105]

In developing countries, these challenges are even more profound, and bureaucratic culture may pose a significant impediment. As Trebilcock and Prado conclude: 'The frailties and failures of public administration in many developing countries have long been documented'.[106] Indeed, Dam argues that cultural and social factors (in the administration and elsewhere) are of critical importance in determining legal institutions and the success of reform.[107] And Putnam, in his seminal comparison of Northern and Southern Italian attitudes to the rule of law, has demonstrated how social and cultural attitudes can impact the effectiveness of legal institutions.[108]

1.5.1.3 Regulatory Capacity

The importance of regulatory capacity and resources to implement and comply with international treaties (or any policy for that matter) is widely

---

[103] O'Toole, 'Interorganizational Relations and Policy Implementation'.
[104] Kenneth I. Hanf, 'American Public Administration and Impacts of International Governance' (2002) 62 *Public Administration Review* 158.
[105] OECD, *Policy Framework for Investment* (OECD Publishing, 2015), 19, 115–24. Quite often such processes for coordination or coherence may be lacking or applied inconsistently. As observed by Wilson, bureaucracies will 'positively resist any effort to set forth their policies in the form of clear and general rules', and 'bureaucratic action is sometimes regular and predictable, but just as often it is irregular and unpredictable'. See Wilson, *Bureaucracy: What Government Agencies Do and Why They Do It*, xvii–xviii. Aware of this challenge, the OECD Best Practice Principles in Regulatory Policy sets out guidance to countries on how to ensure coordination between national and international rules. See also Jurgen Friedrich and Eva J. Lohse, 'Revisiting the Junctures of International and Domestic Administration in Times of New Forms of Governance: Modes of Implementing Standards for Sustainable Development and Their Legitimacy Challenges', 83 ('the degree of institutional organization, the density of domestic regulation of the matter and the underlying legal culture of a particular legal order may lead to different degrees and different ways of implementation').
[106] Trebilcock and Prado, *Advanced Introduction to Law and Development*, 133.
[107] Dam, *The Law-Growth Nexus*.
[108] Robert D. Putnam, *Making Democracy Work: Civic Traditions in Modern Italy* (Princeton University Press, 1993).

recognised in the public policy and law and development literature.[109] In numerous studies, limited regulatory capacity and limited economic and human resources in developing countries have been shown to play an important role in the failure to implement and enforce laws and regulations.[110] Internalisation thus can be undermined by lack of personnel, inadequate training, lack of technical expertise, lack of regulatory infrastructure, and so on.

Kaufmann and Kraay, for example, demonstrate how costly it is to operate legal or regulatory institutions, to train and retain staff and to disseminate information about the law.[111] Similarly, Bach and Newman demonstrate how regulatory capacity affects the enforcement of international insider trading rules.[112] Using Brazil as her case study, McAllister highlights how Brazil's failure to enforce environmental law is a story of regulatory agencies chronically beset by underfunding and understaffing.[113] Regulatory approaches that succeed in developed countries may be inadequate or unworkable in the developing world, where the capacity to enforce basic components of laws may be lacking.[114]

In a similar vein, Chayes' and Chayes' work on 'managerial compliance' has stressed how a lack of state capacity is a barrier to compliance.[115] As noted, the public administrations in developing countries often lack technical, financial or other capacities, which in turn impact their capability to effectively internalise international obligations. Empirical studies in diverse fields of international law – such as environment[116] or human

---

[109] Winter, 'Implementation'; Trebilcock and Prado, *Advanced Introduction to Law and Development*, 56–7.

[110] Lesly K. McAllister, *Making Law Matter: Environmental Protection and Legal Institutions in Brazil* (Stanford University Press, 2008); Jorge Nef, 'Environmental Policy and Politics in Chile: A Latin-American Case Study', in O. P. Dwivedi and Dhirendra K. Vajpeyi (eds.), *Environmental Policies in the Third World: A Comparative Analysis* (Greenwood Press, 1995), 141; Stephen P. Mumme, 'Environmental Policy and Politics in Mexico', in Uday Desai (ed.), *Ecological Policy and Politics in Developing Countries: Economic Growth, Democracy, and Environment* (State University of New York Press, 1998), 183.

[111] Daniel Kaufmann and Aart Kraay, 'Growth without Governance', *World Bank Policy Research Working Paper* 2928 (2013).

[112] Bach and Newman, 'Transgovernmental Networks and Domestic Policy Convergence'.

[113] McAllister, *Making Law Matter*.

[114] *Ibid.*

[115] Abram Chayes, Antonia H. Chayes and Ronald B. Mitchell, 'Managing Compliance: A Comparative Perspective', in Edith Brown Weiss and Harold K. Jacobson (eds.), *Engaging Countries: Strengthening Compliance with International Environmental Accords* (MIT Press, 1998), 39.

[116] Simmons, 'Treaty Compliance and Violation', 286.

rights[117]– have illustrated these problems in practice. Corruption has also been identified as eroding capacity and having a significant impact on compliance with international obligations.[118] Whether subsumed within consideration of regulatory capacity or treated independently, corruption likely stands as a factor affecting internalisation.[119]

Finally, in the field of investment law, Williams has observed a positive link between regulatory capacity and investment disputes, and found that the lower the income and level of development (taken as a proxy for low state capacity), the higher the likelihood that the state will face an investment treaty dispute.[120] This is an especially suggestive finding given that in contrast to other international regimes (e.g. WTO, ILO, World Bank, IMF, IAEA and many more),[121] the investment treaty regime lacks coordinated institutional support for regulatory capacity building, arguably undermining domestic internalisation of investment treaty obligations.[122]

1.5.2   National Context

The internalisation of investment treaties may not only be influenced by the public administration context within which a policy is developed but also by broader national factors. In Shaffer's view, domestic dynamics are the most important factor in understanding the impact of international

---

[117] Wade M. Cole, 'Mind the Gap: State Capacity and the Implementation of Human Rights Treaties' (2015) 69 *International Organization* 405, 405–6.

[118] Nathan W. Freeman, 'Domestic Institutions, Capacity Limitations, and Compliance Costs: Host Country Determinants of Investment Treaty Arbitrations, 1987–2007' (2013) 39 *International Interactions* 54. Freeman relies on the following indicators: the 'Law and Order' and 'Corruption' variables from the International Country Risk Guide (ICRG); the 'Rule of Law' and 'Control of Corruption' variables from the Worldwide Governance Indicators (WGI) Project; and Transparency International's Perceptions of Corruption Index (CPI). See PRS Group, *International Country Risk Guide*, www.prsgroup.com/explore-our-products/international-country-risk-guide/; *Worldwide Governance Indicators*, https://info.worldbank.org/governance/wgi/; and Transparency International, *Corruption Perspectives Index*, www.transparency.org/en/cpi/2020/index/nzl.

[119] Dupont, Schultz and Angin, 'Political Risk and Investment Arbitration' (examining the correlation between the rule of law and corruption with investment treaty claims).

[120] Williams, 'Risky Business or Risky Politics'.

[121] See examples in Moshe Hirsch, 'Developing Countries', in Rüdiger Wolfrum (ed.), *Max Planck Encyclopedia of Public International Law* (Oxford University Press, 2017).

[122] Capacity-building activities do take place with respect to investment treaties of course, but in an uncoordinated, ad hoc way by a variety of disparate actors, including NGOs, international organisations, developed states, international law firms and academic institutions.

rules on the state.[123] Thus, domestic demands, domestic power struggles and domestic culture 'shape how transnational legal norms are received and implemented in practice', and '[s]ometimes they lead to the rejection of transnational law'.[124] Jacobson and Brown Weiss similarly state that: 'The social, cultural, political, and economic characteristics of the countries clearly influence implementation and compliance'.[125]

One notable element of the domestic context that may impact the extent to which states internalise and comply with their international obligations are national elites or other powerful interest groups.[126] This finding corresponds with the insight of liberal theory that the state is 'disaggregated' into different, and at times competing, actors and interests.[127] The work of Williams supports this observation in the investment treaty regime, finding that treaty violations are often a result of domestic interest group pressure.[128]

In addition to interest groups, the research on compliance suggests that political factors such as regime type and ideology of the ruling government may also impact the way in which a state internalises its international treaty obligations. For example, there is support in the literature for the theory that democracies comply better with their international obligations in general,[129] as well as studies asserting that democracies

---

[123] Shaffer, 'The Dimensions and Determinants of State Change', 37: 'Arguably, the most important determinant of state change is the affinity of the transnational legal reform efforts with the demands and discursive frames of domestic constituencies and elites in light of domestic configurations of power and the extent of change at stake'.

[124] Ibid., 43.

[125] Jacobson and Brown Weiss, 'A Framework for Analysis', 7.

[126] See, for example, Xinyaun Dai, International Institutions and National Policies (Cambridge University Press, 2007); Simmons, 'Treaty Compliance and Violation', 286; Shaffer, 'The Dimensions and Determinants of State Change', 43 (noting how the implementation of international environmental obligations can lead to a backlash from commercial groups who are adversely affected by environmental regulations, leading in turn to treaty violation); Patrick Bernhagen, 'Business and International Environmental Agreements: Domestic Sources of Participation and Compliance by Advanced Industrialized Democracies' (2008) 8 Global Environmental Politics 78 (arguing that greater inclusion of NGOs and business in policymaking leads to better compliance).

[127] Moravcsik, 'Taking Preferences Seriously'; Slaughter Burley, 'International Law and International Relations Theory'; Putnam, 'Diplomacy and Domestic Politics'.

[128] Williams, 'Risky Business or Risky Politics'. See also Calamita, 'Are Investments in Water Different?'; Post, Foreign and Domestic Investment in Argentina.

[129] Simmons, 'Treaty Compliance and Violation', 280. See also Todd Landman, Protecting Human Rights: A Comparative Study (Georgetown University Press, 2005) (examining the compliance of democracies with human rights treaties).

comply better with their investment treaty obligations specifically.[130] On the other hand, leftist governments have historically been more likely to expropriate the property of foreign investors.[131] Similarly, governments with strong nationalist ideologies may be more likely to resist complying with international legal restraints than governments of different political leanings.[132] The number of veto players within government also may play a role in internalisation. Some studies, for example, assert that presidential systems – likely due to the small number of veto players – are more likely to violate investment treaties.[133] At the same time, a smaller number of key decision makers may also suggest a smaller group within which effective internalisation is necessary. In the same vein, internalisation may well be more challenging in federal or decentralised states – with a multiplicity of decision makers – rather than in unitary states.

In thinking about these factors, it warrants bearing in mind that the effects of political factors can be particularly pronounced in developing countries. Important insights from the law and development field highlight how crucial political factors and competing political ideologies and interests can be for the successful adoption of legal or regulatory reforms in developing countries.[134] In a series of case studies on reforms in Russia, China, Latin America and the Middle East, Carothers and others have shown how the success of reform has often depended upon political conditions, such as support by political elites, or a change from authoritarian to democratic regime.[135]

1.5.3   International Context

1.5.3.1   Investment Treaties: Treaty Conclusion

The rule of law thesis posits that entering into investment treaties will lead states to internalise these international commitments into their

---

[130]   Nathan M. Jensen, Noel P. Johnson, Chia yi Lee and Hadi Sahin, 'Crisis and Contract Breach: The Domestic and International Determinants of Expropriation' (2020) 15 *The Review of International Organizations* 869; Carl H. Knutsen, 'Democracy, Dictatorship and Protection of Property Rights' (2011) 47 *Journal of Development Studies* 164.

[131]   Quan Li, 'Democracy, Autocracy, and Expropriation of Foreign Direct Investment' (2009) 42 *Comparative Political Studies* 1098.

[132]   Chayes, Chayes and Mitchell, 'Managing Compliance', 39.

[133]   Knutsen, 'Democracy, Dictatorship and Protection of Property Rights'.

[134]   See, for example, Kleinfeld, 'Competing Definitions of the Rule of Law', 55–6 ('achieving rule of law ends requires political and cultural, not only institutional, change'); David Kennedy, 'The "Rule of Law", Political Choices and Development Common Sense', in David M. Trubek and Alvaro Santos (eds.), *The New Law and Economic Development: A Critical Appraisal* (Cambridge University Press, 2006), 95.

[135]   Carothers, *Promoting the Rule of Law Abroad*.

governmental decision making.[136] In other words, the fear of arbitration by foreign investors should act as 'a deterrent mechanism' against short-term policy reversals and 'assist developing countries in promoting greater effectiveness of the rule of law at the domestic level'.[137] In organising our model of factors impacting internalisation, we include the conclusion of investment treaties as a potential factor leading to internalisation. We acknowledge our scepticism that the simple conclusion of investment treaties is likely to give rise to the development of significant internalisation processes. Nevertheless, we recognise the possibility and, given the claims of the rule of law thesis, consider it important to include in the basic outline of our model.

1.5.3.2   Investment Treaties: Arbitral Claims

Investor–state disputes under an investment treaty may act as a trigger for awareness within the government about the saliency of investment treaties. Large awards, high legal costs, and what is often perceived as an intrusion into state sovereignty, can serve to put investment treaties on the radar. The role of claims in the adoption of investment treaties and in their drafting has already been the subject of significant work. Aisbett and Poulsen have shown, for example, that officials in many developing states acted with a kind of 'bounded rationality' in entering into investment treaties, ignoring readily available information about investment claims involving other countries until they themselves were hit by a claim.[138] Similarly, a study by Manger and Peinhardt has shown how investment treaty claims against capital-exporting states have led those states to more precise drafting of successive investment treaties, moving from vague to elaborate rules in an effort to minimise future litigation risks.[139] In the present study, we expect that if investment treaties are serving as mechanisms for governmental reform, investment treaty claims will trigger government awareness and increase the likelihood that the state will develop internalisation processes.

---

[136] See, for example, Salacuse, *The Law of Investment Treaties*, 113–14; Schill, 'International Investment Law and the Rule of Law', 87–93; Dolzer, 'The Impact of International Investment Treaties on Domestic Administrative Law'; Franck, 'Foreign Direct Investment, Investment Treaty Arbitration, and the Rule of Law'.

[137] Echandi, 'What Do Developing Countries Expect from the International Investment Regime?', 13.

[138] Lauge N. S. Poulsen and Emma Aisbett, 'When the Claim Hits: Bilateral Investment Treaties and Bounded Rational Learning' (2013) 65 *World Politics* 273.

[139] Mark S. Manger and Clint Peinhardt, 'Learning and the Precision of International Investment Agreements' (2017) 43 *International Interactions* 920.

1.6 The Case Studies

In the preceding sections, we have conceptually mapped the three main institutional processes or mechanisms through which internalisation would be expected to take place: informational, monitoring or remedial mechanisms. We have also identified some cross-cutting characteristics of these mechanisms, such as whether they are general or specific, ad hoc or consistent, and whether they are formal or informal. Finally, we have sought to flag factors that may impact whether, or the extent to which, internalisation measures are adopted and investment treaties are internalised.

This framework serves as the background for the main body of the book in which we present case studies addressing whether and how a select group of governments in Asia internalise international investment treaty obligations in their decision-making processes. These case studies serve as a foundation for testing our theoretical framework by empirically examining whether and to what extent these governments take investment treaty obligations into account in their governmental decision-making processes, and whether such internalisation has had observable spillover effects on governance in the state more generally.

An empirical assessment of internalisation in individual countries is the only way to develop the evidence necessary to determine the effect of investment treaties on national governance. To that end, the chapters which follow contain qualitative country case studies of eight Asian countries: India, Indonesia, Myanmar, Republic of Korea, Sri Lanka, Singapore, Thailand and Viet Nam. In preparing these case studies, the authors have drawn upon semi-structured interviews conducted with senior- and mid-level government officials and investment lawyers, and the analysis of primary and secondary legal materials. In addition, because the authors are based in the countries about which they are writing, or have deep experience in these countries, they are able to draw upon their own detailed background knowledge of investment governance in the country. We are not aware of any similar empirical studies.

With respect to case selection, the choice of these eight countries for case studies rests on several considerations. The first is principled. The subject of our inquiry – the impact of investment treaties on governance – dictates a primary interest in developing countries, as it is their governance in particular which investment treaties are purported to improve. Thus, six of our eight case studies cover developing countries of different sizes: India, Indonesia, Myanmar, Sri Lanka, Thailand and Viet Nam.

The inclusion of two developed countries (the Republic of Korea and Singapore) provides comparative context that is valuable in understanding the range of factors which affect the internalisation process and the commonality of certain challenges raised by investment treaties, even for the governments of developed economies. In this regard, we note that we have excluded China from the present study due to its magnitude and complex provincial and administrative structure. China itself might form the basis for a single study.

The second driver for covering these eight states is opportunistic. In undertaking an empirical study of the impact of investment treaties on decision making in national governments, we have proceeded on the premise that, in order to be successful, the case studies should be undertaken by locally based authors with knowledge of the laws and government structures of the subject countries. Further, we have looked to authors who are able to gain access to government officials and other stakeholders for the purpose of developing evidence through interviews and other sources. In this respect, the inclusion of countries in this study has depended upon finding the right author for each country covered, rather than deciding *a priori* that certain countries must be included. While admittedly this has introduced a degree of serendipity into our case study selection, we do not believe that it impacts upon the value of the work. In the end, this project does not seek to draw broad conclusions about the impact of investment treaties 'in Asia'. Rather, it seeks to develop a theoretical framework for analysing investment treaty internalisation in government generally and to use that framework to develop an empirical understanding of internalisation in eight Asian countries.

Finally, we have chosen to focus on case studies in Asia, and to work with scholars based in Asia, given our position at the National University of Singapore and the mission of the Centre for International Law which is, *inter alia*, to advance international law research and capacity in the Asia-Pacific region.

2

The Impact of Investment Treaties
on the Rule of Law in India

PRABHASH RANJAN

2.1 Introduction

From 1994 until the end of 2010, India signed close to eighty bilateral investment treaties (BITs) and free trade agreements (FTAs) containing investment chapters.[1] Despite this massive programme, BITs and investment chapters in FTAs ('FTA investment chapters')[2] never occupied an important place in discussions on national governance. Applying Calamita and Berman's analytical framework on internalisation to the case of India,[3] this chapter examines the extent to which India has been able to internalise its investment treaty commitments in governmental decision making. It also relies on their framework in seeking to identify and understand the factors impacting (the lack of) internalisation in India.

As defined in Calamita and Berman's framing chapter (Chapter 1), internalisation refers to the formal and informal processes by which a country's international legal obligations are taken into account in governmental decision making. In the context of investment treaties, this entails an examination of the formal and informal processes followed by the state to ensure that it takes its investment treaty obligations into account when adopting regulatory measures. In other words, the internalisation inquiry asks whether there is evidence that investment treaties are being considered while making regulatory policies or other decisions.[4]

---

[1] For a detailed study of India's BITs, see Prabhash Ranjan, *India and Bilateral Investment Treaties: Refusal, Acceptance, Backlash* (Oxford University Press, 2019).

[2] BITs and the investment chapters in FTAs are referred to collectively as either international investment treaties or international investment agreements (IIAs).

[3] See Chapter 1, N. Jansen Calamita and Ayelet Berman, 'The Internalisation of Investment Treaties and the Rule of Law Promise'.

[4] *Ibid.*

This chapter is organised as follows. After laying out the methodology (Section 2.2), Section 2.3 explains what triggered the debate on internalisation of International Investment Agreements (IIAs) in India. Section 2.4 then documents the tryst of the Indian Parliament with IIAs, especially India's BITs. Section 2.5 addresses the steps undertaken by the Indian government to internalise investment treaty commitments. Section 2.6 discusses the implications of IIAs on civil society and academia in India and Section 2.7 concludes.

2.2 Methodology

Following the methodology of explanatory process tracing, this chapter seeks to understand the internalisation of investment treaties by observing and documenting various events pertaining to IIAs in India. In doing so, this chapter inquires into why these events happened; how, or what, led to their occurrence; and how these developments can be explained.

Research has included documentary review and interviews. Documentary research has included the review of parliamentary records and archives with regard to debate on investment treaties in India. In addition, I have relied upon India's Right to Information Act 2005 (RTI Act) to solicit information on various reports and matters pertaining to IIAs from different government departments such as the Ministry of Finance and the Ministry of Law. Interviews consisted of semi-structured interviews with government officials and non-governmental individuals. The government officials were seven individuals working in central government ministries who have been involved in negotiating investment treaties, who are from ministries whose regulatory measures have been challenged by foreign investors under India's investment treaties, or who work in state government. Out of these seven government officials, five are senior officials (i.e., officials holding positions of Director and above) and two are junior officials (i.e., officials holding positions below the level of Director). The officials were selected for interviews based on their availability and willingness to speak, and because they were from ministries involved in negotiating investment treaties or whose regulatory measures have been challenged by foreign investors in an investor–state dispute settlement (ISDS) claim.

The non-governmental actors interviewed included two people working in think tanks established and funded by the government for the purpose of providing advice to the government on matters of foreign investment law. An additional interviewee had worked on a Law Commission of India

(LCI) report on reforming India's arbitration law. Finally, two lawyers working in law firms who have worked with the government or who have defended the Indian government in ISDS claims were also interviewed.

The interviews were conducted in person in New Delhi from June 2018 to August 2018 and from June 2019 to August 2019. All interviews were anonymous.

2.3   The Internalisation Trigger: *White Industries* v. *India*

Although India signed its first BIT in 1994, in domestic policy circles and even in the academic community, IIAs generally did not occupy a prominent place until the first publicly known BIT arbitral award was issued against India in a case known as *White Industries* v. *India* (*White Industries*),[5] where an ISDS tribunal found that India violated its obligations under the India–Australia BIT (1999).[6] As previous research by this author has shown, prior to the award in *White Industries*, Indian 'policy makers cited absence of BIT claims as proof of lack of interface between Indian BITs and India's ability to adopt regulatory measures'.[7] The fact that BIT cases had been brought by investors against other countries challenging the state's exercise of sovereign power in pursuit of the public interest (such as the actions of the Argentine government in late 1990s and early 2000s to counter a severe financial and economic crisis) had very little impact on the thinking of the Indian government. Instead, most Indian government officials ignored the experience of other countries in considering the impact of BITs on India, until India was hit by its first claim. In this regard, India is no different from many developing countries that did not take their investment treaty commitments seriously until they were faced with their first investor–state claim.[8] This is also consistent with the finding that most countries tended to ignore the experience of other countries in understanding the ramifications of BITs.[9]

---

[5] *White Industries Australia Limited* v. *Republic of India*, UNCITRAL Rules, Final Award (30 November 2011).

[6] *Ibid.*, at para. 16.1.1(a).

[7] Prabhash Ranjan, 'India and Bilateral Investment Treaties – A Changing Landscape' (2014) 29 *ICSID Review – Foreign Investment Law Journal* 419.

[8] Lauge N. S. Poulsen, *Bounded Rationality and Economic Diplomacy: The Politics of Investment Treaties in Developing Countries* (Cambridge University Press, 2015), 155; Lauge N. S. Poulsen and Emma Aisbett, 'When the Claim Hits: Bilateral Investment Treaties and Bounded Rational Learning' (2013) 65 *World Politics* 273, 281–2.

[9] Poulsen, 'Bounded Rationality and Economic Diplomacy', 155.

Debate on the internalisation of India's investment treaty obligations would not have begun had it not been for the *White Industries* award and the slew of other IIA claims against India that followed. Whereas *White Industries* had challenged the functioning of the Indian judiciary, subsequent claims from foreign investors beginning in 2012 challenged a wide range of regulatory measures adopted at the central and sub-national levels of government, such as the imposition of retrospective taxes,[10] revocation of telecom licences,[11] actions of sub-national governments pertaining to the withdrawal of assurances to foreign investors[12] and the denial of tax refunds.[13]

In 2016, another BIT award was issued against India in a case known as *Devas* v. *India*.[14] This case arose out of India's cancellation of an agreement with Devas to lease the capacity of two Indian satellites to provide broadband services.[15] In that case, as well as in a related case brought by

[10] Vodafone issued an arbitral notice to India under the India–Netherlands BIT (1995) for a retrospective taxation measure. The ISDS tribunal ruled in 2020 that India breached the fair and equitable treatment (FET) provision of the India–Netherlands BIT. See *Vodafone International Holdings B.V.* v. *Republic of India (I)*, PCA Case No. 2016-35, Award (25 September 2020). Cairn Energy also dragged India to arbitration under the India–United Kingdom BIT (1994) for a retrospective taxation measure. The tribunal ruled against India holding that the imposition of taxes retrospectively breached the FET provision in the India–United Kingdom BIT. See *Cairn Energy PLC and Cairn UK Holdings Limited* v. *Republic of India*, PCA Case No. 2016-7, Award (21 December 2020).

[11] Tenoch Holdings issued an arbitral notice against India under the India–Russian Federation BIT (1994) and Cyprus–India BIT (2002) for the withdrawal by Indian authorities of an approval to grant telecom licences. See *Maxim Naumchenko, Andrey Poluektov and Tenoch Holdings Limited* v. *Republic of India*, PCA Case No. 2013-23. Although the arbitral award is not in the public domain, according to a press release issued by the Indian government, the tribunal dismissed all the claims of the investor in its entirety. See Ministry of Finance, 'BIT Claims Against India Dismissed', Press Release, 20 January 2020.

[12] *Ras-Al-Khaimah Investment Authority* v. *Republic of India*, Notice of Arbitration, UNCITRAL Rules (8 December 2016).

[13] *Nissan Motor Co. Ltd* v. *Republic of India*, PCA Case No. 2017-37, Decision on Jurisdiction (29 April 2019). India lost the case on the issue of jurisdiction. Some other notices of arbitration include France's Louis Dreyfus Armateurs' case against India under the India–France BIT (1997) challenging a series of measures adopted by the Indian government that allegedly prevented the implementation of a joint venture project to modernise the port in Haldia in Kolkata, India. See *Louis Dreyfus Armateurs SAS* v. *Republic of India*, PCA Case No. 2014-26, Final Award (11 September 2018). The tribunal ruled in favour of India.

[14] *CC/Devas (Mauritius) Ltd, Devas Employees Mauritius Private Limited, and Telecom Devas Mauritius Limited* v. *Republic of India*, PCA Case No. 2013-09, Award on Jurisdiction and Merits (25 July 2016).

[15] *Ibid.*

Deutsche Telekom,[16] India was found to have violated its BIT obligations, notwithstanding its arguments that the measures it had taken were justified on national security grounds.

Due to the cumulative effect of these adverse BIT decisions and BIT arbitration notices, India began the process of reviewing its BITs and debating various aspects of BITs, which had not been deliberated upon earlier. Debates arose as to whether BITs have led to higher foreign investment inflows to India;[17] whether BITs encroach upon India's right to regulate in the public interest; whether BITs should contain ISDS provisions;[18] whether the treaty provisions in BITs are too vague and thus susceptible to overly broad interpretations by ISDS arbitral tribunals; whether the ISDS system works in a transparent way; and so forth.

India's review of its BITs led to three tangible outcomes. First, India adopted a new Model BIT in 2016;[19] second, India issued notices to terminate its BITs to fifty-eight countries;[20] and third, India requested twenty-five of its BIT partner states to issue joint interpretative statements in order to resolve what India described as 'uncertainties and ambiguities that may arise regarding interpretation and application of the standards contained' in India's BITs.[21]

Although BIT disputes against India played an important role in India's decision to terminate a substantial number of its BITs, it would be a mistake to think that BIT claims caused India to exit the BIT system. By developing

---

[16] *Deutsche Telekom AG* v. *Republic of India*, PCA Case No. 2014-10, Interim Award (13 December 2017).

[17] Niti Bhasin and Rinku Manocha, 'Do Bilateral Investment Treaties Promote FDI Inflows? Evidence from India' (2016) 41 *Vikalpa: The Journal for Decision Makers* 275.

[18] Subhomoy Bhattacharjee, 'India Seeks Treaty Revision to Deal with Corporate Suits', *The Indian Express*, 4 April 2012.

[19] Department of Economic Affairs, 'Model Text for the Indian Bilateral Investment Treaty', https://dea.gov.in/sites/default/files/ModelBIT_Annex_0.pdf. It is important to note that the Indian Model BIT contains two dates – 28 December 2015, which is given in the letter accompanying the text; and 14 January 2016, which can be found on the website of the Ministry of Finance, Government of India, as the date of publication of the BIT. This author uses the latter date (i.e., 14 January 2016) and thus refers to the Model BIT as 2016 Indian Model BIT and *not* 2015 Indian Model BIT. See also Prabhash Ranjan and Pushkar Anand, 'The 2016 Model Indian Bilateral Investment Treaty: A Critical Deconstruction' (2017) 38 *Northwestern Journal of International Law & Business* 1.

[20] Nirmala Sitharaman (Minister of State of the Ministry of Commerce & Industry), Lok Sabha, Unstarred Question No. 1290, 'Bilateral Investment Treaties' (25 July 2016).

[21] Government of India, Ministry of Finance, Department of Economic Affairs, *Office Memorandum – Regarding Issuing Joint Interpretative Statements for Indian Bilateral Investment Treaties* (8 February 2016).

a new Model BIT, and by seeking to renegotiate BITs with its former BIT partner states on this basis, India remains a participant in the global IIA regime. In sum, while these BIT claims have triggered a heated debate on investment treaties, they have not resulted in India's exit from the regime.

2.4 The Indian Parliament

2.4.1 Parliamentary Questions

In order to gauge the reaction of the Indian Parliament and to understand its degree of awareness and interest in BITs, this project has carefully examined the questions asked by parliamentarians in the upper (Rajya Sabha) and lower (Lok Sabha) houses of Parliament from 2006 till 2017. Such questioning is an integral feature of India's parliamentary democracy, and a tool whereby Parliament holds the government to account. The period that has been chosen for this examination is five years before and six years after the first BIT arbitral award against India became public in 2011.[22]

The results are revealing. Before 2011, there were very few instances where Indian parliamentarians asked questions to the government about BITs. One notable exception is an occasion in 2010, when a question in the Rajya Sabha asked about the countries with which India had entered into BITs, whether foreign investment was also part of the FTAs that India was signing, and what the advantages were of making investment protection a part of FTA negotiations.[23] The government responded that India had signed BITs with sixty-eight countries,[24] and that foreign investment was made part of FTAs because 'they aim at providing foreign investors with a level of legal assurance regarding the protection of their investments, as also with specific and transparent commitment on the levels of market access available to them.'[25]

In the same year, a question was posed in the Lok Sabha regarding the countries with which India had signed BITs, the salient features of those

---

[22] To search for the questions asked in both houses, the author used each house's respective question search engine. The search terms included 'bilateral investment treaty', 'bilateral investment promotion agreement (BIPA)', 'bilateral investment promotion and protection agreement (BIPPA)'. For the respective search engines in question, see http://164.100.47.194/Loksabha/Questions/Qtextsearch.aspx (Lok Sabha) and http://164.100.47.5/qsearch/qsearch.aspx (Rajya Sabha).

[23] Prakash Javdekar, Rajya Sabha, Unstarred Question No. 2615, 'Bilateral Investment Treaties' (20 April 2010).

[24] Namo Narain Meena (Minister of State in the Ministry of Finance), Rajya Sabha, Unstarred Question No. 2615, 'Bilateral Investment Treaties' (20 April 2010).

[25] Ibid.

BITs, and their advantages.[26] A similar question was asked in the Lok Sabha in 2007 about the number of India's BITs.[27] In response to this latter question, the government of the day replied that BITs 'are intended to provide a common platform for protecting investment flows between India and the country with which, the Agreement has been signed by the Government of India. This results in increase in comfort level of the investors from either country resulting in increased flow of funds for investments'.[28]

Apart from these few occasions, the Indian Parliament showed little interest in BITs till 2011, mainly due to a lack of awareness and understanding about BITs. This lack of awareness about BITs was a result of diverse factors, such as scant media coverage, an absence of BIT disputes, an absence of academic and public commentary on the significance of BITs and ISDS, etc. Another important reason for the lack of awareness and understanding of BITs in Parliament was that BITs rarely required changes in domestic laws. In India, treaties are ratified by the Executive and not by the Parliament and hence, generally speaking, discussion on a treaty takes place when a legislative change is introduced by the Executive in the Parliament in order to meet the obligation imposed by the international treaty.[29] This is not to suggest that the Parliament cannot discuss the significance of BITs if it so desires. Rather, the point is that prior to 2011, it did not do so, mainly because it was oblivious about the significance of BITs. Notably, this is in contrast to the World Trade Organization (WTO) agreements, which have been discussed thoroughly in the Indian Parliament due to the legislative changes required to fulfil India's obligations.[30]

India's 2011 loss in *White Industries* changed things dramatically. India's liability in *White Industries* was based in large part on measures taken by the judiciary which interfered with and delayed the investor's

---

[26] Chandrakant Bhaurao Khaire, Lok Sabha, Unstarred Question No. 5069, 'BIPPA with Countries' (10 December 2010).

[27] Braja Kishore Tripathy, Lok Sabha, Unstarred Question No. 554, 'BIPPA with Ethiopia and Mozambique' (20 November 2007).

[28] Ashwani Kumar (Minister of the State in the Ministry of Commerce and Industry), Lok Sabha, Unstarred Question No. 554, 'BIPPA with Ethiopia and Mozambique' (20 November 2007).

[29] *Union of India* v. *Azadi Bachao Andolan* (2003) 263 ITR 706; (2004) 10 SCC 1 (Supreme Court of India); *M.I. Patel* v. *Union of India* (1970) 3 SCC 400 (Supreme Court of India); *Rosiline George* v. *Union of India* (1994) 2 SCC 80 (Supreme Court of India).

[30] For laws that have been introduced due to India's WTO obligations, see Bureau of Indian Standards Bill 2015, moved by Shri Ram Vilas Paswan in Lok Sabha (2 December 2015); and the amendment to the Patent Act 2005 in order to comply with India's international obligations under the Trade Related Aspects of Intellectual Property Rights (TRIPS) under the WTO.

ability to enforce a foreign commercial arbitral award.[31] In Parliament, the *White Industries* award was viewed as an attack on the Indian judiciary. As one parliamentarian commented, 'this [arbitral award] is an attack on the sovereignty of the Indian Judiciary. The judicial functioning is one of the major sovereign functions of a State. Therefore, it is an attack on the sovereignty of the country'.[32] That said, while much of the criticism of the award focused on alleged overreach by the ISDS tribunal, it is hard not to read criticisms of the award as also reflecting a degree of surprise at the revelation of the scope of India's commitments under its BITs.

Following the *White Industries* award, and a number of other BIT arbitral notices subsequently received by India, the number, frequency, and variety of questions on BITs and ISDS increased in both houses of Parliament. Thus, questions were raised asking the government to supply details of all the BITs that India had entered into and inquiring whether the texts of these BITs were publicly available.[33] Other questions went directly to the policy of including ISDS provisions in India's BITs, asking the government, pointedly, 'whether rattled by threats from foreign companies to drag India to international courts over breach of investment promises, [the] government has decided to erase a key clause in bilateral investment treaties that allow for international arbitration'.[34] Still, other questions asked for information about ISDS claims brought against India,[35]

---

[31] As one parliamentarian accurately summarised, the 'arbitration tribunal criticised the Indian Supreme Court, in particular, and the Indian judicial system, in general, and made the Government of India liable to compensate for the lapse on the part of our Judiciary'. Statement by P. Rajeeve, Member of Parliament, Transcript of the Proceedings of the Rajya Sabha (22 May 2012), 53.

[32] *Ibid*. For another critique of the *White Industries* award as to how it went beyond its mandate, see Manu Sanan, 'The White Industries Award – Shades of Grey' (2012) 13 *Journal of World Investment & Trade* 661.

[33] Pinaki Misra, Anandrao Vithoba Adsul and Dushyant Singh, Lok Sabha, Unstarred Question No. 5870, 'Bilateral Investment Treaties' (11 May 2012). See also M. K. Raghavan and D. Purandeswari (Minister of State in the Ministry of Commerce And Industry), Lok Sabha, Unstarred Question No. 6248, 'Bilateral Investment Treaties' (6 May 2013).

[34] A. Elavarasan, Rajya Sabha, Unstarred Question No. 4236, 'Amending Bilateral Investment Treaties' (15 May 2012).

[35] Baijayant Panda, Lok Sabha, Unstarred Question No. 2391, 'Review of BIPA' (25 July 2014) ('Lok Sabha, Unstarred Question No. 2391'); Ajay Kumar, Lok Sabha, Unstarred Question No. 4322, 'BIPPA with Countries' (22 March 2013) ('Lok Sabha, Unstarred Question No. 4322'). A very specific question was asked about foreign investors suing India as an aftermath of the Supreme Court judgment that cancelled telecom licences of many private companies including foreign investors – Jaya Bachchan, Rajya Sabha, Unstarred Question No. 840, 'Mobile Services under Bilateral Investment Treaties' (30 November 2012).

whether the government had constituted any panel to oversee those BIT disputes,[36] whether India had decided to review,[37] renegotiate,[38] and/or terminate its BITs,[39] and whether India had adopted a new Model BIT.[40] Some parliamentarians questioned the government more fundamentally about whether BITs in fact serve India's interests,[41] or have demonstrable benefits for India.[42] Finally, questions were raised as to the scope of India's obligations under its BITs and whether India's BITs encroach upon 'the domestic decision-making process in the country'.[43]

White Industries was a game changer. Before that case, India's investment treaty commitments barely registered in parliamentary debate. Following India's loss, however, the Indian Parliament became much more deeply engaged with BITs than it had ever before.

2.4.2. Parliamentary Law Making

The increased attention to BITs in Parliament had a knock-on effect. The discussions in Parliament were triggered because of questions posed by opposition parties to the government of the day. In order for the government to answer these questions, the responsible ministers would often need information and other help from officials working in different ministries. As a result, the questions in Parliament led to a kind of ad hoc, informal diffusion of knowledge within the bureaucracies

---

[36] Magunta Srinivasulu Reddy, Lok Sabha, Unstarred Question No. 3926, 'Bilateral Investment Pacts' (5 September 2012) ('Lok Sabha, Unstarred Question No. 3926'); Shrirang Barne, Lok Sabha, Unstarred Question No. 365, 'Bilateral Investment Promotion and Protection Agreement' (11 July 2014) ('Lok Sabha, Unstarred Question No. 365'); Bhagwanth Khuba, Lok Sabha, Unstarred Question No 4834, 'BIPA' (31 March 2017).

[37] Lok Sabha, Unstarred Question No. 2391.

[38] Naresh Gujral, Rajya Sabha, Unstarred Question No. 2927, 'Renegotiation of Bilateral Investment Treaties (BITs)' (28 March 2017).

[39] Lok Sabha, Unstarred Question No. 365; Lok Sabha, Unstarred Question No. 2391; K. Gopal, Lok Sabha, Unstarred Question No. 169, 'Bilateral Investment Treaties' (17 July 2017).

[40] Malla Reddy and Muttamsetti Rao, Lok Sabha, Unstarred Question No. 1290, 'Bilateral Investment Treaties' (25 July 2016); Mallikarjun Kharge, Lok Sabha, Unstarred Question No. 1754, 'Bilateral Investment Treaty' (10 March 2017); A. W. Rabi Bernard, Rajya Sabha, Unstarred Question No. 2635, 'Changes in the Draft Model Bilateral Investment Treaty' (22 December 2015) ('Rajya Sabha, Unstarred Question No. 2635').

[41] Lok Sabha, Unstarred Question No. 365.

[42] Harish Dwivedi, Lok Sabha, Unstarred Question No. 5174, 'BIPA' (24 April 2015).

[43] M. K. Raghavan, Lok Sabha, Unstarred Question No. 6248, 'Bilateral Investment Treaties' (6 May 2013).

on investment treaties,[44] thus leading to greater levels of informational internalisation. In this respect, the mechanism of parliamentary questions has served to help bureaucrats working in responsible ministries to better understand the ramifications of India's BITs.[45] It has also alerted them to the fact that they may be held accountable for negotiating investment treaties or for the ISDS claims brought against India, thus bringing in a degree of caution and circumspection in dealing with investment treaties.[46]

Nevertheless, despite the increased attention shown by Parliament towards investment treaties in the wake of *White Industries*, the Indian Parliament has not developed internalisation processes – as identified by Calamita and Berman – whether informational, monitoring, or remedial,[47] which require or encourage Parliament to take India's international investment treaty obligations into account when it is developing a new law. A search of the parliamentary records on legislative debates in the Lok Sabha since 2010 demonstrates that BITs have only been considered on sporadic occasions while debating legislative changes. In the following text, I lay out three of the rare instances in which BITs have been considered.

The first example arose in the context of discussions concerning the proposed amendment of the Foreign Exchange Management Act in 2012 to allow for 51 per cent foreign investment in the Multi-Brand Retail Trading (MBRT) sector. The policy announced by the national government gave state governments the authority to permit foreign investment in the MBRT sector in their respective states. Concerns were raised that if a state were to deny a licence or a permit to a foreign investor seeking to invest in the MBRT sector, this could lead to a violation of India's BIT obligations.[48] The government allayed these concerns, saying that since India's BITs do not contain pre-establishment provisions, the denial of licences at the time of establishment would not violate India's BITs.

---

[44] Interview Official AA, 2018.
[45] Interview Official BB, 2018.
[46] *Ibid.*
[47] See Chapter 1.
[48] 'Discussion on motion regarding recommendation to withdraw decision to allow 51% Foreign Direct Investment in Multi-Brand Retail Trade and Modifications in Annex "A" and Annex "B" of Notification under Foreign Exchange Management Act, 1999 and Modifications in Annex "B" of Notification under Foreign Exchange Management Act, 1999', Fifteenth Lok Sabha (4 December 2012).

A second reference to BITs was made in the Lok Sabha during debates on the Commercial Courts Bill, which aimed to establish specialised commercial court divisions for faster resolution of commercial disputes.[49] In the course of the debate, parliamentarians argued that India could become an attractive destination for foreign direct investment if it could provide an expeditious judicial forum for settling disputes. Otherwise, these legislators argued, investors would prefer international arbitration under investment treaties for speedier resolution of their disputes. In other words, the desire to speed up dispute resolution with foreign investors so as to avoid ISDS was among the rationales for the creation of separate commercial courts in India.[50]

Third, *White Industries* played an important role in triggering a change in India's arbitration and conciliation law. As noted, India's liability in *White Industries* was based in large part on measures taken by the judiciary which interfered with and delayed the investor's ability to enforce a foreign commercial arbitral award. Indeed, in India, there have long been concerns about judicial interference in arbitration proceedings leading to significant delays in the arbitration process, ultimately negating the benefits of arbitration. This flaw in the Indian arbitration law was recognised in 2014 by the Law Commission of India (LCI).[51] In its report, the LCI offered two reasons for these delays:

> First, the [Indian] judicial system is over-burdened with work and is not sufficiently efficient to dispose cases, especially commercial cases, with the speed and dispatch that is required. Second, the bar for judicial intervention (despite the existence of section 5 of the [Arbitration and Conciliation] Act) has been consistently set at a low threshold by the Indian judiciary, which translates into many more admissions of cases in Court which arise out of or are related to the Act.[52]

The LCI report then went on to recommend amending the Indian Arbitration and Conciliation Act 1996 so as to ensure that international commercial arbitral awards involving foreign parties are dealt with

---

[49] 'Further Discussion on the Motion for Consideration of the Commercial Courts, Commercial Division and Commercial Appellate Division of High Courts Bill, 2015', Sixteenth Lok Sabha (16 December 2015).

[50] *Ibid.*

[51] Government of India, Law Commission of India, Report No. 246, *Amendments to the Arbitration and Conciliation Act 1996* (2014), 15. The commission was entrusted with the task of reviewing the provisions of the Arbitration and Conciliation Act, 1996.

[52] *Ibid.*, at 15–16.

expeditiously by the Indian courts.[53] The LCI report observed that *White Industries* 'serves as a reminder to the Government to urgently implement reforms to the judicial system in order to avoid substantial potential liabilities that might accrue from the delays presently inherent in the system'.[54] Thus, the *White Industries* award weighed heavily on the minds of the drafters of the LCI report as they recommended changes to the Indian arbitration law.[55]

Consequently, the government of the day took the LCI's recommendations into account and introduced a bill in Parliament to amend the Indian arbitration law. In introducing the bill, the government said in Parliament:

> The Law Commission of India in its 246th Report and Supplementary Report has recommended various amendments in the Arbitration and Conciliation Act, 1996, so that India may become a hub of International Commercial Arbitration. Taking into consideration the Law Commission's recommendations and suggestions received from other stake holders we have decided to amend the Arbitration and Conciliation Act, 1996.[56]

Thus, the Indian arbitration law was amended with the aim of reducing judicial intervention in arbitration and excessive delays in the enforcement or setting aside of arbitration awards.

These instances illustrate that while there are no formal rules or institutionalised internalisation procedures or mechanisms in the law-making process, references to investment treaties have been made in an ad hoc manner. Such ad hoc references are often a result of an individual parliamentarian's knowledge or awareness about a particular issue.[57] As mentioned, the absence of institutionalised procedures may be attributed to the fact that BITs in India do not require either parliamentary approval for their enactment or implementation into domestic law. As such, the government's conclusion of BITs with foreign states has had a limited impact on internalisation within Parliament and the government.

---

[53] *Ibid.*, at 16.

[54] *Ibid.*

[55] Interview Lawyer, 2019. The interviewee, who was involved in the drafting of the 246th LCI Report, said, 'the *White Industries* Award acted as an important catalyst to push for the reform in the Indian Arbitration law'.

[56] 'Discussion on the motion for consideration of the Statutory Resolution regarding Disapproval of Arbitration and Conciliation (Amendment) Ordinance, 2015 (No. 9 of 2015) and Arbitration and Conciliation (Amendment) Bill, 2015', Sixteenth Lok Sabha (17 December 2015).

[57] Interview Official CC, 2019.

2.5 The Executive

This section addresses the various internalisation measures that the Indian Executive, in particular the central government, has undertaken on various issues involving BITs and ISDS. It is important to keep in mind that these internalisation measures took shape only after the *White Industries* award and the spate of other ISDS claims against India. In other words, as with Parliament, internalisation in the Executive was driven by India's negative experience with ISDS.

These internalisation measures have largely been a mix of informational, monitoring, and remedial measures. Informational internalisation, by Calamita and Berman in the book's framing introduction,[58] refers to measures adopted by the Executive to diffuse information about investment treaties to government officials. The purpose of informational measures is to ensure that government officials dealing with issues pertaining to foreign investors are aware of the state's international investment obligations such that these obligations are taken into account when they make decisions. Monitoring internalisation refers to those processes by which one agency, or body of the state, screens proposed policies for consistency with international obligations. Remedial internalisation refers to domestic measures aimed at correcting or defending the state's compliance with international investment law obligations. While remedial internalisation measures might often encompass processes for adjusting investor grievances before they rise to the level of an international dispute, they can also include measures aimed at reducing or eliminating the possibility of ISDS claims against the state such as negotiating BITs without ISDS provisions or imposing procedural pre-conditions before an investor is entitled to bring an ISDS claim. These issues are discussed in this section in the context of the Indian Executive.

2.5.1 Informational Internalisation in the Executive

This section addresses informational measures taken by the Ministry of Finance and the Ministry of Commerce and Industry. The former and also the latter to some extent are the two central ministries with responsibility for dealing with BITs and ISDS in the Indian government. Institutionally, these are the agencies, or nodes within the Indian government, with the requisite expertise to diffuse information about the interplay between

---

[58] See Chapter 1.

BITs and domestic policymaking to different wings of the central government and to state governments.

2.5.1.1 Ministry of Commerce Paper

One of the first documents to demonstrate the beginnings of informational internalisation was a paper prepared by the Ministry of Commerce and Industry on BITs in 2011. Following the *White Industries* award, the Department of Industrial Policy and Promotion of the Ministry of Commerce and Industry issued a paper entitled 'International Investment Agreements between India and other Countries'.[59] This paper represented the first-ever comprehensive effort within the government to critically assess India's BITs.

The Ministry of Commerce and Industry's paper proceeded from the view that 'when developing countries enter into BITs, a balance between investor's rights and domestic policy must be ensured'.[60] Thus, the Ministry of Commerce and Industry recognised that although BITs were designed to provide foreign investors with certain rights, 'other legitimate public concerns must not be subordinated to investment protection issues.'[61] In this regard, the paper identified a number of areas of concern in Indian BITs such as an expansive definition of investment, an undefined fair and equitable treatment (FET) provision that could be subject to broad and expansive interpretations, a broad provision on expropriation without any reservations and exceptions, and a wide leverage to investors to freely transfer funds.[62] These broad and unqualified BIT provisions, it found, could result in situations in which India's exercise of regulatory power could be unduly compromised.

The Ministry of Commerce and Industry's paper gave specific examples of situations in which foreign investors could use broad provisions like the FET standard to bring an ISDS claim against India, such as when a licence granted to a foreign investor is 'cancelled on grounds of public policy',[63]

---

[59] Government of India, Ministry of Commerce and Industry, Department of Industrial Policy and Promotion, 'International Investment Agreements between India and Other Countries' (on file with author) ('Ministry of Commerce and Industry Paper'). The paper was not made publicly available but was obtained by members of an NGO through India's Right to Information Act, 2005. The 'Department of Industrial Policy & Promotion' was renamed the 'Department for Promotion of Industry and Internal Trade' in January 2019.

[60] Ministry of Commerce and Industry Paper.

[61] *Ibid.*

[62] *Ibid.*

[63] *Ibid.*, at 11.

'significant changes' are made 'in tax regimes or the administration of taxes',[64] or 'a foreign company' is denied 'environmental clearance, when such clearance has been granted to another company'.[65] The paper also discussed situations in which foreign investors could use a broad Most Favoured Nation (MFN) provision to circumvent a narrow formulation of FET (e.g., one tied to the customary international law minimum standard of treatment) and instead import a broadly phrased, autonomous FET provision from another treaty.[66] In another example, the paper recognised that since the issuance of compulsory licences on patented drugs is not excluded from the purview of expropriation, there could be situations where a patent holder could file a BIT claim against India for issuance of compulsory licences.[67] Finally, the paper highlighted that if India faced 'a balance of payment crisis' and 'capital controls are imposed by the RBI', foreign investors might be able to rely on the transfer of funds provisions in India's BITs to bring ISDS claims against India.[68]

Finally, the Ministry of Commerce and Industry's paper was extremely critical of the ISDS system,[69] questioning the 'impartiality and the objectivity of the present international arbitration'.[70] On the paper's view, the ISDS system creates perverse incentives, where 'a growing number of the arbitration firms take cases on a commission basis' and where 'a percentage of the final claim is agreed upon as fees', which 'increases the incentive for litigation amongst potential clients'.[71] Further, the paper noted 'a growing international business in third party financing of arbitration claims, with private companies making a profit from those cases that are then won'.[72] The paper concluded that these characteristics of ISDS, 'fuelled by a growing awareness of the litigation

---

[64] *Ibid.*
[65] *Ibid.*
[66] *Ibid.*, at 10.
[67] This issue in the context of Indian BITs had been raised earlier. See Prabhash Ranjan, 'Medical Patents and Expropriation in International Investment Law – With Special Reference to India' (2008) 5 *Manchester Journal of International Economic Law* 72. See also Prabhash Ranjan, 'Pharmaceutical Patents and Expropriation in Indian Bilateral Investment Treaties', in Mahdev Mohan and Chester Brown (eds.), *Regulation and Investment Disputes: Asian Perspectives* (Cambridge University Press, 2021), 29–47.
[68] Ministry of Commerce and Industry Paper, 13.
[69] *Ibid.*, at 15–18.
[70] *Ibid.*, at 17.
[71] *Ibid.*, at 17–18.
[72] *Ibid.*

potential of some of the key clauses in the investment agreements[,] have led to a rapid increase in the number of investment treaty claims'.[73]

This paper was a valiant effort at informational internalisation. However, this paper was not widely circulated and read in different ministries of the central government. In fact, it did not reach the state governments at all. A major reason for the limited circulation of the paper was that it was prepared by the commerce ministry, which is not the nodal ministry to deal with BITs and ISDS. Instead, the ministry incharge of BITs and ISDS is the Ministry of Finance.

2.5.1.2   Committee for Reviewing India's International Investment Agreements

Another informational internalisation measure taken by the government following *White Industries* was the establishment of a committee of Ministry Secretaries in April 2013,[74] chaired by the cabinet secretary of India (the topmost executive official and senior most civil servant).[75] The purpose of the committee was to review all of India's BITs and FTA investment chapters to understand their impact on domestic law and policymaking, and to recommend corrective measures to the design of these treaties.[76] The committee established a working group, which was chaired by the Secretary of the Department of Economic Affairs of the Ministry of Finance, and constituted representatives from different ministries, such as the Ministries of Commerce and Industry, Telecommunications, Coal, Revenue, External Affairs, and Law and Justice.[77] The group's mandate included the preparation of a new model BIT, the harmonisation of the provisions in Indian BITs with those in India's FTA investment chapters,

---

[73] *Ibid.*

[74] Government of India, Cabinet Secretariat, Rashtrapati Bhawan, New Delhi (5 April 2013). For clarity, a Secretary to the Indian government is the administrative head of the Ministry or Department and the principal adviser to the Minister on all matters of policy and the administration within the Ministry or Department. See Ministry of Personnel Public Grievances and Pensions, *Central Secretariat Manual of Office Procedure* (2015).

[75] Lok Sabha, Unstarred Question No. 3926. See also Grant Hanessian and Kabir Duggal, 'The Final 2015 Indian Model BIT: Is This the Change the World Wishes to See?' (2016) 32 *ICSID Review – Foreign Investment Law Journal* 216; M. K. Raghavan, Lok Sabha, Unstarred Question No. 6248, 'Bilateral Investment Treaties' (6 May 2013).

[76] Interview Official CC, 2018.

[77] Ministry of Finance, Department of Economic Affairs, *Office Memorandum* (26 March 2013); see also Kavaljit Singh, 'An Analysis of India's New Model Bilateral Investment Treaty', in Kavaljit Singh and Burghard Ilge (eds.), *Rethinking Bilateral Investment Treaties: Critical Issues and Policy Choices* (Both Ends, Madhyam and SOMO, 2016), 81.

and the development of a detailed roadmap for the renegotiation of eighty-two Indian BITs.[78] Another important objective of the review, as claimed by the Indian government, was to 'understand and identify the legal/policy challenges from the existing treaties'.[79] The committee further established an inter-ministerial group to handle ISDS disputes brought against India.[80] In parallel to these developments, in March 2013, the government announced its decision to put all BIT negotiations on hold.[81]

As part of the process of developing a new model BIT, the Ministry of Finance circulated a draft version within the central government[82] for comments in 2015.[83] In that review, the LCI, which works under the aegis of the Ministry of Law and Justice, raised concerns about the circulated draft and decided to take up the draft Model BIT for further study.[84] The LCI communicated this decision to the Ministry of Finance on 8 April 2015.[85]

To carry out its study, the LCI constituted a subcommittee of investment law and investment treaty arbitration experts, of which the author of this chapter was a member.[86] The subcommittee, after studying the draft Model BIT, came up with specific suggestions for modifying several provisions of the draft Model BIT, which later formed the basis of the LCI report submitted to the Law Minister of India on 27 August 2015.[87] The LCI's report stressed that its purpose was to 'assist the government in achieving a balanced negotiating text, that takes into consideration the protection of Indian investors investing abroad, as well as safeguarding the regulatory powers of the State'.[88]

---

[78] *Ibid.*; see also Lok Sabha, Unstarred Question No. 365.

[79] Statement by India at the World Investment Forum, UNCTAD (13–15 October 2014), https://worldinvestmentforum.unctad.org/switzerland2014/2014statements/.

[80] Lok Sabha, Unstarred Question No. 4322; see also Lok Sabha, Unstarred Question No. 2391.

[81] Lok Sabha, Unstarred Question No. 4322.

[82] Draft Model Text for the Indian Bilateral Investment Treaty, www.mygov.in/sites/default/files/master_image/Model%20Text%20for%20the%20Indian%20Bilateral%20Investment%20Treaty.pdf.

[83] See Comments on the 2015 Draft Indian Model BIT, www.mygov.in/group-issue/draft-indian-Model-bilateral-investment-treaty-text/.

[84] Government of India, Law Commission of India, Report No. 260, *Analysis of the 2015 Draft Model Bilateral Investment Treaty* (2015), ii.

[85] *Ibid.*, at 4.

[86] *Ibid.*, at ii. Many of the experts brought in by the LCI had been arguing that the government needed to develop its internal capacity to better understand investment treaties and ISDS.

[87] *Ibid.*, at ii.

[88] *Ibid.*, at 5.

The government adopted its new model BIT in 2016. Aside for some of the LCI's recommendations with respect to the exhaustion of local remedies, which the Ministry of Finance expressly stated it had accepted,[89] it remains unknown whether other recommendations of the LCI report were taken into consideration in the revision of the final model BIT.

Be that as it may, the LCI's intervention in the development of the model BIT stirred a debate within the government[90] and in civil society and academic circles. Such debates contributed to the building of knowledge and awareness within government and society at large and, thus, advanced informational internalisation within the Executive. However, this informational internalisation was limited to the central government with inadequate involvement of state governments and subnational officials.

2.5.1.3   Capacity Building of Government Lawyers

Except for the Ministry of Finance, most government officials involved in line ministries and state government have poor or inadequate knowledge about the implications their policy decisions could have for India's investment treaty obligations.[91] Thus, while officials from the Ministry of Finance display slightly better understanding of the ways in which India's treaty obligations can apply to the day-to-day business of government, in the cases in which BIT claims have been raised against India, there is little indication that officials in the ministries whose measures have led to the dispute are aware of India's obligations or have taken them into account when deciding on the impugned measures.[92]

Following *White Industries* and the slew of other claims brought against India, the Ministry of Finance began taking steps to address the lack of legal capacity and expertise on investment treaties in government. One initiative was the decision by the IIA section of the Ministry of Finance to begin appointing young lawyers and fresh law graduates who have some understanding of international investment law as legal consultants.[93] In doing so, the Ministry of Finance has been able both to

---

[89] See Rajya Sabha, Unstarred Question No. 2635.

[90] An official told this researcher that the LCI Report No. 260 was discussed within the government and it brought a certain degree of rigour towards understanding the implications of BITs on domestic policy making. Interview Official BB, 2019.

[91] Interview Lawyer AA, 2019. The interviewee defended the Indian government in a BIT claim.

[92] *Ibid.* Interview Lawyer BB, 2019. The interviewee defended the Indian government in a BIT claim.

[93] Interview Official DD, 2018.

strengthen its own in-house capacity and to help generalist bureaucrats better understand India's treaty obligations and their possible impact on domestic law making.[94]

However, it appears that the initiative has been unable to build enduring and robust institutional capacity as consultants are appointed only on a contractual basis at a junior level and remain with government for brief tenures of two to three years, after which they tend to move to law firms or higher studies.[95] Moreover, to the extent that these consultants and others within the Ministry of Finance are able to share information with generalist bureaucrats elsewhere in government, these bureaucrats too rotate between departments or ministries, taking their awareness with them and undermining the development of lasting in-house expertise and capacity.

Other informational internalisation measures taken to build knowledge (if not expertise) among state and central government officials, as well as judges, include workshops on international investment treaties. For example, since 2017, the Ministry of External Affairs has been partnering with the Permanent Court of Arbitration to organise a conference and training workshop on the various facets of investment treaty arbitration, which has been attended by many sub-national government officials and judges.[96] Likewise, the Ministry of Finance's Department of Economic Affairs organised a workshop especially for sub-national government officials regarding the implications of investment treaties and ISDS claims.[97] Further, the Ministry of Finance and the Centre for Trade and Investment Law, a think tank funded by the Indian government, also organised workshops to build the capacity of state government officials in 2019[98] and 2021.[99] During this workshop, efforts were made to explain

---

[94] *Ibid.*
[95] Two such consultants after serving short stints in the finance ministry went abroad for their higher studies and are now working in law firms.
[96] Following the inaugural conference, three more conferences were organised in 2018, 2019, and 2020. See, for example, Permanent Court of Arbitration, 'The second PCA India Conference' (26 November 2018), https://pca-cpa.org/en/news/the-second-pca-india-conference/.
[97] Interview Official EE, 2018; Interview Official FF, 2018. Both officials work in the government.
[98] Centre for Trade and Investment Law and Department of Economic Affairs, 'Workshop on Investment Treaties and Investor-State Dispute Settlement System for Government Officials' (8 March 2019), https://ctil.org.in/PrevEventDetails.aspx?id=24.
[99] Centre for Trade and Investment Law and Department of Economic Affairs, 'DEA-CTIL Executive Training Programme on Investment Treaties and Investor-State Dispute Settlement System for Government Officials' (28–30 April 2021), https://ctil.org.in/PrevEventDetails.aspx?id=83. The author was invited to speak at both of these capacity building workshops.

to state officials how India's domestic laws and regulations can implicate India's investment treaty obligations. Thus, it highlighted that state government officials should take India's treaty commitments into account when adopting a policy or a regulation.

From the perspective of effective internalisation, the problem with these workshops has been that they are carried out in an ad hoc manner and largely depend upon the initiative of individual government officials.[100] State government officials interviewed were of the view that such initiatives would be much more beneficial if they were organised on a regular basis.[101] Further, it is notable that on the occasions when these workshops are organised, there has been a tendency within the Indian government to rely more on foreign experts and practitioners than India's own domestic experts within the academic community. This decision to outsource government capacity building tends to undermine the government's goal of long-term, sustainable capacity building within the Indian legal community as a whole.

The need for more and better capacity building has been recognised officially within the Indian government. In 2016, the High Level Committee on Arbitration suggested that there should be targeted capacity-building workshops for government officials on India's investment treaties. This committee was established by the Ministry of Law and Justice, under the leadership of Justice B. N. Srikrishna, to review effectiveness of arbitration in India and to prepare a roadmap to make India a hub of international arbitration.[102] The committee was comprised of retired and serving judges, practising lawyers, industry representatives, and an official of the Ministry of Law.[103] Notably, no academic or expert in international arbitration was appointed to serve as a member of the committee.

The committee, whose mandate included 'focus[ing] on the role of arbitrations in matters involving the Union of India, including bilateral investment treaties (BIT) arbitrations and mak[ing] recommendations where necessary',[104] issued its report in 2017. Seeking to promote arbitration in India, it highlighted, *inter alia*, the need to improve capacity

---

[100] Interview Official, 2019. The interviewee was an official of the think tank that organised the event.

[101] Interview Official MM, 2019. The interviewee was a state official.

[102] Ministry of Law and Justice, 'Constitution of High Level Committee to Review Institutionalisation of Arbitration Mechanism in India', Press Release, 29 December 2016.

[103] *Ibid.*

[104] *Ibid.*

within government. Specifically, the committee recommended that 'there must be targeted capacity building measures within the government to help in policy formulation, decision-making and timeline management to help the state effectively deal with an investment treaty arbitration'. Therefore, it recommended that the government 'undertake a capacity building exercise, whereby mid-level and senior lawyers who appear for or advise the government, as well as senior bureaucrats and potential judges, are sent to attend appropriately tailored courses on investment law and investment treaty arbitration'.[105] It is not known whether this recommendation of the committee especially on training for judges has been followed, although some sporadic capacity-building programmes have been organised, as mentioned before.

2.5.2 Monitoring Internalisation

An important step towards improving monitoring internalisation measures in India was the proposal to establish a Centre–State Investment Agreement (CSIA), mooted by the Ministry of Finance.

2.5.2.1 Centre–State Investment Agreement

One of the greatest challenges to the internalisation of investment treaties in India is the federal structure of its government.[106] Although investment treaties are signed by the central government, they cover many issues that fall within the constitutional competence of sub-national, state governments.[107] Further, within the central government, it is the executive branch that adopts investment treaties. They do not require parliamentary ratification. Thus, parliamentarians representing constituencies in India's states are not called upon to engage with investment treaties in the ordinary course of their constitutional duties. There is, as a result, very little, if any, institutionalised consultation between the central and state governments on the issue of treaty making. Consequently, state governments in India are often not aware of these treaties, let alone aware of their potential ramifications.

---

[105] High Level Committee on Arbitration, *Report of the High Level Committee to Review Institutionalisation of Arbitration Mechanism in India* (2017), 105.
[106] Joseph Stiglitz, 'Preface: Towards a Twenty First Century Investment Agreement', in Lisa E. Sachs and Lise Johnson (eds.), *Yearbook on International Investment Law and Policy 2015–2016* (Oxford University Press, 2018), xiii, xv.
[107] *Ibid.*

In order to build the capacity of the state governments to better understand investment treaties and have some kind of monitoring mechanism, the central government proposed the CSIA. This was introduced for the first time in the 2016 general budget by India's Finance Minister to ensure effective implementation of Indian BITs by state governments.[108] According to the Minister, such an agreement would 'ensure fulfillment of the obligations of the State Governments under these treaties and states which opt to sign these Agreements will be seen as more attractive destinations by foreign investors'.[109] Joining the CSIA would not be mandatory and states were to be given the option not to sign the agreement. Nonetheless, the central government offered a strong incentive for state governments to sign the CSIA, warning that if any state government did not sign the agreement, the central government would suggest to India's treaty partners that these non-participating states are to be viewed as less welcoming to foreign investment.[110]

The critical objective behind introducing the CSIA was to sensitise state governments to India's investment treaty obligations. The CSIA would in turn lead state governments to consider India's international commitments when adopting laws or other regulatory measures and to take steps to ensure that their actions were consistent with India's obligations. An assessment of proposed regulations vis-à-vis investment treaty obligations would ensure a better monitoring of proposed regulations at the level of state governments. This monitoring mechanism might also feed into remedial internalisation processes, as discussed later.

The role of India's state governments as catalysts for international disputes with investors is significant. Indeed, shortly after the CSIA proposal, the Indian government was hit with two claims arising out of measures taken by state governments. In *Rakia v. India* (*Rakia*), the dispute arose out of a memorandum of understanding entered into by India's state government of Andhra Pradesh related to the construction of an alumina refinery in the region.[111] In *Nissan v. India* (*Nissan*), the dispute was based

---

[108] Arun Jaitley (Minister of Finance), 'Budget Speech 2016–2017' (29 February 2016), www.indiabudget.gov.in/budget2016-2017/ub2016-17/bs/bs.pdf.

[109] *Ibid.*; Ministry of Finance (Budget Division), *Annual Report 2016–17*, 29; Arjun Ram Meghwal (Minister of State in the Ministry of Finance), Rajya Sabha, Unstarred Question No. 4369, 'Bilateral Investment Treaty with State Governments' (11 April 2017).

[110] See Prabhash Ranjan and Jay M. Sanklecha, 'Sensitise States, Don't Intimidate Them', *The Hindu*, 26 April 2016.

[111] Dipanwita Gupta, 'UAE Serves Indian Govt Arbitration Notice for Failing on Bauxite Supplies for Andhra Alumina Project', AlCircle, 12 January 2017.

upon an agreement by the state government of Tamil Nadu to provide subsidies as part of deal to set up a car manufacturing plant in the state.[112]

Nevertheless, the CSIA proposal ultimately went nowhere. In response to a query filed under the RTI Act while undertaking this project, the Ministry of Finance disclosed that the CSIA proposal had been shelved in 2017 – ironically, the same year as the *Rakia* and *Nissan* claims.[113] Thus, when asked whether 'the CSIA as envisaged in the 2016–17 budget speech of Arun Jaitley [had] been finalised', the government replied that:

> A draft cabinet note on Centre State Investment Agreement was prepared and submitted to Cabinet for consideration through a Cabinet Note on 22 March 2017. In view of the comments received on draft CSIA from concerned ministries/departments, it was felt that entering into CSIA with state [governments] may have unforeseen and potentially undesirable consequences. Subsequently, the proposal was withdrawn by DEA [Department of Economic Affairs] on 6 June 2017.[114]

Unfortunately, the Ministry of Finance did not elaborate on what these 'unforeseen and potentially undesirable consequences' were.

2.5.3   Remedial Internalisation

The purpose of this section is to address India's attempts to establish remedial internalisation processes. As noted by Calamita and Berman, remedial internalisation processes are designed to correct or defend the state's compliance with its investment treaty obligations. In other words, remedial internalisation processes act in a post hoc manner, after the state has taken a decision or adopted a measure,[115] and seek to address issues related to potential (or actual) disputes with investors. Although the focus of remedial processes is different from informational processes, they are not unrelated. Processes adopted for remedial internalisation may follow measures for informational internalisation. For instance, a capacity-building workshop, with the objective of promoting informational internalisation, might, in turn, lead to remedial internalisation.

---

[112]   Aditi Shah, 'Nissan Sues India over Outstanding Dues; Seeks over $770 Million', *Reuters*, 1 December 2017.

[113]   Information sought under RTI Act, Registration Number, MOOCD/R/2018/50035. Reply of Department of Economic Affairs (DEA), Ministry of Finance (on file with the author).

[114]   *Ibid.*

[115]   In this respect, remedial processes differ from monitoring processes, which Calamita and Berman describe as entailing the review of government measures for consistency with international obligations at or before the time of decision making.

2.5.3.1 Creating Institutional Mechanisms
for Managing BIT Disputes

One step taken in the direction of remedial internalisation has been the creation of an inter-ministerial group (IMG) – a group of officials from different central government ministries – to look into the BIT claims brought against India. The mandate of the IMG is not only to decide on a strategy for litigating claims but also to ascertain if the dispute can be resolved before the start of actual ISDS proceedings. The project has met with resistance. In an interview, an official involved in the IMG told this researcher that many departments are simply not willing to revisit their regulatory measures due to BIT claims.[116] On the contrary, most departments look at BITs as an irritant and an unnecessary obstacle to doing what they deem fit.[117] Often, these different departments question the wisdom of entering into BITs.[118] In light of these attitudes, the possibility of correcting a regulatory measure or fine-tuning it, once problems with the measure have been identified by a foreign investor (and before the dispute has become a formal investment treaty claim), has not enjoyed much support among different ministries of the government.

The High Level Committee on Arbitration, mentioned above, has suggested a number of measures designed to boost remedial internalisation. For better management of BIT disputes, the committee recommended creating an inter-ministerial committee (IMC), comprised of officials from the Ministries of Finance, External Affairs, and Law and Justice; hiring lawyers with investment treaty expertise; creating a designated fund to fight BIT disputes; and appointing counsel qualified in BIT arbitration to defend India against BIT claims.

The most significant recommendation of the committee is the creation of an international law adviser (ILA) to advise the government on international legal disputes, particularly BIT disputes, and who would be responsible for the day-to-day management of BIT arbitrations.[119] The intent behind this suggestion is laudable as it would augment the government's expertise on BITs and create a single authority for managing all BIT arbitrations. That being said, the Legal and Treaties Division in the External Affairs Ministry is in charge of providing international legal advice,

---

[116] Interview Official FF, 2018.
[117] *Ibid.*
[118] *Ibid.*
[119] High Level Committee on Arbitration, 'Report of the High Level Committee to Review Institutionalisation of Arbitration Mechanism in India', 110.

including on investment law, to the government, and has vast experience in dealing with international law disputes before different international tribunals.[120] The creation of a new position thus risks duplicating an existing arrangement, resulting in potential inefficiencies by deepening the red tape and departmental turf wars between ministries. Rather than creating a new position, therefore, a more effective alternative might well be to strengthen and upgrade the current Legal and Treaties Division, which is currently understaffed,[121] and make it the designated authority to deal with all BIT arbitrations, as well as the coordinator of the proposed IMC. Furthermore, since the Ministry of Commerce and Industry deals with India's FTAs, it too should be included in the IMC along with the Ministry of Finance.

While the recommendations of the committee are still under consideration,[122] this report and consultation process clearly highlights the extent of the lack of consistency and coordination within different ministries of the Indian government in dealing with BITs in general and BIT arbitration in particular. In fact, none other than the Finance Minister of India, Arun Jaitley, in a letter written to the Prime Minister's office on 26 May 2017, recognised these problems. This letter was prompted by a note that was handed over to Mr Jaitley by a 'former colleague from the legal fraternity'.[123] The letter shows the various fault lines within the government on the issue of handling of BIT disputes and is worth quoting in full:

> A former colleague from the legal fraternity has handed me a note which I am enclosing. It indicates that under various bilateral treaties, there are 23 arbitrations where Government of India is not being adequately represented. There are some which concern the Department of Revenue which I am bringing to the notice of Revenue Secretary for immediate action. There are others which are dealt by the Ministry of Mines [*Rakia v. India*] and Ministry of Heavy Industries [*Nissan v. India*]. These are illustrative cases only.
>
> In some cases [the Indian government] is defaulting in the matter of appointment of arbitrators. This will result in the international forum usurping our power to appoint the arbitrator. We have engaged lawyers

---

[120] Government of India, Ministry of External Affairs, 'Legal and Treaties Division', www .mea.gov.in/treaty.htm.

[121] A query was raised in the Indian Parliament about the existence of vacancies in the L&T Division in 2017. See Bhagwanth Khuba, Lok Sabha, Unstarred Question No. 5163, 'Vacancies in Legal and Treaties Division' (5 April 2017).

[122] RTI Query (on file with author).

[123] Letter from Arun Jaitley, Minister of Finance, Defence and Corporate Affairs, to Nripendra Misra, Principal Secretary to the Prime Minister, 'Arun Jaitley's Letter to PMO on Vodafone Arbitration' (26 May 2017), www.scribd.com/document/375590061.

who may not have adequate stature to create an impact on these arbitrations. Further, there is no coordinating Ministry which is following up on day to day basis. This needs to be addressed adequately.[124]

2.5.3.2 The Indian Model BIT 2016

A further response to the *White Industries* case was India's reconsideration of its model investment treaty negotiating text. Adopted in 2016, the Indian Model BIT mentioned earlier imposes a number of limits, procedural and otherwise, designed to restrict when a foreign investor can bring an ISDS claim against India.[125] In a sense, this too is a kind of remedial internalisation process whereby officials seek to limit the impact of investment treaty commitments on governmental decision making by limiting the extent of the state's substantive commitments or by making it difficult for foreign investors to bring claims through ISDS or both.[126] As explained by officials, the reasoning is that if the treaty makes it difficult for foreign investors to bring ISDS claims against India, then there will less possibility of Indian regulatory measures being challenged by foreign investors. By the same token, of course, as India limits its commitments to investors, there are likely to be fewer and weaker commitments for Indian officials to internalise in their decision making.

2.6 Academia and the Civil Society

The previous sections have addressed the internalisation of investment treaties within the Indian government, revealing a dynamic in which a distinct lack of attention to investment treaties prior to the *White Industries* award was replaced by a flurry of activity in its aftermath. In many respects, one sees this dynamic mirrored in the experience of Indian academia and civil society.

Within the Indian academic community, before the *White Industries* award, BITs did not attract much attention, barring a few exceptions.[127]

---

[124] *Ibid.*
[125] See Ranjan, *India and Bilateral Investment Treaties: Refusal, Acceptance, Backlash.*
[126] Interview Official AA, 2019.
[127] Sreenivasa Rao, 'Bilateral Investment Promotion Agreements: A Legal Framework for the Protection of Foreign Investments' (2000) 26 *Commonwealth Law Bulletin* 623; Devashish Krishan, 'India and International Investment Laws', in Bimal N. Patel (ed.), *India and International Law*, Vol. 2 (Martinus Nijhoff Publishers, 2008), 277; Prabhash Ranjan, 'International Investment Agreements and Regulatory Discretion: Case Study of India' (2008) 9 *Journal of World Investment and Trade* 209; Ranjan, 'Medical Patents and Expropriation in International Investment Law – With Special Reference to India'.

This academic disregard altered following the award.[128] The existence of
pro-investor obligations within India's BITs and their potential adverse
effects on India's regulatory space were discussed extensively. For instance,
in *White Industries* itself, it was argued that since the *White Industries*
award was an indictment for judicial delays, it encroached upon India's
judicial sovereignty,[129] echoing the same sentiment expressed in the Indian
parliament. Likewise, although some academics had demanded that India
should revisit and review its BITs even before *White Industries*,[130] these
demands gained further traction after the case and the issuance of additional ISDS notices against India.[131]

Similarly, civil society organisations, in the aftermath of *White
Industries* and other ISDS notices against India, urged caution by the
government in ratifying new BITs. For instance, a letter written by a
'Forum against FTAs' to Manmohan Singh, the then Prime Minister of
India, tried to attract the government's attention to some of the problems

---

[128] Ranjan, 'India and Bilateral Investment Treaties – A Changing Landscape'; Prabhash
       Ranjan, 'Comparing Investment Provisions in India's FTAs with India's Stand-Alone
       BITs: Contributing to the Evolution of New Indian BIT Practice' (2015) 16 *Journal of
       World Investment & Trade* 899; Prabhash Ranjan, 'Most Favoured Nation Principle
       in Indian Bilateral Investment Treaties: A Case for Reform' (2015) 55 *Indian Journal
       of International Law* 39; Biswajit Dhar, Reji Joseph and T. C. James, 'India's Bilateral
       Investment Agreements: Time to Review' (2012) 47 *Economic & Political Weekly* 113;
       Smitha Francis and Murali Kallummal, 'India's Comprehensive Trade Agreements:
       Implications for Development Trajectory' (2013) 48 *Economic & Political Weekly* 109;
       Aniruddha Rajput, 'India's Shifting Treaty Practice: A Comparative Analysis of the 2003
       and 2015 Model BITs' (2016) 7 *Jindal Global Law Review* 201; Grant Hanessian and Kabir
       Duggal, 'The 2015 Indian Model BIT: Is This Change the World Wishes to See' (2015) 30
       ICSID Review – Foreign Investment Law Journal 729; Hanessian and Duggal, 'The Final
       2015 Indian Model BIT: Is This the Change the World Wishes to See'; Saurabh Garg,
       Ishita G. Tripathy and Sudhanshu Roy, 'The Indian Model Bilateral Investment Treaty:
       Continuity and Change', in Kavaljit Singh and Burghard Igle (eds.), *Rethinking Bilateral
       Investment Treaties: Critical Issues and Policy Choices* (Both Ends, Madhyam and SOMO,
       2016), 69; Singh, 'An Analysis of India's New Model Bilateral Investment Treaty'; Nish
       Shetty and Romesh Weeramantary, 'India's New Approach to Investment Treaties' (2016)
       18 *Asian Dispute Review* 189; Azernoosh Bazrafkan, 'The (R)evolution of Indian Model
       Bilateral Investment Treaty: Escaping Liability without Mitigating Risks' (2016) 7 *Jindal
       Global Law Review* 245; Deepak Raju, 'General Exceptions in the Indian Model BIT: Is the
       "Necessity" Test Workable?' (2016) 7 *Jindal Global Law Review* 227.
[129] P. K. Suresh Kumar, 'Globalisation and Judicial Sovereignty of India' (2012) 47 *Economic
       and Political Weekly* 27. See also Jayati Ghosh, 'Worrying Trend', *Frontline*, 23 March 2012.
[130] Ranjan, 'International Investment Agreements and Regulatory Discretion'.
[131] See Ranjan, 'Comparing Investment Provisions in India's FTAs with India's Stand-Alone
       BITs'; Dhar, Joseph and James, 'India's Bilateral Investment Agreements'; Francis and
       Kallummal, 'India's Comprehensive Trade Agreements'.

existent in BITs,[132] such as their limiting effects on India's policy space.[133] Indeed, the group argued that the threat of BIT arbitrations 'will have a chilling effect on the ability of different ministries (of the Indian government) to regulate different social and economic needs.'[134] The Forum thus demanded that India should review its BITs and abstain from entering into new BITs.[135]

2.7   Conclusion

While awareness about BITs and ISDS in India has increased after *White Industries* and other BIT claims, India has still not been able to fully internalise the impact and ramifications of BITs. This chapter has shown that India has taken steps towards establishing or improving informational and remedial internalisation processes in terms of BITs. There has been some spillover effects as many specialised government bodies, such as the Law Commission of India, have emphasised the importance and need to internalise BITs in their various reports. However, there continues to be weak coordination between different government ministries in dealing with BITs. Furthermore, given the federal nature and character of the Indian polity, these challenges to internalise BITs remain grave. Some of the recent BIT claims that have arisen due to the actions of the subnational governments reveal this trend quite clearly.

The *White Industries* award and other subsequent ISDS claims marked a turning point with respect to the political salience of investment treaties and the Indian central government's awareness of the potential impact of those commitments. As a result of this shift, this chapter has shown how different elements within the Indian government have tried to take steps towards establishing mechanisms for the informational and remedial internalisation of India's treaty obligations. Yet, as this chapter has

---

[132] Letter from G. Manicandan, Forum against FTAs, to Manmohan Singh, Prime Minister of India, 'We Call upon the Government to Review and Rescind Its Decision to Sign BIT/BIPA with the USA', 26 September 2013, www.bilaterals.org/IMG/pdf/lettter_forum_ag_ftas_us_india_bits_26_sept.pdf.

[133] *Ibid.*

[134] Letter from Santosh M. R., Centre for Trade and Development, to Manmohan Singh, Prime Minister of India, 'Concerns Regarding Proposed US-India Bilateral Investment Treaty', 13 June 2012, https://donttradeourlivesaway.files.wordpress.com/2012/06/civil-society-letter-on-us-india-bit.pdf.

[135] See Letter from G. Manicandan to Manmohan Singh, 'We Call upon the Government to Review and Rescind Its Decision to Sign BIT/ BIPA with the USA'.

demonstrated, although India has undertaken several attempts towards informational and remedial internalisation, most of these initiatives have either been ad hoc or have never come to fruition. Moreover, structural problems within government continue to undermine internalisation. Inter-governmental coordination remains extremely weak, and this is amplified by India's federal structure and the disconnect between state and central governments. These structural problems conspire to create almost insurmountable challenges to internalisation in India, a difficulty reflected quite clearly in the many recent ISDS claims that have arisen due to the actions of sub-national state governments. These findings support Calamita and Berman's theorisation that matters such as public administration coordination, regulatory capacity, and federal structure can have a significant impact on internalisation.[136]

---

[136] See Chapter 1.

3

The Impact of Investment Treaties
on the Rule of Law in Indonesia

JOHN LUMBANTOBING

This chapter probes the extent of internalisation of investment treaties in Indonesia and whether there is evidence of 'spillover effects' on the domestic rule of law. In its assessment, it follows and applies the definitions and analytical framework on internalisation set out by Calamita and Berman.[1] Accordingly, it seeks to examine whether investment treaties are taken into account in governmental decision making – through informational, monitoring or remedial mechanisms – and whether such consideration has resulted in general rule of law improvements.[2]

The chapter concludes that the internalisation of investment treaties has been minimal, especially outside the central Ministry of Foreign Affairs (MoFA) and the National Investment Coordination Board (*Badan Koordinasi Penanaman Modal*) (BKPM). Sectoral ministries and especially regional governments are generally unaware of the state's investment treaty obligations and do not take them into account in decision-making processes. There are also no institutional mechanisms whereby investment treaties are taken into account in the government's dealings with foreign investors, including in regulatory and decision-making processes. Other than a specific and isolated instance in the mining sector, there is little evidence of investment treaties having any impact – positive or otherwise – on the rule of law in Indonesia. The dearth of internalisation is surprisingly persistent even following investment treaty claims faced by the government.

The structure of this chapter is as follows. Section 3.1 contains an overview of Indonesia's investment treaties, providing the backdrop against which the question of internalisation arises. Section 3.2 explains the general process of negotiation, ratification, and dissemination of investment

---

[1] See Chapter 1.
[2] *Ibid.*

treaties within government agencies and gives a first taste of the overall lack of awareness and institutional internalisation mechanisms. Section 3.3 traces the framework and substance of the Indonesian regulatory regime and analyses key provisions governing foreign investment, with a particular focus on their inconsistency with common investment treaty provisions as well as the lack of reference to investment treaties in the *travaux preparatoires* of those laws. Section 3.4 provides an account of investment claims faced by Indonesia with a particular focus on the questions of internalisation and spillover effects. Section 3.5 examines factors that stand in the way of internalisation of investment treaties in Indonesia, synthesising the findings and analyses of previous sections. Section 3.6 concludes.

In terms of methodology, the research has been conducted by examining (1) the content and processes of Indonesian laws and regulations related to foreign investment against the backdrop of investment treaties and (2) the background (and, in a few instances, the aftermath) of investment treaty claims brought by foreign investors. Readers will note that interviews are used fairly extensively in this chapter, hence information regarding the interviews themselves is required as a preliminary matter. Ten interviews involving seven interviewees were undertaken by the author across 2017–2018. Of the interviewees, three individuals were from BKPM, comprising one high-level and two mid-level officials who were involved in recent investment treaty disputes involving Indonesia as well as investment treaty negotiation. One interviewee was a mid-level official in MoFA with intimate knowledge and substantive experience in investment treaty negotiation. A further interview was conducted with one mid-level official from Bank Indonesia who represented the central bank in Indonesia's investment treaty negotiation team. Apart from these government officials, interviews were also conducted with two senior lawyers who represented investors and the Indonesian government, respectively, in recent investment treaty disputes. The interviews were all semi-structured. For the purpose of confidentiality, the names of the interviewees and their institutions are not disclosed in the citations.

3.1   Overview of Indonesia's Investment Treaties Programme

In March 2014, the government of Indonesia announced its intention to terminate its bilateral investment treaty (BIT) with the Netherlands[3]

---

[3] Netherlands–Indonesia BIT (1968).

by not renewing it upon its expiry.[4] At the same time, the government announced its intention to eventually terminate all of its existing BITs.[5] While this caused some uproar among foreign investors at the time,[6] the government repeatedly indicated its openness to the possibility of renegotiating its existing BITs or concluding new ones.[7]

The termination of the Indonesia-Dutch BIT was a turning point in the long history of Indonesian BITs and investment treaties.[8] The country signed its first BIT with Denmark in 1968[9] and subsequently signed more than seventy BITs between 1968 and the 2014 announcement.[10] Separate from the BITs, Indonesia ratified the International Centre for Settlement of Investment Disputes (ICSID) Convention in 1968.[11] In the absence of an ICSID clause in its investment treaties, Indonesia granted access to ICSID through ICSID arbitration clauses in the foreign investment licences issued by BKPM.[12] More recently, Indonesia has become party to a number of the so-called 'third generation' of investment treaties, beginning in the 2000s, including a sizeable number of BITs as well as regional investment agreements (either on their own or as an investment chapter in a multilateral free trade agreement [FTA]).[13] Foremost among these are the

---

[4] Ben Bland and Shawn Donnan, 'Indonesia to Terminate More Than 60 Bilateral Investment Treaties', *Financial Times*, 26 March 2014.

[5] *Ibid.*

[6] For a discussion of the possibility that foreign investors may still benefit from sunset clauses in most BITs as well as a multitude of regional and multilateral investment treaties that remain in force, see Antony Crockett, 'Indonesia's Bilateral Investment Treaties: Between Generations?' (2015) 30 *ICSID Review* 437.

[7] Arif H. Oegroseno, 'Revamping Bilateral Treaties', *The Jakarta Post*, 7 July 2014, *citing* Michael Ewing-Chow and Junianto J Losari, 'Indonesia Is Letting Its Bilateral Treaties Lapse so as to Renegotiate Better Ones', *Financial Times*, 16 April 2014.

[8] For a general overview of the history of foreign investment in Indonesia in the twentieth century, see Louis T. Wells and Rafiq Ahmed, *Making Foreign Investment Safe: Property Rights and National Sovereignty* (Oxford University Press 2007).

[9] Denmark–Indonesia BIT (1968).

[10] See Investment Policy Hub, 'Indonesia', https://investmentpolicy.unctad.org/international-investment-agreements/countries/97/indonesia. While not all of these treaties came into force, more than 60 did.

[11] Law No. 5 of 1968 regarding Settlement of Disputes between the State and Foreign Nationals concerning Investment, 29 June 1968, State Gazette No. 32 ('ICSID Ratification Act').

[12] For instance, ICSID's jurisdiction in the *Amco* case was founded on this clause in Amco's licence even though at the time there was no investment treaty between Indonesia and the United States as Amco's state of origin. See *Amco Asia Corporation, PT Amco Indonesia, Pan American Development Limited v. Republic of Indonesia*, ICSID Case No. ARB/81/1, Decision on Jurisdiction (25 September 1983).

[13] Indonesia has never concluded a bilateral FTA with an investment chapter.

2009 ASEAN Comprehensive Investment Agreement (ACIA)[14] and the 'ASEAN Plus Agreements', concluded by ASEAN member states on the one hand and major trading partners on the other hand.[15] Notably, even though the Indonesian government indicated its intention to terminate its BITs – and, as of this writing it has terminated more than thirty of these treaties – it never indicated a similar intention with respect to these regional and multilateral agreements.

Indonesia's ongoing participation in regional and multilateral agreements,[16] together with its conclusion of new, renegotiated BITs with some of its treaty partners,[17] demonstrates the resilience of investment treaties in Indonesia's foreign investment policy and legal framework. Indeed, even when the Indonesian government was attending to the termination of its older BITs, MoFA and BKPM finalised a Model BIT which they have been preparing since 2014.[18] The question, however, is whether international obligations under these investment treaties are noted and taken into account when the government introduces measures affecting foreign investment. This chapter begins by studying how treaties are concluded and their dissemination within government agencies afterward.

3.2   Negotiation, Conclusion, and Ratification of Indonesian Investment Treaties: Process and Aftermath

The Indonesian government process of drafting, negotiating, concluding, and entering into a treaty is governed by Law No. 24 of 2000 regarding

---

[14] ASEAN Comprehensive Investment Agreement (ACIA) (2009).

[15] ASEAN–Japan EPA (2008); ASEAN–Australia–New Zealand FTA (2009); ASEAN–Korea Investment Agreement (2009); ASEAN–China Investment Agreement (2009); and ASEAN–India Investment Agreement (2014).

[16] See, for example, Regional Comprehensive Economic Partnership (RCEP) (2020), an agreement among ASEAN member states and five ASEAN FTA partners (Australia, China, Japan, New Zealand, and Republic of Korea). RCEP includes an investment chapter, although at the time of signing the parties deferred a final decision on whether to provide for investor–state dispute settlement (ISDS). See RCEP, Art. 10.18.

[17] See, for example, Singapore–Indonesia BIT (2018), replacing the Singapore–Indonesia BIT (2005), which was terminated in 2016.

[18] Interview SG, 2017. The text of the Model BIT is not public and only serves as internal guidance for future treaty negotiations. See also Abdulkadir Jailani, 'Indonesia's Perspective on Review of International Investment Agreements', (2015) 1 *South Centre's Investment Policy Brief* 1, and 2. At the time, Mr Jailani was MoFA's Director for Treaties of Economic, Social and Cultural Affairs.

Treaties ('2000 Treaties Law').[19] Under this regulation, any government entity with a plan for a treaty must consult and coordinate such plan with MoFA.[20] The negotiation can then be led by MoFA or other officials from another ministry, depending upon the issues involved or the ministry's scope of authority.[21] In practice, over the last few years, the process of drafting and negotiating investment treaties has been led jointly by MoFA and BKPM.[22] There is no express or rigid standard procedure apportioning the precise scope and authority for each. But by all accounts, MoFA and BKPM have developed a very good understanding and working relationship that allows them to work together seamlessly.[23] Depending on the circumstances, such as when there is a specific major investment expected from the counterparty in a particular sector, the relevant sectoral ministry or agency will be involved in the negotiation process.[24]

In a fairly recent article, Crockett rejected Poulsen's theory of 'bounded rationality' that developing countries signed BITs and agreed to their investor–state dispute settlement (ISDS) mechanisms without realising the risks posed to their regulatory autonomy – at least as far as Indonesia is concerned.[25] Relying on the text of some early Indonesian BITs and the *Churchill Mining* tribunal's detailed review of the *travaux preparatoires* of the 1976 United Kingdom–Indonesia BIT,[26] he concluded that 'Indonesia has taken a relatively careful and calculated approach to the negotiation of its BITs',[27] and that 'Indonesia has demonstrated that it thinks carefully, and independently, about how the relationship between State and investor ought to be regulated'.[28] However, even if that conclusion is true, it does not automatically translate into stronger internalisation of investment treaties outside of the central government agencies involved

---

[19] Law No. 24 of 2000 regarding Treaties, 23 October 2000, State Gazette No. 185 ('2000 Treaties Law').

[20] 2000 Treaties Law, Art. 5(1).

[21] 2000 Treaties Law, Art. 5(4).

[22] Interview SG, 2017; Interview RB, 2017.

[23] *Ibid.*

[24] Interview SG, 2017. For instance, where the target of FDI inflow from the counterparty is in the mining or banking sector, then the Ministry of Energy and Mineral Resources or Bank Indonesia (the central bank) will be involved, respectively. Interview AT, 2017.

[25] Antony Crockett, 'The Termination of Indonesia's BITs: Changing the Bathwater, But Keeping the Baby?' (2017) 18 *The Journal of World Investment and Trade* 836, 846–52.

[26] See *Churchill Mining Plc v. Republic of Indonesia*, Decision on Jurisdiction, ICSID Case No. ARB/12/40 (24 February 2014), paras. 212–23.

[27] Crockett, 'The Termination of Indonesia's BITs', 847.

[28] *Ibid.*, 850.

in negotiations, for example, to other central government agencies and to subnational governments.

Once investment treaties are concluded, they generally require ratification by state parties.[29] The 2000 Treaties Law requires that ratification in Indonesia be based on a parliamentary act in the event that the treaty concerns, *inter alia*, the 'sovereign rights of the state' and 'the formation of new legal rules'.[30] Otherwise, the treaty may be ratified based on an executive decision in the form of a Presidential Decree.[31] While it is arguable that investment treaties fulfil the two aforementioned conditions due to their restriction on the state's policy space, in practice, the ratification of most investment treaties has not been done through Parliament. Instead, they have been ratified based on presidential decrees.[32] Hence, the ratification process is often limited to the executive branch without the involvement of Parliament. This may explain the very low level of internalisation among members of Parliament, a point that will be discussed with more detail later within the context of drafting domestic investment laws.

After ratification, MoFA maintains a public treaty database[33] where the texts of all Indonesian treaties (including investment treaties) can be accessed together with information regarding the place and date of conclusion, status of ratification (with information on the instrument of ratification), and status of the treaty's entry into force.[34] However, other

---

[29] Ratification is generally required unless provided otherwise by the treaty itself. See Vienna Convention on the Law of Treaties, 23 May 1969, 1155 UNTS 243, Art. 14(1).

[30] 2000 Treaties Law, Art. 10. Other treaties that require parliamentary acts under this provision are those that involve (1) politics and defence, (2) agreements fixing or changing a state's boundary, (3) human rights and the environment, and (4) foreign loan or grants.

[31] 2000 Treaties Law, Art. 11(1).

[32] This can be seen from the information on the instrument of ratification for each investment treaty at Ministry of Foreign Affairs of the Republic of Indonesia, 'International Treaty Search', http://treaty.kemlu.go.id. Even multilateral investment treaties and FTAs with investment chapters were ratified on the basis of a Presidential Decree. For example, the ACIA was ratified by Presidential Decree No. 49 of 2011, 8 August 2011, State Gazette No. 80, and the ASEAN–Australia–NZ FTA was ratified by Presidential Decree No. 26 of 2011, 6 May 2011, State Gazette No. 55.

[33] Ministry of Foreign Affairs of the Republic of Indonesia, 'International Treaty Search', http://treaty.kemlu.go.id.

[34] Admittedly, it may be a bit difficult sometimes to navigate MoFA's treaty database because of the very detailed search tools. However, in the context of investment treaties, there are other alternative databases such as the Investment Policy Hub managed by UNCTAD where anyone can very easily find the list and texts of investment treaties of each state including Indonesia (in the form of both BIT and multilateral agreement). See Investment Policy Hub, 'International Investment Agreements Navigator', https://investmentpolicy.unctad.org/international-investment-agreements.

government agencies are not formally notified of the conclusion of new treaties and generally there is no further coordination between sectoral agencies and MoFA following the conclusion or ratification of a treaty.[35]

There is no national strategy for disseminating information about investment treaties, that is, what Calamita and Berman refer to as informational internalisation measures.[36] Rather, such internalisation measures undertaken by the government are ad hoc and sporadic. For a period, especially from 2014 to 2015, MoFA and BKPM conducted several seminars and workshops in cooperation with, among others, the International Institute for Sustainable Development (IISD), the South Centre, and UNCTAD to disseminate knowledge and raise awareness about investment treaties.[37] These events involved various stakeholders from other central government agencies (sectoral ministries), academia, and subnational governments.[38] The seminars and workshops were ad hoc: not expressly or specifically mandated by law, without any particular standard procedure, and largely dependent upon budgetary availability.[39] Hence, these workshops have not been conducted in the last few years because, in the words of one official, 'there is no more budget'.[40]

A budget is a reflection of priorities and concerns. There was a reason that those seminars and workshops were provided funding in the first place: they coincided or closely followed the government's programme to terminate and renegotiate its BITs as well as the beginning of the government's process of developing a model BIT. The termination and renegotiation of Indonesia's BITs, as well as the development of a model BIT, were encouraged by the ICSID tribunal's decision in 2013 to uphold jurisdiction in the multi-billion dollar *Churchill Mining* arbitration claim,[41] as well as

---

[35] Interview SG, 2017.

[36] See Chapter 1.

[37] This author himself participated in three such events in those two years. One such event was held by MoFA in cooperation with UNCTAD and the International Institute for Sustainable Development (IISD) in January 2015. See the report at IISD's website, IISD, MoFA and UNCTAD, 'Regional Interactive Meeting on the Development of Investment Treaty Models', https://web.archive.org/web/20160911061320/www.iisd.org/pdf/2015/investment-treaty-models-jakarta-report-2015.pdf. The second event was held sometime in May 2015 by MoFA in cooperation with South Centre (invitation and the programme are on file with author). Finally, the third event was held by BKPM in June 2015 to discuss the draft Model BIT with several Indonesian academics (invitation and the programme are on file with author).

[38] Interview NM, 2017.

[39] *Ibid.*

[40] *Ibid.*

[41] See Section 4.2.1.4.

what the government considered as frivolous claims in the *Rafat Ali Rizvi* and *al-Warraq* investment treaty arbitrations,[42] both also brought in 2013. Once the model BIT was completed, however, and the outrage over the investment treaty claims subsided (especially following Indonesia's victory on the merits in those cases), these issues became less salient; consequently, the seminars and workshops stopped.

Even with the workshops, the internalisation of investment treaties – especially among subnational government officials – appears to have been largely unimproved. One official suggested that this was at least partly a consequence of the quality of the participants from local governments: '[w]e explain about investment treaties, and then they ask about other unrelated things'.[43] Beyond issues related to the effectiveness of occasional workshops, however, internalisation has also been limited by poor institutional coordination between central and subnational levels of government – a problem that Calamita and Berman identify as potentially impacting internalisation.[44] Regional government agencies dealing with foreign investment, for example, do not report to BKPM as they are not a provincial office of BKPM. Instead, they are part of the provincial or regency government's structure and are staffed by employees of the local government at large. Most of these employees are regularly rotated every few years among different agencies with different portfolios.[45] Sometimes, the difference between these responsibilities is so extreme that one day, one might be assigned to manage investment issues and the next, to handle agriculture and cows.[46] From the perspective of at least one government official, in many instances, even a mere awareness of investment treaties is practically non-existent, leading to the view that provincial officials 'don't know anything about investment treaties'.[47]

In the absence of a national internalisation strategy for investment treaties, the informational internalisation measures that have taken place have been conducted on an ad hoc basis without coordination among government institutions. Moreover, these measures have been taken in response to unique circumstances in which investment treaties achieved political

---

[42] See Section 4.2.1.3.
[43] Interview NM, 2017.
[44] See Chapter 1 (on the potential impact of intra-governmental coordination on internalisation).
[45] This paragraph is based on Interview NM, 2017; Interview RB, 2017.
[46] Interview RB, 2017.
[47] Interview PD, 2018.

salience in Indonesia. Once those circumstances changed and the political salience of investment treaties waned, internalisation measures similarly receded. Given the lack of coordination and sustained effort, it is no wonder that the level of awareness of investment treaties and their internalisation outside the ambit of MoFA and BKPM – the agencies responsible for developing investment policy – is very low. As discussed in the following section, this point is reinforced with regard to Indonesia's domestic law regulating foreign investment, which is meant to be an instrument to implement investment treaties.

3.3   Indonesian Investment Law: In Search of Internalisation in the Legislative Process

3.3.1   General Overview of Treaty Internalisation in the Legislative Process

At the outset, it should be noted that there is no particular regulation or standard mechanism of general application whereby treaties and other international obligations are incorporated into the legislative process.[48] The basic law regulating such processes is the 2011 Law on Legislative Making.[49] Notably, the 2011 Law requires that any draft parliamentary legislation be preceded by an 'Academic Text' (*Naskah Akademik*), which outlines the theoretical foundations of the rules and provisions proposed in the draft, sometimes with alternative wordings to provide certain flexibility for policy choices.[50] One internal House of Representative's Guideline on Academic Text provides that the materials for an Academic Text should include a review of, among other things, treaties or international agreements.[51] However, that guideline is only for draft legislation

---

[48] On a more fundamental level, the position of international law within the Indonesian domestic legal system is still very much unsettled. Some practices reflect a monist position, while others show a dualist position. See, for example, Simon Butt, 'The Position of International Law within the Indonesian Legal System', (2014) 28 *Emory International Law Review* 1. Among others, this may explain the inconsistent practice when it comes to internalising treaty obligations at a legislative level.

[49] Law No. 12 of 2011 regarding Legislative Making, 22 August 2011, State Gazette No. 82.

[50] *Ibid.*, Art. 43(3). See also Jimly Asshiddiqie, *Perihal Undang-Undang* (Rajawali Pers, 2010), 319–23.

[51] Pusat Perancangan Undang-Undang, Badan Keahlian Dewan Perwakilan Rakyat Republik Indonesia, 'Pedoman Penyusunan Naskah Akademik Rancangan Undang-Undang', www .dpr.go.id/doksetjen/dokumen/reformasi-birokrasi-Quick-Win-Pedoman-Penyusunan-Naskah-Akademik-Rancangan-Undang-Undang-1507775513.pdf, 3.

initiated by Parliament (House of Representatives), while a similar guideline by the Ministry of Law for the use of the executive branch makes no
mention of treaties or international instruments at all.[52] Given the divergence in guidelines, it is no wonder that legislative and executive practices
also differ. Thus, while in many instances, the legislation has clearly considered the treaties applicable in a given area, there are also examples to
the contrary.[53]

As a result of this lack of consistency, the internalisation of treaties
in Indonesia's legislative process must be approached on a case-by-case
basis – in this context, by reviewing the *travaux preparatoires* of the
relevant legislation. However, the archiving of legislative processes in
Indonesia is generally not conducted systematically. Even though the
archives are in principle public documents, they are almost always not
made available online. It is also generally unclear where and from whom
one should ask for the *travaux preparatoires* of a legislation. The author
is fortunate to have obtained the *travaux* for the 2007 Investment Law
from the House of Representatives' secretariat, but even then, the *travaux*
only includes drafts, minutes, and letters pertaining to the process in
Parliament. Crucially, the *travaux* does not contain the Academic Text.
Nevertheless, the available materials do provide some window into the
black box of the legislative process leading to the 2007 Investment Law.

3.3.2   Legal Framework and Key Provisions Related to Foreign Investment

Foreign investment in Indonesia is regulated under an umbrella piece
of legislation, the '2007 Investment Law'.[54] This legislation encompasses
both domestic investment and foreign investment. The 2007 Investment

---

[52] Minister of Law and Human Rights Regulation No. M.HH-01.PP.01.01 of 2008 regarding Guidelines on Academic Text of Draft Legislation, 17 December 2008.

[53] One example is the grounds to refuse recognition and enforcement of foreign arbitral awards in the 1999 Arbitration Law, which are markedly different from the grounds pro-vided in the 1958 New York Convention that Indonesia ratified in 1981. See, for example, Gatot Soemartono and John Lumbantobing, 'Indonesian Arbitration Law and Practice in Light of the UNCITRAL Model Law', in Gary F. Bell (ed.), *The UNCITRAL Model Law and Asian Arbitration Laws: Implementation and Comparisons* (Cambridge University Press, 2018), 300, 339–45.

[54] Law No. 25 of 2007 regarding Capital Investment, 26 April 2007, State Gazette No. 67 ('2007 Investment Law'), with Official Elucidation, Supplement to State Gazette No. 4724 ('2007 Investment Law, Official Elucidation').

Law is further supported by a range of implementing regulations, many of which take the form of 'Head of BKPM Regulation' and are mostly procedural in nature – such as those outlining the processes and requirements to obtain investment licences and investment facilities in the form of tax breaks, etc.[55] Foreign investment is also subject to sectoral regulations, some of which, such as in the mining sector, have given rise to investment disputes. It does not appear that there is any provincial or regency regulation in existence that directly governs foreign investment.

The 2007 Investment Law replaced the 1967 Foreign Investment Law that had previously governed foreign investment.[56] Although the 1967 Law had been enacted within a year of Indonesia's signature of its first BIT in 1968, it does not appear that the obligations of that treaty were considered when drafting the Law. Nonetheless, several provisions of the 1967 Law dealt directly with issues of investment protection, such as a protection from uncompensated expropriation, as discussed further below.

In considering the 2007 Investment Law, it is worth noting that the purpose and the focus of the Law is on investment facilitation, easing of licensing, and pushing for more government coordination between sectoral ministries as well as provincial and regency governments.[57] Nonetheless, a number of provisions are of obvious relevance with regard to state obligations under investment treaties:

- Several articles of the 2007 Investment Law define foreign investment and the form that it must take.[58] Thus, Art. 5(2) provides that foreign direct investment must take the form a limited liability company (*perseroan terbatas* or '*PT*') organised under Indonesian law and domiciled

---

[55] '*Peraturan Kepala BKPM*' or 'Perka BKPM' in Indonesian. For a list and links to these regulations, see online: BKPM, 'Peraturan BKPM', https://jdih.bkpm.go.id/.

[56] Law No. 1 of 1967 regarding Foreign Investment, 10 January 1967, State Gazette No. 1 ('1967 Foreign Investment Law'), with Official Elucidation, Supplement to State Gazette No. 2818 ('1967 Foreign Investment Law, Official Elucidation').

[57] See 2007 Investment Law, Official Elucidation, Section I (General Part), paras. 4–6. Of the Law's forty articles, at least thirteen provisions can be said to be directly addressing these aspects (Arts. 18–30), ten provisions deal with standard issues such as those on definition, scope of application, administrative sanctions, and entry into force (Arts. 1, 2, and 33–40), and two provisions outline the state's general policy and broad principles in regulating investment (Arts. 3 and 4). Meanwhile, other provisions deal with a range of specific issues such as the priority of Indonesian citizens in employment requirements (Arts. 10 and 11), small and medium enterprises (Art. 13), and special economic zones (Art. 31).

[58] See 2007 Investment Law, Art. 1(3) defining 'foreign investment', Art. 1(4) defining 'investor', Art. 1(6) defining 'foreign investor', Art. 1(7) defining 'capital', and Art. 1(8) defining 'foreign capital'.

in Indonesia. This in effect aligns Indonesia's national investment law with the gateway requirements found in most Indonesian BITs that the investment must be made in accordance with the host state's laws and regulations in order to qualify for the treaty's protection.[59]

- Article 6 of the 2007 Investment Law provides for MFN treatment for all foreign investors, with exceptions for those who fall under the scope of investment treaties – meaning that such investors have preferential rights or receive more favoured treatment.[60]
- Article 7 provides for protection from expropriation except as effected by law with compensation according to market value. If no agreement is reached on the amount of compensation between the state and the foreign investor, the matter is to be referred to arbitration.
- Article 8 provides for an investor's right to transfer and repatriate assets (including in foreign currency).
- Article 32, especially Art. 32(4), provides that any dispute between the state and a foreign investor that cannot be settled amicably is to be settled through arbitration which requires the agreement of the parties.
- Articles 35 and 36 provide, respectively, that investment treaties remain in force until the expiration of the individual treaty and that the government must bring the draft of investment treaties currently negotiated in line with the 2007 Investment Law.

3.3.3   Lack of Internalisation in the Process of Making the 2007 Investment Law

While Arts. 35 and 36 of the 2007 Investment Law acknowledge the existence of investment treaties, it is difficult to infer from this that the content of Indonesia's investment treaty obligations has been internalised through the 2007 Investment Law.[61] Instead, looking closely at the 2007

---

[59] For an overview of selected Indonesian BIT provisions defining 'investment', see Alvin Yap, 'Indonesia', in Loretta Malintoppi and Charis Tan (eds.), *Investment Protection in Southeast Asia* (Brill Nijhoff, 2017), 109, 120–22.

[60] Coordinating Ministry for Economy, Response of the Coordinating Minister for the Economy to Questions from the House of Representatives', Special Commission on the Investment Bill, 19 July 2006, 10 (on file with author).

[61] Knörich and Berger have stated that 'the basic structure of Law No. 25/2007 is not too different from that of IIAs'. See Jan Knorich and Axel Berger, 'Friends or Foes? Interactions between Indonesia's International Investment Treaties and National Investment Law', (2014) *Deutsches Institut für Entwicklungspolitik* 66. While this may be true regarding the structure of the Law, the same cannot necessarily be said regarding the content (and thus on the question of internalisation of investment treaty rules).

Investment Law, it is striking how other provisions appear to reflect a certain disconnect with corresponding provisions in investment treaties. That is especially the case with the expropriation and ISDS provisions.

First, on expropriation, Art. 7(1) of the 2007 Investment Law states, 'The government shall not undertake *nationalization* or *take over* the ownership rights of the investor, unless by law'.[62] The choice of the terms 'nationalization' and 'take over' is rather curious inasmuch as this terminology runs contrary to the majority of Indonesia's investment treaties (and indeed international investment law in general), under which expropriation does not necessitate direct nationalisation or the taking of ownership rights; rather, any measure which substantially deprives the investor of the ability to enjoy or exercise its ownership rights may be sufficient to establish expropriation.[63] In this vein, the 1967 Foreign Investment Law more accurately reflected the position under most investment treaties, stating that: 'The government shall not undertake nationalization/revocation of ownership rights in its entirety upon foreign investment company or *undertake measures which deprive the rights to control and/or manage such companies*, [...]'.[64] Thus, on this aspect, the 2007 Investment Law moves away from the understanding of 'expropriation' contained in Indonesia's investment treaties.[65]

A review of the *travaux* of the 2007 Investment Law reveals that the language on expropriation enacted did not undergo any change from the first draft submitted to Parliament.[66] When the provision was discussed in numerous hearings, the concern of virtually all lawmakers was the need to provide legal certainty and protection to foreign investors without there being any question regarding the specific wording of the provision or the specific standard of nationalisation or expropriation.

---

[62] Emphasis added. Translation taken from Yap, 'Indonesia', 117.

[63] See Yap, 'Indonesia', 129 for a review of Indonesian investment treaties on this point. On the notion of expropriation in international investment law generally, see, among others, M. Sornarajah, *The International Law on Foreign Investment* (3rd ed., Cambridge University Press, 2010), 363–411.

[64] Emphasis added.

[65] This discrepancy between the expropriation protection contained in Indonesia's investment treaties and the protection contained in the 2007 Investment Law was recently noted by the OECD as well. See OECD, *Investment Policy Reviews: Indonesia* (OECD Publishing, 2020), 129, 132. For an opposite view, see Knörich and Berger, 'Friends or Foes', 94.

[66] Draft attached to the Letter of the President of the Republic of Indonesia to the House of Representatives, No. R.30/Pres/3/2006, 21 March 2006 (on file with author) ('Draft 2007 Investment Law').

Second, with respect to ISDS, the 2007 Investment Law appears to ignore the arbitration clauses contained in various investment treaties as well as the ICSID Convention that Indonesia has ratified. Article 32(4) of the 2007 Investment Law states, 'In the event of an investment dispute between the Government and a foreign investor, the parties shall settle such dispute before international arbitration which shall be agreed by the parties'. On its face, that wording does not raise an obvious issue as arbitration in general must be based on consent.[67] However, it appears that the government considers its consent to investment arbitration as consisting of a two-step process,[68] that is, that the arbitration clauses in investment treaties do not themselves constitute the government's consent, but instead it is necessary for the investor also to obtain the government's specific consent after the dispute arises (*ex post* consent).[69]

It is telling that the 1968 Act ratifying the ICSID Convention in Indonesia and Indonesia's various investment treaties are nowhere mentioned in the 2007 Investment Law, particularly when it comes to Art. 32(4). Those international instruments appear to be ignored by the 2007 Investment Law. Indeed, the *travaux* of the 2007 Investment Law also revealed that initially the draft provision on investor–state disputes did not even refer to international arbitration. The draft stated that '[...] the parties may settle the dispute through arbitration and alternative dispute resolution or the courts in accordance with the law and regulations'.[70]

In the few instances where the aforementioned draft provision was discussed, many of the comments evidenced an obvious ignorance of the way in which ISDS provisions are often formulated in investment treaties, particularly those referring to ICSID arbitration, by insisting that dispute settlement must be based on Indonesian sovereignty and that any eventual arbitration must be seated in Indonesia.[71] Two exceptions to this

---

[67] See Knörich and Berger, 'Friends or Foes?', 101.

[68] For Indonesia's arguments objecting to the tribunal's jurisdiction, see *Churchill Mining* v. *Indonesia*, Decision on Jurisdiction, paras. 100–121.

[69] Abdulkadir Jailani, 'Indonesia's Experience: IIA Review', Presentation before UNCTAD World Investment Forum (17–21 July 2016).

[70] Draft 2007 Investment Law, Art. 9.

[71] A prominent law professor endorsed this view before a hearing on the draft. See Sutan Remy, Written Comments of the Draft 2007 Investment Law Submitted to the House of Representatives, 30 August 2006, 6 (on file with author). A similar suggestion was made in comments submitted by the Bogor Institute of Agriculture, *ibid.* at 9 (on file with author). However, the value of the Institute's comments is somewhat low in this context as they are not familiar with the legal aspects of foreign investment, since they are not lawyers or legal academics.

ignorance came in (1) a draft proposed by BKPM of what would have been the official 'elucidation'[72] to the provision, clarifying that the arbitration shall be governed by the 1968 ICSID Ratification Act;[73] and (2) a written comment from the Indonesian Chamber of Commerce which suggested that a paragraph be added providing that 'the settlement of dispute ... between the government and foreign investor is conducted pursuant to the investment treaty in force with the state of the investor's origin'.[74] However, there appears to have been no follow-up discussion on BKPM's and the Chamber of Commerce's suggestions.[75]

The elaboration in this section suggests that there has been a low level of internalisation of investment treaty obligations when drafting and passing the 2007 Investment Law. In other words, conformity with investment treaties appears not to have been considered. This conclusion is based upon its content and express wording as well as relevant parts of the *travaux preparatoires*. Further review of the documents contained in the *travaux* does not reveal anything contradictory to the above conclusion. Notwithstanding the focus of the 2007 Investment Law – the treatment of foreign investment in Indonesia – references to investment treaties are very much few and far between. Of the 1200-plus pages in the entire *travaux preparatoires*, there are fewer than 10 references to investment treaties. Moreover, those few references generally go no further than merely acknowledging the existence of investment treaties without delving into the obligations involved or the effects that such obligations might have on the formulation of related provisions in the draft legislation.[76]

---

[72] In Indonesia, an Act or legislation passed by Parliament is always accompanied by a so-called 'elucidation', a document containing clarification or commentaries on the provisions of the Act. In one case, the Constitutional Court held that the Elucidation on Article 70 of the 1999 Arbitration Law is unconstitutional, thus suggesting that the Elucidation itself is also legally binding. See Judgment of the Constitutional Court No. 15/PUU-XII/2014 (11 November 2014).

[73] BKPM, Concept of the Draft Investment Law, 30 December 2004, 9 (on file with author).

[74] See Indonesian Chamber of Commerce, Written Comments in the Hearing on the Investment Law before the 6th Committee of the House of Representatives, 5 July 2006, 3 (on file with author).

[75] In fact, as late as 6 December 2006, lawmakers still envisioned that the dispute settlement provision would require arbitration seated in Indonesia. See Minutes of Meeting with the Minister of Trade regarding the Draft Investment Law, 6 December 2006, House of Representatives Secretariat, 44–45 (on file with author).

[76] One example is a comment by one lawmaker saying that it is important that licences for foreign investors be handled by the central government because of the possibility that the government can be brought to ICSID arbitration by foreign investors under 'bilateral treaties'. The same lawmaker also suggested adding a provision requiring the government to

One side note worth mentioning is that BKPM was not formally in charge of drafting and negotiating the 2007 Investment Law with Parliament. The role instead was performed by the Ministry of Trade. This is due to the technical requirement that only a 'Ministry' (i.e., government institution headed by a Minister) may act as the counterpart to Parliament in the process of legislating and, thus, only a Ministry may formally submit draft legislation.[77] That said, this may not have greatly affected the final legislation because the requirement does not preclude BKPM from providing inputs and substantive support to the Ministry of Trade. In fact, officials from BKPM were also present during parliamentary hearings with the Minister of Trade discussing the draft Investment Law.[78] Furthermore, already by 2007, investment chapters had become an increasingly common feature in FTAs (including in agreements to which Indonesia was a party). Hence, the Ministry of Trade itself might have been thought to have been at least generally aware of Indonesia's international obligations regarding foreign investment. Nevertheless, it seems clear from interviews that such awareness was (and continues to be) lacking among ministerial officials and legislators. This is crucial because investment disputes often arise from sectoral legislation or other measures, as we will turn to in the following section.

Ultimately, the lack of internalisation here is telling because the 2007 Investment Law is the kind of case where one would assume that the government would take investment treaties into account. If internalisation is absent in this context, it is even more unlikely that it would be found elsewhere in the governmental process where particular legislation or measures affecting foreign investors are made. In any case, the next section examines (and largely confirms) that conclusion in the context of investment treaty disputes between foreign investors and Indonesia.

renegotiate investment treaties that prejudice the interest of Indonesia, drawing attention to the example of Bolivia. However, there is no information on whether this suggestion was considered and the suggestion did not make its way to the final text. See Minutes of Meeting with the Minister of Trade regarding the Draft Investment Law, 6 December 2006, House of Representatives Secretariat, 26 and 59 (on file with author).

[77] Interview RB, 2017; Interview SG, 2017. But cf. provisions that appear to allow a nonministerial state organ to propose a legislation, for example, Law No. 12 of 2011 regarding Legislative Making, 12 August 2011, State Gazette No. 82, Art. 27. See also Knörich and Berger, 'Friends or Foes? Interactions between Indonesia's International Investment Treaties and National Investment Law', 66.

[78] In at least one instance, the Head of BKPM himself was also in attendance. See Minutes of Hearing on the Draft Investment Law, 22 June 2006, 4 (on file with author).

3.4 Investment Treaty Claims Involving Indonesia: In Search of Internalisation in Particular Measures Affecting Foreign Investors

As of the time of writing, there have been five known investment treaty claims against Indonesia for which information and materials are available.[79] In addition, there are two other known investment treaty claims, namely *Indian Metals* v. *Indonesia*[80] and *Oleovest* v. *Indonesia*,[81] for which information is not publicly available so as to clearly ascertain the cause of action and factual circumstances. As such, these cases will not be specifically discussed here.

3.4.1 Amco v. Indonesia

This dispute, one of the earliest disputes filed with ICSID, concerned the takeover of a hotel managed by Amco and the revocation of Amco's investment licence by BKPM.[82] In 1968, Amco (an American company) had, through its Indonesian subsidiary PT Amco, entered into a contract with PT Wisma to operate the Kartika Plaza Hotel, which was owned by the latter. PT Wisma was owned by Inkopad, an Indonesian military

---

[79] See the list of cases and relevant links at italaw, www.italaw.com; Investment Policy Hub, 'Indonesia', https://investmentpolicy.unctad.org/investment-dispute-settlement/country/97/indonesia; and ICSID, 'Cases', https://icsid.worldbank.org/en/Pages/cases/AdvancedSearch.aspx. Interestingly, there is also one case where it was the provincial government of East Kalimantan which brought a claim against the investor at ICSID. See *Government of the Province of East Kalimantan* v. *PT Kaltim Prima Coal and Others*, ICSID Case No. ARB/07/3, Award on Jurisdiction (28 December 2009). But this was a case almost entirely concerning the provincial government's claim for divested shares under a commercial contract between KPC and a state-owned mining company, PN Tambang Batubara, which happened to contain an ICSID arbitration clause. Therefore, this case will not be discussed at length.

[80] *Indian Metals & Ferro Alloys Limited* v. *Republic of Indonesia*, PCA Case No. 2015–40. One news article quoted a government official who said that the investor brought the claim because overlapping mining permits by the East Barito Regency in Central Kalimantan disrupted its operations, although it was also noted that no due diligence had been conducted and thus the investor had not been aware that the mining permit at issue was of 'Non-Clean-And-Clear' status and overlapped with seven other permits. See Ayomi Amindoni, 'Indian mining co. sues Indonesia for $581 million', *The Jakarta Post*, 18 November 2015. Apart from this information from the government side, however, there is no more detailed information about the facts of the dispute.

[81] *Oleovest Pte. Ltd* v. *Republic of Indonesia*, ICSID Case No. ARB/16/26.

[82] *Amco Asia Corporation, PT Amco Indonesia, Pan American Development Limited* v. *Republic of Indonesia*, ICSID Case No. ARB/81/1.

cooperative. In 1979–1980, disagreements arose between PT Wisma and Amco regarding several matters, chief among them the amount of profit sharing. Subsequently, PT Wisma, claiming that Amco was in breach of its contractual obligations, took over management of the hotel with the help of the army and police personnel who seized the property. BKPM then revoked PT Amco's investment licence on the grounds that Amco had failed to make sufficient investments in Indonesia, as had been required in exchange for various tax facilities and other benefits already received by Amco. Amco's contract with PT Wisma was later also rescinded by the Indonesian courts.

In January 1981, the Amco companies (including PT Amco) initiated ICSID arbitration against Indonesia. The arbitration case was long and arduous,[83] but for present purposes it suffices to focus on several aspects of the measures giving rise to Amco's claim. First, one cannot miss the fact that the hotel was ultimately owned by the military and at that time the military was all-powerful and omnipotent in Indonesian government and society. The possibility that the military took note of any international obligations pertaining to Amco's investment seems remote. Second, with regard to the revocation of Amco's investment licence, no prior warning was given, and PT Amco had no more than one hour's hearing at the revocation proceedings.[84] Again, there appears to have been no prior consideration of Indonesia's international obligations at the time by the military or BKPM.[85] Given the situation in Indonesia at the time, it would have been inconceivable in the circumstances that government agencies such as BKPM would not have acted in concert with the military's interests. Whether or not there were good reasons to revoke Amco's licence on the merits, the manner and the process leading to the revocation reflects the nature of the then-government as a dictatorship.

---

[83] The arbitration case lasted ten years through a first annulment proceeding, a resubmission proceeding, and a second annulment proceeding. For the case's procedural history, see ICSID, 'Amco Asia Corporation and Others v. Republic of Indonesia, ICSID Case No. ARB/81/1', https://icsid.worldbank.org/en/Pages/cases/casedetail.aspx?CaseNo=ARB/81/1.

[84] Amco v. Indonesia, ICSID Case No. ARB/81/1, Decision on Jurisdiction in Resubmitted Proceeding (10 May 1988), para. 8.

[85] The manner of the revocation was considered a violation of due process and a denial of justice by the first Amco v. Indonesia tribunal, a part of the award that was not annulled. See Amco v. Indonesia, ICSID Case No. ARB/81/11, Award, 1 ICSID Reports 413 (20 November 1984).

3.4.2. Cemex v. Indonesia

This dispute arose because Cemex was denied its option to buy a majority shareholding in a state-owned cement producer, PT Semen Gresik.[86] Cemex Asia Holdings Ltd., a subsidiary of Mexico's cement giant, Cemex SA, had taken a minority stake in PT Semen Gresik in 1998 and held an option to buy a 51 per cent stake by 2001. This option lapsed due to strong opposition by workers and local politicians, and the government also declined to buy back Cemex's minority stake in violation of the share purchase agreement. The ICSID claim subsequently brought by Cemex alleged a 'breach of contract' and 'de-facto expropriation' under the 1987 ASEAN Agreement for the Promotion and Protection of Investments.[87]

The Cemex case was not resolved on the merits. Ultimately, the parties agreed to a settlement, reportedly for USD $337 million, although no further details are publicly available.[88] Cemex is noteworthy, however, for the prominent role played by the regional government in opposing Cemex's option to buy majority shares that gave rise to investment treaty dispute. As we shall see, this is also a prevalent feature in some of the later investment treaty disputes involving Indonesia.

3.4.3 Rafat Ali Rizvi v. Indonesia and al-Warraq v. Indonesia

These two cases, while not entirely identical, mostly arose from the same circumstances – the takeover of Bank Century and the subsequent criminal prosecution of the two claimants.[89] In the early 2000s, Rafat Ali Rizvi and Hesham al-Warraq acquired shares in Bank Century through a Bahamas company, Chinkara Capital Limited. In the midst of the 2008 global financial crisis, Bank Century was on the verge of collapse, given funds through a publicly and politically controversial bailout, and ultimately placed under the administration of Indonesia's Deposit Insurance Agency. Subsequently, the claimants were prosecuted for offences relating to alleged banking irregularities. The two individual investors pursued

---

[86] *Cemex Asia Holdings Ltd* v. *Republic of Indonesia*, ICSID Case No. ARB/04/3.

[87] Luke E. Peterson, 'Cement Firm LaunchesArbitration against Indonesia under Contract, ASEAN Treaty', *INVEST-SD: Investment Law and Policy Weekly News Bulletin*, 6 February 2004.

[88] See ICSID, '*Cemex Asia Holdings Ltd* v. *Republic of Indonesia*, ICSID Case No. ARB/04/3', https://icsid.worldbank.org/cases/case-database/case-detail?CaseNo=ARB/04/3.

[89] See *Rafat Ali Rizvi* v. *Republic of Indonesia*, ICSID Case No. ARB/11/13; *Hesham Talaat M. al-Warraq* v. *Republic of Indonesia*, UNCITRAL Rules.

separate arbitration claims, one in ICSID and one under the UNCITRAL Rules.[90] Both claims were unsuccessful.

The ICSID tribunal in *Rafat Ali Rizvi* v. *Indonesia* dismissed the claim on jurisdictional grounds.[91] The UNCITRAL tribunal in *al-Warraq* v. *Indonesia*, however, ruled on the merits, holding that there was evidence that the claimant had been denied fair and equitable treatment in the manner in which he was prosecuted by the Indonesian authorities. In particular, the tribunal found that, perhaps as a result of the political implications of the bailout, the Indonesian authorities had not taken reasonable steps to ensure that the claimant was informed in a timely manner of the criminal investigation that was being conducted against him, had not sought to take any evidence from him regarding the prosecution, and had tried him *in absentia* in violation of international human rights norms.[92] Nevertheless, Indonesia avoided liability on the ground that the claimant was disentitled to claim for damages on the ground that the investment had been undertaken in violation of Indonesian law.[93]

Notwithstanding the highly public character of the *al-Warraq* case, it is hard to discern any internalisation of investment treaties as a consequence of this dispute. Based on available information, the Indonesian authorities pursued the prosecution of the claimant without regard as to whether, as a foreign investor, he might have been protected by international treaties. This is not to say, of course, that had the authorities taken Indonesia's international obligations into account, they would not have sought to prosecute Mr al-Warraq. Although the case had political overtones, the tribunal found no evidence that the prosecution of Mr al-Warraq was unfounded.[94] Rather, it is to suggest that in the authorities' rush to prosecute Mr al-Warraq and bring him to justice, there appears to have been no appreciation that Indonesia's international obligations could serve as a check on the exercise of prosecutorial power.[95]

[90] This, among others, was because of the different nationalities between the two claimants and thus different applicable investment treaties and ISDS provisions.

[91] *Rafat Ali Rizvi* v. *Indonesia*, ICSID Case No. ARB/11/13, Award on Jurisdiction (16 July 2013).

[92] *al-Warraq* v. *Indonesia*, UNCITRAL Rules, Final Award (15 December 2014), paras. 581–605. The claimant had also made numerous allegations of corruption against the prosecutor and other Indonesian government officials. The arbitral tribunal concluded that the claimant had failed to prove these allegations. See also *ibid.*, para. 614.

[93] *al-Warraq* v. *Indonesia*, paras. 647–52.

[94] *Ibid.*, para. 614.

[95] This appears to have been the case not only with respect to Indonesia's investment treaty obligations, but also its obligations under international human rights law. See *al-Warraq* v. *Indonesia*, paras. 556–621 (relying upon the International Covenant on Civil and Political Rights and other UN instruments in finding that there had been a denial of justice).

3.4.4   Churchill Mining v. Indonesia

Churchill Mining v. *Indonesia*[96] arose following the revocation of certain mining licences held by Churchill Mining's local partner, the Ridlatama Group, for exploration and exploitation in the East Kutai Coal Project (EKCP) area.[97] Churchill Mining's subsidiary in Indonesia had entered into a series of agreements with the Ridlatama Group to provide mining and support services in exchange for 75 per cent of generated revenue from the exploration. Subsequent to Churchill Mining's investment, however, the Regency of East Kutai cancelled the Ridlatama Group's licences on the grounds that they overlapped with mining licences previously granted to other parties and, moreover, had been forged.[98] Following litigation in the Indonesian courts, Churchill Mining commenced arbitration under the United Kingdom–Indonesia BIT.[99]

Ultimately, the tribunal dismissed Churchill Mining's claim, finding that the licences under which the investment was operating under were forgeries. Thus, the tribunal held that Churchill Mining's entire mining operation had been an illegal enterprise, further exacerbated by what the tribunal considered to be the investor's lack of due diligence when making the investment.[100] Notwithstanding Indonesia's avoidance of liability, the *Churchill Mining* case illustrates a major problem faced by Indonesia when putting investment treaty obligations into practice at the provincial or regency level. As noted above, local officials are not well aware of investment treaties and their contents. Institutional design further prevents these officials from becoming familiar with investment treaty obligations due to regular personnel rotation. This, in turn, works against any capacity building or internalisation of investment treaties.

Aside from issues related to internalisation, one other important aspect that can be observed from this case is the disorganised state of licensing, especially in the mining sector, on the provincial and regency level – as shown by the issuance of overlapping mining licences. Such problems arise in the context of decentralisation (*desentralisasi*), whereby provincial and

---

[96] *Churchill Mining Plc and Planet Mining Pty Ltd* v. *Republic of Indonesia*, ICSID Case No. ARB/12/40 and 12/14, Award (6 December 2016). There had been two separate arbitration claims commenced by two different Churchill entities. These proceedings were then consolidated.

[97] *Churchill Mining* v. *Indonesia*, Decision on Jurisdiction, paras. 7–47 (in particular, paras. 15–19 and 38).

[98] *Ibid.*, para. 35.

[99] United Kingdom–Indonesia BIT (1976).

[100] *Churchill Mining Plc and Planet Mining* v. *Indonesia*, Award, paras. 528–29.

regency governments have been vested with very wide authority under Indonesian law,[101] following the fall of President Suharto's very centralised regime in 1998. With the system of decentralisation, provincial and regency governments have been expected to address the interests of their respective regions and optimise their development.[102] One of the powers delegated to regional governments under this system was the issuance of mining licences.[103] Under the system of decentralisation, the number of mining licences skyrocketed without close supervision by the central government, giving rise to *Churchill Mining v. Indonesia*.

Amidst mounting instances of overlapping mining licences, highlighted by the dispute with Churchill Mining – first in the Indonesian courts and then in arbitration – the central government moved to strip regional governments of some of their authority to issue licences in order to minimise instances of overlap through a centralised process.[104] This is probably the most directly visible and arguably positive effect that an investment treaty claim has had on domestic governance in Indonesia.

---

[101] Constitution of the Republic of Indonesia of 1945 (as amended), Art. 18(2). See also Law No. 22 of 2009 on Regional Governments, 7 May 1999, State Gazette No. 60 as replaced by Law No. 32 of 2004, 15 October 2004, State Gazette No. 125 ('2004 Regional Governments Law') as replaced by Law No. 23 of 2014, 30 September 2014, State Gazette No. 244 ('2014 Regional Governments Law').

[102] Junianto J. Losari and Michael Ewing-Chow, 'Difficulties with Decentralization and Due Process: Indonesia's Recent Experiences with International Investment Agreements and Investor-State Disputes' (2015) 16 *The Journal of World Investment & Trade* 981; H. Syaukani HR., 'Peningkatan Kinerja Eksekutif dan Implementasi Otonomi Daerah', in Syamsuddin Haris (ed.), *Desentralisasi dan Otonomi Daerah: Desentralisasi, Demokratisasi dan Akuntabilitas Pemerintahan Daerah* (LIPI Press, 2007), 101, 152.

[103] Law No. 4 of 2009 regarding Minerals and Coal Mining, 12 January 2009, State Gazette No. 4 ('2009 Mining Law'), Arts. 7(1) and 8(1); see also 2004 Regional Governments Law, Arts. 13–14.

[104] 2014 Regional Governments Law, Annex, sub-part on division of authority in energy and mineral resources. Now, the provincial government may only issue mining licences for domestic mining companies which have a mining area located within one province, and cross-provinces licences and mining licences for all foreign-owned companies may only be issued by the Ministry of Energy and Mineral Resources (MoEMR). As an aside, MoEMR – whose portfolio covers mining – also created an integrated system in 2010 to monitor and check any overlapping mining licences. Licences that overlap cannot receive a 'Clean and Clear' ('CnC') status (i.e., these licences will have a 'non-CnC' status), which can become the basis for the revocation of the licence, prevent the renewal of the licence, as well as prevent the issuance of a new/other licence in the same area. Other interested parties may also check the CnC status of a given mining licence – something very useful to avoid acquisitions of overlapping licences like Churchill's. In relation to this study, however, it appears that the Churchill Mining dispute was not the main catalyst of the CnC programme as the programme had started before ICSID proceedings were commenced in 2012.

At the same time, however, the central government issued a Presidential Decree aimed at excluding from the jurisdiction of ICSID any investor–state dispute arising from measures taken by the regency government,[105] which are exactly the type of measures that were at issue in *Churchill Mining* v. *Indonesia*. The Decree is noteworthy because of its breadth. It effectively seeks to exclude *all* investor–state disputes across *all* industry sectors involving regency governments, not just disputes in the mining sector. It shows that while there was governance reform specifically in the mining sector because of Churchill's claim, the government also reacted by broadly limiting the jurisdiction of investor–state arbitration instead of looking for ways to improve domestic governance in other sectors.

Finally, in the context of case management, an episode during the *Churchill Mining* arbitration process also exposed the lack of coordination between government entities in facing investment treaty claims. At one point in the proceedings, the tribunal asked Indonesia for the *travaux preparatoires* of the United Kingdom–Indonesia BIT, which formed the basis of Churchill's claim, but was told that no such documents could be located.[106] Later it appeared, however, that in *Rafat Ali Rizvi* v. *Indonesia*, which involved the same United Kingdom–Indonesia BIT, the Indonesian government had actually submitted the *travaux* for the treaty.[107] This lack of coordination and inconsistency of government action may be attributed to the fact that there were different government entities in charge of the defence in both cases. In *Rafat Ali Rizvi* v. *Indonesia*, it was the Attorney General's office that led the defence and, in *Churchill Mining* v. *Indonesia*, it was the Minister of Law.[108] Following the *Churchill Mining* case, the Indonesian government has responded to each new investment arbitration claim by issuing a presidential regulation to form an ad hoc inter-agency team to represent the state in the proceedings.[109] However, even with this new regulation, given the ad hoc character of the

---

[105] Presidential Decree No. 31 of 2012 regarding Disputes Which Are Not to be Referred to the International Centre for the Settlement of Investment Disputes, 22 September 2012.

[106] *Churchill Mining* v. *Indonesia*, Decision on Jurisdiction, para. 208.

[107] *Ibid.*, para. 209.

[108] Interview PD, 2018. See also, with respect to *Churchill Mining* v. *Indonesia*, Presidential Regulation No. 78 of 2012, 22 September 2012, State Gazette No. 179 ('Presidential Regulation No. 78/2012 re Churchill Mining'), that serve as the basis for the inter-agency team to deal with Churchill's ICSID claim.

[109] See Presidential Regulation No. 78/2012 re Churchill Mining; Presidential Regulation No. 78 of 2014, 24 July 2014, State Gazette No. 179 – for the Newmont case (see below); Presidential Regulation No. 17 of 2016 – for the Indian Metals case.

arrangements, the agency or authority in charge can still be different in each case. Therefore, concerns of poor coordination remain.

3.4.5 Newmont v. Indonesia *(and the Related Freeport Dispute)*

These disputes arose from the promulgation of the 2009 Mining Law and its 2014 implementing regulations.[110] The new legal regime, in particular the implementing regulations, created a requirement that all exported minerals and coal be processed in Indonesia,[111] lest an additional export tax be imposed.[112] These obligations had not existed in the old mining law.

Following the new law, the government put pressure on Freeport and Newmont, two American mining giants, operating the largest gold and copper mines in Indonesia, to build smelters to undertake the newly required processing.[113] Both companies objected on the grounds that their contract of work with the Indonesian government to operate the mines contained a 'stabilisation clause', which they argued protected them from any additional major regulatory obligations and taxes.[114] The government responded by withholding their export permits. After lengthy negotiations stalled, Newmont brought an ICSID claim under the 1994 Netherlands–Indonesia BIT,[115] alleging violation of the treaty's 'umbrella clause', FET clause, and indirect expropriation.[116] The arbitration was soon discontinued, however, as the parties agreed to resume negotiations.[117] Freeport, which had at one point publicly floated the possibility of resorting to international arbitration,[118] also opted to continue negotiating with the government.

---

[110] See, among others, Regulation of the Ministry of Energy and Mineral Resources No. 1 of 2014, State Gazette No. 35 ('MEMR Regulation No. 1/2014'); Regulation of the Ministry of Finance No. 153/PMK.011/2014, State Gazette No. 1061 ('MoF Regulation No. 153/2014').

[111] 2009 Mining Law, Arts. 102–103; see also MEMR Regulation No. 1/2014, Arts. 3 and 5(a).

[112] See MoF Regulation No. 153/2014, Arts. 4A(1)–(2), Annex I (in the column, row no. 1), and Annex II (in the column, row no. 1).

[113] *Nusa Tenggara Partnership B.V. and PT Newmont Nusa Tenggara v. Republic of Indonesia*, ICSID Case No. ARB/14/15 (*Newmont v. Indonesia*).

[114] Interview EN, 2017.

[115] Although an American company, Newmont had structured its investment through the Netherlands, thereby giving it standing to pursue its claims under the Netherlands–Indonesia BIT.

[116] Interview EN, 2017.

[117] *Newmont v. Indonesia*, Order of Discontinuance (29 August 2014).

[118] Fergus Jensen and Wilda Asmarini, 'Freeport Warns of Arbitration as Indonesia Mining Dispute Escalates', *Reuters*, 20 February 2017.

The Newmont and Freeport disputes provide additional insight into the limited internalisation of investment treaty obligations in Indonesia. The measures at issue were part of a major revision of an important area of Indonesian law with obvious impact on large foreign investors. Yet, those treaty obligations appear not to have been considered either by the executive or the legislature when the law, including the contentious mineral processing requirement, was drafted and debated in Parliament.[119]

It is possible to attribute this lack of consideration to the low level of internalisation among sectoral agencies, in this case the Ministry of Energy and Mineral Resources (MoEMR). At the time that the 2009 Mining Law was promulgated, there had not yet been an investor–state dispute in the mining sector. The *Churchill Mining* case had not yet come to the government's attention and, thus, MoEMR institutionally had not yet had first-hand experience with investment treaty commitments. Moreover, a review of the *travaux preparatoires* of the 2009 Mining Law reveals that MoEMR did not consult with or have BKPM or MoFA involved in the process of drafting and negotiating that legislation. Thus, the two principal nodes of knowledge about investment treaty obligations in the Indonesian government were not given the opportunity to bring that knowledge to bear.

It also appears that obligations under investment treaties were never expressly mentioned or featured in any of the written correspondence between Newmont and the government prior to Newmont's ICSID claim.[120] Moreover, it appears as though no references to investment treaty obligations were made in public statements or news media reports at the time either. Behind the scenes, however, both parties 'were aware and did discuss the possibility of the dispute ending up at ICSID'.[121] Thus, in contrast to the circumstances when the 2009 Mining Law was first adopted, the government's awareness of investment treaty arbitration during the Newmont negotiations may be due to the fact that the *Churchill Mining* case was very much ongoing in 2014 and would be known to everyone involved in the Newmont dispute.

---

[119] The author also obtained the *travaux preparatoires* for the 2009 Mining Law from the House of Representatives' secretariat together with the *travaux preparatoires* for the 2007 Investment Law, mentioned above.

[120] Interview EN, 2017 and 2018.

[121] Interview RB, 2017; Interview EN, 2017 and 2018.

3.5   Explaining the Lack of Internalisation:
Synthesising the General Findings

As observed throughout the examples discussed in this chapter, investment treaties have rarely featured in governmental decision making in Indonesia. My findings suggest that certain factors which have been highlighted by Calamita and Berman as potentially impacting internalisation – the absence of institutional internalisation measures, the lack of coordination in the public administration, low regulatory capacity and the political context – have indeed played a role in explaining this lack of internalisation.[122]

First, Indonesia has been unable to establish systematic and concerted institutional internalisation processes, whether they be *informational processes*, which diffuse information and communicate the state's investment treaty obligations to the relevant government agencies; *monitoring processes*, whereby proposed regulations are prepared with a view to ensuring consistency with investment treaty obligations; or *remedial processes* designed to correct or defend Indonesia's compliance with its investment treaty obligations.[123] An example of this difficulty is shown through the inability of the government to build upon or continue the ad hoc training programme on investment treaties by MoFA and BKPM from 2014 to 2015 due to insufficient funds and an absence of political salience.

Second, the lack of institutional internalisation has been exacerbated by factors in the public bureaucracy. In particular, several factors contribute to the difficulties facing internalisation within a *public administration context*. On the one hand is the *lack of coordination* horizontally among different ministries and agencies at the central level and vertically between different levels of government. This can be seen horizontally, for instance, in the promulgation of the 2009 Mining Law leading to the Newmont and Freeport disputes where there was no coordination between MoEMR, MoFA, and BKPM. On a vertical level, this lack of coordination finds its roots in the autonomy enjoyed by provincial and regency governments, which introduces significant barriers to internalisation, especially given the large numbers of subnational entities in Indonesia.[124]

---

[122] See Chapter 1.

[123] See *ibid*. In this regard, see also OECD's specific recommendation for Indonesia to continue developing ISDS prevention and case management tools, drawing on best practices elsewhere. OECD, *Investment Policy Reviews: Indonesia* (OECD Publishing, 2020), 131, 160–61.

[124] Currently, there are 34 provinces and 514 regency or municipal governments.

On the other hand, there is the reality of *low regulatory capacity* across the board in Indonesia. In the first place, in the context of provincial and regency governments, where many of Indonesia's disputes have arisen, there has been little attention given to developing institutional capacity. To the extent that capacity building has been attempted, it has been largely at the central government's level and, even then, only on a sporadic ad hoc basis. While non-governmental 'intermediaries' (as carriers of knowledge about investment treaties at the national and subnational levels) might in principle make up for such a lack of government-led capacity building, there does not appear to have been a strong presence of such intermediaries in the case of Indonesia. International actors such as UNCTAD and NGOs such as IISD and the South Centre have largely been active only at the level of the central government and only for a short period of time when Indonesia started its BIT termination programme and was drafting its new model BIT. Lastly, to the extent that it has been possible to build capacity in government outside of specialised agencies like BKPM and MoFA, that capacity has been undermined by the constant rotation of officials dealing with investment portfolios – an example of the public administration working against the internalisation of investment treaty commitments. Corruption and the dictatorial nature of the military were also noticeable hindrances to the public administration properly internalising investment treaties; however, it is somewhat questionable whether episodes reflecting those aspects such as *Amco* v. *Indonesia* would occur again in contemporary Indonesia.

Third, these public administration factors should be placed within their broader *national context*. As shown in the *Newmont* and *Freeport* disputes, broad economic development policy and rising nationalistic sentiment can drive the government's decision making,[125] taking priority over other considerations and giving rise to investment treaty claims. This is especially evident in economic sectors tied to natural resources such as mining. The timing was also ripe for such a government stance, coming on the heels of Indonesia's victory in *Churchill Mining*, which seems to have prompted a sense among policymakers that the government could pursue policies without needing to carefully consider Indonesia's investment treaty obligations. The victory in *Churchill Mining* was soon followed by

---

[125] More generally, the OECD has commented on the strong desire among Indonesian policymakers and in public sentiment to protect the local economy from foreign investment. See OECD, *Investment Policy Reviews: Indonesia*, 15.

the successful resolution of *Newmont* itself (in the sense that Newmont's withdrawal of its ICSID claim was seen as a victory for Indonesia), and more recently *Indian Metals*, where Indonesia defeated another investment treaty claim in an UNCITRAL arbitration.[126]

Paradoxically, because of Indonesia's success in these disputes, the cumulative effect of Indonesia's experience with investor–state arbitration seems to have lessened the political salience of enacting measures that might serve to ensure their internalisation in future governmental decision making. At the same time, of course, in initiating its BIT termination programme and attempting to renegotiate many of those treaties, interest representation and the perceived legitimacy of the system of investment treaties have been obvious areas of political salience in Indonesia. Thus, while Indonesia's experience with investment treaty disputes seems to have pushed it to engage with its obligations on the international level by seeking reform, on the national level, the experience seems to have had little effect on internalising those commitments into the day-to-day business of government.

3.6   Conclusion

The discussion and analysis in this chapter have shown that there is very minimal internalisation – sometimes even outright ignorance – of investment treaties among government institutions and officials in Indonesia. A high level of awareness and knowledge of the treaties does not appear to extend beyond MoFA and BKPM, the nodes responsible for investment treaties in the central government. This is due to the absence of any formal and concerted mechanism to disseminate investment treaties and monitor or coordinate the implementation of these treaties with sectoral agencies or at the provincial or regency level. As a result, investment treaties do not generally form part of institutional consideration when a government agency takes measures that affect foreign investors. Various factors that contribute to such a low level of internalisation have been pointed out. Ultimately, what follows is the conclusion that investment treaties do not bring about much impact on domestic governance and, consequently, have little impact on developing the rule of law, save for an isolated instance of regulatory and licensing improvement in the

---

[126]   For a report of the case's outcome, see Jack Ballantyne, 'Indonesia Defeats Treaty Claim by Indian Investor', *Global Arbitration Review*, 2 April 2019.

mining sector following the *Churchill Mining* claim. Indeed, although the quality of governance in the country has markedly improved in recent years, at least as evidenced by Indonesia's ascending ranking in the World Bank's 'Ease of Doing Business' and the World Economic Forum's 'Global Competitiveness' index,[127] it is not possible to claim that such improvement is the result of Indonesia's participation in investment treaties.

---

[127] See the 'Ease of Doing Business' data (2020) online at World Bank, 'Ease of Doing Business in Indonesia, www.doingbusiness.org/data/exploreeconomies/indonesia; and the 'Global Competitiveness' data (2019) online at World Economic Forum, 'The Global Competitiveness Report (2019)', www3.weforum.org/docs/WEF_TheGlobal CompetitivenessReport2019.pdf.

The Impact of Investment Treaties
on the Rule of Law in Korea

YOUNSIK KIM

4.1 Introduction

Korea has been actively involved in the global investment regime from the early phase of its development.[1] In 1967, Korea joined the Convention on the Settlement of Investment Disputes between States and Nationals of Other States (ICSID Convention). At present, Korea is a party to ninety-nine bilateral investment treaties (BITs) and more than nineteen free trade agreements (FTAs) containing investment chapters.[2] Since 2012, with the first investor–state dispute settlement (ISDS) case brought against Korea by Lone Star Funds, Korea has faced many investor–state dispute claims. To date, thirteen claims have been filed against it.[3]

---

[1] See Younsik Kim, 'Investor-State Arbitration in South Korean International Trade Policies: An Uncertain Future, Trapped by the Past', in Armand de Mestral (ed.), *Second Thoughts: Investor State Arbitration between Developed Democracies* (Centre for International Governance Innovation, 2017), 449.

[2] See Ministry of Trade, Industry and Energy (MOTIE), List of Korean FTAs, www.fta .go.kr/main/situation/kfta/ov/; Ministry of Foreign Affairs, Lists of Korean International Investment Treaties, www.mofa.go.kr.

[3] The first dispute faced by Korea was the *Lone Star* case in 2012, where a private equity firm brought a claim of USD \$4.6 billion, challenging measures taken by Korea in connection with Lone Star's acquisition and sale of a Korean bank and taxes assessed on Lone Star's investment gains. See *LSF-KEB Holdings SCA and Others* v. *Republic of Korea*, ICSID Case No. ARB/12/37 (BLEU (Belgium–Luxembourg Economic Union)–Korea BIT (2006): pending). Other claims about which information is available publicly include: *Hanocal Holding B.V.* v. *Republic of Korea*, ICSID Case No. ARB/15/17 (Netherlands–Korea BIT (2003): discontinued 2016); *Mohammad Reza Dayyani and Others* v. *Republic of Korea*, PCA Case No. 2015-38 (Iran–Korea BIT (1998): filed in 2015, decided for investors 2018); *Jin Hae Seo* v. *Republic of Korea*, HKIAC Case No. 18117, Final Award (24 September 2019) (KORUS FTA (2007): dismissed 2019); *Elliott Associates, L.P.* v. *Republic of Korea*, PCA Case No. 2018-51 (KORUS FTA (2007): pending); *Mason Capital L.P. and Mason Management LLC* v. *Republic of Korea*, PCA Case No. 2018-55 (KORUS FTA (2007): pending); *Schindler Holding AG* v. *Republic of Korea*, PCA Case 2019-44 (European Free Trade Association (EFTA)–Korea Investment Agreement (2005): pending); *Gale Investments Company LLC*

Until recently, Korea had not instituted any internalisation measures specifically targeted at considering investment treaties in governmental decision making. Although Korea has developed an expert community of international investment lawyers, spanning government, academia and civil society, most expertise within government has been centralised within several ministries. Awareness in line ministries and other public authorities which make decisions impacting foreign investors has been, in contrast, low, potentially explaining the large number of ISDS claims brought against Korea.

The significant number of ISDS claims brought against Korea since 2012 have prompted a change in awareness. Acknowledging the uncomfortable reality that Korea is not immune to investment treaty disputes, Korea has started adopting a series of informational, monitoring and remedial measures aimed at avoiding such disputes. Notably, it has issued a handbook for government officials, is strengthening the position of the Foreign Investment Ombudsman, and has established a standing ISDS response team. Whether these reforms translate into more or better consideration of investment treaty obligations by government officials who deal with foreign investors remains to be seen.

A further development has been the increasing politicisation of Korea's international economic commitments. Over the past ten to fifteen years, Korea has largely concluded FTAs with investment chapters rather than standalone BITs. Unlike the earlier conclusion of Korea's BITs, the conclusion of FTAs has given rise to strong opposition by parliamentarians, civil society, and businesses that see these treaties – in their many different aspects – as causing economic harm to certain groups or sectors. As part of that overall opposition and critique, investment treaties and ISDS have become tied to the contentious political debates on FTAs.

---

v. Republic of Korea (KORUS FTA (2007): notice of intent filed 20 June 2019); Berjaya Land Berhad v. Republic of Korea (Malaysia–Korea BIT (1988): notice of intent filed 17 July 2019); Fengzhen Min v. Republic of Korea, ICSID Case No. ARB/20/26 (China–Korea FTA (2015): pending). Further, based upon information available on the Ministry of Justice's website, Korea has received an additional notice of intent from investors, preparing for the next steps. See Won Tae Yoon v. Republic of Korea (KORUS FTA (2007): notice of intent filed 23 December 2019); Unnamed Claimant v. Republic of Korea (KORUS FTA (2007): notice of intent filed 3 February 2020); Unnamed Claimant v. Republic of Korea (Korea–Canada FTA (2014): notice of intent filed 15 June 2020); Hun Won (a/k/a Jason H. Won) v. Republic of Korea (KORUS FTA (2007): notice of intent filed 14 January 2021). See also for case information and documents, Ministry of Justice, Investment Dispute Information, www.moj.go.kr/moj/220/subview.do.

It might be thought these political tensions would potentially reduce the standing of investment treaties within the country, leading to less internalisation. To the contrary, however, it appears that this political contestation may have ultimately contributed to better internalisation in the sense defined by Calamita and Berman, meaning that they are considered in the formal or informal processes of governmental decision making.[4] The reason for this is that the hot contestation of FTAs, and ISDS in particular, in the media and within government offices has raised awareness about them, including among those public authorities that deal with matters that affect foreign investors. Moreover, these political pressures have led to reforms, which have significantly opened the treaty-making process to increased intra-governmental and public consultation. Overall, these developments have resulted in higher awareness of the existence of investment treaties, raising the likelihood that investment treaties will be considered in decision-making processes.

This chapter is organised as follows: Section 4.2 covers investment treaty making and its impact on internalisation. I first discuss the governmental actors in charge of international trade and investment policy (Section 4.2.1), the investment treaty-making process (Section 4.2.2), and its domestic implementation (Section 4.2.3). Section 4.3 zooms in on internalisation measures. I first lay out the internalisation measures present before the onset of ISDS claims (Section 4.3.1) and then those adopted in the past decade with the rise in ISDS cases (Section 4.3.2). Following Calamita and Berman's typology, discussion of internalisation measures is divided into informational measures (Section (a)), monitoring procedures (Section (b)) and remedial measures (Section (c)). Section 4.4 concludes.

In terms of methodology, this study draws upon relevant primary materials (laws, regulations, government press releases, reports, etc.) and secondary materials, including academic literature and media reports. It also draws on three in-depth semi-structured interviews conducted with government officials in 2017, 2018 and 2021. The first (2017) and the third interview (2021) were with a former mid-level officer at the National Assembly Research Service (NARS) ('Interview A').[5] The second interview, in 2018, was carried out with a former Ministry of Justice (MOJ) officer, who was involved in both investment treaty claims and negotiations as a mid-level officer ('Interview B'). The main objective of these interviews

---

[4] See Chapter 1.
[5] Woomin Shim, Gyeongin University of Education (2011–2017 in NARS).

was understanding and ascertaining the various processes underlying the internalisation of investment treaties in Korea.

4.2 Investment Treaty Making

4.2.1 *The Governmental Actors in Charge of International Trade and Investment Policy*

The purpose of this section is to describe the governmental actors involved in the negotiation and conclusion of BITs and FTAs with investment chapters. As noted, Korea is a party to ninety-nine BITs and more than nineteen FTAs containing investment chapters. In recent years, the Korean government has indicated a preference for comprehensive FTAs with investment chapters over standalone BITs,[6] and most treaties concluded in the past decade have been FTAs.[7]

While the Ministry of Foreign Affairs (MOFA) has been, and remains, responsible for the negotiation of BITs, there have been significant reforms with respect to the ministries and agencies in charge of negotiating FTAs. The conclusion of FTAs has raised many political tensions and it is against this political background that the shifts in governance – which I describe below – are best understood. Following this discussion, I will then assess whether the reforms undertaken in recent years have had any impact on internalisation.

4.2.1.1 Distributed Governance

Historically, or at least since the 1990s, responsibility for the negotiation of international trade agreements was divided between several ministries and agencies: the Economic Planning Board (headed by the Deputy

---

[6] Kim, 'Investor-State Arbitration in South Korean International Trade Policies', 454–56; Younsik Kim, 'The Policy and Institutional Framework for FTA Negotiations in the Republic of Korea', in James Harrison (ed.), *The European Union and South Korea: The Legal Framework for Strengthening Trade, Economic and Political Relations* (Edinburgh University Press, 2013), 41, at 42–3 (describing FTA programmes including international investment policies). As of writing, all of Korea's FTAs, except for the EU–Korea FTA (2010) and the United Kingdom–Korea FTA (2019), include an investment chapter.

[7] Peru–Korea FTA (2011), Turkey–Korea FTA (2012), Australia–Korea FTA (2014) (no ISDS system), Canada–Korea FTA (2014), China–Korea FTA (2015), New Zealand–Korea FTA (2015), Viet Nam–Korea FTA (2015), Colombia–Korea FTA (2013), Central America–Korea FTA (2018), United Kingdom–Korea FTA (2019) (no investment chapter), Regional Comprehensive Economic Partnership (RCEP) (2020) (no ISDS system), Indonesia–Korea CEPA (2020) and Israel–Korea FTA (2021).

Prime Minister), the Ministry of Finance (MOF), the Ministry of Trade and Industry (MTI), and the MOFA. The Office of Foreign Economic Coordination (OFEC), a subsidiary of the Economic Planning Board, coordinated among them.

Being in a bureaucratically lower hierarchical position than the ministries it was tasked with coordinating, OFEC was weak and ineffective in coordinating conflicts that arose among the ministries. This weakness came to bear during Korea's decision to join the World Trade Organization (WTO) in 1995, which was met with much internal political strife. Moreover, large numbers of the public protested against trade liberalisation, especially with respect to the agricultural and rice sector. Faced with divisions within the government and among the public, OFEC was too weak to bridge and coordinate the fragmented bureaucracy and establish a unified governmental position. As a result, the public was confronted with a vagueness as to who was in charge of trade matters, leading to nation-wide discontent.[8]

4.2.1.2   Office of the Minister for Trade

To address the public turmoil caused by Korea's decision to join the WTO, President Kim Dae-Jung decided to establish a specialised agency that would be in charge of trade policy and trade negotiation. To this end, in 1998, it was decided that all trade policy related matters would be transferred to MOFA, which was then renamed the Ministry of Foreign Affairs and Trade (MOFAT). Within MOFAT, the Office of the Minister for Trade (OMT) was assigned the responsibility of trade negotiations. While named a 'minister', the Minister of Trade is ranked below the Minister of MOFAT, and the latter is also the final authority on all trade negotiation matters.[9]

4.2.1.3   Ministry of Trade, Industry and Energy

The duration of MOFAT's tenure in charge of trade policy and trade negotiation was, however, short-lived. When President Park Geun-Hye came into office in 2013, she decided to transfer trade policy and negotiations from MOFAT to the Ministry of Trade, Industry and Energy (MOTIE).

---

[8] See Gi-Hong Kim, 'The Change of Trade Negotiation Agency and Negotiation Power in Korea: Focused on the Office of the Minister for Trade' (2012) 37 *Korea Trade Review* 69, 77.
[9] *Ibid.*, at 77–79 (describing the functioning of OMT at that time).

The background for this reform was to appease those groups that sought to strengthen the position of domestic interests in FTAs. While the goal of trade agreements is to boost the national economy, in practice, the interests of certain groups – notably the agricultural sector – were seen as being harmed by FTAs. In that context, MOFAT was viewed as driving Korea's international position and less concerned with domestic distributional impact.[10] Indeed, many commentators criticised MOFAT's international trade policies for being disconnected from the interests of national industries.[11]

In contrast, MOTIE was seen as being better positioned to forge relationships with domestic industries and better represent the interests of certain public groups.[12] It is thus against this background that President Park Geun-Hye transferred trade policymaking from the hands of MOFAT to MOTIE. Signalling the depreciated political status of trade policy, she also downgraded OMT to a lower bureaucratic level, positioning it under the second vice minister of MOTIE.[13]

MOFAT has not accepted this reform and continues to demand that OMT be returned under its authority. Despite the tug-of-war that has erupted between MOFAT and MOTIE, where both seek control of trade and both compete for expansion of budget and personnel, President Moon Jae-in has decided to keep OMT under MOTIE but, in contrast to his predecessor, has elevated its status back to a ministerial-level public body, suggesting a return of international trade's political status. Finally, it is important to remember that while MOTIE oversees FTAs, MOFA continues to lead on BITs.[14]

---

[10] For example, between the late 80s and early 90s, Korea attempted to conclude a number of BITs with Eastern European countries. The surge of Korean BITs then can be explained by foreign policy at the time which attempted to isolate North Korea by strengthening economic ties with North Korea's former allies. See Kwan-Ho Kim, 'Fifty Years of Korea's Investment Treaties: A Study of the Historical Evolution of the Korean Government's Policies' (2017) 22 *Journal of International Trade and Industry Studies* 19, 33–6.

[11] See for example Kim, 'The Change of Trade Negotiation Agency and Negotiation Power in Korea', 89.

[12] Seok-Bin Hong, 'The Changes and Continuities of Korean Government's International Trade Policy – An Analysis on the Reshuffle of Trade Administrative System of Park Administration' (2014) 39 *Korea Trade Review* 261, 262–3 (describing the controversy surrounding the reforms).

[13] Bomin Ko, 'Analysis on the History of Korea's Trade Administration' (2018) 23 *Journal of International Trade and Industry Studies* 23, 26–9; Hong, 'The Changes and Continuities of Korean Government's International Trade Policy', 287.

[14] See Young Ja Bae, 'A Comparative Study on the Bilateral Investment Treaty in Korea, China, and Japan' (2015) 24 *Journal of Korean Politics* 83, 101.

4.2.1.4   How Does the Shift from MOFAT to MOTIE
Impact Internalisation? An Expert Community

The question that arises is whether this bureaucratic move of OMT and its staff from MOFAT to MOTIE has impacted the internalisation of investment treaties. Indeed, there is an ongoing debate about the impact of this move on Korea's trade and investment policy, with some arguing that the move will result in trade policy falling prey to protectionism and domestic politics.[15]

Despite these concerns, it appears that OMT has maintained its pro-trade stance and that this move has not negatively impacted the acceptance of international trade and investment obligations within the government. One reason for OMT retaining its pro-trade stance is that OMT officials have cultivated a discernible independent organisational identity[16] and, more importantly, see themselves as members of an epistemic community of Korean and international trade and investment lawyers, composed of government officials, practicing lawyers and academics. This is an interconnected network of professionals, especially in respect to their career paths. For example, it is common for university professors to be employed by the government or law firms, or for public officials to be hired by large law firms or universities. This community is also subject to international influences, such as from 'big figures' in global law firms or professors from prestigious international law schools. Local lawyers trained in such global institutions are typically highly regarded within Korea.

The loyalty of OMT staff to the pro-trade and investment ideas of their own peer group thus goes beyond any ministerial affiliation. The cohesiveness of this OMT group is also reflected in the fluidity of its personnel movement, with some OMT staff returning to MOFAT to work on BITs.[17] The move, therefore, is unlikely to have had any impact on their approach to trade policy and international obligations.

---

[15]   Hong, 'The Changes and Continuities of Korean Government's International Trade Policy', 262–64 (mapping out the criticisms regarding the transferring of the trade policymaking function to MOTIE) and 285–86.

[16]   *Ibid.*, at 281.

[17]   A total of seventy-nine workers (thirty-nine general positions plus forty diplomatic posts) were transferred from then MOFAT in 2013. Seventeen of forty people in charge of trade in MOFAT wanted to change their title position into MOTIE and twenty-three remained as transferred workers from MOFA. The personnel of MOTIE has replaced those remaining slots as remaining transferred diplomats have since come back to MOFA. See Sewon Lee, 'Seventeen Diplomats Have Moved to the Ministry of Trade, Industry and Energy', *Yonhap News*, 26 March 2013.

Findings from research surveys completed by OMT officials who had been transferred from MOFA to MOTIE in 2013 support this assertion. The survey found that all interviewees had maintained a liberal policy stance towards trade despite a change in their organisational profiles. Most of the interviewees (62.5%) expected that organisational changes would not affect their individual liberal stances towards trade in performing their duties.[18] These findings suggest that the pool of experts formed and trained by the government under OMT for over twenty years hold relatively homogenous ideological views on trade,[19] and that they share a similar ideology regarding trade policy, irrespective of ministerial affiliation.

To conclude, while politics have driven the relocation of OMT from MOFAT to MOTIE, the pro-trade and investment nature of OMT has not changed and it is unlikely that this move has had any adverse effect on the internalisation of FTAs with investment chapters. In fact, if anything, this relocation reflects the political attention directed at FTAs. As we shall see below, this political attention has led to greater awareness as well as to new treaty-making procedures and adoption of internalisation measures, ultimately increasing the likelihood that investment treaties will be considered in governmental decision-making processes.

4.2.2 The Investment Treaty Negotiation Process: From Secrecy to Transparency

In the past two decades, the Korean government has moved away from BITs and has focused on the conclusion of FTAs with investment chapters. The conclusion of FTAs has been met with much contestation by certain sectors and by civil society, resulting in big headlines in the media and criticisms of these treaties as being made behind closed doors, adversely affecting the agricultural and other sectors, and limiting Korea's autonomy to regulate in its public interest.

In response to these demands for greater transparency and better responsiveness to the public, reforms have been introduced into the treaty-making process in recent years. This section describes the evolution in Korea's treaty-making practices and how FTA making has evolved towards greater parliamentary and public participation. I will then assess how these changes have influenced internalisation of investment treaties in Korea.

---

[18] Hong, 'The Changes and Continuities of Korean Government's International Trade Policy', 274–77.
[19] Ibid., at 279.

4.2.2.1   Before 2003: Legislative Circumvention

Korea's National Assembly has historically played a negligible role in the FTA negotiation process, and virtually no role with respect to BITs. Under Korean constitutional law, National Assembly ratification is only required for constitutionally important treaties, comprising 'treaties pertaining to any restriction in sovereignty', 'treaties which will burden the State or the people with an important financial obligation', or 'treaties related to legislative matters'.[20]

The decision whether a treaty constitutes a constitutionally important treaty is made by working-level officials on a case-by-case basis. Taking advantage of the law's vagueness, MOFAT considered most BITs to fall outside of the scope of a constitutionally important treaty, thereby circumventing legislative control over their conclusion.[21] Only two BITs were ever submitted for ratification to the National Assembly: the 1964 Korea–Germany BIT and the 2002 Korea–Japan BIT.[22]

In contrast, comprehensive FTAs have almost always been submitted to the National Assembly for ratification. That said, the full text of the treaties under negotiation remained confidential until the treaty had been signed. Its content remained unknown to the public or the legislature until it was submitted to the legislature in the form of a bill after the treaty's signature.

This obscure situation resulted in major political turmoil once FTAs were made public and their bills were brought for ratification. For example, when the Korea–Chile FTA was brought for approval, the agricultural sector protested and a major political conundrum erupted between the opposition party which refused to endorse the bill and the ruling party which was pushing for approval.[23]

---

[20] Constitution of the Republic of Korea, Art. 60.
[21] Hyun-Chool Lee, 'Ratification of a Free Trade Agreement: The Korean Legislature's Response to Globalisation' (2010) 40 *Journal of Contemporary Asia* 291, 298–9.
[22] Gap-Yong Jung, 'A Study on the Role of the Related Government Agencies in the Process of the Treaty and the Establishment of the Review Manual for Strengthening the Review of the Ministry of Government Legislation' (2009) *Ministry of Government Legislation Policy Research Paper*, 9.
[23] The Korea–Chile FTA was signed by President Kim Dae-Jung on 15 February 2003 – just ten days before President Roh Moo-Hyun formally took office on 25 February 2003. While both Presidents are from the same party, the legislative approval of the Korea–Chile FTA was a major political issue during the beginning of President Roh's term. See Lee, 'Ratification of a Free Trade Agreement: The Korean Legislature's Response to Globalisation', 294–96. (describing controversies in the National Assembly and in civil society regarding the Korea–Chile FTA).

4.2.2.2 After 2003: The Conclusion Procedure and Implementation of Commercial Treaties Act

Determined to gain broader and more sustained public support for FTAs, President Roh Moo-Hyun, who came into office in 2003, decided to introduce reforms that would improve the accountability of the negotiation process. Accordingly, in 2004 President Roh enacted the 'Presidential Directive on the FTA Conclusion Procedure',[24] a procedure which established new, limited rules on transparency and public participation.

But as the political controversy surrounding the negotiation of the Korea–US Free Trade Agreement ('KORUS FTA')[25] intensified in 2011, so did public demand for even greater transparency and involvement in trade negotiations. The Korean opposition party vehemently criticised the secretive negotiations and the conclusion of the treaty by a handful of high-ranking diplomats.[26] Significant criticism was also directed at the inclusion of provisions on investor–state arbitration and protections for indirect expropriation, which were seen as limiting the government's autonomy to regulate in the public's interest. Opposition parties and civil society asserted that through such closed-door negotiations, the government was concealing the latent public policy risks of investment arbitration.[27] In response to these pressures and seeking to secure the opposition party's support for the ratification of the FTA, the government, on 17 January 2012, passed the Act on The Conclusion Procedure and Implementation of Commerce

---

[24] Kim, 'The Policy and Institutional Framework for FTA Negotiations', 44–45 (describing the development of an institutional framework for FTA negotiations in Korea before the establishment of KORUS FTA).

[25] The United States and Korea signed the KORUS FTA on 30 June 2007. The KORUS FTA entered into force on 15 March 2012. In 2017, the United States notified Korea of its desire to renegotiate parts of the agreement. After nearly one year of discussions, the United States and Korea signed a protocol amending the FTA on 24 September 2018. The amendments did not make significant changes to the investment chapter. See KORUS FTA Protocol (2018).

[26] Soun-Young Eum, 'The Globalization of Law: The Legal Character of the Treaty-Making Power and of the Consent of the Legislature to Treaty-Making' (2006) 32 *Democratic Legal Studies* 183, 207–8; Dong Suk Oh, 'A Critical Study on the Negotiation of KORUS FTA' (2006) 32 *Democratic Legal Studies* 151. See also Lee, 'Ratification of a Free Trade Agreement', 293–94 (discussing the democratic deficit in concluding the KORUS FTA).

[27] Hi-Taek Shin and Liz (Kyo-Hwa) Chung, 'Korea's Experience with International Investment Agreements and Investor-State Dispute Settlement' (2015) 16 *The Journal of World Investment & Trade* 952; Kim, 'The Policy and Institutional Framework for FTA Negotiations in the Republic of Korea', 49–52; Kim, 'Investor-State Arbitration in South Korean International Trade Policies', 458–64 (explaining controversies and the relevant social backgrounds about the KORUS FTA).

Treaties ('CTP Act').[28] The purpose of the law was to enhance public participation and legislative control at the earlier stages of the negotiation process of 'commerce treaties'.[29]

The CTP Act thus ushered in a new era of transparent treaty making. The CTP Act regulates the entire process of negotiating, concluding, and implementing FTAs and has opened up the treaty-making process, mandating broad-based consultations with governmental and non-governmental stakeholders.[30] It should be noted, however, that while the CTP Act has introduced changes regarding FTAs, the CTP Act's notion of 'commerce treaty'[31] has been interpreted not to cover BITs. Thus, its procedures are only followed in the context of the negotiation of FTAs (which include investment chapters), whereas BIT negotiations continue to be run by MOFA. In practice, however, this division is of little significance, as BITs now play a negligible role in Korean trade policy. As mentioned above, Korea prefers concluding FTAs with investment chapters rather than standalone BITs and, since 2013, has only concluded four BITs (2014 Korea–Myanmar BIT; 2014 Korea–Kenya BIT; 2013 Korea–Cameroon BIT; 2018 Korea–Armenia BIT).

In what follows I lay out the procedures under the CTP Act.

---

[28] Act on the Conclusion Procedure and Implementation of Commerce Treaties. Act No. 11149, 17 January 2021.

[29] Lee, 'Ratification of a Free Trade Agreement', 298–306 (explaining the social backgrounds that called for the Bill of the CTP Act at that time).

[30] See generally Lee Jae Min, 'Korea's FTA Drive and Enactment of Trade Treaty Conclusion Procedure Act of 2011 – Its Legal Implications and Practical Consequences' (2012) 19 *Seoul International Law Journal* 31; Hye-Sun Choi, 'Study on Content of Trade Treaty Conclusion Procedure Act and Its Revision Direction' (2015) 26 *Han Yang Law Review* 143.

[31] Art. 2 of the CTP Act reads: The terms used in this Act shall be defined as follows:

1. The term 'commerce treaty' means any treaty subject to consent of the National Assembly under Art. 60(1) of the Constitution of the Republic of Korea among the following treaties, concluded either by the Republic of Korea's accession to any international organisations, such as the World Trade Organization, or to any economic unions, or by the Republic of Korea with other countries, etc.
   (a) Treaties concluded at the level of international organizations, such as the World Trade Organization, with the aim of comprehensive opening to overseas markets;
   (b) Regional or bilateral treaties, such as regional trade agreements or free trade agreements, concluded with the aim of comprehensive opening to overseas markets;
   (c) Other treaties that have a significant influence on the national economy by entailing opening to overseas markets in each field of economy and commerce; [...]

In this chapter, Korean statutes are translated by reference to the Korea Legislation Research Institute and Korea Law Translation Center Website, which can be accessed at https://elaw.klri.re.kr/eng_service/main.do.

(a) **Treaty Conclusion Plan**   Once MOTIE decides to initiate a trade negotiation, it must first establish a 'trade treaty conclusion plan'[32] before beginning such negotiations. In establishing the conclusion plan, MOTIE undertakes an economic feasibility assessment of the proposed treaty and holds public hearings for relevant parties and experts.[33] MOTIE may also consult non-governmental stakeholders through its Civilian Advisory Committee on Trade Negotiations.[34]

Thereafter, the Trade Steering Committee considers the plan. The Trade Steering Committee is chaired by MOTIE and is composed of vice ministers from twenty trade-related ministries and agencies such as the Ministry of Economy and Finance, MOFA, the Ministry of Food and Drug Safety and the Korea Customs Service. The Trade Steering Committee deliberates as to whether to recommend starting FTA negotiations to the Ministerial Meeting on Foreign Economic Affairs (MMFEA), a ministerial-level decision-making body on international economic issues.[35] When significant issues warrant further inquiry, the Committee may also recommend first carrying out preliminary negotiations or other joint research with the prospective treaty party before embarking on full negotiations.[36] When MOTIE submits the treaty conclusion plan to the National Assembly, all relevant subcommittees are immediately informed.[37]

---

[32] Art. 6(1) of the CTP Act prescribes that the Plan shall include the following issues:

1. Objectives and main details of commercial negotiations;
2. Schedules for, and expected effects of, commercial negotiations;
3. Major issues expected in commercial negotiations and direction-setting for addressing such issues;
4. Trends of major countries involved in commercial negotiations; and
5. Other matters deemed necessary by the Minister of Trade, Industry and Energy.

[33] The procedure of public hearing is governed by Section 3 of Chapter II of the Administrative Procedures Act. Moreover, 'any citizen may present his/her opinion to the Government about commerce negotiations or commerce treaties' throughout the treaty-making process. In such cases, the Government shall endeavour to reflect the opinions so presented in making its policies whenever they are deemed reasonable. See CTP Act, Art. 8. See also CTP Act, Art. 7 and Regulations on Establishment and Operation, Etc. of the Trade Steering Committee ('TSC Regulations'), Art. 11.

[34] Previously, this committee, based on administrative rules, was called the FTA Civilian Advisory Committee and was established formally under the jurisdiction of the FTA Steering Committee (currently the Trade Steering Committee), which consisted of assistant ministers. The FTA Civilian Advisory Committee worked at the inter-ministerial level.

[35] Presidential Decree on the Ministerial Meeting for Foreign Economic Affairs, Arts. 1 and 2. MMFEA is chaired by the Minister of Strategy and Finance.

[36] TSC Regulations, Art. 12.

[37] CTP Act, Art. 6(1).

(b) The Negotiation Process   The CTP Act has significantly opened the negotiation process to a diverse set of governmental and non-governmental stakeholders. The negotiation team circulates the draft treaty for comments to other government ministries, departments or agencies in the early phases of the negotiation.[38] MOTIE's Trade Steering Committee carries out formal or informal consultations with relevant governmental and non-governmental stakeholders. Further, MOTIE must expediently report any significant issues to the National Assembly so that the latter may present its opinions.[39]

Once agreement on the draft treaty has been reached, the Minister must carry out an impact assessment, which it then also submits to the parliament when it seeks ratification.[40] Once signed by the President, MOTIE must submit a report to the Trade, Industry, Energy, SMEs and Startups Committee of the National Assembly and notify the public.[41]

4.2.2.3   The Treaty-Making Process and Internalisation

While the negotiation and conclusion of BITs by MOFA remains largely untransparent and not open to public participation, the rules on FTA negotiations have instituted a new paradigm of transparent treaty making, which involves the whole range of stakeholders from government, parliament and the public.

These differences in the treaty-making process between BITs and FTAs arguably have significant consequences for internalisation. The involvement at the treaty-making stage impacts the levels of awareness, buy in, and acceptance of the diverse stakeholders from government departments, the National Assembly, and the public that are involved in the process. For example, by commenting and providing feedback on drafts sent out by the Trade Steering Committee, the awareness of ministries, departments, and agencies increases, generating a learning process across government agencies as to investment treaties. FTAs have also drawn much more media attention, raising awareness in society at large.

---

[38] Interview B, 2018.
[39] CTP Act, Art. 10.
[40] CTP Act, Arts. 11 and 13. Notably, Art. 11 prescribes that the impact assessment covers the following issues: (1) overall impacts of the commerce treaty on the domestic economy; (2) impacts of the commerce treaty on national finances; (3) impacts of the commerce treaty on the domestic industries involved; and (4) impacts of the commerce treaty on domestic employment.
[41] CTP Act, Art. 12.

The renegotiation of the KORUS FTA provides an example of how this mechanism works in practice. The Korean government stated that it would undertake broad public consultations in cooperation with the National Assembly.[42] Then, when on 13 July 2017 the Office of the US Trade Representative (USTR) convened a special committee session of the Joint Committee, Korea conducted a feasibility assessment (October–November 2017) and two public hearings (10 November 2017 and 18 December 2017) in line with the CTP Act. During these hearings, Korean farmers raised objections to the Trump administration's demands that Korea grant the United States more access to the automotive and agricultural sectors.[43] In stark contrast to these objections, there were no serious public objections to matters pertaining to the investment chapter, although Korean negotiators – in light of the experience gained with respect to investment claims – did seek amendments to secure a clearer delimitation of regulatory space.[44]

Thus, while awareness as to BITs appears to remain low, awareness as to FTAs across the government and in society has risen to a high degree. That, on its face, reduces the likelihood that FTA obligations are not considered in governmental decision making, though more empirical work would need to be carried out to confirm the impact of this difference between BITs and FTAs in practice.

4.2.3 Implementation of Investment Treaties

Once an international treaty has been concluded, the Ministry of Government Legislation examines whether implementing legislation is required. If needed, the executive introduces a bill to the National Assembly. For example, if a trade agreement imposes specific technical obligations, such as the application of a new scheme for a tax refund, a custom rate, the elimination of a trade barrier, or an adjustment to market access, implementing laws will be adopted.

BITs, however, do not require implementing legislation. Neither do investment chapters in FTAs. The lack of implementing legislation can

---

[42] See Hyo-sik Lee, 'Korea to Reflect Public Opinion on FTA Renegotiation', *The Korea Times*, 3 November 2017.

[43] See Julie Kim Jackson, 'Agriculture Remains Hot Button Issue at 2nd FTA Public Hearing', *The Korea Herald*, 1 December 2017.

[44] See KORUS FTA Protocol (2018). See also for more background on the KORUS FTA renegotiation, Simon Lester, Inu Manak and Kyounghwa Kim, 'Trump's First Trade Deal: The Slightly Revised Korea-U.S. Free Trade Agreement', *Free Trade Bulletin* No. 73, 13 June 2019.

be attributed to the fact that the Korean government considers foreign investment protections as being already integrated in existing domestic investment laws. Notably, the Foreign Investment Promotion Act[45] largely mirrors the main principles found in investment treaties. Further, the government considers that foreign investors are also protected under domestic property laws, which apply equally to foreign and domestic investors, and which, in the government's view, provide the same degree of protection as contained in Korea's investment treaties.

4.3 Internalisation Measures

4.3.1 Internalisation Before Korea's ISDS Experience

Prior to its shift away from BITs towards the conclusion of FTAs, the Korean government had paid little attention to the internalisation of investment treaties. With the negotiation of the KORUS FTA, however, and the increased attention paid to that treaty within government and civil society, Korea's approach to internalisation began to change. For the first time, Korea developed dedicated informational tools for internalising its treaty commitments within the government. The FTAs, however, did not bring about changes with respect to the monitoring of government decision making or the remediation of potential treaty violations. In this regard, research indicates that prior to the rise of ISDS cases beginning in 2012, the Korean government had not developed any internalisation processes aimed at monitoring or remediating the application of its investment treaty obligations. Moreover, to the extent that there existed general mechanisms in Korean law and rulemaking designed to monitor the legality of government action, it does not appear that these mechanisms were used to internalise investment treaty obligations. Lastly, although Korea had established a specialised system for addressing the grievances of foreign investors in 1999 – the Foreign Investment Ombudsman – that system was developed and has operated as a process of investment aftercare rather than a process for monitoring and remediating potential investment treaty disputes.

4.3.1.1 Informational Measures

In this section, I describe the two main informational measures for internalising investment treaties adopted by the Korean government prior to

---

[45] Foreign Investment Promotion Act, Act No. 14839, 26 July 2017.

its experience with ISDS: dissemination and training within government and knowledge capacity building in the Korean legal community.

(a) Dissemination and Training within Government   Following the conclusion of the KORUS FTA, the MOJ published two handbooks in 2010 on Korea's investment treaty obligations: *Easy Understandable ISDS Cases*[46] and *Easy Understandable ISDS Cases by Policy Type*.[47] The principal purpose of these handbooks was to create a set of tools for disseminating information to non-specialist government officials and others regarding Korea's investment treaty obligations and their operation.

The two handbooks are complimentary. *Easy Understandable ISDS Cases* is seventy-nine pages long, laid out with short paragraphs and cartoons, and written in an approachable style. The handbook introduces the concept of ISDS through detailed examples in a question-and-answer format, with the objective of helping central and local government officials avoid investment disputes. *Easy Understandable ISDS Cases by Policy Type* provides a case-specific companion. Across eighty-seven pages, *Cases by Policy Type* focuses on examples of investor–state disputes drawn from arbitral case law and organised by the type of policy involved in the dispute. The idea behind the organisation of the handbook is to provide central and local government officials with practical examples of the application of investment treaty disciplines, thereby giving those officials operational insight into the way in which investment treaties apply to the day-to-day business of government. In addition, the document is also intended to assist Korean companies with investments in overseas markets to refer to cases of investment agreement violations by various policy types, if they believe their rights have been affected by the host state.

At the time of their release, the handbooks were met with much criticism by civil society groups and media which viewed them as encouraging 'regulatory chill' and conceding the public interest to foreign investors.[48] MOJ, however, maintained that these criticisms were exaggerated, and that the handbooks were being issued for educational purposes only.[49]

---

[46] Ministry of Justice, *Easy Understandable ISDS Cases* (알기 쉬운 국제투자분쟁 가이드) (2010).

[47] Ministry of Justice, *Easy Understandable ISDS Cases: By Policy Type* (알기 쉬운 정책유형별 투자분쟁 사례) (2010).

[48] Eun-Ha Chae, 'MOJ's "Self-Defeating" Warning of the Danger of ISDS', *Pressian*, 7 November 2011.

[49] *Ibid.*

While the debate about the impact of investment treaties on public policies and social rights continues in Korea, the government has updated and used these handbooks for training government officials for more than ten years.[50] Indeed, within the MOJ, the training of officials regarding Korea's treaty obligations is a specific portfolio, involving monthly MOJ-conducted training sessions around the country.[51]

(b) Legislation Support Service   The National Assembly Research Centre (NARS), a body similar to the U.S. Congressional Research Service, is currently not designed to cope with international investment law issues, but its research publications could potentially be used as an instrument for enhancing awareness regarding investment treaty commitments.

NARS provides expert research support to members of the National Assembly in the submission of a legislation or in the preparation of parliamentary inquiries.[52] NARS prepares research reports and informational materials such as briefs and newsletters. Typically, NARS is tasked by National Assembly members or committees, but it also has discretion to issue reports on its own initiative on matters it considers important or necessary.

NARS' primary function is to educate and not to monitor. In other words, NARS researchers do not monitor for conformity with international investment law.[53] That said, through its educational activities, NARS' research increases awareness within the National Assembly and the public with respect to Korea's treaty obligations. For instance, in the context of the KORUS FTA negotiations and renegotiations (in 2012 and 2018, respectively) NARS issued research reports and short news briefs on related policy and legislation.[54]

---

[50] Both handbooks were updated in 2016 and 2019 in response to the claims brought against Korea in *Lone Star* and other cases. *Easy Understandable ISDS Cases: By Policy Type* was again updated in 2021 under the leadership of the newly established International Dispute Settlement Division of the MOJ.

[51] These trainings are not limited only to investment, although investment is a specific component.

[52] Interview A, 2021.

[53] Interview A, 2017.

[54] For example, Min-Jung Chung, 'KORUS FTA Implementation Legislations' (2011) 334 *Issues and Controversies 1*; Min-Jung Chung, *Issue Reports No. 318: KORUS-FTA Renegotiation Procedures and Government's Negotiation Strategies* (NARS, 2017); Min-Jung Chung, *Legislation & Policy Report No.21: Investor-State Dispute Settlement (ISDS) in Revised KORUS-FTA, and Future Issues* (NARS, 2018); NARS (ed.), *Special Report: Critical Policy and Legislative Issues after the Establishment of the KORUS FTA* (NARS, 2012).

Nevertheless, NARS lacks sufficient expert knowledge on trade and investment law related issues. International investment legal issues are typically dealt with by the Foreign Affairs and National Security Team under the Politics and Administration Research Office, which does not specialise in trade and investment. To boost such expertise, some have called for establishing a specialised trade team.[55]

(c) **Knowledge Capacity Building in the Korean Legal Community**   In addition to taking steps to disseminate information and build capacity among government officials, the Korean government developed informal informational measures to strengthen knowledge capacity in the community of investment law experts. The Korean Commercial Arbitration Board (KCAB) – which MOTIE supports – plays a meaningful role in this regard.[56] In 1970, KCAB was incorporated as a statutory independent arbitration body under the Arbitration Act. It conducts both domestic and international arbitrations. Aside from arbitrations, in 2007, it established the Centre for International Investment Arbitration, which serves as a knowledge and research centre on international investment law,[57] bringing together the international investment community in Korea from varied sectors such as the government, private practice, and civil society. In this capacity, it organises events, sends newsletters and provides a forum for information exchange on current events for the international investment law community. It also collaborates with other centres, holding joint events with the Centre for International Trade and Transaction Law at the Seoul National University. Government officials also advertise their policies in this forum as a way of receiving informal comments from the expert community.

4.3.1.2   Monitoring Measures

In this section, I describe two mechanisms in Korean law and rule-making designed to monitor the legality of government action. These mechanisms were available prior to Korea's development of new, specialised monitoring processes in the wake of its ISDS experiences, and

---

[55] Bomin Ko, 'Korea's Strategies for Becoming an Advanced Trading Nation – A Focus on Trade Legislation and Trade Administration' (2015) 7 *Legislation and Policy Studies* 439, at 450–1.

[56] See KCAB International, www.kcabinternational.or.kr/main.do.

[57] KCAB, 'Introduction of the Centre for International Investment Arbitration', www.adr .or.kr/html/kcab_kor/monitering/monitering01.jsp.

theoretically could have been used to promote the internalisation of Korea's investment treaty commitments in government decision making. The mechanisms described are general mechanisms, originally designed to assess the legality of government action vis-à-vis principles of Korean law.[58] Critically, they were not designed to monitor investment law or international obligations.[59] As a consequence, perhaps, even though they might have permitted the consideration of investment treaty obligations in principle, in practice it does not appear that they were ever used in this way.

(a) Monitoring of Regulations through Regulatory Impact Analysis   When an agency of the executive branch attempts to introduce a new regulation or amend an existing regulation in the form of primary or secondary law, it must conduct a regulatory impact analysis (RIA). An RIA is designed to evaluate the feasibility of the regulation by predicting and analysing its effects.[60] The agency must prepare a report concerning its regulatory impact according to specific guidelines.[61] The guidelines require the agency to check the severity of any regulatory burden by reference to 'global standards'.[62] Further, the Regulatory Reform Committee established under the President may scrutinise the feasibility of 'important regulations', which covers excessive and unreasonable regulations 'by comparison with international standards'.[63]

Although it may have been possible in principle, it does not appear that Korea's investment treaty commitments ever played a role in the RIA process. Indeed, given the chronic lack of international investment law experts within Korean government agencies, it is questionable whether RIA officers and the Regulatory Reform Committee are equipped to take investment treaty obligations into account in their reviews.[64] Nevertheless, it may be that the RIA process is able to contribute indirectly to reducing the risk of investment disputes in any case because many domestic elements of the rule of law incorporated in the RIA guidelines (e.g., due process or proportionality) are shared with investment treaties. Although the extent

---

[58] See Chapter 1.
[59] *Ibid.*
[60] Framework Act on Administrative Regulations, Art. 2(1)–5.
[61] Framework Act on Administrative Regulations, Art. 7.
[62] Office for Government Policy Coordination, Guideline for Preparing the Regulatory Impact Analysis Guideline (2019) 17.
[63] Enforcement Decree of the Framework Act on Administrative Regulations, Art. 8–2.
[64] Interview A, 2021.

to which this occurs is not clear, it thus becomes possible that the RIA process may incidentally ameliorate potential problems, not by its internalisation of international commitments, but through the way in which those international commitments mirror the content of existing Korean law.[65]

(b) Monitoring of Regulations through Notice and Comment Procedures Under the Korean Administrative Procedures Act, when the executive develops regulations, it must undertake a notice and comment procedure enabling the public to voice its opinion and concerns with respect to the proposed rule.[66] Stakeholders may then present their opinions in writing, orally, or through information and communication networks.[67] When deemed necessary, the government may also hold a closed or a public hearing.[68] Moreover, when the government plans to establish a new regulation or add restrictive measures to existing regulations, it must undertake public or expert hearings or both.[69] In principle, such notice, comment and consultation procedures are an avenue through which issues relating to investment treaty obligations could have been raised by the public, and then considered by the government. With one exception, research has revealed no examples of these procedures being used in this way prior to the first ISDS cases against Korea.

The exception occurred in October 2011, when the Korean Postal Service pre-notified the public that it was revising the Enforcement Rules of the Postal Savings and Insurance Act to give effect to its confirmation letter under Chapter 13 of the KORUS FTA. Under the KORUS FTA, any rise in the value limit on insurance sales by the Korean Postal Service was made subject to approval by the Financial Supervisory Commission (FSC). The consequence of this requirement was that any amendment of this limit by the Korean Postal Services could now face difficulties. Thus, before enacting this limitation, in November 2011, the Korean Postal Service decided to amend the pre-notification and to increase the value limit by 50 per cent, reflecting fourteen-year inflation.[70]

---

[65] See Jung-In Choi, 'Indirect Expropriation', in NARS (ed.), *Special Report: Critical Policy and Legislative Issues after the Establishment of the KORUS FTA* (NARS, 2012) 669–70.

[66] See Administrative Procedures Act, Art. 21 (for administrative measures), Art. 41 (for secondary laws), and Art. 46 (for other types of administrative actions).

[67] Administrative Procedures Act, Arts. 22, 44, 46 and 50.

[68] Administrative Procedures Act, Arts. 22(1) and (2).

[69] Framework Act on Administrative Regulations, Art. 9.

[70] Ji-hwan Kim, 'Korea-U.S. FTA, Post Office Insurance?', The Weekly Kyunghyang, 17 January 2012.

Under the Administrative Procedures Act,[71] the American Chamber of Commerce in Korea (AMCHAM Korea) challenged this proposal. It argued, among other things, that the revision process was in breach of KORUS FTA's transparency clause[72] and its Confirmation Letter (Cross-Border Financial Services).[73] Following these and other comments, the government withdrew the proposal in 2012,[74] and has never reintroduced it. Some commentators think that this reluctance is explained by concerns that AMCHAM Korea would again object on the basis that the amendment is not in conformity with KORUS FTA.[75]

4.3.1.3   Remediation Measures

As with its monitoring measures of internalisation, prior to Korea's ISDS experiences, there were no mechanisms in Korea designed to remediate potential investment treaty violations. Although in 1999, prior to Korea's move towards the conclusion of FTAs, Korea had already established the Foreign Investment Ombudsman (FIO), a mechanism specifically tasked with addressing the grievances of foreign investors, FIO lacked both the mandate and the capacity to address grievances in terms of Korea's treaty obligations. The FIO mechanism is discussed in the following text.

(a) The Korean Foreign Investment Ombudsman   In 1999, the FIO mechanism was established under the Foreign Investment Promotion Act as an alternative mechanism for resolving disputes arising from the business activities of foreign investors in Korea.[76]

---

[71]   Administrative Procedures Act, Art. 44.

[72]   KORUS FTA (2007), Art. 13.11(9).

[73]   Exchange of Letters between Hyun Chong Kim, Minister for Trade, Republic of Korea and Susan C. Schwab, US Trade Representative, regarding KORUS FTA, Chapter 13 (Financial Services) (30 June 2007). In its challenge, AMCHAM Korea also raised procedural claims under the Administration Procedures Act, Art. 43. According to the provision, the period for pre-announcement of legislation shall be determined at the time of the pre-announcement and shall not be less than forty days in the absence of exceptional circumstances. In this case, the notice period for the amendment was only eight days.

[74]   Ministry of Information and Communication, '[Press Release] Government's Comment on the Newspaper Article, Retracts Expand Postal Insurance to AMCHAM's Objections to Korea's Plan to Expand Post Office Insurance', 5 January 2012.

[75]   *Ibid.*

[76]   The President appoints the FIO upon the recommendation of the Minister of MOTIE, which is based on the deliberation of the Foreign Investment Committee. See Foreign Investment Promotion Act, Art. 15-2(2). The Foreign Investment Committee is established under MOTIE to deliberate on important issues concerning the basic policies and schemes for foreign investment. The Minister of MOTIE is the Chairperson of the Foreign Investment Committee, and its members are deputy ministers of relevant ministries.

The government set up FIO as part of its policy to attract foreign investment following the 1997–1998 financial crisis.[77] Notably, Korea's investment treaty obligations did not drive the decision to establish the FIO mechanism. Rather FIO was set up as an investment aftercare process, designed to enable the early adjustment of investor grievances in order to facilitate investments and avoid having grievances with foreign investors develop into formal disputes.[78] FIO is an independent body which works closely with MOTIE and the Korea Trade-Investment Promotion Agency (KOTRA) but is not controlled by them.[79]

The 'Foreign Investors Aftercare Office' (FIAO) within FIO serves as the grievance committee to which foreign investors can submit petitions and complaints.[80] There are two alternative paths for submission of complaints by a foreign investor. The investor may submit a claim to an executive consultant, also referred to as a 'home doctor', who receives the complaints on behalf of FIAO. Each consultant specialises in a certain field, such as tax, legal affairs, construction, finance, foreign exchange, visas and labour. Each consultant is also exclusively assigned to a specific foreign company, allowing for the development of close ties between consultants and their designated companies as well as the provision of proactive care services.[81] In the alternative, a foreign investor can submit complaints directly to FIAO by e-mail or in person.

While considering complaints, FIO is authorised to demand cooperation from relevant public authorities, such as requiring them to explain

---

[77] Foreign Investment Ombudsman (FIO) (2019) *2018 Foreign Investment Ombudsman Annual Report*, 34–6.

[78] See, for example, Ministry of Justice (2010) *Easy Understandable ISDS Cases*, 38.

[79] KOTRA was established in 1962 as the 'Korea Trade Promotion Agency' under the Korea Trade Promotion Agency Act. This state-funded organisation under MOTIE initially purported to promote international trade, especially national exports to international markets. Since 1995, this agency has been expanded to cover investment issues with a new name, 'Korea Trade-Investment Promotion Agency'.

[80] Foreign Investment Promotion Act, Art. 15-2(10). This organisation is translated as 'Grievance Committee' by the Korea Law Translation Centre under the Korea Legislation Research Institute. However, KOTRA branded the Grievance Committee as 'Foreign Investors Aftercare Office'. See Foreign Investment Ombudsman, 'Organisational Charter'. This chapter refers to 'Grievance Committee' of the Foreign Investment Promotion Act as the 'Foreign Investors Aftercare Office (FIAO)' as adopted by KOTRA because the latter term appears more appropriate to express the main function of the organisation and leads to a better understanding of its functions. See Enforcement Decree of the Foreign Investment Promotion Act, Art. 21-4(2).

[81] Enforcement Decree of the Foreign Investment Promotion Act, Art. 21-4(5).

their actions, requesting site visits,[82] or demanding the provision of information if necessary for 'investigating whether a foreign investment-related system complies with international practices or standards'.[83] The public authority must respond to the request within seven days.[84]

Upon completion of the investigation, FIO may make a recommendation. FIO's recommendations, including corrective measures, are not legally binding,[85] but the public authorities must present reasonable reasons to reject them. They must also notify FIO within thirty days as to the actions they have taken to remedy the situation in light of the recommendation.[86] FIO also has the authority to verify and inspect if and how their recommendations for corrective measures have been implemented.[87] When recommendations issued by FIO are not implemented, FIO may raise the issue before the Foreign Investment Committee.[88] FIO submits a quarterly 'Report on Grievance Resolution for Foreign-Invested Companies' to MOTIE,[89] which is then regularly distributed to local governments and major public bodies.[90]

The FIO system has attracted significant interest and use from foreign investors in Korea. According to FIO, between 2008 and 2017, FIO resolved over 3,800 grievances by foreign investors across the Korean economy through the help of 'home doctors', the enactment of legislative changes, and adjustments to administrative decision making.[91] While it is not possible to know definitively whether any of these grievances would have developed into formal legal challenges had they not been addressed through the FIO mechanism, it seems clear that the FIO mechanism has proven a useful mechanism for the facilitation of foreign investment in Korea.

Nevertheless, there are reasons to doubt whether FIO has contributed to the internalisation of investment treaties. As noted above, FIO was not set up to review international investment law when settling complaints.

---

[82] Foreign Investment Promotion Act, Art. 15-2(3).
[83] Enforcement Decree of the Foreign Investment Promotion Act, Art. 21-3(3).
[84] Enforcement Decree of the Foreign Investment Promotion Act, Art. 21-4(3).
[85] Foreign Investment Promotion Act, Art. 15-2(4).
[86] Enforcement Decree of the Foreign Investment Promotion Act, Arts. 15-2(5) and 21-3(5).
[87] Enforcement Decree of the Foreign Investment Promotion Act, Art. 21-3(6).
[88] Foreign Investment Promotion Act, Art. 15-2(6).
[89] Enforcement Decree of the Foreign Investment Promotion Act, Art. 21-4(7).
[90] However, detailed contents of this report are not open to the public because relevant case information is confidential material. FIO, *2018 Foreign Investment Ombudsman Annual Report*, 51.
[91] FIO (2018) *2017 Foreign Investment Ombudsman Annual Report*, 38.

Indeed, historically, there has been a lack of awareness with respect to investment treaties within FIO. Unless the compatibility of a government measure with an investment treaty commitment is raised directly by the foreign investor, there is no mechanism within FIO, and no institutional capacity either, for FIO to identify potential treaty breaches on its own. FIAO houses no consultant with international investment law expertise. Moreover, in terms of institutional competence, FIO lacks the legal authority to compel government ministries, such as MOJ, MOTIE or MOFA, to disclose information.

Moreover, it appears that investment treaties have only rarely, and very recently, been raised by investors in their FIO grievances. Although FIO does not publish all its decisions, FIO's website lists 'best practice cases' each year for different types of grievance. None of these publicly available cases clearly indicate that they were resolved by reference to FTAs or BITs. Further, in FIO's annual reports, although there is an indication of issues related to FTAs arising in rare cases, it does not appear that these issues have been related to the FTAs' investment chapters. Instead, the issues identified have concerned trade, competition and other substantive areas covered by FTAs.[92]

4.3.2   Internalisation after the ISDS Cases

The influx of ISDS cases brought against Korea in the past decade, especially the high-profile *Lone Star* case, has been a catalyst for change in the internalisation of Korea's investment treaty obligations. Most significant among these changes has been the 2019 'Regulation on International Investment Dispute Prevention and Response', which established a lead agency responsible for improving internalisation through informational, monitoring and remedial tools dispute prevention and management in the Korean government.[93] This section discusses the changes brought about by the 2019 Regulation.

---

[92] In the 2017 annual report, for example, the one reference to a grievance involving an FTA concerned a trade-related matter, that is, setting country of origin marking requirements for the India–Korea CEPA (2009). See FIO (2018) *2017 Foreign Investment Ombudsman Annual Report*, 76. In the 2018 report, the grievances concerned product safety certification and the competition provisions of the EU–Korea FTA (2010). See FIO (2019) *2018 Foreign Investment Ombudsman Annual Report*, 78–81. In 2019, FIO reported grievances with respect to the prospective conclusion of an FTA with the United Kingdom. See FIO (2020) *2019 Foreign Investment Ombudsman Annual Report*, 82 and 85.

[93] Hyong-Ki Park, 'Gov't Sets up ISDS Response Team', *The Korea Times*, 5 April 2019.

4.3.2.1   Regulation on International Investment
Dispute Prevention and Response

As noted, since 2012 Korea has been subject to a dozen, large-scale ISDS claims and yet, until 2019, Korea responded to those claims in an ad hoc way. Thus, when Korea received notices of intent to arbitrate from foreign investors,[94] the government would set up an ad hoc joint response system, consisting of the Office for Government Policy Coordination and other relevant ministries such as the Ministry of Strategy and Finance, MOFA, MOJ and MOTIE.

The joint response system consisted of a consultation body of the relevant ministries and a Dispute Response Task Force. The consultation body was presided over by the Vice Minister of the Office for Government Policy Coordination, which is under the control of the Prime Minister, and composed of vice ministers from the concerned ministries. The consultation body was responsible for all strategic decision making regarding the arbitration. The Task Force consisted of Director-General level officials from the ministries and oversaw all practical issues arising during the arbitration proceedings. Typically, the consultation body would appoint the ministry most relevant to the dispute to chair the Task Force.[95]

This ad hoc system suffered from various inefficiencies. Notably, ministries did not volunteer to lead the Task Force as defeat in an investment dispute entailed high political risks.[96] Further, in some cases, in order to avoid reprimand from their seniors or negative public opinion, officials in charge of a dispute are understood to have deliberately (and rather dangerously) taken a passive attitude and sought to delay the arbitration process as much as possible, with the hope that the blame would shift to their successor(s).[97] Moreover, the temporary ad hoc system failed to create robust and permanent expertise in the management

---

[94] This notice was received by the Office of International Legal Affairs.

[95] Interview B, 2018.

[96] *Ibid.*

[97] While it is impossible to prove that this risk-avoiding approach prevails in Korea's ISDS response, this attitude of self-preservation is said to be prevalent in the Korean bureaucracy. See Jungho Park, 'Implications of Organizational Behavior Theories to Proactive Public Administration' (2019) 18 *Korean Public Personnel Administration Review* 283, 286. This is called a 'blame game', typically found in advanced democratic politics and bureaucracy. See Christopher Hood, *The Blame Game: Spin, Bureaucracy, and Self-Preservation in Government* (Princeton University Press, 2010).

of ISDS disputes. All learning and expertise were temporary and not institutionalised.[98]

The increasing numbers of cases received by Korea between 2012 and 2019 exposed the problems of the ad hoc system and the need for reform. The government, therefore, decided to launch an ambitious project for efficient resolution of investment disputes.[99] The President issued a Presidential Directive entitled the 'Regulation on International Investment Dispute Prevention and Response', which established a standing body called the International Investment Dispute Response Team.[100] Under the Regulation, the Dispute Response Team is headed by the Head of the MOJ Legal Affairs Bureau and is comprised of executive members (senior officers from the Office for Government Policy Coordination, the Ministry of Strategy and Finance, MOFA, and MOTIE) and non-executive members (temporarily serving in particular cases).[101] The team is staffed and supported by the International Dispute Settlement Division.[102] The Regulation not only establishes a new body but it also sets out a detailed procedure, which incorporates the three types of internationalisation mechanisms identified by Calamita and Berman: informational, monitoring and remedial.[103]

(a) Informational Procedures   In terms of informational processes, the Dispute Response Team is required to prepare guidelines whose purpose is to educate government officials so as to prevent international investment disputes. To support this function, the Response Team must conduct research on foreign investment-related policies, trends, government measures and ombudsman cases.[104]

---

[98] See Jin-Soo Im, 'Easy Target by Global Hedgefunds? In the Need of the ISDS Response System', *Nocut News*, 23 May 2019; Deok-Young Park, *Study on the ISDS Prevention and Response Systems of States* (Ministry of Justice Policy Research Paper, 2014), 98–102.

[99] Ministry of Justice, 'Response to International Investment Disputes (ISDS) will be Strengthened', 29 August 2019.

[100] Hyong-Ki Park, 'Gov't Sets up ISDS Response Team', *The Korea Times*, 5 April 2019.

[101] International Investment Dispute Regulation, Art. 2 para. 5.

[102] The International Dispute Settlement Division was separated from the International Legal Affairs Division in August 2020 with the reformation of the investment dispute response system. See also Jae-hyuk Park, 'Korea Launches Organization to Defeat Lone Star', *The Korea Times*, 20 August 2020.

[103] See Chapter 1.

[104] International Investment Dispute Regulation, Art. 3(2) paras. 1, 7, and 8.

In this regard, one may recall the two handbooks published by MOJ in 2010 following the conclusion of the KORUS FTA.[105] Although the relation of these handbooks to the mandate of the Dispute Response Team is not yet clear, it is worth noting that following Korea's experience in *Lone Star* and other ISDS cases, MOJ has updated these handbooks in 2016 and again in 2019. Moreover, MOJ has used these handbooks over the past decade for training government officials. Indeed, within MOJ, training officials regarding Korea's treaty obligations had become a specific job portfolio by 2016, involving monthly MOJ-conducted training sessions around the country.[106] Notwithstanding these efforts, however, the effectiveness of the MOJ trainings remains unclear. For all of the resources dedicated by MOJ to training officials across government, those efforts face a constant challenge from the perpetual rotation of civil servants within and across ministries and in and out of government.

(b) Monitoring Procedures The Dispute Response Team also has a duty to monitor whether governmental measures may give rise to potential investment treaty disputes.[107] The monitoring process is not applied on a standing basis but is rather only activated when government agencies issue specific types of policies, measures, rules, legislation and other actions as listed in Art. 7 of the International Investment Dispute Regulation. To this end, governmental authorities and administrative organs are under a duty to inform the Response Team about their undertakings with foreign investors, both before and once a dispute erupts. For example, they must inform the Response Team whenever they enter contracts with a foreign investor from a state which is a party to a Korean FTA or BIT and whenever their contracts with a foreign investor include dispute resolution procedures.[108] The Dispute Response Team will also be brought into action following a preliminary assessment of investment dispute risk identified by government agencies or other administrative organs. When they find that their existing or planned laws, regulations or policies potentially infringe on the property rights of

---

[105] *Easy Understandable ISDS Cases* (2010); *Easy Understandable ISDS Cases: By Policy Type* (2010).

[106] These trainings are not limited only to investment, although investment is a specific component.

[107] International Investment Dispute Regulation, Art. 3(2) para. 2.

[108] International Investment Dispute Regulation, Art. 7 (1) paras. 1 and 2.

foreign investors, or when they identify any other potential investment dispute, these agencies or organs must refer the case to the Dispute Response Team.[109]

(c) **Remedial Measures**   The framework established by the Regulation also sets up a detailed procedure for dispute prevention and management. The main rules encompass the following procedures.

First, according to the Regulation, the public authority must inform the Dispute Response Team whenever foreign investors file lawsuits challenging statutes, regulations or policies; and whenever a foreign investor mentions its intention to pursue an international investment dispute.[110] Also, once public authorities have been notified by a potential claimant of its intention to initiate an investment arbitration claim, they are required to inform the Response Team without delay.

Upon receiving the notification, the Response team must promptly review the possibility of an international investment dispute and, thereafter, notify the department heading the relevant authority or administrative organ, if that is the case. This process can serve as a warning to the relevant government actors that certain actions may lead to investment disputes, giving them notice to work on a preventive measure.

Once a dispute is underway, the Response Team plays a pivotal role in dispute management by providing relevant legal advice and establishing an international dispute response strategy for the administrative organs and relevant authorities.[111] The Response Team hires and supervises law firms that represent administrative organs or relevant authorities in the investment arbitration.[112] The Response Team can also request the concerned authorities to present facts and opinions on issues related to the arbitration.[113]

The International Investment Dispute Regulation mandates that the administrative organs and relevant authorities must cooperate with the Response Team.[114] MOJ or the ministers of the central government departments in charge of implementing the measure implicated in

---

[109]   International Investment Dispute Regulation, Art. 7 (1) paras. 3 and 6.
[110]   International Investment Dispute Regulation, Art. 7 (1) paras. 4 and 5.
[111]   International Investment Dispute Regulation, Art. 3(2) paras. 3 and 4.
[112]   International Investment Dispute Regulation, Art. 3(2) paras. 4 and 5.
[113]   International Investment Dispute Regulation, Art. 3(2) para. 6.
[114]   International Investment Dispute Regulation, Art. 6.

investment treaty disputes may convene a meeting of relevant ministries to decide how to respond to the investment dispute, including
its prevention if necessary.[115] This ministerial-level deliberative body
is established on an ad hoc basis when active cooperation is necessary
to reach politically or legally important decisions. The body is chaired
by the head of the central government department, which convened
the relevant ministerial meeting. The members of the meeting are to
be nominated by the vice-ministerial officials of ministers from the
Ministry of Strategy and Finance, MOFA, MOTIE, and other heads of
authorities concerned with the dispute. The relevant ministerial meeting must be convened with the attendance of most of the members;
further, all decisions must be approved by a majority of the members
present.[116]

   To conclude, the International Investment Dispute Regulation
introduces important informational, monitoring, and above all remedial measures for the internalisation of investment treaties. However,
this framework is not perfect. For instance, the Dispute Response
Team's dispute resolution function (located under MOJ) potentially
creates some overlap with FIO (which is under MOTIE). At the time
of writing, MOJ and FOI signed a memorandum of understanding for
enhancing cooperation for the prevention of investment disputes.[117]
MOJ undertook to establish an information-sharing system for dispute prevention and to cooperate with FIO for improving the FDI
environment. MOJ and FIO agreed to hold a joint session for hearing
the grievances of foreign investors. They also agreed to cooperate on a
diverse set of issues, from personnel exchange through intra-network
sharing. This being a very new development, how successful such
cooperation shall be in practice remains to be seen.[118] This is an area
for future consideration.

---

[115] International Investment Dispute Regulation, Art. 9(2). However, the Head of the Office
for Government Policy Coordination may convene a meeting of relevant ministries if necessary, to coordinate opinions among departments and organs related to international
investment disputes or to closely coordinate cooperation systems for international investment disputes.

[116] International Investment Dispute Regulation, Art. 9(3).

[117] Byung-yeul Baek, 'KOTRA, Ministry of Justice Join Forces to Prevent International
Investment Disputes', *The Korea Times*, 30 April 2021.

[118] Ministry of Justice, '[Press Release] Establishment of a Preemptive Cooperation System to
Prevent International Investment Disputes with Foreign-Invested Companies', 30 April
2021.

4.4 Conclusion

While Korea has been an active member of the international investment regime, until it began facing ISDS cases and concluding FTAs, not much attention had been directed to its investment treaty commitments. Investment treaty expertise was centralised in the hands of experts in several ministries such as MOFA, MOTIE and MOJ, while most officials dealing with the domestic measures that potentially affect foreign investors lacked necessary investment law awareness and expertise. However, in the past decade, there have been two interrelated developments which will likely have a gradual positive impact on the internalisation of investment treaties in Korea.

The first is the shift from BITs to FTAs with investment chapters. Due to their significant distributional effects, FTAs have been subject to much political contestation within Korea, with some notable FTAs such as the KORUS FTA generating heated public debate. In response, the Conclusion Procedure and Implementation of Commercial Treaties Act introduced transparency and participation into treaty making. Such openness – leading to greater governmental, parliamentary and public awareness – is likely to have a positive impact on the consideration of FTAs with investment chapters in governmental decision-making processes, including beyond the central ministries. Notably, BITs do not follow such an elaborate political vetting procedure, and this may potentially lead to different levels of internalisation of BITs and FTAs. Further empirical research would be needed to inquire into the scope and degree of this difference.

The second is the rise in ISDS cases brought against Korea, especially the *Lone Star* case, which caused significant disturbance and gave rise to public disapproval. In response, the government adopted several internalisation measures. In the first instance, it revised the two handbooks originally published by MOJ in 2010 following the conclusion of the KORUS FTA, and set upon continuing MOJ's nationwide program of training for government officials. More recently, and most notably, Korea adopted the Regulation on International Investment Dispute Prevention and Response and set up a standing International Investment Dispute Response Team. Through this new framework, Korea has established new institutional structures and centralised responsibility for the development and implementation of informational, monitoring and remedial internalisation tools to prevent disputes from emerging.

Whether these new structures will be effective in practice remains to be seen. Inasmuch as different informational, monitoring and remedial mechanisms are now available, they will amount to little if the involved authorities have insufficient levels of awareness and do not use them properly. Nonetheless, awareness within government, parliament and the public as to investment treaty obligations has significantly increased in recent years and thus there is reason for optimism that these informational, monitoring and remedial measures will slowly but surely break the vicious cycle and foster a virtuous circle of internalisation.

5

The Impact of Investment Treaties
on the Rule of Law in Myanmar

JONATHAN BONNITCHA

5.1 Introduction

Supporters of investment treaties argue that investment treaties encourage respect for the rule of law in countries that are bound by them. According to this argument, the legal obligations contained in investment treaties align with normatively attractive conceptions of the rule of law.[1] Conscious that the risk of breaching these obligations entails financial liability, states then reform their systems of domestic governance in order to ensure compliance.[2] Critics argue that investment treaties discourage legitimate, public interest regulation of foreign investment. On this view, investment treaties impose broad, ill-defined obligations on states to refrain from interfering with foreign investment. Conscious that breaching these obligations entails financial liability, investment treaties make

---

[1] In making this argument, supporters of investment treaties invoke a broad conception of the rule of law that combines both procedural and substantive elements. Vandevelde, for example, characterises the rule of law as comprising the principles of 'reasonableness, consistency (or security), nondiscrimination, and transparency' in all state conduct: see Kenneth J. Vandevelde, *Bilateral Investment Treaties: History, Policy, and Interpretation* (Oxford University Press, 2010), 51–52. This conception of the rule of law differs from formalist/procedural theories of the rule of law and from more sociological accounts of the rule of law. For a formalist theory of the rule of law, see Joseph Raz, 'The Rule of Law and Its Virtue' (1977) 93 *Law Quarterly Review* 195. For a sociological account, see Martin Krygier, 'Rule of Law', in Michel Rosenfeld and András Sajó (eds.), *The Oxford Handbook of Comparative Constitutional Law* (Oxford University Press, 2012), 233. It also differs from other influential substantive theories of the rule of law, which emphasise respect for human rights: see Tom Bingham, *The Rule of Law* (Allen Lane, 2010). In earlier work, I have criticised the broad conception of the rule of law that supporters of investment treaties invoke – see Jonathan Bonnitcha, *Substantive Protection Under Investment Treaties: A Legal and Economic Analysis* (Cambridge University Press, 2014), 42–43. Nevertheless, for the purpose of this chapter, I adopt, without endorsing, this broad conception of the rule of law.

[2] Roberto Echandi, 'What Do Developing Countries Expect from the International Investment Regime?', in José E. Alvarez and Karl P. Sauvant (eds.), *The Evolving International Investment Regime: Expectations, Realities, Options* (Oxford University Press, 2011), 3.

states reluctant to impose new regulations on foreign investment. In other words, investment treaties lead to 'regulatory chill'.[3]

The claims of both the supporters and the critics rest on a set of empirical assumptions about the impact of investment treaties on government institutions and decision making within those institutions, in the states that are bound by them. To date, these assumptions have been subject to little investigation. The handful of studies that have examined these questions have raised questions about the claims of both supporters and critics.[4] In light of these studies, the claims of supporters seem particularly implausible. The legal obligations that investment treaties impose on state parties constrain *all* state conduct that affects covered foreign investments, regardless of the responsible organ of government (e.g., legislature, responsible Minister, specialised regulatory agency, or judiciary) and the subject matter of the measure (e.g., environment, public health, energy policy, or tax). As such, the claims of supporters depend on the obligations contained in investment treaties being deeply and systematically internalised across a wide range of government decision-making processes.

In this context, this chapter examines the impact of investment treaties on domestic rule of law through a single, detailed case study of Myanmar. Myanmar is a powerful case study because, if investment treaties do have effects on the domestic rule of law, it is a country where one would expect to see such effects. This is for three reasons. First, according to investment treaties' supporters, the treaties' positive impact on the rule of law is the result of a simple incentive effect: states are concerned about the cost of being held liable for breaching an investment treaty and therefore reform systems of domestic governance to ensure compliance.[5] The strength of this supposed incentive to reform depends on the perceived gap between existing standards of domestic governance and the standards required by the treaties' obligations. Myanmar is a least developed country that is perceived – both internally and externally – to have a poor standard of

---

[3] Kyla Tienhaara, *The Expropriation of Environmental Governance: Protecting Foreign Investors at the Expense of Public Policy* (Cambridge University Press, 2009); Kyla Tienhaara, 'Regulatory Chill and the Threat of Arbitration: A View from Political Science', in Chester Brown and Kate Miles (eds.), *Evolution in Investment Treaty Law and Arbitration* (Cambridge University Press, 2011), 606.

[4] Mavluda Sattorova, *The Impact of Investment Treaty Law on Host States: Enabling Good Governance?* (Hart Publishing, 2018).

[5] Stephan W. Schill, *The Multilateralization of International Investment Law* (Cambridge University Press, 2009), 377. For a more detailed elaboration of this argument, see Chapter 1.

domestic governance.[6] Hence, one would expect the incentive that investment treaties create for reform in Myanmar to be much larger than in states that are already perceived to be meeting the standards required by investment treaties.

Second, the research for this project was conducted primarily in 2018 and 2019, with documentary sources and events described by interviewees spanning a broader period of 2012 to 2020. This corresponds to an era of quasi-democratic reform in Myanmar. In 2011, Myanmar began a major transition from military to quasi-civilian rule, which tragically ended with the military coup of February 2021.[7] In the intervening period, attracting new foreign investment was a key priority of the Myanmar government. Foreign development assistance to Myanmar also dramatically increased in this period,[8] much of it focused on economic reform and the domestic business environment. Financial capacity and high-level political support are two dimensions of the national context that one might expect to be associated with a positive relationship between investment treaties and the domestic rule of law,[9] in the sense that both factors ease practical constraints that might limit the positive impact of investment treaties on domestic governance.

Third, Myanmar had a relatively early experience as a respondent in investor–state dispute settlement (ISDS), an experience that previous empirical work has shown often triggers reflection and learning within government on the implications of participation in the investment treaty regime.[10]

---

[6] For example, in 2019, Myanmar was ranked 182nd out of 209 states on the World Bank's Worldwide Governance Indicators 'Rule of Law' metric. See World Bank, 'Worldwide Governance Indicators', https://info.worldbank.org/governance/wgi/.

[7] So far as it is possible to tell, Myanmar's laws and bureaucratic processes governing foreign investment remain largely unaffected by the coup, see, for example, Directorate of Investment and Company Administration (DICA), 'Policy and Law', www.dica.gov.mm/en/policy-and-law. Nevertheless, the coup has had a dramatic effect on the business environment and, in particular, the willingness of Western companies to continue operating in the country – for example, see the recent divestment by Norwegian telco Telenor, one of three major network operators in Myanmar: Victoria Klesty, 'Telenor quits Myanmar with $105 mln sale to Lebanon's M1 Group', *Reuters*, 8 July 2021.

[8] OECD, *Development Aid at a Glance, Statistics by Region: Asia* (OECD Publishing, 2019), 7.

[9] The role of national context and capacity constraints in mediating the impact of investment treaties on domestic governance are explored in more detail in the introductory chapter to this volume, see for example Figure 3.

[10] See for example Lauge N. S. Poulsen and Emma Aisbett, 'When the Claim Hits: Bilateral Investment Treaties and Bounded Rational Learning' (2013) 65 *World Politics* 273; Lauge N. S. Poulsen, *Bounded Rationality and Economic Diplomacy: The Politics of Investment Treaties in Developing Countries* (Cambridge University Press, 2015).

Nevertheless, this chapter casts doubt on the claim that investment treaties promote the rule of law, as well as complicating critics' claims about regulatory chill. The overall finding is that investment treaties have only limited and ad hoc effects on domestic rule of law, primarily mediated through processes within the executive branch of government. Investment treaties have no discernible impact on the judicial system in Myanmar, and little impact on legislation or regulatory rule-making processes. While these findings challenge many of the assumptions implicit in debates about investment treaties, they are broadly consistent with the wider literature on law and development, which tends to emphasise both complexity and the uncertain effects of legal interventions.[11]

5.1.1   The Normative Implications of Empirical Research?

Before launching into the substance of the chapter, a brief word of caution is necessary to readers who might draw normative conclusions from this chapter. The chapter empirically examines how investment treaties affect the institutional structure of government in Myanmar, and decision making within that institutional structure. Because the rule of law is used as an organising concept throughout this volume, and because the rule of law is generally considered to be a good thing,[12] some readers might assume that the *empirical* conclusion that investment treaties have relatively little impact on government decision making in Myanmar implies a *normative* conclusion that Myanmar should do more to ensure that the investment treaties are internalised within the state apparatus.

This conclusion would be seriously mistaken for two reasons. First, as already noted, claims that investment treaties promote the rule of law rely on a particular – and contentious – conception of the rule of law.[13] Second,

---

[11] See for example David M. Trubek, 'Law and Development: Forty Years after "Scholars in Self-Estrangement"' (2016) 66 *University of Toronto Law Journal* 301.

[12] E. P. Thompson famously described the rule of law as 'an unqualified human good', although his conception of the rule of law differs sharply from the conception adopted by proponents of investment treaties. See E. P. Thompson, *Whigs and Hunters: The Origin of the Black Act* (Pantheon Books, 1975), 266.

[13] For example, a normative commitment to ensuring consistency in government conduct over time (which is an element of Vandevelde's conception of the rule of law) may well be in tension with other normative goals, such as the responsiveness of democratic institutions to the views of their citizens and to new information. For an exploration of Vandevelde's conception of consistency as an element of the rule of law, see Kenneth J. Vandevelde, 'A Unified Theory of Fair and Equitable Treatment' (2010) 43 *New York University Journal of International Law and Politics*, 43, 69–78.

even if one accepts that the obligations contained in investment treaties reflect a normatively attractive conception of the rule of law, there remains a question of priorities. Governments everywhere operate under resource and information constraints; it is obviously not feasible, for example, that all conduct across a state's entire governmental apparatus be reviewed for compliance with every obligation under international law. Decisions of resource allocation and relative priority are required, particularly in developing countries. In a transitional context like Myanmar from 2012 to 2020, any argument that 'more should be done' to ensure internalisation of investment treaties within the state apparatus would need to consider whether other governance reforms might be more urgent – for example, reforms to address the dominance of the military and military-linked companies in the economy, and associated efforts to reconsider the terms of existing investment contracts and long-term land lease arrangements.[14]

5.1.2 Research Methods and Methodology

The research relied on a process-tracing methodology, which sought to identify the causal chain of actors, mechanisms, and events linking investment treaties to actual effects on government decision making. The first step in this methodology involved identifying nodes within government that have, or might be expected to have, direct contact with investment treaties – for example, the agencies of government responsible for negotiating investment treaties, managing investor–state disputes, and providing legal advice on questions of international law. The second step involved examining the impact of investment treaties on government decision making within these agencies. The third step involved identifying further processes or mechanisms emanating from these nodes by which investment treaties might influence government decision making more widely – for example, the informational, monitoring and remedial processes described by Calamita and Berman in the introductory chapter to this volume.[15]

The choice of methodology reflects the assumption that, beyond nodes of government that have direct responsibility for investment treaties, government officials in Myanmar are highly unlikely to have any independent

---

[14] Such competing reform priorities may also be in tension with the conception of the rule of law that prevails in scholarship on investment treaties, which emphasises the importance of consistency in state action over time and the security of contractual entitlements.
[15] See Chapter 1.

knowledge of investment treaties. In other words, absent internalisation processes and mechanisms linked to nodes of knowledge of investment treaties, the assumption is that investment treaties have little impact on governance in Myanmar. This assumption is justified for three related reasons. First, the extant literature on governance in Myanmar suggests a very low level of capacity within the government in general.[16] Government officials are poorly paid and under-resourced. Half a century of military rule has created a culture within the bureaucracy of deference to authority, rather than accountability to the public. In an environment where government agencies struggle to perform their own core functions, the idea that government officials are evaluating their conduct in light of the disciplines imposed by investment treaties seems fanciful. Second, this assumption is consistent with my own direct personal experience working on investment governance within the Myanmar government over several years prior to the commencement of this study. This experience included engagement on issues of investment governance with government officials in Myanmar both within and beyond nodes of knowledge of investment treaties. Third, this assumption is consistent with research on the general awareness of investment treaties among government officials in other developing countries, including countries that are wealthier than Myanmar and have significantly more experience as respondents in high-profile investment treaty claims.[17]

While these three reasons provide strong grounds for the assumption that government officials outside nodes of contact with the investment treaty system do not have any independent knowledge of investment treaties, it is also important to acknowledge that this project did not *directly* verify the accuracy of this assumption. Due to difficulties in access, no interviews were conducted with officials from line Ministries, specialised agencies, or sub-national levels of government themselves. Nevertheless, the interviews that were conducted strongly suggest that this assumption

---

[16] For example, Su Mon Thazin Aung and Matthew Arnold draw attention to the lack of high-level policy coordination between different ministers and ministries of the national government. See Su Mon Thazin Aung and Matthew Arnold, *Managing Change: Executive Policymaking in Myanmar* (The Asia Foundation, May 2018). For a deeper look into the low level of capacity to draft and scrutinise legislation, see Melinda Thet Tun, 'Making better laws for Myanmar', *Frontier Myanmar*, 24 October 2017. Others have also explored the significant capacity challenges facing state- and region-level governments; see Hamish Nixon et al., *State and Region Governments in Myanmar* (The Asia Foundation, September 2013).

[17] Sattorova, 'The Impact of Investment Treaty Law on Host States?' See also chapters in this volume.

was justified. There was consensus among everyone interviewed as part of this project – government officials working within identified nodes of contact with investment treaties, external consultants, and foreign investment lawyers – that there was little awareness of investment treaties within government in Myanmar beyond the nodes of government with direct responsibility for dealing with the treaties.[18]

The research methods involved a combination of semi-structured interviews and analysis of primary and secondary documents. Over the course of this project, I interviewed a total of eight senior and four junior government officials in eight separate interviews. Senior, in this context, refers to government officials with Director-level positions or higher. A Director in the Myanmar public service leads a Division and would normally have between twenty to forty people working under them. Junior, in this context, refers to government officials below the level of Director. Officials who are junior in this sense may still have management oversight over a small team and significant influence on decision making within their areas of responsibility.

I conducted nine further interviews with foreign investment lawyers based in Myanmar and foreign advisors to the Myanmar government on investment governance. Some interviewees fell into both categories. All the foreign lawyers who I interviewed had personal experience of representing foreign investors in regulatory interactions with the Myanmar government. In the case of the foreign advisors, I was able to verify independently that all had indeed advised the Myanmar government on investment governance issues and that their advice had been taken seriously by senior government officials. All interviews were based on sets of reference questions developed for different classes of interviewees. As the research progressed, many interviews also included additional questions to cross-check information uncovered elsewhere, or to elicit additional context.

Of the seventeen interviews, twelve were conducted in person in Myanmar, four were conducted by phone or through Skype, and one was by written response to questions by email. All interviews were conducted in English. Given the sensitivities of the subject matter, the interviewees preferred this option to having a professional translator present. All interviews were conducted one-on-one, with the exception of one group interview. The group interview format was used once, at the request of the

---

[18] These findings are elaborated in the section on internalisation within the Executive (Section 5.2.4.).

interviewees, to deal with a situation where interviewees felt unsure about expressing themselves in English and asked to have colleagues present to clarify the meaning of their responses in English. All interviewees were guaranteed anonymity. To avoid inadvertently identifying interviewees, some of the information provided has been further anonymised. Even though not reported in this chapter, the level of detail that many interviewees provided was important in facilitating verification of the events and practices they described, through cross-checking with other interviewees or with documentary sources.

The interviews were complemented by primary and secondary documentary sources. Relevant primary sources included treaty texts as well as domestic laws and regulations in Myanmar. Relevant secondary sources include the nascent scholarly literature on investment governance in Myanmar, documents and PowerPoint slide-decks prepared by international organisations, such as the International Finance Corporation (IFC), and press reports of investment disputes.

My own experience working on investment treaties within the government of Myanmar from 2014 to 2016 provided a further source of background knowledge. For example, my background knowledge of the internal structure of the Myanmar government assisted in the initial identification of nodes of knowledge of investment treaties within the government of Myanmar, and in preparing reference questions for different classes of interviewees. It is important to acknowledge that my background may also be a source of bias. In particular, my own impression of the government officials I interviewed was of honest people, working long hours, in challenging conditions, for what they understand to be the best interests of their country.

5.2   The Impact of Investment Treaties on the Rule of Law in Myanmar

This section of the chapter reports the findings of the research. It begins, in Section 5.1.1, with a brief overview of the institutional architecture within the government of Myanmar, as it relates to investment governance. Section 5.1.2 then examines how Myanmar decides whether to enter into investment treaties and how it participates in the process of treaty negotiations. While this analysis does not speak directly to the question of investment treaties' impact on the rule of law in Myanmar, it does provide important context. Participation in negotiations is one way that officials may become aware of investment treaties, and the conclusion of a new treaty might plausibly trigger subsequent processes to implement treaty commitments across government.

With this context in mind, this section then examines the impact of investment treaties on domestic governance through legislation and legislative processes (Section 5.2.3), executive mechanisms and processes (Section 5.2.4), and through the judicial system (Section 5.2.5). The overall finding is that investment treaties' effects on domestic governance are primarily mediated through executive processes and that these effects are limited and often ad hoc. Investment treaties have no discernible impact on the judicial system in Myanmar, and little impact on legislation or regulatory rule-making processes.

5.2.1   Basic Institutional Architecture

The Myanmar Investment Commission (MIC) is the most visible government body involved in the regulation of investment in Myanmar. It is a high-level decision-making committee, comprised of thirteen members from different Ministries.[19] Some of its members are Ministers themselves, but most are senior civil servants. Under the Myanmar Investment Law 2016 (MIL),[20] as was also the case under the earlier investment laws which it replaced, the MIC is vested with the power to regulate the admission of foreign investment by issuing investment permits and investment endorsements. It meets roughly twice a month.

The Directorate of Investment and Company Administration (DICA) acts as the Secretariat to the MIC. DICA has several hundred permanent staff, so it is a very different type of institution compared to the MIC. DICA carries out the day-to-day work of the MIC, among other functions, which include drafting laws and regulations related to investment and negotiating investment treaties.[21] It is also the main point of contact for foreign investors in Myanmar. DICA's role as a point of contact for foreign investors is closely related to two of the MIC's main decision-making functions. The first relates to the admission of new foreign investment, and includes the granting of investment permits in sectors where entry is regulated and the grant of investment endorsements required for

---

[19] DICA, 'About the MIC', www.dica.gov.mm/en/information-myanmar-investment-commission-mic.

[20] Myanmar Investment Law, Pyidaungsu Hluttaw Law No. 40/2016, 18 October 2016 ('Myanmar Investment Law 2016').

[21] Myanmar Investment Law 2016, ss. 99 and 100.

investors to benefit from fiscal incentives available under the Myanmar Investment Law.[22] The second function relates to the management and resolution of investor–state disputes. DICA provides advice, information and recommendations to the MIC, which form the bases for these decision-making functions.

DICA, itself, is divided into several divisions. The Policy and Legal Affairs Division has ongoing responsibility for negotiating investment treaties and also had the responsibility for drafting the MIL.[23] It is widely perceived as the central node of knowledge of investment treaties within the government of Myanmar. In the course of this research, interviewees from both within and outside government routinely referred me back to the Policy and Legal Affairs Division as the authoritative source of information on Myanmar's engagement with investment treaties.[24] Despite its name, the Policy and Legal Affairs Division is not a legal office and most of its staff are not lawyers.[25] (DICA does not have a permanent in-house legal division.) Other divisions of DICA have responsibility for supporting the MIC in issuing investment permits and for the performance of DICA's other functions, including investment promotion, investment monitoring, company registration, and collection of investment statistics.[26]

In contrast to DICA, the Union Attorney General's Office (UAGO) is staffed by lawyers and is responsible for legal affairs across government. It has four departments, of which two are potentially relevant to investment governance.[27] The first is the Legal Advice Department, which includes both the International Law and ASEAN Affairs Division and the Commercial Contract Division. The second is the Legislative Vetting and Legal Translation Department. The International Law and ASEAN Affairs Division within the Legal Advice Department is the primary node of institutional knowledge of international law within the government of Myanmar. It is responsible for legal review of all treaties concluded by Myanmar, including investment treaties.[28]

---

[22] *Ibid.*, ss. 36–39.
[23] See Section 5.2.2.
[24] Interview 7, 2018; Interview 14, 2019; Interview 15, 2019.
[25] Interview 16, 2019.
[26] DICA, 'Values, Development and Structure', www.dica.gov.mm/en/values-development-and-structure.
[27] The other two departments are the Prosecution Department and the Administrative Department.
[28] Interview 2, 2018.

5.2.2 Negotiating and Entering into Investment Treaties

Due to its limited capacity, Myanmar does not initiate negotiations for new investment treaties.[29] In the case of bilateral investment treaties (BITs), this means that the proposal to open negotiations inevitably comes from Myanmar's counterparty. As a result, such negotiations are invariably conducted on the basis of that state's model BIT.[30] ASEAN investment treaties, of which there are several, are somewhat different, as the decision to commence negotiations is made at the regional level.

DICA is the lead agency, which is responsible for negotiating investment treaties.[31] In the case of proposed BITs, DICA is normally responsible for receiving and evaluating proposals to begin negotiations for an investment treaty. This evaluation is guided by the potential benefits of the treaty to Myanmar,[32] but any evaluation of benefits appears to be more impressionistic than systematic. Interviewees did not refer to any framework for assessing or valuing costs and benefits, and there is no publicly available information to suggest that such a framework for policy evaluation exists.[33] On the basis of this evaluation, DICA makes a recommendation to the Minister of Finance and Planning.

In deciding whether to recommend launching negotiations of a new BIT, the main consideration appears to be whether the counterparty is, or has the potential to be, a significant source of investment for Myanmar. Interviewees from both DICA and UAGO, which does not play a direct role in this evaluation, suggested that DICA's leadership tends to have a more positive view of the potential benefits of investment treaties than both UAGO and specialists within DICA's own Policy and Legal Affairs Division.[34] DICA's leadership's focus on the perceived benefit of attracting foreign investment is consistent with DICA's mandate as an investment promotion agency.[35] In contrast, UAGO, which would play a significant role in defending any investment treaty claim against Myanmar, is more conscious of the legal risks associated with the treaties, including at the leadership level.

---

[29] Interview 6, 2018.
[30] Ibid.
[31] Interview 1, 2018.
[32] Ibid.
[33] Myanmar is certainly not unique in this respect. See generally Poulsen, *Bounded Rationality and Economic Diplomacy: The Politics of Investment Treaties in Developing Countries*.
[34] Interview 3, 2018; Interview 4, 2018; Interview 13, 2019.
[35] Interview 15, 2019.

5.2.2.1   Government Knowledge of Investment Treaties
Associated with Participation in Negotiations

During discussions about the negotiation of investment treaties, some members of DICA's negotiating team showed familiarity with global legal and policy debates about investment treaties. One interviewee cited the difficulties that India has had in convincing other states to enter into investment treaties based on the new Indian model BIT.[36] Another referred specifically to 'next generation' investment treaty provisions being promoted by UNCTAD, as a way to mitigate some of the legal risks associated with investment treaties. When Myanmar proposed the inclusion of such language, its negotiating partner insisted on its preferred – more investor-friendly – language, arguing that Myanmar had previously accepted such provisions in investment treaties with other states.[37] Despite this evident familiarity with investment treaties as shown by key officials within the Policy and Legal Affairs Division, some interviewees also described situations in which these key officials struggled to grapple with technical issues arising in the course of negotiations.[38]

Formally, UAGO's only role during the negotiations of investment treaties is to provide a legal opinion on the proposed text of an investment treaty *after* negotiations have been concluded. Reopening the negotiated text at this point in response to any concerns identified in the legal review is exceedingly difficult.[39] As a practical workaround, some DICA and UAGO staff have established a pattern of discussing legal concerns about investment treaties under negotiation informally, while negotiations are still ongoing.[40] For present purposes, this practice is relevant because it illustrates some level of knowledge of investment treaties within UAGO and at least some sharing of information between these two key nodes of knowledge about investment treaties.

Beyond DICA and UAGO, other government agencies are sometimes involved in investment treaty negotiations – specifically, the Internal Revenue Department, Ministry of Natural Resources and Environmental Conservation, the Ministry of Industry, the Ministry of Commerce, and the Central Bank.[41] Representatives from these agencies regularly attend

---

[36] Interview 6, 2018.
[37] Interview 4, 2018.
[38] Interview 15, 2019.
[39] Interview 3, 2018; Interview 4, 2018.
[40] Interview 4, 2018.
[41] *Ibid.*; Interview 7, 2018; Interview 6, 2018.

BIT negotiating rounds held in Myanmar. They appear to play a minor role in the negotiation process, only raising issues perceived as falling within the mandate of the agency in question – for example, concerns around free transfer of funds in the case of the Central Bank.[42] Due to financial constraints, they do not attend negotiating rounds held overseas, but are invited to comment on draft texts emerging from these rounds.[43] Regional investment treaties and investment chapters of regional free trade agreements (FTAs) are handled differently, and other agencies would not necessarily be present in the negotiating room.[44]

The involvement of representatives of these agencies in the negotiation process demonstrates that there is at least some awareness of investment treaties beyond DICA and UAGO. Due to the challenge of accessing these agencies, this project did not directly investigate the depth of knowledge of investment treaties' implications within these agencies. That said, interviewees expressed doubts about the breadth of understanding of investment treaties among these representatives, few of whom have a legal background.[45] These doubts are consistent with the consensus among interviewees that there is negligible awareness of investment treaties across the government in Myanmar.[46]

Once the final text of an investment treaty has been agreed to, the treaty must be approved by the Economic Committee of Cabinet (in the case of BITs), or by parliament (in the case of regional investment treaties and FTAs).[47] There is no evidence that these processes have ever blocked the entry into force of an investment treaty. On the contrary, the fact that ministerial visits were the catalyst for negotiations of some investment treaties suggests a generally positive attitude towards these treaties.[48] At

---

[42] Interview 13, 2019.

[43] Interview 7, 2018.

[44] Interview 4, 2018.

[45] Interview 13, 2019; Interview 16, 2019.

[46] See Section 5.2.3.1.

[47] Interview 6, 2018. Section 108 of the Myanmar Constitution provides that parliament must approve ratification of treaties, but also that the parliament may confer on the President the authority to enter into treaties. Presumably, such a conferral has been provided in relation to bilateral investment treaties, although there is no publicly available English language record of it.

[48] The decision to negotiate the Japan–Myanmar BIT (2013) had its origins in the President of Myanmar's visit to Japan: Interview 6, 2018. Similarly, current negotiations of the EU–Myanmar BIT were also initiated following a Ministerial visit: Interview 1, 2018. See also European Commission, Press Release, 'EU and Myanmar/Burma to Negotiate an Investment Protection Agreement', 20 March 2014.

least one interviewee suggested that there was little real understanding of the content or implications of investment treaties at the Ministerial level or in cabinet.[49]

5.2.2.2 Implementation of Investment Treaties Following Negotiation

One way in which the conclusion of new investment treaties might, in principle, influence domestic governance is by triggering a process to embed the treaty in decision making across government. However, Myanmar's conclusion of a new investment treaty does not trigger any 'monitoring process' to review the consistency of existing laws and government practices with the treaty.[50] Moreover, this project did not identify any case where the conclusion of a particular investment treaty had led to ad hoc changes in Myanmar's laws or regulations.

Since 2016, DICA has sent letters to line Ministries as well as state- and region-level governments following the conclusion of new investment treaties.[51] The purpose of these notifications is not to explain the details of investment treaties or their implications to other organs of government. Rather, it is to alert them to the basic fact that foreign investment covered by MIC permits may also be covered by BITs and regional agreements. The rationale is to encourage these arms of government to contact DICA for advice before interfering with a foreign investment. DICA is particularly concerned about the risk of line Ministries acting inconsistently with investment liberalisation obligations in investment treaties – for example, the ongoing practice of some ministries to block or impose additional conditions on foreign investment in sectors in which Myanmar has agreed to allow foreign investment on a non-discriminatory basis.[52] However, interviewees also acknowledged that, as of July 2018, there were no cases in which a line Ministry or state or regional government had sought advice from DICA as a result of these notifications.[53] This suggests that this practice of sending formal notifications, or what the introduction chapter to this book refers to as informational internalisation measures,[54] has not yet had a significant impact on the decision making of these arms of government.

---

[49] Interview 10, 2018.
[50] Interview 7, 2018; Interview 4, 2018.
[51] Interview 6, 2018; Interview 4, 2018.
[52] Interview 4, 2018.
[53] Interview 6, 2018.
[54] See Chapter 1.

5.2.2.3   Policy Feedback Loops
in Investment Treaty Negotiation?

Previous research on investment treaties suggests that a state's experience with the investment treaty regime – particularly, its first experience as a respondent in investment treaty arbitration – encourages a state to reconsider the negotiation of new investment treaties.[55] Myanmar's investment treaty program does not fit this pattern. Myanmar does have one experience as a respondent in investment treaty arbitration, in the case of *Yaung Chi Oo* v. *Myanmar* during the military era.[56] Notably, there appears to be little awareness of this case among DICA officials who are responsible for Myanmar's current investment treaty program.[57] There was more awareness of this case within UAGO, although interviewees could not recall any changes to Myanmar's approach to investment treaties as a result of that arbitration.[58]

More generally, there is no institutionalised process through which Myanmar's experience with existing investment treaties, or its wider experience managing foreign investment, is fed back into its negotiation strategy for new investment treaties. Interviewees were unable to think of any examples where problems relating to investment treaties or foreign investment had led to a change in Myanmar's position in investment treaty negotiations.[59]

5.2.3   Internalisation of Investment Treaties
in Legislation and Legislative Processes

Myanmar is a dualist country. International law does not automatically become part of the domestic legal system, unless it is incorporated through laws or regulations. However, investment treaties could still affect the content of Myanmar law (in a formal sense) in several ways, including

---

[55] Poulsen and Aisbett, 'When the Claim Hits'.

[56] *Yaung Chi Oo Trading Pte Ltd* v. *Government of the Union of Myanmar*, ASEAN I.D. Case No. ARB/01/1, Award (31 March 2003). The case concerned the military takeover of a brewery jointly owned by Singaporean company in 1998 and the alleged freezing of certain bank accounts of the investor. The final award in the arbitration was rendered in March 2003 and the dispute was decided in favour of the state.

[57] At this point, it is important to note that the transition from military to quasi-civilian rule in 2011 was a high-level political transition that was not accompanied by a purge, or even major reform, of the bureaucratic apparatus. The fact of the transition does not, in itself, provide an explanation for a loss of bureaucratic memory.

[58] Interview 3, 2018.

[59] Interview 4, 2018; Interview 5, 2018.

through the enactment of laws transposing Myanmar's obligations under investment treaties into domestic law and, more broadly, through processes of review intended to ensure consistency between new laws and regulations and Myanmar's investment treaty obligations (Calamita and Berman refer to such mechanisms as internalisation through monitoring processes).[60] Insofar as investment treaties do affect the content of Myanmar law by any one of these mechanisms, further questions arise as to how these effects on Myanmar law shape the exercise of government authority in practice.[61]

When asked about whether investment treaties were incorporated in Myanmar's laws and law-making processes, several interviewees referred to the provisions of the new Myanmar Investment Law 2016. It was only when explicitly asked about wider legislative processes that some interviewees discussed the consistency of other legislation with investment treaties.[62] This dynamic is interesting in itself, as it suggests that many interviewees did not perceive the obligations contained in investment treaties to be relevant to Myanmar's domestic laws except insofar as those laws were addressed explicitly to the notion of 'investment'. This understanding sits uneasily with patterns of litigation under investment treaties. Laws that nominally address issues such as environmental protection, land rights, tax and public health regulation have been the subject of investment treaty claims.

5.2.3.1   Internalisation of Investment Treaties in Legislation and Regulation Generally

In Myanmar, new laws and regulations are normally drafted by the relevant line Ministry.[63] For example, the Mining Regulations 2018[64] were drafted by the Division of Mines within the Ministry of Natural Resources and Environmental Conservation,[65] whereas the Myanmar Companies Regulations 2018 were drafted by DICA.[66] Laws and regulations are often

---

[60] See Chapter 1.
[61] These issues are dealt with in Section 5.2.4, focusing particularly on the executive action under the framework established by the Myanmar Investment Law 2016.
[62] Interview 3, 2018; Interview 4, 2018.
[63] Interview 2, 2018; Interview 12, 2018.
[64] Ministry of Natural Resources and Environmental Conservation, Notification No. 13/2018, 13 February 2018.
[65] Kyaw Lin Htoon, 'Long-Delayed Mines Law Comes into Effect', *Frontier Myanmar*, 2 March 2018.
[66] Ministry of Planning and Finance, Notification No. 66/2018, 23 July 2018.

poorly drafted, reflecting, in part, the fact that line Ministries generally have no in-house legal capacity.[67] Occasionally, new laws are drafted by the Union Government – that is, the national executive – or by members of parliament themselves.[68] These groups also lack basic legal expertise, and are unlikely to be aware of investment treaties. As such, it is exceedingly unlikely that the content of investment treaties is reflected in the initial drafting of laws and regulations.

An example of the compartmentalisation of legislative drafting within responsible agencies is the new Companies Law, which DICA began drafting in 2014 and was enacted in 2017. The law was drafted by the Companies Affairs Division within DICA, with the support of external consultants funded by the Asian Development Bank. Both the Companies Law 2017,[69] and the Companies Act 1914,[70] which it replaced, distinguish between 'Myanmar companies' and 'foreign companies' on the basis of the percentage of foreign ownership.[71] Classification as a foreign company under the Companies Act 1914 meant that an entity was subject to a range of discriminatory restrictions on operation in various sectors.[72] The original rationale for revising the Companies Act 1914 was to lift the threshold for classification as a foreign company, thereby making it easier for foreign investors to acquire stakes in local businesses.[73] In this way, the revision to the Companies Act 1914 squarely raised questions of compliance with the investment liberalisation obligations contained in Myanmar's investment treaties – notably, the ASEAN Comprehensive Investment Agreement,[74] and the Myanmar–Japan BIT.[75] For this reason, one might have expected

---

[67] Interview 3, 2018; Interview 10, 2018.

[68] Melinda Thet Tun, 'Making Better Laws for Myanmar'; Victoria Hasson and Franklin de Vrieze, *The Union Assembly of Myanmar: Context Analysis* (Westminster Foundation for Democracy, 2016).

[69] Myanmar Companies Law, Pyidaungsu Hluttaw Law No. 29/2017, 6 December 2017.

[70] Burma Companies Act, 1 April 1914.

[71] Myanmar Companies Law 2017, s. 1(c)(xiv); see also Berwin Leighton Paisner, *Guide to the Myanmar Companies Law* (undated).

[72] Interview 15, 2019; Thompson Chau, 'Examining the Companies Act', *Myanmar Times*, 5 September 2017; Duane Morris LLP, *New Myanmar Companies Law 2017: Implications for Foreign Companies and Investors* (Duane Morris LLP, 13 December 2017).

[73] Interview 15, 2019.

[74] ASEAN Comprehensive Investment Agreement (2009).

[75] Japan–Myanmar BIT (2013). Julien Chaisse and Sufian Jusoh, *The ASEAN Comprehensive Investment Agreement: The Regionalisation of Laws and Policy on Foreign Investment* (Edward Elgar, 2016), 67; Jonathan Bonnitcha, 'The Myanmar-Japan Bilateral Investment Treaty', International Institute for Sustainable Development (March 2014), 6.

the new Companies Law to have been drafted with compliance with Myanmar's obligations under investment treaties in mind. However, the potential intersections between them were not considered in any meaningful way even though different divisions in the same Yangon office of the same agency – DICA – were responsible for the new Companies Law and for investment treaties.[76] In terms of the introductory chapter of this volume, this speaks to the absence of not only formal, but also informal and ad hoc monitoring processes, even in relation to laws that clearly intersect with Myanmar's investment treaty obligations.

A distinct mechanism by which investment treaties could influence Myanmar's laws and regulations is through centralised processes of legislative and regulatory review. The Legislative Vetting and Translation Department of UAGO has the responsibility to review all new laws and regulations in Myanmar.[77] In principle, the Legislative Vetting and Translation Department has the role of vetting laws and regulations for consistency with Myanmar's Constitution and compliance with international law.[78] In practice, however, this project did not uncover any examples of changes that had been made to the draft text of proposed laws or regulations reflecting concerns about consistency with investment treaties.

Several interviewees from outside the Legislative Vetting and Translation Department said that, so far as they were aware, the legislative vetting process did not review, or monitor, new laws or regulations for consistency with investment treaties, and provided additional information to corroborate their view.[79] One recounted an experience of receiving comments on a draft law from the Legislative Vetting and Translation Department that 'focused on the form, rather than the substance of the law' and showed both a lack of 'technical expertise [and] policy understanding'.[80] Others described the Department as, 'chaotic', 'over-stretched', and '[lacking] the capacity to scrutinise legislation effectively'.[81]

Unfortunately, it was not possible to interview any government officials from within the Legislative Vetting and Translation Department to directly confirm that they did not review draft legislation for compliance with investment treaties. Interviewees suggested that, for reasons

---

[76] Interview 15, 2019.
[77] Interview 2, 2018.
[78] Interview 3, 2018; Interview 12, 2018.
[79] For example, Interview 3, 2018.
[80] Interview 15, 2019.
[81] Interview 12, 2018; Melinda Thet Tun, 'Making Better Laws for Myanmar'.

unrelated to investment treaties, there was a degree of sensitivity around discussing the legislative vetting process.[82] Nevertheless, the suggestion that the legislative vetting process in Myanmar does not include review for consistency with investment treaties is unsurprising. Even in countries with much greater bureaucratic capacity than Myanmar, reviewing all new laws and regulations for consistency with the entire corpus of international law would be a demanding task. In Myanmar, any oversight is made even more challenging due to a sharp increase in new law making across a wider range of areas since the 2011 transition.

In relation to new laws specifically, a final stage in the legislative process involves review through parliamentary committees – including the Bills Committee of each of the two houses of Myanmar parliament.[83] While the committee process has attracted attention from reformers seeking to support the functioning of Myanmar's democratic institutions,[84] none of the interviewees mentioned the committee process when responding to questions about the role of investment treaties in legislative processes. There is no evidence that the members of these parliamentary committees have any meaningful awareness of investment treaties,[85] much less that they have modified draft laws in light of concerns about their consistency with investment treaties.

To conclude, there is no evidence of any monitoring processes, whether formal or informal, that seek to ensure consistency between new laws and regulations and Myanmar's obligations under investment treaties.

---

[82] Interview 12, 2018.

[83] Renaud Egreteau, *Parliamentary Development in Myanmar: An Overview of the Union Parliament, 2011–2016* (The Asia Foundation, May 2017).

[84] Victoria Hasson and Franklin de Vrieze, *The Union Assembly of Myanmar: Context Analysis*; Melissa Crouch, *The Constitution of Myanmar: A Contextual Analysis* (Hart Publishing, 2019).

[85] The records of committee proceedings are not publicly available. The records of parliamentary debates are publicly available, but only in Burmese and not in an easily searchable format. The New Light of Myanmar – an official government newspaper that reports in English on parliamentary proceedings – has a searchable online archive of its reports going back to August 2014. An electronic search of this archive revealed only a handful of mentions of investment treaty in reports of parliamentary proceedings, all of which involved generic references to the benefits of the ACIA in debates to approve the amendment of that treaty. See Aung Ye Thwin and Aye Thant, '2nd Pyidaungsu Hluttaw 6th Session 3rd Day Meeting', *New Light of Myanmar*, 25 October 2017; Myanmar News Agency, 'Pyidaungsu Hluttaw Holds Tenth-day Meeting, Releases Peace Conference statement', *New Light of Myanmar*, 30 August 2016; Myanmar News Agency, 'Pyidaungsu Hluttaw Approves Bill Amending the 2016 Union Budget Law', *New Light of Myanmar*, 23 August 2016.

5.2.3.2   Internalisation of Investment Treaties
in the Myanmar Investment Law 2016

While investment treaties have had little impact on Myanmar law and legislative processes in general, they have had at least some impact on the MIL. In 2012, in the early stage of its transition from military rule, Myanmar adopted two new, nearly identical, laws: the Foreign Investment Law 2012 and the Myanmar Citizens Investment Law 2012. In 2013, the IFC proposed that these two new laws should be replaced by a single, revised investment law addressing both domestic and foreign investment.[86] Early drafts of this law were prepared for DICA by the IFC.[87] These drafts focused on issues of investment protection and, in contrast to the two laws they were intended to replace, followed the structure and content of investment treaties closely.[88] Following a public consultation process in the first half of 2015, several comments were made about these proposals.[89] These comments evidently influenced the drafting process, as the final version of the Law contains more careful language limiting the scope of protections guaranteed to investors, as well as far more detail on the operation of Myanmar's investment admission and governance regime.

The final version of the MIL, as enacted, covers investors of all nationalities, including Myanmar investors. As such, on the basis of purely formalist analysis, the MIL extends new legal rights to investors that do not benefit from the protection of an investment treaty. These rights are found in Chapters 11 to 15 of the MIL. However, the MIL also appears to confer *less* protection on investment than would be the case under some of Myanmar's investment treaties. For example, section 48 of the MIL guarantees investors fair and equitable treatment, but only in respect of:

(a) the right to obtain the relevant information on any measures or decision which has a significant impact on the investors and their direct investments;

---

[86] Interview 14, 2019.

[87] See Jonathan Bonnitcha, Lauge N. S. Poulsen and Michael Waibel, *The Political Economy of the Investment Treaty Regime* (Oxford University Press, 2017).

[88] Myanmar Investment Law, Draft, 29 August 2014 (on file with author); Myanmar Investment Law, Draft, 24 February 2015 (on file with author); Interview 16, 2019.

[89] See for example Comments from Vicky Bowman, Director, Myanmar Centre for Responsible Business, to Directorate of Investment and Company Administration, 'Comments on the Myanmar Investment Law' (27 March 2015), www.myanmar-responsiblebusiness.org/pdf/2015-03-30-MCRB-Comments-on-draft-Myanmar-Investment-Law.pdf, 3; Sandar Lwin, 'DICA Calls for More Local Feedback on Draft Investment Law', *Myanmar Times*, 7 May 2015.

(b) the right to due process of law and the right to appeal on similar measures, including any change to the terms and conditions under any license, a Permit or an Endorsement granted by the Government to the investors and their direct investments.[90]

Another difference is that section 53 appears to envisage circumstances where compensation for expropriation could be less than an investment's full market value.[91] Most investment treaties do not recognise such circumstances.[92]

These discrepancies are relevant to debates about whether investment treaties lead to legal 'spillover effects' into the domestic legal system, which then benefit investors not covered by investment treaties. While awareness of Myanmar's investment treaties did influence the drafting of the MIL, the standards of investment protection contained in the latter are defined independently of the former. In other words, there has been *some* spillover effect to the Myanmar legal regime, but there has also been some adaption of the transplanted standards in the process.

A further issue arises in relation to the scope of the MIL. As a matter of Myanmar law, it seems that the MIL is intended to prevail over other laws in the event of conflict. Section 94 of the MIL provides that: '[n]otwithstanding anything contained in any other law, matters relating to any provision in this Law shall be carried out in accordance with this Law'.

In addition to conferring rights on foreign investors, the MIL also affirms investors' responsibilities. Section 65 provides that the investor must comply with licence terms, conditions imposed by relevant Ministries, labour laws, and the Environmental Conservation Law, among others. As a formal matter of Myanmar law, it is not clear what would happen if – for example – Myanmar took action against an investor for failure to comply with the Environmental Conservation Law and the investor subsequently argued that this action breached its rights as provided under Chapters 11 to 15 of the MIL. In contrast, it is clear that action taken against an investor for failure to comply with domestic law

---

[90] Myanmar Investment Law 2016, s. 48.

[91] This appears to reflect concerns that could arise from the nationalisation of investments that were originally transferred by the military regime to investors on a non-arm's length basis, see Bonnitcha, Poulsen and Waibel, 'The Political Economy of the Investment Treaty Regime'.

[92] For investors covered by an investment treaty, these discrepancies are resolved by section 91 of the MIL, which provides that the provisions of Myanmar's treaties prevail over the MIL to the extent of any inconsistency.

may well breach the rights that investment treaties guarantee to foreign investors.[93] This is another potential point of difference between the scope of the rights that investment treaties confer on foreign investors and the scope of the investors' rights transposed into domestic law.

In any event, a formal legal analysis of the rights conferred by the MIL, their scope, and their similarity to the legal standards found in investment treaties, tells us little about investment governance in Myanmar in practice. The following section examines some of the ways in which investment treaties shape the exercise of government authority in Myanmar in practice, including the actions of Myanmar's investment authorities responsible for administering the MIL.

5.2.4　Internalisation of Investment Treaties through Executive Processes and Institutions

Even by the standards of developing countries, the executive branch of government in Myanmar has a low level of capacity.[94] Investment lawyers described basic problems of coordination between Ministries and agencies, including some Ministries' refusal to allow investment in sectors open to foreign investment under the MIL, and another agency's refusal to make the hard copy of an application form for a licence available to the investor even though the investor was required to obtain the licence as a precondition for investing.[95] In this general context, it is unsurprising to find little evidence of internalisation of investment treaties in decision making across the executive branch.

This section begins with a general overview of the level of awareness of investment treaties across the government in Myanmar. Subsections (2) and (3) examine the impact of investment treaties on decision making in DICA, the MIC and other executive processes. Subsections (4) and (5) then examine the management of investor–state disputes within the executive branch

---

[93] For example, *Técnicas Medioambientales Tecmed* v. *United Mexican States*, ICSID Case No. ARB(AF)/00/2, Award (29 May 2003); *Occidental Petroleum Corporation and Occidental Exploration and Production Company* v. *Republic of Ecuador (II)*, ICSID Case No. ARB/06/11, Award (5 October 2012).

[94] World Bank, 'Worldwide Governance Indicators', http://info.worldbank.org/governance/wgi/. For the purpose of this paper, the executive branch of government is understood broadly to include the Union Government – that is, the national executive – its Ministries, agencies and officials, and the officials and administrative apparatus of sub-national levels of government.

[95] Interview 8, 2018.

of government in Myanmar. Such disputes, and the processes by which they are managed and resolved, constitute mechanisms by which investment treaties could, in principle, have an impact on domestic governance.

5.2.4.1 Awareness of Investment Treaties across Government in Myanmar

Following Myanmar's transition to nominally civilian rule in 2011, many development actors began engaging in capacity building with the Myanmar government. Among other forms of training and advice, this included conducting workshops and capacity building activities in relation to investment treaties, which fall within the conception of 'informational processes' outlined in the Introduction chapter to this volume.[96] At least four international law firms and four more development NGOs have provided some form of capacity building on investment treaties, ranging from one-off workshops to sustained engagement over years. These activities are funded by UNDP and the IFC, among other donors. This engagement focused primarily on the divisions in DICA and UAGO, which are responsible for the negotiation of, and the provision of legal advice on, investment treaties, although officials from other Ministries also attended ad hoc workshops and training events.[97]

These activities suggest that there are some government officials outside DICA and UAGO who are aware of the existence of investment treaties, even if only at a basic level. Nevertheless, the consensus among interviewees was that, beyond a handful of individuals in DICA and UAGO, there is negligible awareness of investment treaties across the government in Myanmar.[98] As one interviewee explained, Myanmar government officials' 'level of knowledge [of investment treaties] is often most strongly informed through direct experience, rather than formal training'.[99] Several other interviewees expressed similar views. One remarked that the 'majority of government officials ... pay little attention to investment treaties. Except for within our Policy and Legal Affairs Division, the other Divisions [of DICA] are not very familiar with investment treaties'.[100] Another observed that '[o]utside DICA things are hopeless. I don't think there is any awareness of investment treaties'.[101]

---

[96] See Chapter 1.
[97] Interview 16, 2019.
[98] For example, Interview 10, 2018.
[99] Interview 16, 2019.
[100] Interview 13, 2019.
[101] Interview 14, 2019

Information provided by other interviewees corroborates these views. For example, interviewees could not recall any occasion on which a Ministry or state or regional government had sought advice from DICA or UAGO on investment treaties.[102] (If there was some awareness of investment treaties in Ministries that interact with foreign investors, one might expect occasional communication with DICA or UAGO in situations that raise concerns about treaty compliance.) And foreign investment lawyers described having to educate officials about the content of Myanmar legislation that the Ministry in question has direct responsibility for administering.[103] If line Ministries struggle to understand laws for which they have portfolio responsibility, it seems unlikely that they are appraised of the wider issues of international law. Foreign investment lawyers also said that it would be exceedingly rare for a foreign investor to invoke the existence of investment treaties in their dealings with government.[104]

To understand why the occasional participation of government officials beyond DICA and UAGO in training events does not lead to sustained understanding of the implications of investment treaties across line Ministries, or any associated effects on government decision making, some reference to the wider 'public administration context'[105] may be useful. The transitional period in Myanmar saw an influx of international organisations and development agencies operating in Myanmar. Many of these organisations had mandates that encompassed the training of government officials. As well as being poorly paid and under-resourced, senior government officials often attended multiple training workshops each month on disparate and unconnected topics. For government officials who do not understand themselves as having direct responsibility for 'investment' issues, training sessions on investment treaties may have seemed of limited relevance, when considered among the many other workshops, issues and imperatives competing for their attention.

In addition to the general public administration context, interviewees also identified two particular obstacles to the diffusion of knowledge of investment treaties across the executive branch. Several interviewees referred to a wider challenge of legal capacity within the government.[106]

---

[102] Interview 6, 2018; Interview 3, 2018; Interview 7, 2018.
[103] Interview 10, 2018; Interview 11, 2018.
[104] Interview 6, 2018; Interview 11, 2018; Interview 8, 2018; Interview 9, 2018.
[105] To adopt the terminology of Calamita and Berman in Chapter 1.
[106] Interview 10, 2018; Interview 3, 2018.

Line Ministries do not have in-house lawyers. Occasionally, retired legal officers from UAGO are posted to Ministries. However, these individuals normally have a background in criminal prosecution; they do not have an understanding of commercial issues or investment law.[107] In response to these concerns, in 2017, the President decreed that Ministries should appoint in-house legal advisors. To date, this decree has not been widely implemented, due to a lack of qualified individuals in practice.[108]

The second obstacle relates to bureaucratic culture. Several interviewees drew a distinction between a Ministry's 'own' laws – laws which that Ministry has the portfolio responsibility to administer – and the wider legal environment. The general impression among interviewees was that Ministries are generally motivated to comply with their own laws, even if they sometimes struggle to understand and implement them.[109] In contrast, Ministries were likely to regard other legal issues as beyond their responsibility. If an official were to learn of investment treaties, they would likely regard it as something that was the responsibility for the part of government that had entered into it.[110]

Although it is not part of the executive branch, it is also important to consider the position of the Myanmar military, known as the Tatmadaw. Under the 2008 Constitution, the Tatmadaw is not subject to civilian control or oversight and holds 25 per cent of the seats in Myanmar's parliament. The Tatmadaw also participates actively in the economy through military-linked enterprises,[111] and its actions were responsible for the only investment treaty claim against Myanmar to date. Obvious limitations in access made it impossible to examine the impact of investment treaties on decision making within the Tatmadaw, even prior to the coup. But it is reasonable to assume that there is also little knowledge of investment treaties with Tatmadaw, not least because of the lack of civilian oversight and wider culture of impunity.

Understanding the role of the Tatmadaw in investment governance will be even more important now, following the coup of February 2021, which occurred after research for this chapter had been completed. For the time being, the military regime is publicly professing to welcome

---

[107] Interview 3, 2018.
[108] *Ibid.*; Interview 10, 2018.
[109] Interview 11, 2018
[110] Interview 10, 2018.
[111] These entitles are called 'special companies' and are governed differently to ordinary companies under Myanmar law. The two most prominent are Union of Myanmar Economic Holdings Limited and Myanmar Economic Corporation.

foreign investment and has asserted that the legal regime governing foreign investment remains unchanged.[112]

5.2.4.2   The Impact of Investment Treaties on Decision Making by DICA and the MIC

The foregoing sections show that there is clearly some awareness of investment treaties within DICA and UAGO. The question then arises as to whether this awareness of investment treaties has any effect on DICA and the MIC's decision making – that is, the extent to which investment treaties lead to actual impact on investment governance. (This question does not arise in relation to UAGO, as UAGO is not a primary decision maker in interactions with investors.) In this subsection, I focus on the MIC's most prominent decision-making function, which is to regulate the admission of new foreign investment through a system of permits and endorsements prescribed by the MIL.[113]

Interviewees were conscious of the relevance of investment treaties to the MIC's decision-making processes on whether to admit new foreign investment.[114] However, interviewees explained that the chain of causation ran from Myanmar's investment policy, which is then reflected in Myanmar law (currently, in Notification No. 15/2017 under the MIL),[115] which is the basis for Myanmar's schedules of liberalisation commitments under various investment treaties. According to this account, investment treaties do not require any liberalisation beyond what is required under Myanmar law.[116] Consistent with this view, interviewees said they were unable to recall any cases in which foreign investors had used the existence of an investment treaty to argue that they should be granted permission to invest in sectors that were restricted to foreign investment as

---

[112] Chan Mya Hywe, 'Senior General Min Aung Hlaing to Maintain Foreign, Economic Policies', *Myanmar Times*, 9 February 2021; 'Myanmar Coup Leader Vows to Protect China-Backed Enterprises', *The Irrawaddy*, 24 May 2021.

[113] Myanmar Investment Law 2016, ss. 36–39.

[114] Interview 7, 2018. In March 2017, approval of new foreign investment projects below the value of USD $5 million was devolved to governments at the state and regional level. This devolution was effected by the MIC; see Myanmar Investment Commission, Notification No. 11/2017, 3 March 2017. This project did not directly probe the impact of investment treaties on governance at the state and region level. Due to their lack of direct involvement in investment treaty negotiations, it is reasonable to assume that state and regional investment commissions have a lower level of awareness of investment treaties than officials in DICA.

[115] Myanmar Investment Commission, Notification No. 15/2017, 10 April 2017.

[116] Interview 6, 2018; Interview 7, 2018.

a matter of Myanmar law.[117] Interviewees also did not report any situations in which the MIC considered applying restrictions on new foreign investment but had been precluded from doing so by liberalisation commitments that had been 'locked in' through investment treaties. In short, while some DICA officials are aware that investment treaties are relevant to their role in the admission of foreign investment, it is not clear that the existence of the treaties have significantly affected the way they carry out this responsibility.

5.2.4.3   Informational and Monitoring Processes to Ensure Executive Action beyond DICA Is Consistent with Investment Treaties

A wider question is whether investment treaties have any impact on decision making in the executive branch beyond DICA. DICA does have a practice of notifying Ministries and sub-national levels of government of the conclusion of new investment treaties.[118] Beyond this practice of notification, there does not appear to be any monitoring processes to ensure the compliance with investment treaties across the executive branch of government.[119] It does not have mechanisms to require or encourage officials to seek advice on the consistency of proposed measures with investment treaties. Neither DICA nor UAGO appears to have ever conducted a diagnostic exercise to ascertain whether the practices of Ministries and other agencies of government are consistent with the standards of investment protection that investment treaties guarantee. Myanmar does not have a handbook on investment treaties – or any similar document – that is distributed to officials across the government with a view to informing them of the implications of investment treaties for their role.[120] Given the low level of awareness of investment treaties across the government in Myanmar and the absence of informational and monitoring processes to ensure compliance with them, it is reasonable to conclude that investment treaties have a negligible ex ante impact on decision making in the executive branch in Myanmar beyond DICA itself.

---

[117]   Interview 7, 2018.
[118]   This practice is discussed in Section 5.2.1.
[119]   Interview 6, 2018.
[120]   One interviewee suggested that, as of mid-2018, Myanmar was, with the support of an unidentified external partner, in the process of finalising a handbook on investment treaties for distribution *within* DICA: Interview 4, 2018. Other interviewees were unable to confirm the existence of such a document – for example Interview 16, 2019 – which, in any case, would be of limited relevance to ensuring the consistency of executive action *beyond* DICA.

Situations in which the investor raises the existence of an investment treaty in its dealing with the government – for example, in the context of a disagreement or dispute – raise distinct issues.[121] Even if government officials are generally unaware of investment treaties, the investor's invocation of the treaties in particular instances could provide a mechanism through which the treaties influence government decision making. This could occur either within the institutional structure of formal remedial processes of the sort theorised by Calamita and Berman in the Introductory chapter or in the context of more informal interactions. The following subsections examine this possibility.

5.2.4.4   The Development of Processes to Manage Investment Disputes

The MIL contains a new provision that requires the MIC to 'establish and manage a grievance mechanism to resolve and prevent the occurrence of disputes, and carry out relevant inquiries for the investment issues before reaching the stage of a legal dispute'.[122]

This provision is similar to other provisions included in earlier drafts of the MIL prepared by the IFC.[123] A commentary to the February 2015 draft prepared by the IFC argued that one of the rationales for such a mechanism is to resolve investors' grievances before they escalate into investor–state arbitrations, including arbitrations initiated under an investment treaty.[124] In interviews, some government officials agreed that one purpose of establishing a grievance mechanism was to reduce the risk of investment disputes triggering investor–state arbitration against Myanmar, whether initiated under an investment contract or an investment treaty.[125] Other government officials described investor grievance mechanisms (IGMs) as a way to build trust among investors, thereby improving investment retention,[126] and as a way to formalise the ad hoc role the MIC was already playing in resolving investor–state disputes.[127] Thus, overall, it seems that the existence of investment treaties was one factor that indirectly

---

121 Bonnitcha, 'Substantive Protection Under Investment Treaties', 118.
122 Myanmar Investment Law 2016, s. 82.
123 Myanmar Investment Law, Draft, 29 August 2014 (on file with author), s. 20; Myanmar Investment Law, Draft, 24 February 2015 (on file with author), s. 20.
124 Myanmar Investment Law, Draft, 9 March 2015 (on file with author), Explanatory Note; similarly, see World Bank Group, 'Investor Grievance Mechanisms: Concept and Practice', presentation slides (13 February 2018) (on file with author).
125 Interview 3, 2018.
126 Interview 5, 2018; Interview 14, 2019.
127 Interview 5, 2018; Interview 1, 2018.

influenced the decision to adopt an IGM.[128] The mechanism thus falls into what Calamita and Berman refer to as a remedial mechanism, albeit one that is not exclusively (or even primarily) 'designed to correct or defend the state's compliance with its international obligations'.[129] The remainder of this section explores the impact of that decision on the process by which investment disputes are resolved in Myanmar.

Through the Myanmar Investment Rules 2017 promulgated under the MIL,[130] the MIC established an Investor Assistance Committee (IAC). The IAC temporarily implements the mandate of section 82 of the MIL; it is only intended to exist until a new IGM with greater powers and a more formalised legal structure can be established. Many interviewees referred to the detail of ongoing discussions about the design of a future IGM. However, as of February 2021, a new IGM had not been established and it now seems doubtful if the institution will ever come into existence. This section focuses on the IAC, as it operated in 2018, when the bulk of the research for this project was conducted.

Like the MIC, the IAC is a cross-ministerial institution. Its chairman is the Permanent-Secretary – the most senior public servant – of the Ministry of Commerce. Its nine ordinary members comprise three senior officials from different divisions within DICA, as well as one senior official each from UAGO, the Internal Revenue Department, the Land Record Department, the Environment and Conservation Department, the Trade Department, and the Customs Department.[131]

The IAC is available to both Myanmar and foreign investors. Rule 170 of the Myanmar Investment Rules enumerates types of grievances and disputes that investors may submit to the IAC:

An Investor may submit notice of their grievance or dispute to the IAC who believes in good faith that:

(a) a decision of governmental department or governmental organisation in respect of their Investment was incorrectly made;

(b) that an application for a permit, licence, registration or approval was incorrectly refused by governmental department or governmental organisation; or

(c) that any right, protection or Approval benefiting them under the Law has been frustrated.

---

[128] Interview 14, 2019.
[129] See Chapter 1.
[130] Ministry of Planning and Finance, Notification No. 35/2017, 30 March 2017.
[131] Interview 5, 2018.

Once the investor has submitted its complaint, the IAC determines whether the complaint is justified.[132] Essentially, this involves a determination of whether the investor was treated in accordance with Myanmar law.[133] In its evaluation of the investor's complaints, the IAC does not routinely consider whether investors are treated in accordance with the protections guaranteed by investment treaties, although interviewees said that the provisions of an applicable investment treaty would be considered if the issue was raised by the investor.[134] Section 5.2.4.6 describes one such case involving a proposed coal power station.

In its evaluation of the investor's complaint, the IAC seeks to involve relevant line Ministries and government agencies. This practice reflects the IAC's limited powers. The IAC's ultimate decision on the complaint takes the form of a recommendation to the MIC.[135] It does not have any legal force of its own. In acting on the IAC's recommendation, the MIC does not have the power to award compensation to an investor,[136] or to compel the concerned Ministry to resolve the dispute in a particular way.[137]

The operation of the IAC in this respect is also consistent with the wider practice of the MIC in seeking to resolve disputes with investors, including those that are never submitted to the IAC process, through negotiations.[138] This does not mean that the resolution of these disputes is costless to Myanmar. For example, the MIC has resolved several disputes – including the well-known Marga Landmark dispute – by granting valuable rights to use public land to the investor.[139] Although neither the MIL nor the Myanmar Investment Rules refer to rights of appeal against the MIC's action in response to an investor complaint, interviewees explained that an investor that is unhappy with the way the MIC has resolved its complaint is entitled to appeal that decision to Cabinet, which is able to award compensation.[140]

As of July 2018, when the majority of the interviews for this project were conducted, investors had submitted five disputes to the IAC. Three of these disputes involved foreign investors, while two involved Myanmar investors.

---

[132] Interview 1, 2018.
[133] *Ibid.*; Interview 5, 2018.
[134] Interview 1, 2018.
[135] *Ibid.*
[136] *Ibid.*
[137] Interview 5, 2018.
[138] *Ibid.*; Interview 6, 2018.
[139] Kyaw Phyo Tha, 'Education Ministry Wants to Take Bank Rangoon Land from Property Developer', *The Irrawaddy*, 29 November 2016.
[140] Interview 1, 2018.

Two had been resolved as of July 2018, while three were ongoing. Four of the five disputes related to land rights authorisation, while the fifth – which is described in Section 5.2.4.6 – related to a line Ministry's refusal to issue a permit required for an investment to go ahead.[141] This is consistent with the wider pattern of disputes described by foreign investment lawyers, the most of which also relate to land use authorisation or regulatory permits.[142]

5.2.4.5 Processes to Manage Threats of Investor–State Arbitration Specifically

Myanmar does not appear to have a specific policy to manage threats of investor–state arbitration. UAGO provides advice on investment treaties in relation to investment disputes that it becomes aware of, but this is not linked to any formalised notification process designed to make UAGO aware of disputes with a treaty dimension.[143] Consistently with the absence of such a mechanism, in at least one, or probably two of the three cases described in the following section, the investor's invocation of an investment treaty did not lead to any legal evaluation of the strength of the investor's treaty claim.

Myanmar does not have a formal policy in place to manage the defence of investment treaty claims.[144] In the case of investment disputes more generally, the line Ministry whose conduct gave rise to the dispute is responsible for defending the claim. UAGO is also involved in the defence through the provision of legal advice.[145] It appears that this practice was followed in Myanmar's only experience of investment treaty arbitration to date – *Yaung Chi Oo* v. *Myanmar* – in which Myanmar was represented at the hearing by employees of Myanmar Foodstuff Industries (an agency of Ministry of Industry) and UAGO.

5.2.4.6 Myanmar's Response to Investors' Invocation of Investment Treaties: Three Case Studies

Foreign investment lawyers explained that they are involved in regulatory interactions and low-level disagreements with government officials in Myanmar 'every day'.[146] The most common sources of disputes

[141] Interview 5, 2018.
[142] Interview 9, 2018; Interview 8, 2018.
[143] Interview 3, 2018.
[144] *Ibid.*
[145] *Ibid.*
[146] Interview 8, 2018.

are land use authorisation and issues relating to permits and licensing.[147] Notwithstanding the frequency of these interactions, both government officials and foreign investment lawyers stated that it would be exceedingly rare for a foreign investor to invoke the existence of investment treaties in their dealings with the government.[148] Interviewees have remarked that they 'have no experience relying on BITs [when dealing with government] in Myanmar' and that there is 'no confidence that you'd be able to rely on them to get the protection that you need'.[149]

Instead, these day-to-day disputes are framed as requests to the government either to address practical obstacles facing investors or to comply with national law.[150] Only one foreign investment lawyer said they had raised investment treaties in their dealings with the Myanmar government, and even then, only on one occasion. In that case, the reference to the treaty was a strategy to encourage the government to engage with the investor; the investor did not present any particularised legal claims based on the treaty or threaten arbitration explicitly.[151]

Nevertheless, this research identified at least three instances in which a foreign investor, or a foreign investor's home state, had invoked an investment treaty in the context of an investment dispute with some part of the Myanmar state apparatus. No one interviewee was familiar with all three of these instances. This reflects the fact that each of these instances occurred in a different regulatory/institutional context, that Myanmar lacks any mechanism to notify or escalate disputes with an investment treaty dimension to a single government agency, and that none of the instances involved the investor taking any practical steps to initiate arbitration.

The first instance involved an investor's attempt to dissuade the Ministry of Health from adopting a new tobacco labelling requirement of graphic health warnings. The investor had become aware that the Ministry in question was considering adopting the regulation and sought the intercession of the MIC to engage the Ministry of Health. The MIC arranged a meeting at which the investor and Ministry representatives were both present. At this meeting, the investor requested that the Ministry modify the proposed measure, linking this request to the protection to which it was entitled under an investment treaty. The Ministry responded that the measure was justified according to another international treaty (presumably, the

---

[147] *Ibid.*; Interview 9, 2018.
[148] Interview 6, 2018; Interview 8, 2018; Interview 17, 2021.
[149] Interview 11, 2018.
[150] Interview 6, 2018.
[151] Interview 9, 2018.

Framework Convention on Tobacco Control) and that the Ministry was not entitled to meet directly with foreign investors to discuss regulatory processes in any event. The Ministry subsequently declined the investor's requests for further meetings and the measure was introduced. The investor did not take any further legal action. Throughout the process, the MIC did not seek to influence the Ministry's consideration of the investor's request and no advice on the legal merits of the investor's potential treaty claim was provided to the Ministry at any point.[152]

The second instance concerned the invocation of an investment treaty by the investor's home state in parallel to the consideration of the dispute through the IAC. The dispute concerned a line Ministry's refusal to issue an environmental permit required for a coal power station to proceed. The Thai investor approached their embassy in Myanmar and embassy officials then raised the investment treaty in communications with the relevant Myanmar Minister. The reference to the treaty was general in nature; it did not involve specification of particular treaty provisions that Myanmar was alleged to have breached. The investor's strategy to involve home state officials was successful in escalating the dispute in a way that engaged the relevant Myanmar minister, and ultimately led to the permit being issued. It appears that no advice on the legal merits of the investor's potential treaty claim was provided to the Ministry at any point, and that concerns about the possibility of investor–state arbitration were not a factor that influenced the decision to grant the permit.[153]

A third instance concerns an investment dispute of significant political sensitivity. In this instance, the investor's home state raised the existence of an investment treaty in high-level government-to-government discussions about the resolution of the dispute. Although lawyers at UAGO were involved to some extent, it is unclear if they provided formal advice on the legal merits of the investor's potential treaty claim.[154] The dispute remained unresolved at the time of writing.

5.2.5 Internalisation of Investment Treaties through Judicial Processes and Practices

In principle, investment treaties could also affect governance in Myanmar through their interaction with judicial processes and practices. One possible example would be Myanmar judges taking investment treaties into account

---

[152] Interview 4, 2018.
[153] Interview 5, 2018.
[154] Interview 3, 2018.

when deciding cases. Myanmar is a dualist country, so judges cannot apply investment treaties directly to cases before them. But – hypothetically – judges might interpret section 91 of the MIL as incorporating investment treaties into Myanmar law. Or, if parties referred to the existence of investment treaties in their arguments, it might influence the judges' approach to cases governed by Myanmar law beyond the MIL. More broadly, investment treaties might influence the development of judicial institutions in Myanmar over time, by diverting litigation and reform energy toward arbitration at the expense of the domestic judicial system.[155]

This project did not uncover any evidence of investment treaties impacting the Myanmar judicial system. For example, interviewees did not mention any training or information sessions on investment treaties that had been organised for judges, even when asked directly.[156] On the contrary, a clear picture emerged of profound disconnection between investment governance in Myanmar (including but not limited to investment treaties) and the domestic judicial system. There was a consensus across all classes of interviewees that Myanmar courts did not constitute a viable forum for the resolution of investor–state disputes, with the possible exception of minor regulatory disputes.

This consensus was expressed in several different ways. It was reflected explicitly in government officials' comments that they were not aware of any investor–state disputes that had been litigated in Myanmar courts.[157] It was also reflected implicitly in government officials' discussions of the IAC and the development of the IGM – institutions to resolve investment disputes without court proceedings. Government interviewees did not mention any link between the design of the IAC/IGM and the Myanmar court system,[158] even when asked follow-up questions about the role of Myanmar courts in investment disputes.[159] It was also reflected in interviews with foreign investment lawyers, who referred to the problem of corruption in local courts, the local courts' reluctance to make decisions against powerful local actors, as well as legal barriers such as requirements relating to standing to bring a constitutional writ.[160] Investment lawyers

---

[155] Tom Ginsburg, 'International Substitutes for Domestic Institutions' (2005) 25 *International Review of Law and Economics* 107.
[156] Interview 13, 2019.
[157] Interview 4, 2018; Interview 5, 2018.
[158] Interview 1, 2018; Interview 6, 2018; Interview 14, 2019.
[159] Interview 4, 2018; Interview 5, 2018.
[160] Interview 9, 2018.

further described local court proceedings as slow and referred to uncertainty about how Myanmar courts would interpret and apply Myanmar law.[161] They indicated either that they had never heard of a foreign investor bringing a claim against the state in Myanmar courts[162] or, if they had, that they would strongly advise against it.[163] These views are consistent with external metrics that purport to measure the rule of law across countries.[164]

In this context, one striking finding of this project is that the investment policy community's efforts to build institutions to resolve investor–state disputes in Myanmar are focused entirely on strengthening institutions than can *substitute* for the Myanmar court system. There is no analogous impetus to strengthen the Myanmar court system's ability to handle investor–state disputes. To be sure, there is a great deal of energy being expended on the reform of the Myanmar court system generally by foreign donors and international organisations. However, these efforts focus on issues such as criminal justice reform, judicial corruption, and access to justice for victims of human rights abuse and land grabbing.[165] They do not focus on investor–state disputes, and there is no evidence that they are motivated by a perceived need to implement Myanmar's investment treaty obligations as they relate to the judiciary.

The development of the IAC and IGM is discussed earlier.[166] These mechanisms are intended to substitute for, rather than complement or strengthen, the Myanmar court system. A further example is the proposal to establish a Myanmar international arbitration centre. This proposal originally came from the investment policy community in Myanmar, but also found support within government.[167] The proposal relates primarily to investment disputes between private parties, but could also provide a forum for arbitration of investor–state disputes. According to its proponents, the rationale for the centre is that, since foreign investors do not

---

[161] Interview 11, 2018.

[162] *Ibid.*; Interview 8, 2018; Interview 11, 2018; Interview 14, 2019.

[163] One foreign investment lawyer said they were aware of a case in which a foreign investor had disputed a small back-tax assessment imposed by the Internal Revenue Department on their investment in Myanmar courts: Interview 8, 2018.

[164] The World Justice Project ranked Myanmar 100th out of 113 countries in its 2017–18 rule of law index. See World Justice Project, *World Justice Project: Rule of Law Index 2017–2018*.

[165] For example, Scott Ciment, 'Fair Trial Guidebook to Support Law Officers Do their Work Better', 31 May 2018, UNDP Myanmar, www.mm.undp.org/content/myanmar/en/home/blog/2018/fair-trial-guidebook-to-support-law-officers-do-their-work-bette.html; Interview 12, 2018.

[166] See Section 5.2.4.3.

[167] Interview 12, 2018; Interview 10, 2018.

trust Myanmar courts, they will inevitably insist on arbitration of disputes. If disputes related to investments are to be resolved through arbitration, it is preferable that arbitration occur in Myanmar rather than offshore. If this proposal does come to fruition, its supporters hope it will allow Myanmar lawyers to gain exposure to the litigation of business disputes and strengthen the rule of law within Myanmar.[168]

While the research for this project suggests that a great deal of reform energy is being devoted to developing substitutes for the resolution of investor–state disputes to the domestic court system, it is less clear that this dynamic is driven by the existence of investment treaties. Investment treaties did play some role in justifying the need for the IAC and IGM,[169] but it is doubtful that these initiatives diverted energy that would otherwise have been directed to the reform of the Myanmar court system. The IFC, which played a central role in driving the development of the IGM,[170] does not have a mandate that extends to justice sector reform, and fundamental judicial reform is vastly more difficult than developing a new mechanism to resolve investor–state disputes within the executive branch. More generally, there is no evidence that more litigation would be channelled through domestic courts in the absence of investment treaties. This is both due to the infrequency of investor–state arbitration under investment treaties, and to the apparent reluctance of foreign investors to litigate investor–state disputes through Myanmar courts regardless of whether they are protected by an investment treaty.

In summary, the findings of this project suggest that investment treaties have not had any significant impact – whether positive or negative – on the domestic judicial system in Myanmar. These findings challenge the claims of investment treaties' proponents, who argue that investment treaties lead to improvements in the rule of law in countries that are bound by them. They also cast doubt on Ginsburg's argument that investment treaties tend to weaken domestic judicial systems by diverting reform energy away from efforts to improve local courts.[171]

5.3   Conclusion

Debates about investment treaties are based on a series of embedded assumptions about the treaties' impact on domestic governance. Through

---

[168] Interview 10, 2018.
[169] See Section 5.2.4.3.
[170] Interview 14, 2019; Interview 15, 2019.
[171] Ginsburg, 'International Substitutes for Domestic Institutions'.

a single detailed case study of Myanmar, this chapter empirically examines whether these assumptions are justified. The research involved a combination of semi-structured interviews and analysis of primary and secondary documents. My experience working on investment treaties within the Government of Myanmar from 2014 to 2016 provided an additional source of background knowledge and facilitated access to government officials.

The findings cast serious doubt on supporters' claims that investment treaties promote good governance and the rule of law. There is no evidence that investment treaties have had any significant impact – whether positive or negative – on the domestic judicial system in Myanmar. If anything, the existence of investment treaties has indirectly strengthened efforts to construct substitutes for the domestic judiciary, such as the proposal to develop an IGM.

Similarly, there is little evidence that investment treaties play a role in the development or review of new legislation or regulation: no monitoring processes are in place to review consistency of new or existing laws with Myanmar's investment treaty obligations. The drafting of the Companies Law 2017 provides a striking example. The new Companies Law was drafted by the Companies Affairs Division of DICA. Meanwhile, the Policy and Legal Affairs Division of DICA, which is located in the same Yangon office, has primary responsibility for Myanmar's investment treaty program. The process of drafting the new Companies Law was well-resourced, through the technical and financial support of the Asian Development Bank. Nevertheless, the overlaps between the two workstreams 'were never really flushed out or resolved'.[172]

The one identified occasion on which investment treaties have had some relevance to a process of legislative development was in the drafting of the new Myanmar Investment Law. But, even in this case, the causal mechanism by which the treaties influenced the process was very different to that assumed by the treaties' proponents. Myanmar did not implement the provisions of investment treaties in its national investment law out of a concern to avoid the risk of claims under investment treaties. Rather, foreign consultants, who had been engaged in the legislative drafting process, used provisions from varying investment treaties as a model in preparing a first draft of the new law. Subsequent consultations on and revisions of the draft led to a final version of the law that resembles provisions from investment treaties to some extent, but also there are also

---

[172] Interview 15, 2019.

novel and unexpected variations. These changes were driven, in part, by concerns that draft was *too similar* in its terms to an investment treaty and that 'having a national law that resembled an international investment treaty could have negative impacts'.[173]

Finally, the findings show that Myanmar's obligations are not deeply or systematically internalised across the executive branch of government. Consistent with previous research in other countries, the picture that emerged during this project was of little-to-no awareness of investment treaties beyond the key nodes of knowledge within government that have direct responsibility for the treaties: DICA and UAGO. For example, this project did not identify any monitoring or informational processes to ensure the compliance with investment treaties across the executive branch of government, such as mechanisms which require officials to seek advice on the consistency of proposed measures with investment treaties or handbooks distributed to officials across government with a view to informing them of the implications of investment treaties for their role. Neither DICA nor UAGO appears to have ever conducted a diagnostic exercise to ascertain whether the practices of Ministries and other agencies of government are consistent with the standards of investment protection that investment treaties guarantee.

Investment treaties did play some role in the resolution of investor–state disputes outside formal processes of litigation. The examples described in Section 5.2.4.6 fall outside the concept of internalisation developed by Calamita and Berman in the Introductory chapter. In any case, given the frequency of investor–state disputes, one remarkable finding of this project is how infrequently investors invoked the existence of the treaties. Even when invoked, the treaties' role in the process of resolving dispute differed from that assumed by both supporters and critics of the treaties.

In one compelling example, a tobacco company attempted to prevent the Ministry of Health Ministry from strengthening graphic health warnings on tobacco products. This was – to adopt the terminology of investment treaties' critics – a clear attempt at 'regulatory chill'. Yet, it proved unsuccessful. The Ministry introduced the measure over the investor's objections. It justified its action by referring to another international treaty and by strategically invoking the limitations of its own mandate to engage directly with foreign investors. This case suggests that even states with low bureaucratic capacity can avoid acceding to investors' demands under certain conditions.

---

[173] Interview 16, 2019.

In another case, a foreign investor successfully sought the intercession of officials from its home state, who raised the investment treaty in communications with the relevant Myanmar Minister. In contrast to the assumptions of treaties' supporters, this was not a case where the treaty provided an impartial forum for the adjudication of investment disputes.[174] Rather, it was a case where the investor used the treaty as a resource to escalate its grievance through diplomatic channels. This case suggests that one way in which investment treaties benefit foreign investors is by providing another weapon to their armoury in the messy process of negotiations.

Looking forward, the findings of this project point to a need for further empirical research on investment treaties' impacts on domestic rule of law and governance. Myanmar is only one case study and detailed empirical work across other countries would assist in building a more comprehensive picture. In the meantime, participants in debates about these treaties should be much more cautious in making claims about their impact. Investment treaties still matter, as the billions of dollars currently at stake in hundreds of unresolved arbitrations attest. But they may not matter for domestic governance in the way we assumed that they did.

[174] Cf. Ibrahim F. I. Shihata, 'Towards a Greater Depoliticization of Investment Disputes: The Roles of ICSID and MIGA' (1986) 1 *ICSID Review – Foreign Investment Law Journal* 1; *Corn Products International, Inc.* v. *United Mexican States*, ICSID Case No. ARB(AF)/04/1, Separate Opinion of Andreas F. Lowenfeld (Award) (18 August 2009), paras. 1–4.

6

The Impact of Investment Treaties
on the Rule of Law in Singapore

DAFINA ATANASOVA[*]

6.1 Introduction

To what extent has Singapore internalised its international investment obligations? And what explains whether and how it has internalised such obligations? The purpose of this chapter is to try to answer this question by opening the black box of Singapore and undertaking an empirical qualitative investigation as to the inner government workings of its internalisation process. In doing so, the chapter applies Calamita's and Berman's internalisation framework, as elaborated in the introduction to this book, and seeks to shed light on the impact of investment treaties on the rule of law in Singapore.[1]

Specialised government ministries and agencies in Singapore possess a high level of knowledge and expertise with respect to Singapore's investment treaty commitments, and there are diverse internalisation measures employed by the government, spreading awareness of investment treaties across the broader administration. At the same time, these internalisation measures are of a general nature (as defined by Calamita and Berman) and not consistently calibrated to situations commonly giving rise to investment disputes. Moreover, the impetus for such internalisation measures has not been – as the rule of law theory laid out in Calamita's and Berman's introduction posits – driven by investment treaties, but, instead, has been triggered by other factors, notably international trade law obligations. There is also limited evidence suggesting investment treaties have led to general improvements in the rule of law in Singapore.

[*] I am indebted to Marcus Teo for providing valuable research on the Singaporean legal system. I thank N. Jansen Calamita, Ayelet Berman, Jonathan Bonnitcha, Eugenio Gomez Chico and the participants in the Centre for International Law (CIL) NUS workshops held as part of the Investment Treaties and National Governance Project for their valuable comments. All mistakes remain, of course, mine.
[1] See Chapter 1.

While most other studies on internalisation focus on developing countries,[2] Singapore is a developed country that scores very high on many factors, which are considered conducive to the internalisation of international obligations: it has a highly efficient bureaucracy, manageable size, and a strong commitment to the respect of international law. As such, the city-state offers a 'most likely' case study for testing the plausibility of claims regarding the effects of investment treaties on domestic governance and the rule of law. Yet, the mixed evidence regarding Singapore's experience with the internalisation of investment treaties suggests that even in the most conducive of governance conditions,[3] their internalisation poses important challenges and has a complex relationship with claims of the treaties' broader governance effects. It also suggests that limited internalisation may be related to some of the other factors captured in Calamita's and Berman's introductory framework and which may warrant further research.

This chapter is organised as follows. Section 6.2 outlines research methods and methodology. Section 6.3 explains why Singapore is a 'most likely'

---

[2] See, for example, Mavluda Sattorova, *The Impact of Investment Treaty Law on Host States: Enabling Good Governance?* (Hart Publishing, 2018); Josef Ostřanský and Facundo Pérez Aznar, 'Investment Treaties and National Governance in India: Rearrangements, Empowerment, and Discipline' (2021) 34 *Leiden Journal of International Law* 373; Anna Sands, 'Does the Investment Treaty Regime Promote Good Governance? The Case of Mining in Santurbán, Colombia', *Investment Treaty News*, 19 December 2020. One notable exception is that of Canada, which is, however, a federal state, entailing a certain degree of administrative complexity; see Christine Côté, 'A Chilling Effect? The Impact of International Investment Agreements on National Regulatory Autonomy in the Areas of Health, Safety and the Environment', PhD thesis, The London School of Economics and Political Science (2014); Gus Van Harten and Dayna N. Scott, 'Investment Treaties and the Internal Vetting of Regulatory Proposals: A Case Study from Canada', *Osgoode Legal Studies Research Paper* No. 26/2016.

[3] It is important to note that the assessments of how conducive the Singaporean environment is to internalisation in this chapter are made in order to test the plausibility of the rule of law theory on its own terms, that is, they do not offer a value judgment on the desirability of internalisation of investment treaties. Indeed, the question of the desirability of internalising investment treaties requires an assessment going beyond the scope of this chapter. Importantly, this question seems to operate at two different levels and the answers to it are also likely to depend on those levels. At a systemic level, the desirability of internalising investment treaties is a question intimately related to the desirability of investment treaties themselves: the cost of internalisation constitutes a negative factor to take into account in the cost–benefit analysis of investment treaties as a policy tool. At the level of decision making of an administrative agency confronted with an existing investment treaty portfolio (and pending decisions on systemic modification), the desirability of internalisation seems more directly related to the litigation risk incurred under them: the cost of internalisation can, under these circumstances, be justified if and to the extent that it limits that litigation risk proportionately.

case study for the internalisation of investment treaties. Sections 6.4 through Section 6.6 present the mechanisms that Singapore has put in place to internalise its investment treaty obligations in the executive, legislature, and judiciary. Section 6.7 concludes.

6.2   Research Methods and Methodology

This research followed an explanatory process-tracing methodology, which sought to identify the causal chain of actors, mechanisms, and events linking investment treaties to actual effects on government decision making.[4] Process tracing is preferred because it serves to illuminate a decision-making process through an inquiry into the *why* and *how* behind the observable result.[5] It aims to identify the causal link between the actions of relevant actors, institutions, and the observable results, allowing for a nuanced understanding of a given process.

In devising the chain of internalisation for the purposes of this research, I adopted a top-down approach, tracing internalisation processes from their point of origin.[6] Namely, I enquired into the activities of the expert agencies in Singapore presumed to possess the greatest knowledge of investment treaties and traced any steps they have taken towards internalising investment treaties within the Singapore government more broadly. I further traced any internalisation processes through their path in the administration, that is, through bureaucrats in non-expert agencies that must transmit the internalisation policy forward for it to be

---

[4]   See, for example, Derek Beach and Rasmus B. Pedersen, *Process-Tracing Methods: Foundations and Guidelines* (University of Michigan Press, 2013); Andrew Bennett, 'Process-Tracing: A Bayesian Perspective', in Janet M. Box-Steffensmeier, Henry E. Brady and David Collier (eds.), *The Oxford Handbook of Political Methodology* (Oxford University Press, 2008), 702; Alexander L. George and Andrew Bennett, *Case Studies and Theory Development in the Social Sciences* (MIT Press, 2005).

[5]   Bennett, 'Process-Tracing'; Robert K. Yin, *Case Study Research: Design and Methods* (Sage Publications, 2003), 32–3.

[6]   The reason for adopting a top-down approach is grounded in the assumption that bureaucrats in non-expert agencies are unlikely to have independent knowledge of investment treaty obligations, absent active measures aiming at the transmission of knowledge by expert agencies. This assumption is supported both by the general literature on internalisation of international obligations domestically (see Chapter 1) and prior research conducted on the impact of investment treaties more specifically in both developing and developed countries. See Sattorova, 'The Impact of Investment Treaty Law on Host States'; Christine Côté, 'Is It Chilly Out There? International Investment Agreements and Government Regulatory Autonomy' (2014) 16 *AIB Insights* 14; Van Harten and Scott, 'Investment Treaties and the Internal Vetting of Regulatory Proposals'.

effective.[7] Finally, to enhance the explanatory value of the study, I completed the research with an inquiry into the development of these processes over time. To do so, I included a search of significant events which preceded (and possibly prompted) the way in which the different agencies involved in internalisation deal with investment treaties today.[8]

The research relied on a combination of data sources, namely semi-structured interviews, and the analysis of domestic archival documents, complemented by a review of secondary literature providing contextual understanding of Singaporean governance.

I conducted thirteen interviews with government officials in Singapore, selected through a combination of purposive and snow-ball sampling.[9] As a first step, interviewees were selected on the basis of the relevance of their official position in the management of investment treaties in the Singaporean administration. As a second step, interviewees from this first pool identified further relevant persons within the administration that could be contacted. Nine of the interviewees come from the two main expert agencies on international investment law, the Attorney General's Chambers (AGC) and the Ministry of Trade and Industry (MTI). Their relevant professional experience ranges from four to over twenty years,[10] with varying supervisory responsibilities of up to forty people. One further interviewee is a high-ranking Singaporean official with past professional experience in one of the expert agencies. The remaining three interviews were conducted with officials with ten or more years of legal experience in three different Singaporean line (i.e., non-expert) agencies, allowing for a partial assessment of the effective reach of the internalisation processes put in place by expert agencies.

In addition, the research included extensive research into government documents, namely documents of several government agencies,[11] as well as systematic surveys of parliamentary debates for the past ten years[12] and judicial decisions. Both surveys relied on a two-step process. First, a priori

---

[7] Beach and Pedersen, 'Process-Tracing Methods', 45–67.

[8] Yin, 'Case Study Research', 125–7.

[9] Oisín Tansey, 'Process Tracing and Elite Interviewing: A Case for Non-Probability Sampling' (2007) 40 *PS: Political Science & Politics* 765.

[10] This includes experience at their current posts, other posts within the government relevant to international investment law, and for one interviewee, other relevant international investment law experience outside the government.

[11] These included the annual reports of activities and records of public consultations conducted by relevant agencies, where these were available.

[12] The Parliamentary debates studied were from the period 1 January 2009 to 1 April 2019.

relevant documents were identified in online databases[13] on the basis of key-word searches.[14] Second, in the case of parliamentary debates, I conducted a textual analysis and coded these documents across seven categories of variables pertaining to the extent of internalisation of investment treaties that they show.[15] In the case of judicial decisions, in view of the limited number of a priori relevant documents, I only conducted a textual analysis.

Finally, my research was especially facilitated by my appointment as a research fellow at the Centre for International Law (CIL) at the National University of Singapore (NUS) between 2017 and 2019. During this time, I developed an understanding of the Singaporean legal and political system. In addition, CIL has lasting working relations with Singaporean government agencies, such as AGC and the Ministry of Foreign Affairs (MOFA) of Singapore, which facilitated access to officials from these institutions for interviews. While this work experience facilitated my research, I acknowledge that this may have also been a potential source of bias, due to my prior professional acquaintance with some of the interviewees and my personal impressions of the Singaporean bureaucracy.

6.3 Singapore: A 'Most Likely' Case Study for the Internalisation of Investment Treaties

As a party to over seventy investment treaties (bilateral investment treaties (BITs) and other treaties with investment provisions), and a member of several international and regional economic integration organisations,

---

[13] These online databases are Singapore Parliament Official Reports – Parliamentary Debates (Hansard) and Singapore LawNet.
[14] The keywords used are the following: international investment agreement(s)/IIA(s); free trade agreement(s)/FTA(s); bilateral investment treaty(ies)/BIT(s); investment guarantee agreement(s); investment obligation(s); international investment; investment arbitration/investor–state arbitration; and investor state dispute settlement/ISDS.
[15] The categories of variables are:

   (i) number of mentions of a keyword in any given document;
  (ii) existence of investment-treaty-related content in the document (for documents identified under broader keywords such as FTA and international investment; here, I further distinguish between documents discussing investment treaties in the context of outward investment and inward investment);
  (iii) type of reference to an investment treaty (here I distinguish between references to the existence of the investment treaty, specific standards of protection, and investor–state dispute settlement);
  (iv) the investment treaty standard of protection mentioned, if any;
  (v) type of reference to investor–state dispute settlement, if any;
  (vi) whether the mention of an investment treaty is related to a specific domestic measure in Singapore; and

Singapore is an active participant in the international investment regime. Singapore is also a high-income country with a unitary government and an efficient, capable, and organised administration which considers the rule of law material to its prosperity. In line with Calamita's and Berman's framework, these national and public administration characteristics suggest that internalisation of Singapore's investment treaties is highly likely.[16] In what follows, I elaborate on these characteristics, describe Singapore's active role in the investment treaty regime, and expound on Singapore's national characteristics and public administration.

6.3.1 Singapore's Engagement with the Investment Treaty Regime

Singapore – known as the 'Asian miracle' – has one of the world's highest per-capita GDPs.[17] Being a port state with few natural resources, Singapore's economy has historically relied on international trade and investment and is the hub (alongside Hong Kong) for investment flows to and from Asia. Indeed, Singapore is consistently ranked high on openness to trade[18] and business-friendly environment rankings,[19] and is the fourth largest recipient of foreign direct investment in the world.[20]

Viewing regional and global economic integration as critical for its survival and prosperity, since the 1970s, Singapore has been actively involved in the regional and international trade and investment regimes. It is a founding member of the Association of Southeast Asian Nations (ASEAN) and a member of the Asia-Pacific Economic Cooperation (APEC) forum. Singapore is also one of the preferred arbitration seats in Asia, including for investment arbitration disputes.[21]

(vii) if the mention is connected to a specific measure in Singapore as per (vi), whether it is done *ex ante*, in the process of adoption of the measure, or *ex post*, when the measure is already in place.

[16] For a discussion regarding the factors that influence whether or the extent to which international obligations are internalised, see Chapter 1.

[17] International Monetary Fund, *World Economic Outlook Database, October 2019: Global Manufacturing Downturn, Rising Trade Barriers*. Despite its moderate size and population, Singapore's GDP, at USD $364.16 billion, puts it in the top forty economies in the world; see World Bank Data, 'Singapore', https://data.worldbank.org/country/SG.

[18] World Economic Forum and Global Alliance for Trade Facilitation, *The Global Enabling Trade Report 2016*.

[19] World Bank, *Doing Business 2020: Comparing Business Regulation in 190 Economies*.

[20] UNCTAD, *World Investment Report 2019: Special Economic Zones*, 4.

[21] See, for example, Queen Mary University of London, School of International Arbitration and White & Case LLP, *2018 International Arbitration Survey: The Evolution of International Arbitration*, 9.

As regards its treaties, Singapore signed its first BIT in 1972,[22] and it is currently party to forty-eight BITs in total,[23] as well as twenty-six free trade agreements (FTAs) and other treaties that include foreign investment protection.[24] In 2018, Singapore concluded a comprehensive FTA and BIT with the European Union[25] and has negotiated several other new investment treaties in the past five years.[26] Moreover, Singapore has been an active participant in ambitious mega-regional initiatives in the Asia-Pacific region, such as the Comprehensive and Progressive Agreement for Trans-Pacific Partnership (CPTPP)[27] and the Regional Comprehensive Economic Partnership (RCEP).[28]

Despite being a party to many investment treaties, Singapore has never faced an investment treaty claim.[29]

6.3.2   National and Public Administration Characteristics

As outlined in the introductory chapter, a number of structural factors at the international, national, and administrative levels can influence the

---

[22] The country's first BIT, the Netherlands–Singapore BIT, was signed in 1972. For a detailed analysis of Singapore's investment treaty portfolio, see Charis Tan and Kate Lan, 'Singapore', in Loretta Malintoppi and Charis Tan (eds.), *Investment Protection in Southeast Asia: A Country-by-Country Guide on Arbitration Laws and Bilateral Investment Treaties* (Brill Nijhoff, 2017), 297.

[23] See Ministry of Trade and Industry, 'International Investment Agreements (IIAs)', www.mti.gov.sg/Improving-Trade/International-Investment-Agreements; UNCTAD, 'Investment Policy Hub: International Investment Agreements Navigator', https://investmentpolicy.unctad.org/international-investment-agreements.

[24] Of these twenty-six FTAs, fifteen are FTAs signed by Singapore and another eleven are agreements signed as part of ASEAN. For a list, see Enterprise Singapore, 'Singapore FTAs', www.enterprisesg.gov.sg/non-financial-assistance/for-singapore-companies/free-trade-agreements/ftas/singapore-ftas.

[25] EU–Singapore FTA (2018); EU–Singapore IPA (2018).

[26] Including Myanmar–Singapore BIT (2019), Armenia–Singapore Agreement on Trade in Services and Investment (2019), Sri Lanka–Singapore FTA (2018), Kazakhstan–Singapore BIT (2018), Indonesia–Singapore BIT (2018), Qatar–Singapore BIT (2017), Nigeria–Singapore BIT (2016), and the Iran–Singapore BIT (2016).

[27] Comprehensive and Progressive Agreement for Trans-Pacific Partnership (CPTPP) (2018).

[28] Regional Comprehensive Economic Partnership (2020) (RCEP).

[29] As of writing, only seventeen countries have not been respondents under investment treaties according to the UNCTAD Investment Dispute Settlement Navigator. In 2014, Minister Lim Hng Kiang, Minister of Trade, also confirmed in a written response to Parliament regarding ISDS claims that '[t]o date, no multinational company has challenged or threatened to challenge Singapore.' See *Singapore Parliamentary Debates, Official Report*, vol. 92, 5 August 2014 (Mr Gerald Giam Yean Song, Mr Lim Hng Kiang).

internalisation of international norms at the domestic level.[30] International factors relate to international treaties or institutions.[31] National factors pertain to a country's specific characteristics from a geographical, organisational, political, or legal standpoint. Finally, the organisation, cultural resources, and capacity of the public administration play a significant role too.

With respect to national factors, Singapore has several characteristics that support internalisation. First, it is a unitary dominant-party parliamentary republic. While its parliamentary system follows the Westminster model,[32] since its establishment in 1965 the country has been governed by the People's Action Party (PAP), which enjoys a supermajority in Parliament.[33] Over this period of more than fifty-five years, there have only been three Prime Ministers.[34] Under the Singaporean Constitution, legislative initiative lies primarily with the executive, which allows for a coordinated/centralised approach to law making. In addition, thanks to the PAP's majority, bills normally do not undergo modifications once they are introduced to Parliament. While the suitability of such a high level of centralisation is questionable for a democracy, it simplifies internalisation by minimising the number of key actors whose agreement is needed for this process.[35]

Second, the international rule of law is perceived as central to Singapore's success and prosperity. It is a central tenet of Singaporean policy that the international rule of law is the only way for a small state to survive in a world where 'might is right'.[36] Both economic relevance and promoting international legality are part of the core principles of its foreign policy.[37] The government is also committed to maintaining its

---

[30] See Chapter 1.

[31] *Ibid.*

[32] Constitution of the Republic of Singapore. See also *Halsbury's Laws of Singapore*, vol. 1, 'Administrative and Constitutional Law' (Butterworths Asia, 2012).

[33] See Kevin Y. L. Tan, *The Constitution of Singapore: A Contextual Analysis* (Hart Publishing, 2015), 218–21.

[34] *Ibid.*

[35] See Chapter 1.

[36] Ministry of Foreign Affairs, 'Transcript of Remarks by Minister for Foreign Affairs Dr Vivian Balakrishnan at the MFA Townhall on 17 July 2017', www.mfa.gov.sg/Newsroom/Press-Statements-Transcripts-and-Photos/2017/07/Transcript-of-Remarks-by-Minister-for-Foreign-Affairs-Dr-Vivian-Balakrishnan-at-the-MFA-Townhall-on.

[37] *Ibid.* See also Ministry of Foreign Affairs, 'S Rajaratnam Lecture 2019 by The Honourable Chief Justice Sundaresh Menon – The Rule of Law, the International Legal Order, and the Foreign Policy of Small States', www.mfa.gov.sg/Newsroom/Press-Statements-Transcripts-and-Photos/2019/10/20191015-S-Raj-Lecture.

international reputation as a country which respects the international rule of law and guarantees an open economy.[38] In this vein, there is the sense among officials that Singapore *must* respect and uphold the legitimacy of international economic law, including investment treaties.[39]

Third, with a territory of 719 square km, a population of 6 million, and a public service comprised of about 150,000 public officers,[40] Singapore is a small and centralised city-state. In comparison with the other case studies on larger or federal states found in this volume,[41] the complexity and the number of links in the chain of transmission are considerably reduced, making it easier for an international norm to penetrate from a high-level entry point into the bureaucracy.[42]

Moreover, Singapore's public administration arguably represents a nearly ideal environment for the internalisation of international obligations.[43] The administration has high regulatory capacity, is composed of a robust and competent civil service, and is very efficient.[44] Singapore also dedicates significant resources to the achievement of its policies.[45] Indeed,

---

[38] It is anecdotally known that Singapore ensures that it is able to comply with an international treaty before entering into it and is thus selective with regard to the international commitments that it undertakes. By way of example, Singapore is among a very small minority of countries that has yet to ratify three of the Fundamental International Labour Organization Conventions (Convention 87 – *Freedom of Association and Protection of the Right to Organise Convention* (1948); Convention 105 – *Abolition of Forced Labour Convention* (1957); and Convention 111 – *Discrimination (Employment and Occupation) Convention* (1958)). This is the case despite a commitment to do so under the recent EU–Singapore FTA, namely under Art. 12.3.4. (For an interpretation of the legal nature of similar commitments within the context of the EU–Republic of Korea FTA (2010), see generally European Commission, 'Panel of experts confirms Republic of Korea is in breach of labour commitments under our trade agreement', https://trade.ec.europa.eu/doclib/press/index.cfm?id=2238.)

[39] See also *Singapore Parliamentary Debates, Official Report*, vol. 85, col. 687–692, 28 May 2009 (Mr Lim Hng Kiang).

[40] Data.gov.sg, 'Public Service Staff Strength (Civil Service & Statutory Board)', https://data.gov.sg/dataset/public-service-staff-strength-civil-service-statutory-board?view_id=3bebe6b2-2396-4072-9b9a-8d9602bc2887&resource_id=899105b0-af9b-47ed-85d2-ab1c2a8be0e5.

[41] For example, see the chapters on India and Indonesia.

[42] See Chapter 1.

[43] *Ibid.*

[44] See David S. Jones, 'Governance and Meritocracy: A Study of Policy Implementation in Singapore', in Jon S. T. Quah, *The Role of the Public Bureaucracy in Policy Implementation in Five ASEAN Countries* (Cambridge University Press, 2016), 297.

[45] *Ibid.*

in international rankings such as the World Bank Worldwide Governance Indicators, Singapore regularly scores at the top for regulatory quality and government effectiveness.[46] At the same time, it also scores very low for corruption.[47]

Taken together, these national and public administration characteristics suggest that Singapore is structurally in an excellent position to internalise its investment treaty commitments, that is, it is a 'most likely' case study of the internalisation of investment treaties.

In what follows, I lay out the internalisation measures found in the executive, legislature, and judiciary.

6.4   Internalisation Measures: The Executive

In the following sub-sections, I address the internalisation measures found in the different branches of government. This section is focused on the executive, where most internalisation measures and processes are found.

6.4.1   The Institutional Framework: Ministries and Agencies in Charge of Investment Treaties

MTI, AGC, and the Ministry of Law are the three main ministries and government agencies involved in the negotiation and management of Singapore's investment treaties. The International Trade Cluster (ITC, the Cluster) at MTI is mandated with protecting and advancing Singapore's international economic policy. Since the 2000s, the Investment Section within ITC has managed Singapore's investment treaty portfolio,[48]

---

[46] World Bank, 'Worldwide Governance Indicators', https://info.worldbank.org/governance/wgi/Home/Reports. See also Daniel Kaufmann, Aart Kraay and Massimo Mastruzzi, 'The Worldwide Governance Indicators: Methodology and Analytical Issues', *World Bank Policy Research Working Paper* No. 5430 (September 2010). Singapore scores similarly high on the quality of its public administration under the expert Variety of Democracies indicator. See V-Dem Institute, *Autocratization Turns Viral: Democracy Report 2021*.

[47] Under the Worldwide Governance Indicators, Singapore has ranked in the top ten percentile since 1996; under the V-Dem indicators, the country is among the countries within the 'maximum' score (over 3) for the indicator 'Rigorous and impartial public administration'; under the Transparency International Corruption Perception Index, Singapore ranked 3 out of 198 in 2018 and it has ranked in the top 10 countries since the creation of the index in 1995.

[48] See, for example, Ministry of Trade and Industry, 'People at MTI', www.mti.gov.sg/About-Us/People-at-MTI.

including investment treaty negotiations and implementation. In the course of negotiations, the ITC coordinates with other ministries and agencies to ensure both policy coherence and Singapore's capacity to meet new obligations.[49] The Investment Section consists of five officers working closely with the ITC Goods and Services Section.[50] At times, depending on staffing needs, officers from other MTI divisions, such as the ASEAN Division, take part in investment-related work.[51] Prior to the establishment of the ITC, investment treaty negotiations were under the purview of the Economic Development Board (EDB),[52] an agency that holds, *inter alia*, functions approximating those of an investment promotion agency (Figure 6.1).[53]

AGC is the government's legal advisor on all matters, and represents the government before international courts and tribunals.[54] The International Affairs Division (IAD) at AGC concentrates on international law, including international investment law.[55] IAD plays an important role throughout the life-cycle of an investment treaty: providing legal support to MTI in the course of negotiations, monitoring the compliance of domestic law with existing investment treaty obligations, and representing the government in the event of investment disputes. AGC dedicates important resources to developing expertise in international law: since its creation in 1995, IAD has grown from six legal officers to forty in 2019.[56] This expansion began in the 2000s with the conclusion of Singapore's first FTAs.[57]

[49] Interview B2, 2019; Interview C5, 2019; Interview C6, 2019.
[50] Interview A1, 2019; Interview C6, 2019.
[51] Interview C6, 2019.
[52] Interview C5, 2019; Interview C6, 2019.
[53] The approximation of the role of EDB to that of an investment promotion agency is only meant for heuristic purposes and remains an imperfect description. The EDB was established almost immediately after Singapore's independence in 1961 and is considered to have held a key role in the country's economic development. The EDB has held different roles over time which go beyond investment promotion, including with respect to the development of a broad industrialisation strategy. For the current functions and role of the EDB, see Economic Development Board Singapore, 'About EDB', www.edb.gov.sg/en/about-edb/who-we-are .html; for a historical account, see Belinda Yuen, 'Singapore Local Economic Development: The case of Economic Development Board (EDB)', presented at 'Workshop on City Economic Development: The Agency Question', World Bank, Washington, DC (May 2008).
[54] Interview C5, 2019.
[55] *Ibid.* Interviewees point that the core of international lawyers in government are at IAD (Interview C5, 2019; Interview C6, 2019), with one exception, namely the Ministry of Defence which holds the expertise on international humanitarian law (Interview C5, 2019).
[56] Interview E9, 2019; Interview C5, 2019.
[57] Interview E9, 2019.

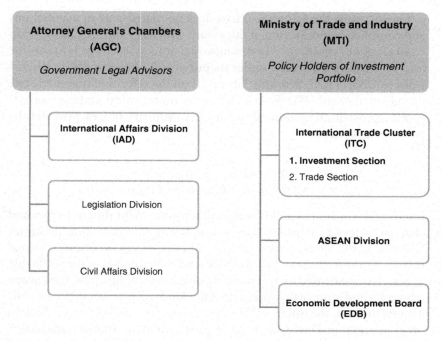

Figure 6.1   Simplified organisational charts of expert agencies[58]

Because these new FTAs included compulsory dispute resolution mechanisms,[59] the government considered that it was important to monitor the implementation of and compliance with them.[60] IAD dedicates important resources to the field of international investment law more specifically. Around ten to fifteen officers at IAD regularly work on investment law matters, and all new IAD officers receive general training in core areas of international law, which interviewees confirmed includes international investment law.[61]

---

[58] The chart presents the divisions/sections of AGC and MTI referred to in this chapter only and is not meant to constitute an accurate exhaustive organisational chart of either of these agencies.

[59] *Ibid.* It is interesting that at least one interviewee identified compulsory dispute settlement as a relevant factor for the continuous presence of an AGC officer during treaty negotiations, as opposed to a more limited backstopping role on the part of the AGC (Interview C5, 2019).

[60] Interview E9, 2019; Interview B2, 2019.

[61] Interview B2, 2019; Interview B5, 2019. One interviewee described the level of engagement of these ten to fifteen lawyers as having 'negotiated or advised on or taken part in potential disputes to a much greater depth'.

Finally, while the Ministry of Law does not participate in negotiations and compliance monitoring, it does work with MTI and AGC to develop strategic policy positions.[62] In this informal process, each agency takes the lead on matters that come under its purview.[63] For example, in discussions in UNCITRAL Working Group III on the reform of investor–State dispute settlement (ISDS), AGC has a say on technical matters, such as specific procedural mechanisms, while the Ministry of Law provides the policy perspective.[64]

6.4.2   The General and Informal Nature of the Internalisation Processes

Building on Calamita's and Berman's description of the different types and characteristics of internalisation measures, the internalisation processes followed in the Singapore executive tend to be of a general and informal nature. As shown below, the processes tend to be general in the sense that although they are used for internalising investment obligations, their scope is broader and is normally applied to other kinds of international legal obligations. Indeed, the origin of these processes can often be traced back to other international law disciplines, in particular international trade law.

Further, most communication and coordination within the administration is characterised by a certain level of informality and a culture of collegiality. There are no formal laws and regulations on managing any of the aspects of investment obligations in the domestic sphere and the division of labour among and within agencies in this respect is not formalised either.[65] Similarly, a number of specific practices in law making, such as public consultations,[66] inter-agency, or inter-department consultations[67]

---

[62] Interview D8, 2019. Examples include the negotiations of the UNCITRAL rules on transparency and ensuing United Nations Convention on Transparency in Treaty-based Investor-State Arbitration (New York, 2014) (otherwise referred to as the Mauritius Convention), or the current work on the reform of investor–state dispute settlement (ISDS) at Working Group III of UNCITRAL. Other examples include the ongoing work of the open-ended intergovernmental working group on transnational corporations and other business enterprises with respect to human rights (OEIGWG). See United Nations Human Rights Council, *Report on the fourth session of the open-ended intergovernmental working group on transnational corporations and other business enterprises with respect to human rights*, A/HRC/40/48 (2 January 2019).

[63] Interview D8, 2019.

[64] *Ibid.*

[65] *Ibid.* Interview B3, 2019; Interview C6, 2019.

[66] *Ibid.*

[67] Interview B3, 2019.

are a matter of convention rather than formalised rules.[68] Both communication and internalisation measures are also defined by a culture of collegiality.[69] Interviews revealed an important reliance on the competence and diligent work of individual officers to handle situations adequately even in the absence of hard rules. This reliance manifests itself in two ways. Experts have confidence that line ministry officials and street-level bureaucrats will act with caution and in line with the law.[70] Conversely, non-expert agencies also have confidence in the correct assessment on the part of expert officers in the agencies in charge of investment treaties.[71]

6.4.3 The Role of Treaty Negotiation and Ratification in the Internalisation Process

An investigation as to the governmental actors involved in the negotiation process provides additional insights with respect to the internalisation process. Notably, government agencies involved in the negotiation process are aware of the existence of investment treaties, and, as such, are nodes through which information about investment treaty obligations could potentially spread to the bureaucracy. Surveying Singapore's experience with internalisation partially confirms this hypothesis and offers ways to refine it.

In this section, after a short summary of the negotiations and ratification process itself, I describe the main features of negotiations that can be conducive to internalisation, namely intra-governmental consultations and the composition of the negotiating team.

6.4.3.1 The Investment Treaty Negotiation Process

MTI, with legal support from AGC, leads and oversees investment treaty negotiations.[72] Once a political decision to start negotiations has been made, a feasibility study on the economic and policy aspects of a treaty is carried out.[73] MTI then establishes a negotiating team that runs the negotiations.[74] In the course of negotiations, intra-governmental consultations

---

[68] Therefore, a majority of information about Singapore is gathered through interviews and, to the extent available, complementary archival documents.
[69] Interview C5, 2019; Interview C6, 2019; Interview D8, 2019. One interviewee put this characteristic in terms of a general national culture in Singapore.
[70] Interview B2, 2019; Interview B3, 2019; Interview C5, 2019.
[71] Interview B3, 2019; Interview C5, 2019.
[72] Ibid.; Interview B2, 2019.
[73] Interview B2, 2019.
[74] Ibid.; Interview C5, 2019.

with respect to certain treaty provisions are carried out – in particular those deviating from the preferred Singaporean model treaty or template.[75] Once signed, AGC handles the formal ratification process,[76] and MTI determines, in consultation with other agencies, whether implementation measures are necessary.[77] I elaborate on the limited role of Parliament in these processes below.[78]

6.4.3.2   The Role of Intra-governmental Consultations

Since the negotiation of its first FTAs at the beginning of the 2000s, including the United States–Singapore FTA, intra-governmental consultations have become an integral part of the BIT and FTA negotiation process.[79] Through such consultations, awareness as to the existence of investment treaties spreads across government. As such, consultations can arguably be understood as an informational internalisation tool.

The consultation process typically begins when MTI sets out the internal template for negotiations and, in that process, consults with other agencies. Then, during the negotiations, MTI consults other relevant ministries, in particular, when a deviation from Singapore's model treaty or preferred position is being considered.[80] Further, Singapore's model treaty is periodically reviewed and updated to address emerging issues,[81] and it is within this context that intra-governmental consultations are also carried out.

The scope and frequency of intra-governmental consultations is significant: consultations typically involve many of Singapore's government ministries and agencies,[82] and are carried out with respect to around 30

---

[75] Interview B2, 2019; Interview B4, 2019; Interview C5, 2019; Interview C6, 2019.

[76] Interview B4, 2019.

[77] Interview A1, 2019; Interview C6, 2019.

[78] See Section 6.5.

[79] Interview C6, 2019; Interview B3, 2019; Interview C5, 2019. Between 2000 and 2003, Singapore concluded ambitious FTAs with several of its important trading partners, namely New Zealand (2000), Japan (2002), EFTA (2002), China (ASEAN–China Framework Agreement (2002)), Australia (2003) and the United States (2003), which required broad consultations and mapping of the economy. In this context, one interviewee mentioned that the negative list approach to liberalisation in the United States–Singapore FTA (2003) required an important level of coordination.

[80] Interview B2, 2019. To the contrary, if there are no substantial changes, MTI will negotiate without consulting on the basis of this understood consensus.

[81] Interview A1, 2019.

[82] Interview B2, 2019. Several interviewees mentioned agencies with an economic portfolio such as the EDB, Enterprise Singapore, and the Monetary Authority of Singapore (which is responsible for financial regulation); agencies with domestic regulatory portfolios such

per cent of negotiated treaties.[83] As Singapore is very active in the conclusion of economic treaties,[84] respective ministries are regularly involved in consultations.

MTI's negotiation team initiates consultations and identifies the relevant stakeholders within government.[85] Prior to the consultations, MTI and AGC provide background information on the negotiations to the respective ministry, including their potential policy implications,[86] and the ministry in turn provides its input and policy objectives.[87] Taking considerations arising from such consultations into account, MTI and AGC will finalise the specific treaty language.[88]

Most consultations relate to pre-establishment commitments,[89] especially where a treaty incorporates a negative list approach to investment and trade liberalisation.[90] In such instances, MTI sends out a 'blast to every single agency'.[91] Other instances where consultations take place relate to specific exceptions or carve-outs.[92] Consultations on classic investment protection standards such as fair and equitable treatment or minimum standard of treatment are rare,[93] as they are considered legal matters, and are under the purview of MTI and AGC.[94] The discussion with the solicited agency takes place regarding the policy implications of the provision. The legal language to implement the agreed upon policy is then supplied by MTI and AGC.[95]

---

as the Ministry of National Development, Ministry of Defence, and Ministry of Home Affairs; and sectoral agencies such as the Ministry of Law, Infocomm Media Development Authority, the Ministry of Health, the Inland Revenue Authority, and the Ministry of Education (Interview B2, 2019; Interview B3, 2019; Interview C5, 2019).

[83] Interview B2, 2019.
[84] For instance, Singapore signed two new treaties with investment provisions in both 2020 and 2019, five in 2018, two in 2017, and three in 2016.
[85] Interview B3, 2019; Interview A1, 2019.
[86] One interviewee referred to it as a 'crash course' on the subject matter (Interview C5, 2019; Interview C6, 2019).
[87] Interview B2, 2019.
[88] Ibid.; Interview B3, 2019; Interview B4, 2019.
[89] Interview B2, 2019; Interview B3, 2019; Interview A1, 2019; Interview C6, 2019; Interview C7, 2019.
[90] Interview C5, 2019; Interview C6, 2019.
[91] Interviewees described a 'blast' as a form which provides information about the potential content of the treaty and seeks the feedback of line agencies on provisions that are relevant to them (Interview C6, 2019; Interview C5, 2019; Interview B2, 2019).
[92] Interview B2, 2019; Interview B4, 2019.
[93] Interview C5, 2019; Interview C6, 2019; Interview A1, 2019.
[94] Interview C5, 2019; Interview B2, 2019; Interview F11, 2019.
[95] Interview B2, 2019; Interview B3, 2019; Interview B4, 2019; Interview C5, 2019; Interview C6, 2019.

To conclude, thanks to the practice of intra-governmental consultation, which in the past two decades has become an integral part of the negotiation process, awareness as to the existence of international investment treaties has likely increased across a wide range of ministries, in turn likely increasing the informational internalisation within diverse ministries. That being said, it is important to point out that despite similar consultation processes, in practice, the level of involvement with respect to FTAs is higher than with respect to BITs. This is so because, as noted above, involvement with respect to investment pre-establishment obligations is more intense as compared to post-establishment protections. In the Singaporean context, only FTAs liberalise trade and investment, with consultations in turn being more extensive and more common for them. By contrast, Singapore's BITs do not contain liberalisation provisions,[96] but rather are limited to standards of protection, such as fair and equitable treatment or expropriation, which are seen as within the purview of MTI and AGC, thus prompting less consultations than FTA chapters that include liberalisation.[97] A systematic understanding of how or to what extent these differences between FTAs and BITs impact informational internalisation is an area for further research.

6.4.3.3   The Role of the Negotiation Team

In addition to consultations with respect to treaty negotiations, it might be hypothesised that the composition of the negotiating team itself also plays a role in internalisation. Composed of members from different ministries, such members might act as nodes for the spread of awareness and information about investment treaty obligations from the international level (at which the negotiations take place) to the governmental level (at which the obligations are applied). This might be especially true in FTA negotiations, where negotiation teams tend to be quite large and inclusive. In Singapore, however, my inquiry suggests that negotiation team membership has had a limited impact on informational internalisation.

The composition of negotiating teams in Singapore differs depending upon whether the negotiations concern a BIT or an FTA. BIT negotiation teams normally consist of several MTI and AGC officers (in total, two to four officers).[98] Although AGC's participation depends in principle on

---

[96] See, for example, Tan and Lan, *Investment Protection in Southeast Asia*, 297.
[97] Interview C6, 2019.
[98] Interview B2, 2019; Interview C5, 2019.

the complexity of the negotiations, because investment treaties include compulsory dispute settlement provisions, AGC generally participates.[99]

FTA negotiation teams include members from other ministries alongside MTI and AGC officers,[100] such as the Ministry of Law, the Monetary Authority of Singapore, the Ministry of Environment, the Ministry of Manpower, and the Intellectual Property Office.[101] As a consequence of this broad participation, it might be thought, as noted above, that FTA negotiations would serve to spread awareness and information about investment treaty obligations across the participating ministries and agencies. This proves not to be the case. As with BITs, MTI and AGC run the negotiations, while the participation of specialised ministries or agencies is on an 'in-and-out' basis, that is, limited to the particular issues falling within their respective areas of responsibility.[102] Thus, the knowledge of these specialised ministries and agencies tends to be narrow and limited to those issues which are specific to them, which generally do not include the treaty's investment provisions. Indeed, in the interviews conducted for this chapter, FTA negotiators from specialised ministries and agencies showed limited awareness of the content of investment chapters and the relevance of these chapters to the work of their ministries.[103]

6.4.4   Internalisation Measures Pertaining to Domestic Rule and Decision Making

Once an investment treaty is in place, Calamita and Berman describe three institutional processes – informational, monitoring, or remedial – through which obligations are or could be internalised.[104] In what follows, I lay out the main internalisation processes which have been implemented in Singapore. Compared to the majority of other countries surveyed in this book where investor claims have triggered the adoption of internalisation measures, in the case of Singapore, it was the adoption of FTAs with compulsory dispute settlement, along with the growing importance of AGC that gave rise to the adoption of internalisation processes towards the end of the 2000s and beginning of the 2010s.[105]

---

[99] Interview C5, 2019.
[100] Interview B2, 2019; Interview C7, 2019.
[101] Ibid.; Interview A1, 2019; Interview D8, 2019; Interview F11, 2019; Interview F12, 2019.
[102] Interview D8, 2019.
[103] Interview E9, 2019; Interview F11, 2019; Interview F12, 2019.
[104] See Chapter 1.
[105] Interview F10, 2019; Interview B2, 2019; Interview B3, 2019.

6.4.4.1   Informational Processes

As is common to most other case studies in this volume, there is no systematic practice for intra-governmental notification of the entry into
force of new treaties, including investment treaties.[106] Thus, although it
might have been hypothesised that that the conclusion of a treaty and its
notification within government could arguably increase informational
internalisation, in Singapore this does not appear to be the case.

Instead, there are two main informational processes aimed at educating
the entire public administration in Singapore regarding investment treaty
obligations and the relevance of investment treaties to the work of line agencies. Both processes are consistently implemented and targeted at their relevant audiences in a sophisticated manner. Yet, despite these processes, the
collected data suggests that certain concerns remain about their effectiveness in raising officials' awareness about the relevance of investment obligations to most economic sectors and across different areas of government.

The first informational process, 'trade advisories', has been put in place
by MTI. Trade advisories are short documents sent to line ministries and
agencies on matters of international economic law.[107] They aim to explain
the types of obligations that Singapore has undertaken in its treaties.[108]
They are either sent at the time of entry into force of an FTA or are based
on specific themes.[109] Although the trade advisories practice is consistent,
the actual decision to send out a trade advisory is ad hoc, need-based, and
takes place on average once per year or once every two years.[110]

The second informational process is driven by AGC. IAD gives lectures
on international economic law, including international investment law,
as part of different training programmes for the civil service and more
specifically for lawyers working in the public sector. According to interviewees, an important message in these training programmes is to pay
closer attention when dealing with foreign companies and, in particular,
in cases where an envisaged measure may negatively impact them, that is,
impact their 'pockets'.[111] The fora at which this type of training takes place
varies. They include, among others, the Public Sector Law Forum and the
Civil Service College, where AGC offers an International Law Seminar as

---

[106] Interview B4, 2019.
[107] Interview C6, 2019; Interview C5, 2019.
[108] Interview B2, 2019; Interview C6, 2019.
[109] Interview C6, 2019.
[110] *Ibid.*
[111] Interview C5, 2019; Interview B2, 2019.

an elective course.[112] Interviewees provided varied information regarding the frequency with which international economic law topics form part of these training programmes. It seems to be somewhere between once per year or once biannually.[113]

Both the trade advisories and the training programmes are what Calamita and Berman define as measures of a 'general nature', that is, they inform the administration broadly about international economic law rather than narrowly focus on international investment law. The training programmes conducted by AGC were described as 'international economic law 101', rather than 'international investment law 101'.[114] Similarly, the design of the trade advisories favours informing line agencies about types of issues, such as public procurement or non-discrimination standards of protection, covering all relevant sources of law on the relevant issue.[115]

In addition to regular implementation, Singapore's informational measures display a markedly sophisticated approach. Particular care is taken to ensure that information is provided at an appropriate level for non-experts in line agencies and at an appropriate frequency. Thus, when describing some of the training sessions, one interviewee pointed out that focusing only on investment law would have been 'too nerdy' and unlikely to attract people to the session.[116] Similarly, interviewees suggested that sending out trade advisories every six months or making them too long may lead other agencies to consider them repetitive and thus not pay that much attention to them.[117] Furthermore, for both the trade advisories and training programmes, the chosen register is adapted for an audience of non-specialists. As one interviewee put it regarding the trade advisories, there is an effort to 'laymanise' the concepts.[118] MTI and AGC also make an effort to capture the attention of the audience by showing the relevance of the concepts through relatable case studies, taken from the practice of investment and trade disciplines.[119] By way of example, AGC training sessions sport titles such as 'International Economic Law: It Concerns You More Than You Know' and bring forward unexpected connections, such as the relevance of investment arbitration for

---

[112] Interview B2, 2019; Interview B4, 2019.
[113] Interview B2, 2019; Interview B3, 2019.
[114] Interview B2, 2019.
[115] Interview C6, 2019.
[116] Interview B2, 2019.
[117] Interview A1, 2019; Interview B6, 2019.
[118] Interview B6, 2019.
[119] Interview B2, 2019.

seemingly unrelated areas of governmental decision making, such as criminal extradition requests.[120]

Despite the informational processes put in place, a lack of appreciation of the relevance of investment treaties to the administration writ large persists in certain quarters. Indeed, it appears that many line ministries and agencies remain relatively unaware about investment treaties or do not consider that their work relates to investment treaties. Thus, for example, there is limited awareness of investment treaty obligations in the National Environment Agency,[121] despite the relative prevalence of environmental measures as a source of investment treaty disputes worldwide and evidence of the impact of environmental investment disputes have on domestic governance in high capacity countries.[122] Moreover, it is telling that a majority of the line agency officials interacting with the private sector that I invited for interviews directed me to contact MTI, as they considered that their work is unrelated to investment obligations. Finally, not all officers, including in expert agencies, had equal knowledge of the informational mechanisms in place or the same sensitivity about the need to inform line agencies of the content of investment treaties in the first place. My question regarding disseminating information to line agencies was met with disparate answers. More than once, the mechanisms that interviewees gave as examples were of informational processes that are unlikely to further awareness in line agencies, because they are meant to further expert knowledge or do not, in fact, feature investment treaty obligations in their programs.[123]

6.4.4.2   Monitoring and Remedial Processes

(a) The Role of the International Affairs Division at AGC   The IAD of AGC is the main agency responsible for monitoring Singapore's compliance with international law, including investment standards

---

120 *Ibid.* The reference is to an investment tribunal enjoining Romania from pursuing its extradition request against the principal shareholder of the claimant in the case. See *Nova Group Investments, B.V. v. Romania*, ICSID Case No. ARB/16/19, Procedural Order No. 7 Concerning the Claimant's Request for Provisional Measures (29 March 2017).

121 Interview B3, 2019. The observation was also made with respect to the National Environment Agency's parent, the Ministry of Sustainability and the Environment and one more agency. It is interesting to note that the interviewee considered that this unawareness derives from the notion that the work of these agencies is not related to investment treaties.

122 Tarald L. Berge and Axel Berger, 'Do Investor-State Dispute Settlement Cases Influence Domestic Environmental Regulation? The Role of Respondent State Bureaucratic Capacity' (2021) 12 *Journal of International Dispute Settlement* 1.

123 See Interview B4, 2019; Interview C7, 2019 (referring to programmes designed to further the qualifications of specialists in the field, such as the Hague Academy Course in Singapore or

of protection.[124] This monitoring process serves as an informal early warning system for nascent disputes and thus fulfils the role of a remedial internalisation process. Below, after detailing the general characteristics of the process, I discuss the administration's response to two recent situations that presented high litigation risk.

As with the rest of Singapore's internalisation processes, the monitoring of rule and decision making tends to be informal. In practice, it relies for the most part on questions being addressed to the relevant expert agency, namely IAD,[125] although, on occasion, IAD takes the initiative to provide advice on a matter that it considers to raise a question of international law.[126] There are two main avenues, both equally used, through which IAD becomes involved in the rule- and decision-making process. First, the line agency that proposes a change in policy may request IAD's views on the compliance of that policy with Singapore's international obligations.[127] Second, other divisions within AGC may identify such questions in carrying out their own responsibilities and bring them to IAD's attention.[128] This may occur, for example, either when the Civil Division of AGC receives a question regarding a policy's compliance with Singaporean domestic law or when a proposed measure is sent to the Legislation Division, which is in charge of drafting all legislative acts in Singapore.[129]

Through these avenues, IAD reviews measures proposed by a broad range of line agencies,[130] with interviewees pointing out anecdotally that since the establishment of the informational processes described above, there has been a rise in the number of queries.[131] Most often the inquiries pertaining to international investment law originate from MTI and the

---

the internal training programmes undertaken by AGC's IAD lawyers); Interview B2, 2019; Interview C5, 2019; Interview E9, 2019 (referring to the 'Trade Academy' organised by MTI, which offers courses relevant for investment promotion and for informing Singaporean investors of opportunities and investment protections outside of Singapore).

[124] However, for straightforward questions with respect to investment treaty obligations, the ITC at MTI may also sometimes take that advisory role (Interview B4, 2019; Interview C5, 2019; Interview C6, 2019).

[125] Interview B3, 2019; Interview C5, 2019.

[126] Interview B2, 2019.

[127] Interview C5, 2019. When international economic law is at stake, the line agency may request the advice of MTI, which would then forward the question to IAD, if their expertise is needed.

[128] Interview B2, 2019; Interview B3, 2019; Interview C5, 2019.

[129] For an overview of the functions of the Legislation Division, see Attorney-General's Chambers, 'Overview of Functions', www.agc.gov.sg/our-roles/drafter-of-laws/overview.

[130] Interview B2, 2019; Interview B3, 2019; Interview B4, 2019.

[131] Interview B2, 2019; Interview C7, 2019.

Ministry of Law.[132] On other occasions, inquiries may not be so specific and IAD will be responsible for identifying the international law obligations implicated, including investment law obligations.[133]

According to interviewees, IAD addresses around ten investment treaty-related matters a year.[134] Most often, these matters raise questions pertaining to compliance with the indirect expropriation and fair and equitable treatment (FET) standards,[135] although certain interviewees also mentioned non-discrimination standards of treatment.[136] Interviewees unanimously agreed that the government has modified measures in the past to ensure compliance with investment treaty obligations based on the advice of IAD.[137] Interviewees pointed out upon prompting, however, that it has seldom been the policy goal itself that is modified, but rather the means used by the government for achieving that policy goal.[138] As an example, interviewees described the kinds of advice often provided by IAD with respect to complying with the FET standard of treatment. Interviewees noted that IAD's suggestions are often addressed to the process by which government decisions are made, such as recommending that an agency take steps to establish a stronger evidentiary basis for a particular policy,[139] undertake a comparative analysis of international approaches to assess whether a proposed measure by Singapore would be an outlier,[140] or include consultations with potentially affected economic actors as part of its decision making.[141] A final feature of this process shows the particularly high capacity of the Singaporean administration, as it requires intimate knowledge of the economic actors on the ground. Part of the risk assessment of a measure by IAD officers is also to distinguish between what one interviewee described as the 'legal risk' and the 'litigation risk' associated with it.[142]

---

[132] Interview B4, 2019; Interview B3, 2019.
[133] *Ibid.*; Interview B2, 2019; Interview C7, 2019. In addition, sometimes questions are phrased in hypothetical terms when line agencies want to plan for the future.
[134] Interview B2, 2019; Interview B3, 2019; Interview B4, 2019; Interview C7, 2019; Interview D8, 2019.
[135] Interview B3, 2019; Interview C7, 2019.
[136] Interview B2, 2019; Interview C6, 2019.
[137] Interview B2, 2019; Interview B4, 2019; Interview C7, 2019.
[138] Interview B3, 2019.
[139] Interview C7, 2019.
[140] *Ibid.*
[141] *Ibid.*; Interview C6, 2019.
[142] Interview B4, 2019.

Namely, if a particular course of action could potentially constitute a breach of an international obligation (i.e., legal risk), officers will go on to verify if there is actual discontent on the part of affected economic actors in Singapore (i.e., litigation risk) before advising whether a modification is warranted.

The only specific example of substantive modification of a policy that interviewees shared was with respect to the Additional Buyer's Stamp Duty (ABSD) for purchase of residential property in Singapore.[143] Under Singaporean law, foreigners are liable to pay a supplementary tax (as compared to Singapore citizens) when purchasing residential property.[144] The ABSD was put in place in 2011, after Singapore had entered into FTAs with the United States and the European Free Trade Association (EFTA), under which it accorded national treatment to nationals of these countries with respect to taxation and investment, both pre- and post-establishment.[145] As a result of these commitments and upon advice from IAD, the authorities limited the originally proposed scope of the ABSD.[146] Contracting partners' citizens and, for EFTA states, permanent residents, were given an exemption to ABSD liability, entitling them to rights equivalent to those of Singaporean citizens.[147]

Finally, on the rare occasions where IAD has had to address an individual investor's grievance,[148] interviewees pointed out that monetary

---

[143] Once prompts on the potential risk of the ABSD regulation reached IAD, one interviewee put it that 'all the alarms went off'. Both the legal service of IRAS and the legislative division at AGC had alerted IAD to the issue (Interview C5, 2019).

[144] See Stamp Duties Act (Cap 312, 2006 Rev Ed), First Schedule; Inland Revenue Authority of Singapore, 'Additional Buyer's Stamp Duty (ABSD)', www.iras.gov.sg/IRASHome/Other-Taxes/Stamp-Duty-for-Property/Working-out-your-Stamp-Duty/Buying-or-Acquiring-Property/What-is-the-Duty-that-I-Need-to-Pay-as-a-Buyer-or-Transferee-of-Residential-Property/Additional-Buyer-s-Stamp-Duty--ABSD-/.

[145] United States–Singapore FTA; EFTA–Singapore FTA (2002).

[146] Interview B4, 2019; Interview C5, 2019; *Singapore Parliamentary Debates, Official Report*, vol. 90, 16 September 2013 (Mr Gerald Giam Yean Song, Mr Tharman Shanmugaratnam); *Singapore Parliamentary Debates, Official Report*, vol. 89, 9 April 2012 (Mrs Lina Chiam, Mr Lim Hng Kiang). It is worth noting that interviewees clearly indicated that there was an investment related aspect to the ABSD, even though parliamentary debates only refer to national treatment regarding taxation.

[147] Inland Revenue Authority of Singapore, 'Foreigners Eligible for ABSD Remission under Free Trade Agreements (FTAs)', www.iras.gov.sg/irashome/Other-Taxes/Stamp-Duty-for-Property/Claiming-Refunds-Remissions-Reliefs/Remissions/Foreigners-Eligible-for-ABSD-Remission-under-Free-Trade-Agreements--FTAs-/.

[148] Interviewees pointed out that such grievances are limited (Interview B3, 2019; Interview B4, 2019; Interview C7, 2019).

compensation would be exceptional.[149] The government prefers finding a compromise with the aggrieved investor. Where the administration is confident in the legal basis of the putative decision or measure, they may simply focus on preserving the relationship with the investor.[150]

Interviewees consistently relayed that IAD's advice is generally followed.[151] However, an important feature of the monitoring process is the shared understanding that the final decision on proceeding with a particular measure lies with the ministry or agency designing it.[152] There are stages of advice on legal risk and if the line agency wants to implement a particular policy that presents such risk, the relevant officers from IAD would advise on mitigation measures.[153]

(b) Types of Rules and Decisions Monitored Law is codified in Singapore in two ways: as Acts of Parliament, which are bills adopted by Parliament,[154] and as subsidiary legislation, which refers to any administrative rule made by an executive officer applying to a class, rather than individuals.[155] In terms of internalisation, the monitoring process seems to be used most systematically for legislative proposals, as compared to subsidiary legislation. Moreover, administrative decisions that concern individual investors are similarly not subject to systematic monitoring either.[156] Thus, given that most investment claims arise out of administrative measures rather than legislative or judicial ones,[157] Singapore's monitoring process, despite its sophistication, may not be fully tailored to the risks that investment treaties pose.

IAD is more likely to review the content of legislative measures than subsidiary legislation for two related reasons. First, the Legislation Division of AGC drafts only primary legislation. By contrast, subsidiary

---

149   Interview B3, 2019. Despite asking the question to a number of subjects, interviewees were unwilling to confirm whether or not Singapore has actually provided monetary compensation in the past.
150   Interview B3, 2019.
151   Interview C5, 2019; Interview C7, 2019.
152   Interview B4, 2019; Interview C6, 2019; Interview C7, 2019.
153   Interview B4, 2019; Interview C7, 2019.
154   Kevin Y. L. Tan, 'Parliament and the Making of Law in Singapore', in Kevin Y. L. Tan (ed.), *The Singapore Legal System* (2nd Ed) (Singapore University Press, 1999), 123, 140.
155   The definition can be found in *Cheong Seok Leng* v. *Public Prosecutor* [1988] 1 SLR(R) 530, [1988] SGHC 48 at [42] (Singapore High Court).
156   Interview C5, 2019; Interview B3, 2019; Interview C7, 2019.
157   Zoe P. Williams, 'Risky Business or Risky Politics: What Explains Investor State Disputes?', unpublished PhD thesis, Hertie School of Governance (2016), 42.

legislation is often drafted by the line agency holding the relevant port-folio.[158] Therefore, one of the possible avenues for IAD review – referral by the Legislative Division – is absent for subsidiary legislation, leaving it to the competent line agency to request IAD's advice (or not) on its own. Second, there appears to be a sense among some officials from line agencies that subsidiary legislation is less likely to raise questions of com-pliance with international (including investment) law obligations.[159] As a consequence, the review of subsidiary legislation is less systematic as compared to draft primary legislation.

Moreover, the Singaporean monitoring process does not systemati-cally cover decision making. That is, there is no process for the regular review of line agency decision making with respect to individual actors, for example, a decision to grant or renew a permit or a license, the conclu-sion of a contract with an individual investor, etc. As with subsidiary leg-islation, there appears to be a sense among some officials that individual decisions are less relevant to the question of compliance with investment treaty obligations.[160]

(c) **Examples of the Monitoring Process**   Singapore's response in two recent situations illustrates the functioning of the monitoring-remedial mechanism in practice. The first scenario relates to the only notice of investment claim that Singapore has received to date; the second is the Singaporean administration's approach to the regulation of tobacco plain packaging. Singapore's experience in these situations shows a high internal capacity to assess the risk involved and proceed with a calibrated response, even in the face of an impending threat by an investor to initiate proceedings.[161]

---

[158] Interview D8, 2019. See also *Halsbury's Laws of Singapore*, vol. 1, 'Administrative and Constitutional Law' (Butterworths Asia, 1998), paras. 10.020–10.022.

[159] Interview D8, 2019. This understanding stems from the rule under which subsidiary legislation must be consistent with its parent legislation and any Act of Parliament (Interpretation Act (Cap 1, 2002 Rev Ed), s 19(c)). See M. P. Jain, *Administrative Law of Malaysia and Singapore* (4th Ed) (LexisNexis, 2011), 63–4.

[160] Interview C5, 2019.

[161] While Moehlecke classifies Singapore as a developing country, that is, averse to the risk of undergoing investment proceedings independently of the likelihood of ensuing lia-bility, the data gathered during this study and outlined in this section suggest that the country has an approach similar to that of developed countries. See Carolina Moehlecke, 'The Chilling Effect of International Investment Disputes: Limited Challenges to State Sovereignty' (2020) 64 *International Studies Quarterly* 1.

(i) Notice of an Investment Claim   As mentioned above, Singapore is one of a small minority of countries that have not faced a formal investment treaty claim to date. Recently, the country was served with its first formal notice of a dispute under one of its FTAs and undertook consultations with the investor, as required by the treaty.[162] Interviewees preferred to remain discreet regarding the factual details of the case and the nationality of the claimant, but they did specify that the dispute pertained to an administrative decision by an agency (but not MTI or AGC) specifically concerning the aggrieved investor.[163] As noted above, a decision of this type would not have come before IAD for review prior to its being made.

As per the provisions in most of Singapore's FTAs, the notice of claim was sent to MTI. IAD, which represents Singapore in all international litigation, was informed 'immediately'[164] and coordinated the consultations.[165] While interviewees remained vague as to the composition of the task force for the consultations, it was clear that it included, at least, officers from MTI, AGC, and the line agency whose decision was being challenged.[166] Again, as with most other questions of internalisation in the executive branch, there was no formal procedure in order to decide on the composition of the consultations task force,[167] and it resulted from the operational needs of the case.

When discussing the notice of claim and the process of handling it with interviewees, two things stood out which characterise Singapore's experience – the internal expertise of the country and the confidence in the existing internalisation processes. Interviewees revealed that Singapore relied entirely on its own internal governmental expertise to address the notice of claim at the consultations stage. Moreover, officials felt confident to assess the claim on their own, ultimately concluding that the claim was without merit.[168] This reflects important in-house capacity and expertise as well as the willingness of officials to take responsibility at personal and agency levels.

---

[162] Interview B3, 2019; Interview C5, 2019.
[163] Interview C5, 2019.
[164] *Ibid.*
[165] Interview B3, 2019.
[166] *Ibid.*; Interview C5, 2019.
[167] Interview C5, 2019.
[168] Interviewees were not afraid to refer to it as 'not legitimate' (Interview B3, 2019; Interview C5, 2019).

Although the consultations were not successful, at the time of the interviews the investor had not filed a formal claim.[169] Discussing the process by which the underlying agency decision had been made, interviewees expressly stated that the notice of claim had not triggered a change in the government's approach to internalising investment obligations.[170] In part, this appears to have been motivated by the fact that the administration did not consider the claim substantiated. However, it remains noteworthy that neither AGC nor MTI have since increased their efforts to monitor ministry or other government decisions which, as detailed above, are less monitored than regulatory measures. Further, interviewees did not seem to consider these decisions more relevant to their work as a result of the notice of claim having been triggered by such an individual decision.[171]

(ii) Tobacco Plain Packaging   Singapore has one of the strictest regulatory frameworks for tobacco control in the world, and has been a pioneer on smoking reduction policies in Asia and the world. It was the first country in the world to ban tobacco product advertising in 1971[172] and the first in Asia to introduce graphic warnings on cigarette packs in 2004.[173] Thus, it is revealing that the Ministry of Health only proceeded formally with its decision to implement tobacco plain-packaging requirements in October 2018.[174] The country adopted the necessary legal amendments in February 2019[175] and the regulatory framework became effective on 1 July 2020.

The timing of Singapore's adoption of plain-packaging regulations was informed by the administration's awareness of the investment and

---

[169] Interview B3, 2019; Interview C5, 2019.

[170] Interview C5, 2019.

[171] *Ibid.* The interviewee pointed to the unsubstantiated character of the claim, as well as to the consultation processes at the time of negotiations to explain that there was no need to modify the existing processes in place.

[172] Gianna G. H. Amul and Tikki Pang, 'Progress in Tobacco Control in Singapore: Lessons and Challenges in the Implementation of the Framework Convention on Tobacco Control' (2018) 5 *Asia & Pacific Policy Studies* 102.

[173] See Smoking (Control of Advertisement and Sale of Tobacco) (Labelling) Regulations 2003 (No. S 378/2003).

[174] Ministry of Health, 'Singapore to Introduce Standardised Packaging and Enlarged Graphic Health Warnings', Press Release, 31 October 2018.

[175] Tobacco (Control of Advertisements and Sale) (Amendment) Act 2019 (Act 9 of 2019); Tobacco (Control of Advertisements and Sale) (Appearance, Packaging and Labelling) Regulations 2019 (No. S 480/2019); WTO notification: G/TBT/N/SGP/49, 1 July 2019.

trade litigation risks involved in introducing such measures. Interviewees confirmed that the government only decided to go ahead with its plain-packaging measures following the favourable resolution of claims concerning plain packaging that had been brought against other states under investment treaties[176] and at the WTO.[177] Indeed, the Singaporean government had long been aware of the legal risks posed by introducing plain packaging and the relevance of the experiences of other states. In 2013, the Minister of Health noted the following in response to a question on plain packaging by a Member of Parliament (MP):

> The tobacco companies and several countries have challenged the legality of the [Australian plain packaging] measures. … the question of whether the legislation infringes on intellectual property rights and violates global trade laws is pending dispute resolution between state parties at the World Trade Organisation. Australia has also been challenged by a tobacco company through the Hong Kong-Australia Bilateral Investment Treaty on grounds of unlawful expropriation of its investments and valuable intellectual property without compensation. My Ministry is closely monitoring the developments in Australia and around the world on this plain packaging, with regard to the legal issues as well as its effectiveness.[178]

Singapore's appreciation of the legal risks posed by the introduction of plain-packaging measures also influenced its approach to the way in which the regulations were formulated and adopted. The procedure leading to the plain-packaging measures was lengthier and more transparent than usual practice. It took over five years to come to fruition. Three consecutive rounds of public consultations took place during that period, one in 2015 and two in 2018.[179] Further, the government made public a substantial amount of the scientific data on which the plain-packaging

---

[176] *Philip Morris Asia Ltd* v. *Commonwealth of Australia*, PCA Case No. 2012-12, Award on Jurisdiction and Admissibility (17 December 2015); *Philip Morris Brands Sàrl, Philip Morris Products S.A. and Abal Hermanos S.A.* v. *Oriental Republic of Uruguay*, ICSID Case No. ARB/10/7, Award (8 July 2016).

[177] WTO Panel Report, *Australia – Certain Measures Concerning Trademarks, Geographical Indications and Other Plain Packaging Requirements Applicable to Tobacco Products and Packaging*, WT/DS435/R, WT/DS441/R WT/DS458/R, WT/DS467/R (28 June 2018). Interviewees specified that Singapore decided not to wait for a decision by the WTO Appellate Body (Interview B4, 2019; Interview C5, 2019).

[178] *Singapore Parliamentary Debates, Official Report*, vol. 90, 14 January 2013 (Mr Gan Kim Yong).

[179] See Ministry of Health, 'Singapore to Introduce Standardised Packaging and Enlarged Graphic Health Warnings', Press Release, 31 October 2018, together with documents mentioned in it.

proposal for the 2018 consultations was based, as well as all responses to both rounds of 2018 consultations.[180]

The government's approach to plain packaging was, to the author's knowledge, a unique departure from Singapore's usual administrative practice, which is less transparent. Public consultations are not mandatory in Singapore and, while they do occur, their format is at the discretion of the responsible agency.[181] In this respect, the number of consultations regarding plain packaging, and their manner, appear to have been unprecedented. Moreover, the results of consultations are not consistently published in Singapore and, when they are, usually take the form of a government prepared summary.[182] In this case, as noted, the government provided the full responses that participants submitted. By way of comparison, according to the Ministry of Health's website, at least three public consultations on other health-related regulations have taken place since the 2018 plain-packaging consultations. None have led to the publication of the scientific background data on which the regulations are based or the publication of the public's responses.[183]

From the perspective of internalisation, the procedure leading to the adoption of the plain-packaging regulation is of great interest. Importantly, just as with the situation involving Singapore's receipt of a notice of claim, the approach followed for plain packaging has not led to a broader change in procedure. Rather, it remains an outlier, perhaps best understood as a targeted ad hoc litigation avoidance measure.

This example of the government's use of the monitoring process offers evidence of narrow (in scope) and limited (in time) regulatory chill

---

[180] See Ministry of Health, 'Public Consultation on Proposed Tobacco-Control Measures in Singapore', www.moh.gov.sg/proposed-tobacco-control-measures.

[181] Interview D8, 2019; Interview F11, 2019.

[182] See, for example, Ministry of Health, 'MOH to Introduce Measures to Reduce Sugar Intake from Pre-packaged Sugar-sweetened Beverages', Press Release, 10 October 2019. For more general archives of public consultations conducted by Singaporean agencies at REACH (Reaching Everyone for Active Citizenry @ Home), see REACH, 'Archives', www.reach.gov.sg/participate/public-consultation/archives.

[183] Ministry of Health, 'Public Consultation on Measures to Reduce Sugar Intake from Pre-packaged Sugar-sweetened Beverages', Press Release, 4 December 2018; Ministry of Health, 'Public Consultation on Proposed Amendments to the Medical Registration Act', Press Release, 28 September 2018; Ministry of Health, 'Public Consultation on Proposed Amendments to Infectious Diseases Act', Press Release, 27 June 2018. The most detailed information on the outcome of the public consultation is available regarding sugar-sweetened drinks and it still takes the form of a summary of received responses: Ministry of Health, 'MOH to Introduce Measures to Reduce Sugar Intake from Pre-packaged Sugar-sweetened Beverages', Press Release, 10 October 2019.

consistent with existing literature on the way in which high-income countries respond to the risk of investment treaty claims.[184] Importantly, this instance, together with the notice of claim and the ABSD legislative modification described above, also show a conversely narrow focus on compliance, with no evidence of intent to implement broader policy changes on the part of the administration. They thus offer a novel nuance regarding the role of governmental capacity and its relation to the impact of investment treaties on national governance: the high capacity to tailor a precise response to a risky situation may, based on the Singaporean experience, in fact, limit the likelihood of broader rule of law improvements.

6.5   Internalisation Measures: The Legislature

International treaties, including investment treaties, do not need to undergo ratification by Parliament in Singapore. This presents a first limit to the ability of the legislature to internalise those treaties, as they are not necessarily included in the parliamentary process. In addition, as in most other countries, no implementing legislation for investment treaty obligations exists in Singapore.[185] Indeed, interviewees were unable to recall any instances of implementation measures pertaining to an investment treaty or investment chapter of an FTA.[186] In contrast, the FTAs to which Singapore is a party include a wide range of commitments, which have required implementation legislation and other implementing measures for non-investment chapters such as customs,[187] intellectual property,[188] competition,[189] and financial services.[190]

---

[184] Moehlecke, 'The Chilling Effect of International Investment Disputes'. The evidence is also complementary to the findings of Berge and Berger who study the chilling effect of investment claims on environmental regulation and find that regulatory capacity is a predicate for regulatory chill; see Berge and Berger, 'Do Investor-State Dispute Settlement Cases Influence Domestic Environmental Regulation?'.

[185] Singapore does not have a specific legislation on foreign investment, in which certain investment treaty obligations could have otherwise been mirrored.

[186] Interview B2, 2019; Interview B4, 2019; Interview C6, 2019.

[187] Interview B6, 2019. The United States–Singapore FTA was relevant, *inter alia*, for the revision of legislation on patents, trademarks, and medicines, namely the Patents Act (Cap 221, 2005 Rev Ed), Trade Marks Act (Cap 332, 2005 Rev Ed), and Medicines Act (Cap 176, 1985 Rev Ed) respectively. More recently, the EU–Singapore FTA gave the impetus for the adoption of the Geographical Indications Act 2014 (Act 19 of 2014).

[188] Interview B2, 2019.

[189] The United States–Singapore FTA served as a basis for the adoption of the Competition Act (Cap 50B, 2006 Rev Ed).

[190] Interview B2, 2019; Interview B4, 2019. The implementation measures did not require a legislative modification, however.

The process under which Acts of Parliament are adopted in Singapore is efficient. While any MP may introduce a bill, in practice, bills are first formulated by government ministries,[191] then vetted by both AGC and the Ministry of Law,[192] before being introduced to Parliament. Given the ruling party's considerable majority, bills are often not amended after being introduced to Parliament.[193]

A survey of ten years of archival records from parliamentary debates confirmed that there is a low level of awareness of investment treaties and their relevance for domestic governance in the legislative branch. The narrative that emerges from the review of parliamentary debates is that the government speaks from an expert position and debates are limited. In this role, governmental interventions before Parliament are geared towards instilling respect for international economic law obligations and an underlying narrative reiterating the benefits for Singapore of doing so.[194]

Both the number and type of references to investment treaties in parliamentary debates suggest only a superficial involvement by parliamentarians with these treaties. For example, although research identified fifty-eight parliamentary documents that referred to investment treaties,[195] these documents show a limited awareness regarding the content or relevance of investment treaty obligations for the domestic governance of Singapore. Typically, parliamentarians' questions and the answers from the executive relate to the outward dimension of investment treaties. Forty of all fifty-eight documents pertaining to investment obligations relate to outward investment, compared to only seventeen that concern inward investment. These figures suggest that officials see the treaties primarily as a means of creating positive conditions for Singaporean companies investing and trading abroad, while their relevance for domestic governance remains unaddressed.

---

[191] Tan, *The Constitution of Singapore*, 140–1.

[192] *Ibid.*

[193] *Ibid.*, 153. A Bill is read in Parliament three times, and it is often during the second reading that comments (if any) are made on its content.

[194] See, for example, *Singapore Parliamentary Debates, Official Report*, vol. 92, 5 August 2014 (Mr Gerald Giam Yean Song, Mr Lim Hng Kiang); *Singapore Parliamentary Debates, Official Report*, vol. 94, 2 March 2018 (Asst Prof Mahdev Mohan).

[195] Through a first selection based on a keywords search, I identified 142 potentially relevant archival parliamentary records. I then analysed these results qualitatively according to their level of actual engagement with Singapore's investment obligations. Out of the 142 originally identified documents, 28 were false positives and thus discarded as irrelevant. Another 56 only contained a nominal mention of a broad economic agreement, such as an FTA or discussed exclusively trade-related aspects of such an agreement. As such, they too could not constitute evidence of awareness in Parliament of investment obligations.

In addition, the archives reveal that parliamentary debates only exceptionally contain references to the content and specific obligations in investment treaties. Often, treaties are simply mentioned as deliverables in the context of activities' reports by the MOFA and MTI to Parliament for the purposes of budgeting oversight.[196] Indeed, only fifteen of the reviewed documents contain a reference to a specific investment obligation and about half of those documents bear no relation to the domestic governance of Singapore or the potential effect of investment treaties on domestic governance. Instead, these debates typically discuss the advantages of future treaties for Singaporean investors in terms of investment liberalisation or access to ISDS,[197] securing Singapore's place as a preferred arbitration hub, including for ISDS,[198] or the successful ratification of the EU–Singapore FTA.[199]

The remaining handful of parliamentary references touch upon international investment law's effect on domestic governance concerns such as tobacco plain packaging,[200] the impact of ISDS on Singapore's right to regulate,[201] and the ABSD.[202] Relevant as these queries are, their limited depth prompts the conclusion that there is only superficial awareness among MPs of the relevance of investment obligations for Singapore's governance, and only superficial oversight of the government's treaty making. Indeed, of all the parliamentary materials reviewed, MPs only twice raised questions as to whether Singapore's investment treaty obligations

[196] Forty-five out of a total of 142 documents containing relevant terms were either Committee of Supply or Budget related documents. The finding is in line with Poulsen's finding that investment treaties serve to justify bureaucrats' budget and status in the administration; see Lauge N. S. Poulsen, *Bounded Rationality and Economic Diplomacy: The Politics of Investment Treaties in Developing Countries* (Cambridge University Press, 2015).

[197] See *Singapore Parliamentary Debates, Official Report*, vol. 94, 19 November 2018 (Mr Desmond Choo, Mr Chan Chun Sing); *Singapore Parliamentary Debates, Official Report*, vol. 94, 7 November 2016 (Mr Thomas Chua Kee Seng, Mr Lim Hng Kiang); *Singapore Parliamentary Debates, Official Report*, vol. 94, 16 August 2018 (Mr Chan Chun Sing, Mr Ang Wei Neng).

[198] *Singapore Parliamentary Debates, Official Report*, vol. 94, 7 November 2017 (Asst Prof Mahdev Mohan, Mr K Shanmugam).

[199] *Singapore Parliamentary Debates, Official Report*, vol. 94, 7 November 2017 (Dr Koh Poh Koon, Asst Prof Mahdev Mohan).

[200] *Singapore Parliamentary Debates, Official Report*, vol. 90, 14 January 2013 (Mr Gan Kim Yong).

[201] *Singapore Parliamentary Debates, Official Report*, vol. 92, 5 August 2014 (Mr Gerald Giam Yean Song, Mr Lim Hng Kiang).

[202] *Singapore Parliamentary Debates, Official Report*, vol. 89, 9 April 2012 (Mrs Lina Chiam, Mr Lim Hng Kiang).

might impinge upon Singapore's ability to govern (or 'right to regulate').[203] In the other situations in which parliamentary references directly addressed the impact of investment treaty obligations on Singapore, it was the Minister's response to a broader question that introduced the issue (e.g., the relevance of the pending plain-packaging investment arbitration against Australia to Singapore's own regulations).[204]

Finally, it warrants noting that it is not only MPs' questions which are superficial. Often, the ministerial responses are as well. For instance, when asked about measures being taken by the government to ensure that Singapore's right to regulate would be preserved in the context of ISDS, MTI's response included a blanket statement that 'FTAs, including the TPP, do not restrict Singapore from adopting measures for legitimate public policy reasons, including the protection of public health and the environment'.[205] The Ministry of Law also pointed out briefly that '[they] actively participate in discussions on possible reform of ISDS mechanisms, so that any future disputes on trade agreements can be fairly and effectively resolved'.[206] No further details were provided in support of either of these statements. Moreover, in none of these instances did MPs demand such details in later sessions.

6.6 Internalisation Measures: The Judiciary

Singapore is a dualist State; thus, international treaties, including investment treaties, do not have force of law in the country[207] and must be subject to implementing legislation to acquire such force.[208] As a consequence,

---

[203] *Singapore Parliamentary Debates, Official Report*, vol. 94, 2 March 2018 (Asst Prof Mahdev Mohan); *Singapore Parliamentary Debates, Official Report*, vol. 92, 5 August 2014 (Mr Gerald Giam Yean Song).

[204] Parliamentary discussion regarding the ABSD reflects the same dynamic, although in that situation even the responding Minister did not expressly mention investment obligations in her answer. Only through interviews have I conclusively ascertained the relevance of investment treaties to the ABSD. This example is particularly revealing to the limited level of internalisation of investment obligations in Parliament, given that the ABSD is the only example of a policy modification based on investment obligations that interviewees unanimously referred to (see Section 6.4).

[205] *Singapore Parliamentary Debates, Official Report*, vol. 92, 5 August 2014 (Mr Lim Hng Kiang).

[206] *Singapore Parliamentary Debates, Official Report*, vol. 94, 2 March 2018 (Mr K Shanmugam).

[207] Centre for International Law and British Institute of International and Comparative Law, *Workshop on Treaty Law and Practice (16–19 January 2012): Workshop Report*, 44.

[208] *Ibid.*

unless there has been domestic legislation implementing a treaty, rights arising under the treaty (as well as the interpretation of the treaty) are non-justiciable in Singapore's courts.[209] Reflecting that position of treaties in Singaporean law, a review of Singaporean case law does not reveal any case in which a court has referred to an investment treaty in the course of adjudicating a domestic dispute.

As in other common law countries, the Singaporean courts follow a canon of statutory interpretation under which domestic laws are presumed to be consistent with Singapore's international law obligations ('presumption of consistency'),[210] so long as the statute's wording is amenable to such interpretation.[211] Research, however, does not reveal any instance in which this presumption has been applied in connection with an investment treaty. Indeed, there is some doubt in Singaporean law as to whether the presumption of consistency should apply to investment treaty obligations.

Singaporean case law is divided on whether the presumption of consistency applies in all cases or only in those in which the court concludes that an interpreted statute has been enacted specifically to give effect to a particular international obligation.[212] If the rule is the latter, of course, this would mean that investment treaties would effectively never be taken into account in statutory interpretation as Singapore has adopted no laws specifically to give effect to their investment obligations, a position that can be contrasted with certain other FTA obligations.[213] Moreover, even if

---

[209] *Lee Hsien Loong* v. *Review Publishing Co. Ltd* [2007] 2 SLR(R) 453, [2007] SGHC 24 at [97] (Singapore High Court).

[210] F. A. Mann, *Foreign Affairs in English Courts* (Oxford University Press, 1986), 130.

[211] *Yong Vui Kong* v. *Public Prosecutor* [2015] 2 SLR 1129, [2015] SGCA 11 at [49]–[50] (Singapore Court of Appeal).

[212] In *The 'Sahand'* [2011] 2 SLR 1093, [2011] SGHC 27 at [34] (Singapore High Court), the High Court opined that Singapore's international obligations were only relevant materials guiding the interpretation of written law in 'appropriate cases', such as when those laws were '*expressly* made to give effect to Singapore's international obligations' – but no such qualification appears a subsequent High Court judgment, namely *Public Prosecutor* v. *Tan Cheng Yew* [2013] 1 SLR 1095, [2012] SGHC 241 (Singapore High Court).

[213] By way of example, Singaporean courts discussed the obligations undertaken under the United States – Singapore FTA in several trademark-related disputes under the relevant implementing legislation, such as: *Louis Vuitton Malletier* v. *Megastar Shipping Pte Ltd* [2017] SGHC 305 at [78]–[79], [85]–[86], and [93]–[101] (Singapore High Court); *Novelty Pte Ltd* v. *Amanresorts Ltd and Another* [2009] SGCA 13 at [161]–[229] (Singapore Court of Appeal); *Zyfas Medical Co. (Sued as a firm)* v. *Millenium Pharmaceuticals, Inc.* [2020] SGCA 84 at [44]–[45] (Singapore Court of Appeal); *Samsonite IP Holdings Sarl* v. *An Sheng Trading Pte Ltd* [2017] SGHC 18 at [62] (Singapore High Court).

the presumption of consistency were to be applied more broadly, difficult issues might arise as to its application in individual cases. Because different investment treaties grant different (albeit similar) rights to the nationals of different states, applying the presumption of consistency to these treaties might entail adopting different interpretations of Singapore's domestic laws in different cases depending on the litigant-investor's nationality. This approach would be unprecedented in Singaporean statutory interpretation, and has been frowned upon by the High Court in relation to the interpretation of statutes relevant to other bilateral treaties.[214]

The only context in which the Singaporean courts have addressed investment treaty issues is where Singapore has been the seat of an investor–state arbitration[215] and the courts have been called upon to exercise their supervisory jurisdiction over the arbitral tribunals.[216] On these occasions, the Singaporean courts, assisted on certain unique questions by court-appointed *amici curiae*,[217] have demonstrated a sophisticated understanding of the procedural and jurisdictional issues that arise in investment disputes. It must be noted, however, that due to the limited nature of the courts' jurisdiction in these cases, the Singaporean courts have not needed to address the substantive obligations contained in investment treaties, which would tend to restrict the possibility for their internalisation in the judiciary.

6.7 Conclusion

Singapore demonstrates a high level of internalisation of investment treaty obligations in its governance. This high level of internalisation appears to be a product of the general characteristics of the country,

---

[214] *Public Prosecutor* v. *Tan Cheng Yew* at [62], concerning the interpretation of Singapore's Extradition Act (Cap 103, 2002 Rev Ed) and the (ir)relevance of Singapore's bilateral extradition treaties thereto.

[215] To date, Singapore has been the seat of nine known investor-state arbitral proceedings based on an investment treaty.

[216] See the annulment proceedings in the cases: *Sanum Investments* v. *Lao People's Democratic Republic (I)* [2016] 5 SLR 536, [2016] SGCA 57 (Singapore Court of Appeal); *Swissbourgh Diamond Mines (Pty) Limited* v. *Kingdom of Lesotho* [2019] 1 SLR 263, [2018] SGCA 81 (Singapore Court of Appeal); *Republic of India* v. *Vedanta Resources plc* [2021] SGCA 50 (Singapore Court of Appeal); *Republic of India* v. *Vodafone International Holdings B.V.*, SIC/OS 6/2021 (Singapore International Commercial Court) (pending).

[217] In *Sanum Investments* v. *Lao*, the Singapore Court of Appeal appointed Professors Simon Chesterman and Locknie Hsu, together with J. Christopher Thomas QC. In *Swissbourgh Diamond* v. *Lesotho*, the Court of Appeal appointed Professor N. Jansen Calamita and J. Christopher Thomas QC. In *India* v. *Vodafone*, the Singapore International Commercial Court appointed Professors Andrea Bjorklund and N. Jansen Calamita.

the characteristics of its public administration, and its development of a national internalisation strategy. Capacity and knowledge regarding international investment law is high in ministries and specialised agencies and there is a sustained effort to disseminate relevant information across the entire administration. Both AGC and MTI have taken active steps to increase awareness of investment obligations in line ministries and the administration at large. Moreover, the collaborative style of the Singaporean administration, especially with line agencies typically taking expert agencies' advice into account, buttresses the effectiveness of these efforts. These findings support Calamita and Berman's arguments regarding the diverse public administration and national factors that impact internalisation.[218]

The causal link between investment treaties and Singapore's internalisation practices, however, remains unclear. Based upon my research, it would appear that compliance with investment treaties across the administration is more a result of the general culture of respect for the law which prevails in the civil service, than of anything particular to investment treaties as such. Moreover, research reveals that the principal impetus for the creation of Singapore's internalisation processes has come from its international trade law commitments. Thus, as noted, Singapore's internalisation processes are general in scope rather than specifically related to investment treaties.

In addition, despite Singapore's sophisticated internalisation process and conducive environment for internalisation, this chapter has revealed certain calibration problems in the government's approach. There is a lingering mismatch between the focus of internalisation measures and the types of government action that are most likely to give rise to investment disputes. Thus, during treaty negotiations, line agencies are most engaged in the negotiation of pre-establishment provisions rather than in the negotiation of the post-establishment protections that generally lead to disputes. Moreover, the processes for reviewing executive or administrative decisions are less systematic than that for legislation, again in contrast to the types of government actions that most often lead to investment claims. Singapore's administration at times still considers the relevance of investment treaties along the lines of sectoral competence, even though past investment disputes have touched upon several economic sectors and areas of government. This suggests that even in the highly conducive

---

[218] See Chapter 1.

environment of a developed and effective administration, the internalisation of investment treaties presents challenges. In turn, these findings in a
'most likely' case study may warrant further research on other factors that
Calamita and Berman identify as relevant for investment treaty internalisation, such as the characteristics of treaties and the institutional framework of which they are a part.

Finally, with respect to the impact of Singapore's investment treaties
on the rule of law in Singapore, there is little evidence to support such a
conclusion. Singapore's overall approach to the internalisation of investment treaties is highly targeted to the object of those treaties – namely foreign investors and investments – which renders spill-over effects unlikely.
As regards the possibility of 'regulatory chill' alluded to in the literature,
Singapore's experience in situations involving high litigation risk suggests that with high regulatory capacity and expertise in investment law,
regulatory chill is limited in scope and time. Importantly, both instances
discussed in this chapter where compliance with investment treaty obligations led to tangible changes[219] were narrowly calibrated to the cases
at hand and there is no evidence that they triggered broader modifications to governance practices. Existing informational processes also caution bureaucrats only about their dealings with foreign investors. Given
Singapore's overall high level of internalisation, this finding casts doubt
over the plausibility of the hypothesis that investment treaties, if internalised, lead to improvements in governance and the rule of law.[220]

---

[219] See Section 6.4.4.2 on ABSD and Tobacco Plain Packaging.
[220] This statement is further supported by the fact that determining that there has been a positive impact on governance practices requires a high threshold, as identified in the existing
literature. See Jonathan Bonnitcha, *Substantive Protection under Investment Treaties: A
Legal and Economic Analysis* (Cambridge University Press, 2014), 133–9.

The Impact of Investment Treaties
on the Rule of Law in Sri Lanka

SACHINTHA DIAS*

7.1 Introduction

This chapter assesses the 'internalisation'[1] of Sri Lanka's obligations under its international investment agreements (IIAs)[2] and the impact of those obligations on the rule of law in Sri Lanka. The methodology adopted for this exercise is a mixture of semi-structured interviews with relevant stakeholders and an examination of documentary material related to three factual scenarios of the recent past that concerned international investments in Sri Lanka.

The findings reveal that although there is some awareness of Sri Lanka's IIA obligations within higher-level state organs,[3] such internalisation is lacking at the level of government agencies belonging to different fields that interact with foreign investors on a day-to-day basis. Despite the role of the Board of Investment of Sri Lanka (BOI) as the agency tasked with

---

* This piece is written in the author's personal capacity and in no way reflects the views of the Attorney General's Department of Sri Lanka. The author notes with gratitude the excellent research assistance provided by Ms. Hasini Rupasinghe of the Faculty of Law, University of Colombo.

1 See Chapter 1.
2 I use the shorthand 'IIA obligations' to refer to both standalone investment treaties and the investment chapters of free trade agreements.
3 By 'higher level state organs' I refer to state organs engaged in the formulation of laws, regulations and policy with respect to investment, including the Cabinet of Ministers, Parliament, the higher judiciary (i.e., the Supreme Court and the Court of Appeal), the Ministry of Foreign Affairs, the Ministry of Finance, the Central Bank, the Attorney General's Department, the Ministry in charge of industry and commerce and the Board of Investment. By 'lower-level state organs' I refer to state agencies which implement the policies, rules and regulations formulated by higher-level organs. This includes line ministries not directly involved in law and policy with respect to foreign investment (e.g., the Ministry of Power and Energy, the Ministry of Environment) and particularly project approving and licensing agencies. For a list of such agencies see footnote 53.

investment promotion and facilitation, there are no informational processes[4] in place to disseminate awareness of IIA obligations. Further, with the exception of Art. 157 of the Constitution, which establishes a basis for some monitoring during the legislative process, there are no monitoring processes for systematically considering IIA obligations when making decisions that potentially affect foreign investments.[5]

Even in higher levels of government, where there is evidence of an awareness of IIA obligations, the impact of such obligations on decision making appears minimal. Consequently, given that there is minimal evidence of the internalisation of IIA obligations, there is very little, if any, evidence of a spillover effect of such obligations on the rule of law and good governance in general. Thus, with respect to Sri Lanka, the 'rule of law' thesis[6] fails, and emphatically at that.

The chapter is structured as follows. Section 7.2 sets out the methodology of the research, followed by Section 7.3, which gives an overview of the legal regime for investment protection in Sri Lanka. Thereafter, Section 7.4 looks at the mechanisms of internalisation of IIA obligations within Sri Lanka's government structures through material gathered from interviews.

Section 7.5 focuses on three specific factual scenarios in the recent past, which implicated Sri Lanka's IIA obligations. These scenarios were spread over a period of roughly a decade and provide instructive case studies on the internalisation of IIA obligations and their impact on the rule of law within Sri Lanka. Section 7.5.1 assesses the oil hedging agreements concluded between the Ceylon Petroleum Corporation (CPC) and, *inter alia*, Deutsche Bank AG in 2008, which resulted in arbitration before the International Centre for Settlement of Investment Disputes (ICSID). Section 7.5.2 examines Parliament's passage of the Revival of Underperforming Enterprises or Underutilized Assets Act, No 43 of 2011 ('RUEUA Act'), a unique piece of legislation aimed at transferring to the government specified enterprises or assets which were considered 'underperforming' or 'underutilized' under the Act. Section 7.5.3 analyses the suspension and recommencement of the 'Port City' project – a project to build a city on reclaimed land near the Colombo Port carried out by a Chinese state-owned agency.

---

[4] Informational processes or measures, as defined by Calamita and Berman in Chapter 1.
[5] Monitoring processes or measures, as defined by Calamita and Berman in Chapter 1.
[6] See Chapter 1.

Having examined each of these scenarios, looking in particular at parliamentary debates, court decisions, and reports by government agencies, Section 7.6 assesses how and to what extent IIA obligations were taken into account in each case. Finally, Section 7.7 concludes with a discussion of the wider question of whether IIAs have had an impact on the rule of law in Sri Lanka.

7.2 Methodology

The research methodology employed in this project has been a mixture of semi-structured interviews and examination of primary and secondary documentary sources in order to identify the processes for and the extent of internalisation of IIA obligations in Sri Lanka.

With respect to the interviews, government institutions and stakeholders involved in (1) negotiating IIAs on behalf of the Government of Sri Lanka, (2) facilitating international investment within Sri Lanka, and (3) managing dispute resolution under IIAs were identified. Thereafter, interviews were conducted with representatives of the relevant government institutions.[7] With respect to the government officials who were interviewed, all officials were mid- to high-level officials within their institutions. Some of the officials had a degree of specialisation[8] in IIAs, whilst others had no such specialisation though they had experience dealing with foreign investors within the scope of their work. A total of ten interviews were conducted and all interviews were one-on-one.

The reason for a majority of the interviews being with officials from more senior government institutions was the assumption that any impact IIA obligations might have on the decision making of agencies further down the state hierarchy would have to stem from these nodes of

---

[7] Interviews were conducted with representatives of the following government agencies: Ministry of Foreign Affairs (Interview A1); the Attorney General's Department of Sri Lanka (Interviews B1, B2); the Board of Investment of Sri Lanka (Interviews C1, C2); National Agency for Public Private Partnership (Interview D1); and several government agencies involved in dealing with foreign investors in the power sector (Interviews E1, E2). Two further interviews were conducted with a lawyer of the private bar who represented an investor in an investor–state dispute against Sri Lanka (Interview F) and an independent consultant from the energy sector with experience assisting foreign investors (Interview G).

[8] All of the officers interviewed worked on matters relating to IIAs amongst other types of work. For instance, at the Attorney General's Department, the officers interviewed were those who would be typically allocated IIA-related work though the same officers would also handle matters relating to various aspects of domestic law as a matter of course. The percentage of each interviewee's worktime taken up by work related to IIAs differed.

government. This assumption was based on the experience of the author working with several government agencies and lower line ministries in his capacity as a government lawyer as well as the information borne out of the interviews themselves.[9] It is also supported by documents on Sri Lanka's institutional and regulatory capacity.[10]

The information gathered through the interviews was supplemented by reference to primary and secondary documentary sources. The primary sources considered include the Constitution of Sri Lanka, acts, regulations, parliamentary debates (Hansard), and case law. Secondary sources include reports, newspaper articles, and online resources.

7.3   The Legal Regime and Regulatory Environment for Investment Protection in Sri Lanka

7.3.1   Local Laws Governing Foreign Investment

IIAs are the only type of international treaty and, more generally, the only source of international law to receive constitutional protection in Sri Lanka. Article 157 of the Constitution[11] reads as follows:

> Where Parliament by resolution passed by not less than two-thirds of the whole number of Members of Parliament (including those not present) voting in its favour, approves as being essential for the development of the national economy, any Treaty or Agreement between the Government of Sri Lanka and the Government of any foreign State for the promotion and protection of the investments in Sri Lanka of such foreign State, its nationals, or of corporations, companies and other associations incorporated or constituted under its laws, such Treaty or Agreement *shall have the force of law in Sri Lanka and otherwise than in the interests of national security no written law shall be enacted or made, and no executive or administrative action shall be taken, in contravention of the provisions of such Treaty or Agreement.*[12]

---

[9] Especially Interview B1.

[10] See Government of Sri Lanka, Ministry of Finance, National Agency for Public Private Partnerships, *Framework Development and Infrastructure Financing to Support Public Private Partnerships: Environmental Assessment & Management Framework (EAMF) – Executive Summary* (18 July 2018), ii; Malathy Knight-John, Shantha Jayasinghe and Andrew Perumal, 'Regulatory Impact Assessment in Sri Lanka: The Bridges That Have to be Crossed', Centre on Regulation and Competition, University of Manchester, Working Paper No. 74 (June 2004).

[11] Constitution of the Democratic Socialist Republic of Sri Lanka (1978). Article 157 was part of the original Constitution as drafted in 1978.

[12] Emphasis added.

Thus, IIAs that are approved by Parliament as set down in Art. 157 are incorporated into the laws of Sri Lanka and are protected from written law[13] as well as executive and administrative action contrary to the provisions of such IIAs,[14] other than in the interests of national security. Article 157 therefore not only 'implements' IIAs,[15] but it also renders it unconstitutional to enact legislation and to take executive or administrative action that contravenes their provisions.

The process of ratifying IIAs in Parliament has been made mandatory. A Circular issued by the Presidential Secretariat indicates that treaties or agreements 'for the promotion and protection of investments are *required* to be tabled in Parliament' in order to secure constitutional protection.[16] This constitutional protection given to IIAs is in contrast to other sources of international law, which are only mentioned as principles of state policy. Article 27(15) of the Constitution states that the State shall *endeavour* to foster respect for international law and treaty obligations in dealings among nations.[17]

The reason for the inclusion of Art. 157 in Sri Lanka's Constitution probably lies in the political climate that existed when the Constitution of 1978 was drafted. One of the newly elected United National Party Government's central election pledges at the time was to liberalise the economy and attract foreign investment following the severely controlled economy under the rule of Sirimavo Bandaranayake's Sri Lanka Freedom Party from 1956 to 1977.[18] Article 157 is likely a product of the United National Party's constitutional reform project and its enthusiasm to create a stable investment climate to attract foreign investment. To understand the history and politics behind the constitutional protection of IIAs, further research – which goes beyond the scope of this chapter – would be required.

---

[13] Written law is defined in Art. 170 of the Constitution as 'any law and subordinate legislation [and includes statutes made by a Provincial Council], Orders, Proclamations, Rules, By-laws and Regulations made or issued by any body or person having power or authority under any law to make or issue the same'.

[14] For the definition of executive and administrative action in relation to fundamental rights, see for example, *Perera* v. *University Grants Commission* [1978–1979–1980] 1 SLR 128 (Sri Lanka Supreme Court).

[15] See Chapter 1.

[16] Presidential Secretariat, 'Interaction by Government Ministries/Departments with Foreign States and International Organizations' Circular No. SP/CA/01/11 (14 January 2011)   http://env.gov.lk/web/images/pdf/circulars/circular_in_deplomatic_relations.pdf (emphasis added).

[17] Constitution, Art. 27(15).

[18] See K. M. de Silva, *A History of Sri Lanka* (Vijitha Yapa Publications, 2005), 626–80.

The domestic law concerning foreign investment in Sri Lanka[19] includes the Board of Investment Act as amended ('BOI Act'),[20] which details the procedure on investing in Sri Lanka. The BOI may grant approval for investments in Sri Lanka under sections 16 and 17 of the BOI Act. Projects that are approved under section 17 may be exempted from the application of specific laws including customs and exchange control regulations. Other legislation regulating foreign investments include the Strategic Development Projects Act.[21] This Act gives the BOI the authority to nominate certain projects as 'strategic development projects', with the result that such projects enjoy the benefits stipulated under the Act.

In the past decade, several new laws and amendments have been enacted in order to boost investment protection and promotion in Sri Lanka. For example, the amendments to the Land (Restriction on Alienation) Act[22] in 2017 and 2018 relaxed restrictions related to purchasing of land and condominium parcels by foreigners.[23] The Inland Revenue Act[24] adopted a new incentive regime, moving past traditional tax holidays for investments.[25] Finally, under the Commercial Hub Regulation,[26] made under the Finance Act as amended,[27] a new enterprise established in Sri Lanka engaging in specified business activities, where at least sixty-five per cent of the total investment is from foreign sources, has been made exempt from, *inter alia*, the Customs Ordinance and the Exchange Control Act.[28]

Beyond these acts that regulate investments at the entry point, there is no legislation which provides substantive protection to investors for the duration of the investment. This is perhaps due to Art. 157 of the Constitution, which, if the process therein were followed, incorporates the protections under the relevant IIAs into domestic law.

---

[19] For a detailed overview, see Dilini Pathirana, 'An Overview of Sri Lanka's Bilateral Investment Treaties: Status Quo and Some Insights into Future Modifications' (2017) 7 *Asian Journal of International Law* 287, 293–5.

[20] No. 4 of 1978.

[21] No. 14 of 2008.

[22] No. 38 of 2014.

[23] Land (Restrictions on Alienation) Amendment Act, No. 3 of 2017, s. 2; Land (Restrictions on Alienation) (Amendment) Act, No. 21 of 2018, s. 2.

[24] No. 24 of 2017.

[25] Inland Revenue Act, No. 24 of 2017, Schedule II.

[26] No. 1 of 2013.

[27] No. 12 of 2012.

[28] No. 24 of 1953; see Finance Act – Commercial Hub Regulation, No. 1 of 2013, s. 2(1).

7.3.2   Processes in Place for the Negotiation of IIAs
and the Regulation of Foreign Investment

The entity tasked with coordinating the negotiation of investment treaties is the Ministry of Foreign Affairs. The negotiations also involve
representation from the BOI and the Attorney General's Department.[29]
The Ministry of Foreign Affairs claims to use a model text in these negotiations, which has been under review for several years.[30] However, some
interviewees denied the existence of a formal policy when entering into
negotiations for IIAs.[31]

The entity in charge of investments once they are admitted is the BOI,
which promotes itself as 'a central facilitation point for investors, offering convenience, easy access and information'.[32] The Ministry of Foreign
Affairs liaises with foreign state entities in the event of an investor–state
dispute, but it is the Attorney General's Department that is in charge of
handling dispute settlement with foreign investors.[33] There is evidence of
coordination between the Ministry of Foreign Affairs, the BOI, and the
Attorney General's Department during the process of treaty negotiations and to a lesser extent at the stage of dispute resolution. But crucially,
there seems to be little regularised coordination between these agencies
in between these stages, where IIA obligations are to be implemented in
day-to-day interactions with foreign investors.[34]

7.3.3   International Investment Obligations

Sri Lanka's international investment commitments include bilateral
investment treaties (BITs) with twenty-eight countries.[35] It is also party to
several broader economic agreements with investment chapters including the recently concluded Singapore–Sri Lanka Free Trade Agreement.[36]

---

[29] Interview A1.
[30] *Ibid.*; for a text of the Sri Lanka Model Bilateral Investment Treaty (undated), see
       UNCTAD Investment Policy Hub, 'Sri Lanka', https://investmentpolicy.unctad.org/
       international-investment-agreements/countries/198/sri-lanka.
[31] Interview B1.
[32] Board of Investment of Sri Lanka, 'Who We Are', https://investsrilanka.com/about-us/.
[33] Interview B1.
[34] Particularly Interviews A1, B1, B2, and C1.
[35] For a full list of these BITs, see Board of Investment of Sri Lanka, 'Investment Protection',
       http://investsrilanka.com/services/investment-protection/.
[36] Singapore–Sri Lanka FTA (2018). For an overview of all such agreements, see UNCTAD
       Investment Policy Hub, 'Sri Lanka', https://investmentpolicy.unctad.org/international-
       investment-agreements/countries/198/sri-lanka.

Sri Lanka is a party to the Convention on the Settlement of Investment Disputes between States and Nationals of Other States (ICSID Convention) and a founder member of the Multilateral Investment Guarantee Agency, an agency of the World Bank which provides safeguards against expropriation and non-commercial risks.

7.3.4 Investor–State Disputes

Sri Lanka has been the responding party in five investor–state arbitrations before the International Centre for the Settlement of Investment Disputes to date. These cases are *Asian Agricultural Products Ltd.* v. *Sri Lanka*,[37] *Mihaly International Corporation* v. *Sri Lanka*,[38] *Deutsche Bank AG* v. *Sri Lanka*,[39] *Eyre* v. *Sri Lanka*,[40] and most recently *KLS Energy* v. *Sri Lanka*.[41] The first and the third of these arbitrations were decided against Sri Lanka whilst the second and fourth were decided in favour of the State. Proceedings are still underway in *KLS Energy* v. *Sri Lanka*.[42]

7.3.5 Sri Lanka's Commitment to Attracting Foreign Direct Investment (FDI)

Attracting FDI has been a policy priority of successive governments since the liberalisation of the economy in 1977.[43] Budget allocations have been

---

[37] *Asian Agricultural Products Ltd. (AAPL)* v. *Democratic Socialist Republic of Sri Lanka*, ICSID Case No. ARB/87/3, Award (27 June 1990).

[38] *Mihaly International Corporation* v. *Democratic Socialist Republic of Sri Lanka*, ICSID Case No. ARB/00/2, Award (15 March 2002).

[39] *Deutsche Bank AG* v. *Democratic Socialist Republic of Sri Lanka*, ICSID Case No. ARB/09/2, Award (31 October 2012).

[40] *Raymond Charles Eyre Montrose Developments (Private) Limited* v. *Democratic Socialist Republic of Sri Lanka*, ICSID Case No. ARB/16/25, Award (5 March 2020).

[41] *KLS Energy Lanka Sdn. Bhd.* v. *Democratic Socialist Republic of Sri Lanka*, ICSID Case No. ARB/18/39.

[42] In the interests of full disclosure, the author is currently part of the Respondent's counsel team in *KLS Energy* v. *Sri Lanka*.

[43] See among many examples, *Parliamentary Debates (Hansard)*, vol. 195(1), 119, 22 November 2010 (Hon. Mahinda Rajapaksa) (Budget Speech on the investment climate); *Parliamentary Debates (Hansard)*, vol. 192(3), 590, 4 August 2010 (Hon. Sriyani Wijewickrama) (referencing the need to rejuvenate the legal framework to boost investor confidence and suit the development of commerce and industry); *Parliamentary Debates (Hansard)*, vol. 19(1), 192, 5 July 2010 (Hon. Harsha De Silva) (referencing the need to strategically approach the international community in a way that Sri Lanka can have leverage in maximising investment inflow). For statistics from 1977 to 2018, see CEIC, 'Sri Lanka Foreign Direct Investment', www.ceicdata.com/en/indicator/sri-lanka/foreign-direct-investment.

made to reform the institutional mechanisms to improve the investment climate and attract large, quality investments that add value to the economy.[44] The concerted effort to attract FDI has resulted in an increase in FDI in nominal terms. Sri Lanka's FDI inflows reached an all-time high of USD 961 million in the fourth quarter of 2017 but has dipped significantly since.[45]

Parliament has also made mention of IIAs in its endeavour to attract FDI.[46] It has been noted on occasion that the lack of the rule of law within the investment regime has led to expropriation and diminished investor confidence.[47]

7.4   Internalisation Generally: Interviews

Interviewees provided significant insight into the conditions of internalisation in Sri Lanka, revealing the non-existence of formal processes for internalising investment treaty obligations into government decision making. The clarity with which one interviewee answered the key inquiry of this paper was startling. Asked what formal and informal processes Sri Lanka had in place to 'internalise' its IIA obligations, defined as ensuring that the content of such obligations were known and taken into account in decision making at all levels of government, the interviewee replied, 'None. Absolutely none'.[48]

The interviewee illustrated the lack of coordination between organs of government *vis-à-vis* Sri Lanka's international obligations by referring to

---

[44] *Parliamentary Debates (Hansard)*, vol. 195(1), 119, 22 November 2010 (Hon. Mahinda Rajapaksa) (English text of the Budget Speech 2011).

[45] Board of Investment Sri Lanka, 'Sri Lanka Achieves Highest Ever FDI in 2017', 25 January 2018, https://web.archive.org/web/20180204080601/http://www.investsrilanka.com/news/story/4212/Sri-Lanka-Achieves-Highest-Ever-FDI-in-2017; Trading Economics, 'Sri Lanka Foreign Investment – Net Inflows', https://tradingeconomics.com/sri-lanka/foreign-direct-investment.

[46] See for example *Parliamentary Debates (Hansard)*, vol. 191(4), 974, 8 July 2010 (Hon. Risad Badhiutheen) (where the expansion of Sri Lanka's foreign trade relations through bilateral, regional and multilateral agreements is viewed as laying a solid foundation to promote investment); *Parliamentary Debates (Hansard)*, vol. 205(14), 2711, 17 December 2011 (Hon. Risad Badhiutheen) (referencing the Asia Pacific Free Trade Agreement, India–Sri Lanka Free Trade Agreement, and the Trade and Investment Framework Agreement with USA as arrangements that enable investment and trade opportunities).

[47] *Parliamentary Debates (Hansard)*, vol. 197(4), 634, 7 January 2011 (Hon. Lakshman Kiriella); *Parliamentary Debates (Hansard)*, vol. 206(4), 627, 20 January 2012 (Hon. Lakshman Kiriella).

[48] Interview B1.

Sri Lanka's tax commitments under the WTO regime. For instance, the interviewee stated that the offering of tax incentives by the BOI evinces a complete disconnect with the Department of Commerce, which enters into international agreements relating to trade and taxation on behalf of the government. It was stated that this disconnect between different government departments results in there being no transmission of the content of IIA obligations to line ministries and state agencies that come into contact with investors. This view was shared by several other interviewees, who agreed that there were no informational processes[49] for the internalisation of IIA obligations.[50] This view is corroborated by documents such as the Government Procurement Manual, where there is but a solitary reference to Sri Lanka's international obligations, located in a single sentence within the section on objectives.[51] Indeed, on the evidence provided, it appears that it is only through direct exposure to investor–state arbitration that officials from lower-level government agencies such as licensing authorities acquire any knowledge of IIA obligations.[52]

With respect to monitoring processes, Parliament has considered the need to strengthen monitoring and compliance in order to attract more FDI.[53] However, there seem to be few, if any, monitoring mechanisms in place to ensure that policy decisions as well as decisions by line ministries that affect foreign investors comply with IIA obligations. There is no legal requirement and no established practice to consider the views of the Attorney General's Department before making decisions which affect foreign investments. This was borne out by the interviews[54] and

---

[49] See Chapter 1.
[50] Interviews A1, B1, D1, and F. Other interviewees were slightly more hesitant to reveal that there were no such processes in place, for example, Interview C1.
[51] National Procurement Commission, Draft Government Procurement Manual 2017: Selection and Employment of Consultants, para. 18. The relevant sentence is 'adhering to prescribed standards, specifications, local laws, rules and regulations and international obligations'. An identical, solitary reference could also be found in the National Procurement Commission's Guidelines on Selection of Employees and Consultants, August 2007.
[52] Interviews E1 and E2. Licensing authorities for investment projects include, for instance, Divisional Secretaries in charge of state land, the Central Environmental Authority in charge of environmental approval, the Coast Conservation Department in charge of projects in the Coastal Zone and the Sustainable Energy Authority in charge of licensing projects relating to renewable energy resources.
[53] See for example, *Parliamentary Debates (Hansard)*, vol. 195(1), 118, 22 November 2010 (Hon. Mahinda Rajapaksa) (referencing the need to devote time to monitor and follow up on foreign investments).
[54] In particular, Interview B2.

is substantiated by the analysis of the Port City project below.[55] Whilst development projects are scrutinised against, for instance, environmental standards[56] and Regulatory Impact Assessments have been conducted in specific sectors,[57] there appears to be no mechanism to assess the impact of regulation and decision making on Sri Lanka's international obligations.

Sri Lanka does not have remedial mechanisms in place to review and correct its compliance with IIA obligations. There is no role such as that of an ombudsman to review decisions taken with respect to foreign investors ex ante and matters reach the Attorney General's Department at a very late stage once notice of arbitration has been received.[58] Though there is a process of consulting the Attorney General on matters of legality before contracts are signed, there does not seem to be a similar formal process of consultation when decisions are taken to suspend such contracts.[59]

There may, however, have been some changes to remedial mechanisms brought about through Sri Lanka's history of investor–state disputes. One interviewee pointed to the recently concluded Singapore–Sri Lanka FTA which includes a consultation mechanism, followed by the need to exhaust local remedies, before disputes are referred to arbitration. They stated that such a mechanism was included as a reactionary measure to Sri Lanka's investor–state disputes.[60] It was also noted that steps were being taken to reformulate Sri Lanka's model BIT and that several government organs were keen to begin a process of re-evaluating and renegotiating Sri Lanka's BITs.[61] Whether such efforts will bear fruit remains to be seen.

In sum, the evidence provided by interviewees reveals an almost total lack of formal processes for the internalisation of IIA obligations.

---

[55] See Section 7.5.3.
[56] The National Environment Act lays down detailed guidelines with respect to carrying out Environmental Impact Assessments (EIAs) for development projects. See National Environment Act, No. 47 of 1980 (as amended); see also Central Environmental Authority, 'Environmental Impact Assessment (EIA) Procedure in Sri Lanka', www.cea.lk/web/index.php/en/environmental-impact-assessment-eia-procedure-in-sri-lanka.
[57] For example, see Indunil Hewage, 'Country on Journey towards UN Guidelines on Consumer Protection', *Daily News*, 10 January 2018.
[58] Interviews B1 and B2.
[59] See for example 'Hedging Deal Consigned to the Dustbin?', 23 August 2017, Daily FT (where it is reported that the Attorney General was never consulted on the hedging agreements).
[60] Interview B2.
[61] Interviews A1 and B2.

7.5   Examination of Internalisation with Respect to Three Scenarios

This section will assess three events in the recent past which concerned Sri Lanka's IIA obligations. These scenarios were spread over a period of roughly a decade, involved legislative, judicial, and executive action which implicated Sri Lanka's IIA obligations, and received significant public attention. In the author's view, they provide instructive case studies on the level of internalisation of IIA obligations and their impact on the rule of law within Sri Lanka.

7.5.1   The Oil Hedging Agreements of 2007–2008

In 2007 and 2008, CPC entered into oil hedging agreements with several foreign and local banks to protect Sri Lanka against the impact of rising oil prices.[62] The focus of this section will be on the hedging agreement entered into between CPC and Deutsche Bank in July 2008.[63]

The drastic fall in oil prices in mid-2008 resulted in CPC having to make payments amounting to millions of dollars to the banks under the hedging agreements. CPC was exposed to a particularly high level of risk as there was no cap on the downside of the agreements (i.e., the liability of CPC in the event of a drop in oil prices), though the liability of the banks was capped in the event that oil prices remained above a specified amount for a specified period of time.[64]

With CPC having made the first few payments to Deutsche Bank under the agreement, the parties discussed renegotiation and subsequently, in December 2008, Deutsche Bank issued early termination notice on the basis that the ISDA Master Agreement had not been signed within the relevant time. The close out payment payable by CPC was calculated at USD 60,368,993.

The payments due to Deutsche Bank were halted by a Supreme Court decision and, subsequently, a Central Bank investigation. Deutsche Bank successfully claimed that the Supreme Court decision, the Central Bank

---

[62] For the fluctuations in oil price in the period concerned, see David Hugh and Cassie Barton, 'Oil Prices', Briefing Paper No. SNSG 02106, House of Commons Library (7 March 2016), 10–11.

[63] For a detailed chronology of the facts of the matter, see *Deutsche Bank* v. *Sri Lanka*, paras. 12–63.

[64] For an overview of the financial implications of the agreements, see Finance Training Course, 'Ceylon Petroleum Corporation (CPC) Oil Hedging 2007 – Case study', https://financetrainingcourse.com/education/2014/04/ceylon-petroleum-corporation-cpc-oil-hedging-2007-casestudy/

investigation, and the stop payment decision violated the fair and equitable treatment (FET) standard as well as constituted an expropriation under the Germany–Sri Lanka BIT.[65]

This section will assess whether and, if so to what extent, Sri Lanka's obligations under the Germany–Sri Lanka BIT were considered by the Supreme Court, the Central Bank, and Parliament when making decisions regarding payments under the hedging agreements.

7.5.1.1   The Supreme Court

Several fundamental rights applications were lodged in the Supreme Court of Sri Lanka alleging that the petitioners' right to equality before the law and equal protection of the law, guaranteed by Art. 12(1) of the Constitution, had been violated by the hedging agreements into which CPC had entered.[66] The Supreme Court adopted an interim order two days after the applications were filed. The interim orders required, *inter alia*, the suspension of payments by CPC to the banks under the hedging agreements on the basis that the petitioners had made a strong *prima facie* case that the agreements in question had not been entered into lawfully.[67] Thereafter, the Supreme Court made two more interim orders concerning the regulation of the price of petroleum-related products in Sri Lanka and investigations into the transactions.

The government followed the court order suspending payments to the banks, but it did not reduce the prices of petroleum products in accordance with the orders of court. The Supreme Court discontinued proceedings in January 2009 and vacated all previous orders on the basis that 'the applications have been filed in the public interest which would not be advanced in a situation of non-compliance with the order of Court by the Executive'.[68]

What is interesting for present purposes is that there was no mention of Sri Lanka's investment treaty obligations in the court's orders. This is

---

[65] Germany–Sri Lanka BIT (2000); *Deutsche Bank* v. *Sri Lanka*, paras. 474, 479–80, 484, 489–91 and 520–1.

[66] Supreme Court of the Democratic Socialist Republic of Sri Lanka, S.C. (FR) No. 535/2008 and S.C. (FR) No. 536/2008. Under Art. 126(1) of the Constitution, the Supreme Court has sole and exclusive jurisdiction to hear and determine any question relating to the infringement or imminent infringement by executive or administrative action of any fundamental right or language right declared and recognised by Chapter III or Chapter IV of the Constitution.

[67] *Ibid.*, Supreme Court minutes of 28 November 2008.

[68] *Ibid.*, Supreme Court minutes of 27 January 2009.

all the more noteworthy because the petitioner[69] had brought Sri Lanka's IIA obligations to the notice of court, arguing that the hedging agreements did not come within the scope of 'investments' protected under such agreements.[70] The CPC Chairman, in his affidavit, had stated that a default by the CPC on the payments due to the banks would amount to sovereign default and would have serious consequences for the country and its growth prospects, but did not refer to Sri Lanka's IIA obligations in resisting the fundamental rights applications.

The presiding judge in the case, the Chief Justice at the time, stated later in an interview that the decision was made to 'pass on the benefit [of reduced oil prices] to the people'. He also stated, referring to the claims made against Sri Lanka internationally that '[t]here are huge claims and I can't imagine how we are going to meet them. Internationally, we have no defence. This is a difficult fight'.[71]

The foregoing demonstrates that the Supreme Court was aware of Sri Lanka's IIA obligations and that its order could potentially violate these obligations. The IIA obligations did not however impact the court's decision to order that the payments be stopped.

7.5.1.2 The Central Bank

The Central Bank of Sri Lanka undertook an official investigation into the hedging agreements between CPC and the banks in question in November 2008. On 16 December 2008, the Monetary Board of the Central Bank sent a letter to the banks, referring to the Supreme Court's order of 28 November 2008 and requesting the banks not to proceed with or give effect to the transactions in question as the Central Bank considered them 'materially affected and substantially tainted'.[72]

Subsequently, in January 2009, the Central Bank issued its report into the hedging agreements concluding, *inter alia*, that the banks had not obtained the necessary approvals from the Board of Directors of CPC, had

---

[69] The petitioner in the main fundamental rights application was Nihal Sri Amarasekere, a former Chairman of the Public Enterprise Reform Committee. Other petitioners included Ravi Karunanayake, a Member of Parliament.

[70] See the Petition in Supreme Court S.C (FR) No. 481/2009, www.consultants21.com/pdf/public%20interest%20litigations/HEDGE-4-5.pdf, para. 11.

[71] Namini Wijedasa, 'Why Mahinda Rajapakse and Sarath Silva Became Enemies: An Interview with the Former Chief Justice', *TransCurrents*, 3 January 2010. See *Deutsche Bank* v. *Sri Lanka*, para. 479.

[72] *Deutsche Bank* v. *Sri Lanka*, para. 57.

not undertaken a proper risk assessment, and that CPC did not have the authority to enter into the hedging agreements. After the Supreme Court proceedings were terminated, the Central Bank confirmed that the directions in its letter of 16 December 2008 would remain in force in spite of the Supreme Court vacating its order suspending payment.[73] As a result, Sri Lanka refrained from making payments under the hedging agreements. There appears to have been no consideration of Sri Lanka's obligations under IIAs in the decision of the Central Bank to issue and then keep in force its order prohibiting CPC from proceeding with the payments under the agreements.

7.5.1.3   Parliamentary Proceedings

A survey of the parliamentary debates concerning the hedging agreements[74] shows no explicit consideration of Sri Lanka's obligations under IIAs. Instead, the focus of the debates was on the illegality of the agreements and the impact on Sri Lanka's economy of not being able to benefit from reduced oil prices and having to pay large amounts to the banks under the agreements.

The hedging agreements were a highly incendiary political issue at the time with opposition MPs referring to it as 'robbery' and akin to 'gambling'.[75] References were made in Parliament to the Supreme Court order of 28 November 2008 with opposition MPs claiming that since the Supreme Court had ordered the suspension of payment under the agreements, some relief could be passed to consumers by reducing petroleum prices.[76]

The Minister of Petroleum and Petroleum Resources Development at the time, Hon. A. H. M. Fowzie, made a statement to Parliament

---

[73] Central Bank of Sri Lanka, Press Release, 'CBSL direction re the Oil Hedging Transactions of several banks with the Ceylon Petroleum Corporation (CPC)', 27 January 2009.

[74] The Sri Lanka Parliament website offers a keyword search function for Hansard. The method adopted for searching Hansard for reference to Sri Lanka's IIA obligations in relation to the hedging agreements was to first isolate debates referring to the hedging agreements. This was done by searching for keywords related to the hedging deals through the search function. Once the relevant debates referring to the hedging agreements were isolated, the debates were checked for references to Sri Lanka's international obligations. This methodology applies to all searches of Hansard in this chapter.

[75] See for example *Parliamentary Debates (Hansard)*, vol. 179(10), 2100, 28 November 2008 (Hon. Sagala Ratnayake) (translated from Sinhalese).

[76] *Parliamentary Debates (Hansard)*, vol. 179(10), 2184, 28 November 2008 (Hon. John Amaratunga).

regarding the hedging agreements on 3 December 2008.[77] Though there was reference in the Minister's statement to the fact that Sri Lanka would be in default of its sovereign debt obligations if the CPC were to suspend payment to the banks, there was no mention of Sri Lanka's IIA obligations.

Following the award in *Deutsche Bank AG* v. *Sri Lanka*, which found Sri Lanka in violation of the Germany–Sri Lanka BIT's FET standard and expropriation clause, an MP who petitioned the Supreme Court on the hedging agreements stated his view that if the Supreme Court's injunctions had been 'allowed', Sri Lanka would have been able to avoid making payments to Deutsche Bank on the basis that it was prevented from doing so by the local courts.[78] This view, which is inaccurate as a matter of international (and Sri Lankan) law, evinces a broader lack of awareness of the content of IIA obligations throughout the legislature.[79]

7.5.2 The Revival of Underperforming Enterprises or Underutilized Assets (RUEUA) Act

The RUEUA Act[80] was a unique piece of expropriatory legislation which identified one enterprise and thirty-six assets as 'underperforming' and 'underutilized' respectively. It made provision to vest ownership of the identified enterprise and assets in the Government 'in order to ensure the effective administration, management or revival of such enterprises or assets, through alternate methods of utilization, such as restructuring or entering into management contracts'.[81]

Under the RUEUA Act, an 'underperforming enterprise' was defined as any company or body established under or by any written law in force, in which the Government owns shares and where the Government has

---

[77] *Parliamentary Debates (Hansard)*, vol. 179(10), 2818, 3 December 2008 (Hon. A. H. M. Fowzie).

[78] *Parliamentary Debates (Hansard)*, vol. 213(7), 1360–61, 26 November 2012 (Hon. Ravi Karunanayake).

[79] International Law Commission, 'Draft Articles on Responsibility of States for Internationally Wrongful Acts, with Commentaries' (2001) 2 *Yearbook of the International Law Commission* 146, Art. 4.

[80] Revival of Underperforming Enterprises or Underutilized Assets (RUEUA) Act, No. 43 of 2011, now repealed by Revival of Underperforming Enterprises or Underutilized Assets (Repeal) Act, No. 12 of 2019.

[81] RUEUA Act, Preamble.

paid contingent liabilities of such enterprise. Another feature was that the Government must be engaged in protracted litigation with regard to such enterprise, which is prejudicial to the national economy and public interest.[82] An 'underutilized asset' was defined as either:

(a) land which had been alienated by the Government on freehold or leasehold basis within a period of twenty years prior to the coming into operation of the Act under conditions such as that the operations related to it would bring about public benefit including generating employment or generating foreign exchange earnings, but with respect to which such benefits had not materialised; or

(b) land owned by a person that within a period of twenty years prior to the coming into operation of the Act had been granted incentives such as tax incentives or incentives under the BOI Law, on the condition that that the proposed operations would bring about public benefit, but with respect to which such benefits had not materialised.[83]

In schedules to the Act, the specific enterprise and assets to which the provisions of the Act would apply were identified.

The Act provided for the establishment of a Compensation Tribunal to receive claims for compensation by the shareholders of the 'underperforming enterprise' and the owners of the 'underutilized assets'.[84] The Act provided that the shareholders and owners would 'be entitled to receive prompt, adequate and effective compensation . . . '.[85]

The Act had potential implications for Sri Lanka's IIA obligations insofar as the enterprise and some of the assets identified had foreign ownership. For example, the sole enterprise identified as 'underperforming' under the Act, Hotel Developers (Lanka) PLC, had Japanese shareholders,[86] who would have been covered under Sri Lanka's IIA with Japan.[87]

This section will examine the consideration of Sri Lanka's IIA obligations in the Supreme Court Special Determination and the parliamentary proceedings with respect to the Act. It will also discuss the Central Bank's reaction to the criticism of the Act.

---

[82] RUEUA Act, s. 9.
[83] *Ibid.*
[84] *Ibid.*, ss. 5–6.
[85] *Ibid.*, s. 4.
[86] Nihal S. Amerasekere, *Settlement of a Fraud Colombo Hilton Hotel Construction: Fraud on Sri Lanka Government* (Author House, 2012), 678.
[87] Japan–Sri Lanka BIT (1982).

7.5.2.1   The Special Determination of the Supreme Court

The Bill introducing the RUEUA Act was declared 'urgent in the national interest' by the Cabinet of Ministers under the now repealed Art. 122(1) of the Constitution. The practical consequence of this designation was that the Bill did not need to be gazetted prior to it being placed on the Order Paper of Parliament. A further consequence was that the President was required to request a special determination of the Supreme Court as to whether the Bill or any of its provisions were inconsistent with the Constitution.

The Special Determination of the Supreme Court on the Bill referred specifically to Art. 157 of the Constitution. The Supreme Court discussed the impact that the legislation might have on Art. 157 in its discussion of clause 4 of the draft Bill, which dealt with vesting in the Secretary to the Treasury the shares of the underperforming enterprise and the underutilised assets concerned. The Court stated that the Bill would not be in contravention of any relevant investment treaties or agreements because it provided for prompt, adequate, and effective compensation.[88] The Court also noted that the Act was not in violation of Art. 157 as the vesting would take place for a public purpose. Accordingly, the Court found the Bill not to be inconsistent with the provisions of the Constitution.

Thus, in its consideration of the Bill, the Supreme Court considered Sri Lanka's obligations under IIAs by virtue of its consideration of Art. 157 of the Constitution. It was satisfied that Sri Lanka's obligations were met by the inclusion of a provision for prompt, adequate, and effective compensation and due to the fact that the takings were for a public purpose.

7.5.2.2   Parliamentary Proceedings

The Special Determination of the Supreme Court was tabled in Parliament on 8 November 2011 and the Bill was debated and passed in Parliament on 9 November 2011. During the debate, several opposition MPs raised the issue of the impact of the Bill on Art. 157 of the Constitution. Referring to foreign investments in two of the entities/assets identified in the Act, namely Hotel Developers (Lanka) PLC and Sevanagala Sugar Industries (Pvt) Ltd, one opposition MP stated that the Act was in direct contravention of Art. 157 of the Constitution as the takings were not for reasons of national security. The MP stated that the Act would violate the provisions

---

[88] RUEUA Act, s. 4(2).

of Sri Lanka's IIAs with the states of nationality of the investors in these enterprises and that this would have a devastating effect on the economy.[89]

Another opposition MP referred to Art. 157 and stated that the bilateral and multilateral investment agreements entered into by Sri Lanka for the protection of foreign investments would be rendered redundant by the Act.[90] Other Members raised concerns regarding the Act's impact on investor confidence and the flow of foreign direct investment to Sri Lanka.[91] Still others argued that the Act directly violated agreements that some of the entities concerned had entered into with the BOI.[92]

It is clear from the foregoing that Members of Parliament were aware of Sri Lanka's obligations under its IIAs by virtue of Art. 157 of the Constitution, and took these obligations into account in considering the RUEUA Act. It is also clear that despite the concerns raised by some MPs, the Act was passed into law.

7.5.2.3   Reaction by the Central Bank

An interesting development following the passage of the Bill into law was that the Central Bank issued a press release explaining the purpose of the Act and offering assurances that the Act did not in any way constitute a nationalisation or expropriation of private assets.

A part of the press release reads as follows:

> [T]he Revival of Underperforming Enterprises and Underutilized Assets Act does not, in any way, constitute the nationalization or the expropriation of private assets, but instead, is designed to ensure the productive use of assets that have hitherto been lying abandoned or have been seriously underutilized.[93]

The press release appeared to be a reaction to the views expressed by several local and international bodies that the Act amounted to expropriation and would hurt investment in Sri Lanka.[94] Thus, whilst the proximate reason for the press release was the Central Bank's interest in ensuring that

---

[89] *Parliamentary Debates (Hansard)*, vol. 203(7), 988, 9 November 2011 (Hon. Wijeyadasa Rajapakshe).

[90] *Parliamentary Debates (Hansard)*, vol. 203(7), 1074, 9 November 2011 (Hon. Kabir Hashim).

[91] *Parliamentary Debates (Hansard)*, vol. 203(7), 1067–8, 9 November 2011 (Hon. D. M. Swaminathan).

[92] *Parliamentary Debates (Hansard)*, vol. 203(7), 1062, 9 November 2011 (Hon. Harsha de Silva).

[93] Central Bank of Sri Lanka, Press Release, 'Revival of Underperforming Enterprises and Underutilized Assets Act', 17 November 2011.

[94] See for example LBO, 'Sri Lanka Expropriations Will Hurt Economy: EIU', *Lanka Business Online*, 21 November 2011; LBO, 'Sri Lanka: Expropriations Will Hurt Investment: Fitch', *Lanka Business Online*, 16 November 2011.

local and foreign investor confidence would not be not adversely affected, one could surmise that the desire to avoid breaching IIA obligations in a manner that might damage the investment climate would also have affected the Central Bank's decision making. This view is bolstered by the fact that the *Deutsche Bank* proceedings, in which the Central Bank's role was severely criticised, were underway at this point in time.

7.5.3 The 'Port City' Project

The 'Port City' project is an ongoing project to reclaim 269 hectares of land adjacent to the Galle Face Green in Colombo for the purpose of constructing a state-of-the-art city with investment from a Chinese state-owned agency. The government led by President Mahinda Rajapaksa signed the agreement for the project in 2013. Upon the election of Maithripala Sirisena as President in January 2015, and the formation of a United National Party led government, however, the Port City project was suspended based on allegations of corruption by the Rajapaksa administration and the absence of required clearances and permits for the project. The project was recommenced in 2016 after renegotiations between Sri Lankan state organs and the Chinese state-owned company.[95] This section will assess whether Sri Lanka's IIA obligations were considered in the suspension and recommencement of the project.[96]

7.5.3.1 The Suspension of the Project

A Cabinet Decision was made in March 2015 to suspend the operations of the project with immediate effect and to inform the company carrying out the project to produce valid permits/approvals within two weeks. The Decision was taken pursuant to a proposal made by Hon. Ranil Wickremasinghe, the Prime Minister, which in turn was based on the interim report of a committee of experts appointed to review the project.[97] It was noted in interviews conducted for this chapter that the Attorney General was not consulted prior to the suspension of the project.[98]

---

[95] For an overview of the project, see Anjelina Patrick, 'Revival of Colombo Port City Project: Implications for India', 27 October 2016, www.maritimeindia.org/View%20 Profile/636131464409108056.pdf.

[96] See China–Sri Lanka BIT (1986).

[97] Office of the Cabinet of Ministers, 'Port City Development Project', Press Briefing of Cabinet Decision on 2015-03-04, www.cabinetoffice.gov.lk/cab/index.php?option=com_content &view=article&id=16&Itemid=49&lang=en&dID=5976.

[98] Interview B1.

The reasons provided for the suspension of the project were the apparent lack of Cabinet approval, environmental concerns, and the lack of proper feasibility studies carried out prior to entering into the agreement.[99] The re-evaluation of the Port City project and of China's presence and investment in the country generally was, however, a key election pledge of President Sirisena and it was noted in the media that the decision to suspend the project contained strong political overtones.[100]

Following the suspension of the project, concerns were raised in Parliament regarding the impact of the suspension on Sri Lanka's investment prospects as well as on the IIAs to which Sri Lanka was a party.[101] Despite these concerns, the Sirisena administration continued its suspension of the project for over a year.

7.5.3.2   The Renegotiation of the Port City Agreement

In June 2015, the Cabinet approved a proposal by the Prime Minister to vest the activities of the project with the Urban Development Authority,[102] to instruct the Central Environment Authority to commence a comprehensive Environment Impact Assessment, and to consider the recommencement of the activities of the project.[103] By December 2015, the Government indicated that the project would be allowed to resume and, in March 2016, ahead of a visit by Prime Minister Ranil Wickremesinghe to China, the Cabinet Committee on Economic Management recommended that the Colombo Port City project be resumed.[104]

As a result of the project's suspension, the Project Company had claimed USD 125 million in compensation for losses caused by the delay to the project. In interviews, officials revealed that the claim was based on the contract with the Project Company and that the Sri Lanka–China BIT was not invoked at that point in time.[105] The claim reached the Attorney

---

[99]   *Parliamentary Debates (Hansard)*, vol. 232(9), 940, 18 February 2015 ('Present Situation of the Port City Project: Statement by the Hon. Ranil Wickremasinghe, Prime Minister').

[100]   See Taylor Dibbert, 'Sri Lanka's Port City Project Is Back in Business', *The Diplomat*, 12 March 2016.

[101]   See *Parliamentary Debates (Hansard)*, vol. 233(5), 541, 20 March 2015 (Hon. Lakshman Yapa Abeywardena).

[102]   A statutory body tasked with managing matters of urban development under the Urban Development Act, No. 41 of 1978.

[103]   Office of the Cabinet of Ministers, 'Colombo Port City Development Project', Press Briefing of Cabinet Decision taken on 2015-06-17, www.cabinetoffice.gov.lk/cab/index .php?option=com_content&view=article&id=16&Itemid=49&lang=en&dID=6149.

[104]   Kelum Bandara, 'Proposal to Resume Colombo Port City Project', Daily Mirror, 10 March 2016.

[105]   Interview B1.

General's Department who were preparing their defence of the claim.[106] However, the claims were dropped in August 2016 as a result of additional land being offered to the Project Company under a renegotiated contract.[107] On 12 August 2016, a new tripartite agreement was signed between the Sri Lankan government, its Urban Development Authority, and the Chinese firm managing the Project locally.[108] The Cabinet Decision to recommence the project made reference to the claim made by the Chinese investor.[109]

7.6   Analysing Internalisation in Sri Lanka

Despite interviews revealing few formal processes in place to internalise IIA obligations, the above scenarios display evidence of some awareness of IIA obligations at the higher-level institutions concerned with formulating laws, regulations and policy with respect to investments.

In the oil hedging cases, for example, the Supreme Court was well aware of the relevance of Sri Lanka's IIA obligations with respect to the hedging agreements through the petitioner's pleadings, and despite not addressing the impact of these obligations in its orders, the presiding judge's subsequent interview reveals an awareness of their impact on Sri Lanka's international responsibility. Similarly, in the Supreme Court Special Determination on the RUEUA Act, the Supreme Court had to consider whether the Bill was in accordance with Art. 157 of the Constitution and by extension, Sri Lanka's IIA obligations.

The parliamentary debates concerning the Port City project likewise reveal that Sri Lanka's IIA obligations were discussed, particularly by opposition MPs opposing the government's suspension of the project. Parliament also showed awareness of Sri Lanka's IIA obligations during the passage of the RUEUA Act. Similarly, the Central Bank, though not explicitly, displayed an awareness of Sri Lanka's IIA obligations, particularly in its press release concerning the RUEUA Act.

The reasons for Sri Lanka's IIA obligations being considered in the manner in which they were in the three factual cases are important for present purposes. The following sections will assess these reasons and

---

[106] Interview B2.
[107] 'Sri Lanka Says Chinese Firm Drops Claim Over Colombo Port City's Delay', Reuters, 2 August 2016.
[108] Patrick, 'Revival of Colombo Port City Project', 2.
[109] 'Decisions Taken by the Cabinet of Ministers at its Meeting held on 01-08-2016', News.lk, 2 August 2016.

draw inferences from the manner in which IIA obligations were considered. This will be followed by some conclusions on internalisation and possible spillover effects on the rule of law in Section 7.

7.6.1   Reasons for the Consideration of IIA Obligations

7.6.1.1   Article 157 of the Constitution

It is clear that Art. 157 of the Constitution has, in practice, proven to be the most significant catalyst for the internalisation of Sri Lanka's IIA obligations. The Article does not merely incorporate Sri Lanka's IIA obligations into domestic law, it is also the means through which decision-making organs of government are required to consider these obligations.

In the Supreme Court Special Determination, as well as in the parliamentary debates on the RUEUA Act, it was the Act's impact on Art. 157 that was considered. Moreover, under Art. 77 of the Constitution, the Attorney General is required to assess whether any Bill that is placed before parliament is required to be passed by a special majority (i.e., whether the Bill is inconsistent with the Constitution).[110] This requires the Attorney General to consider if the Bill violates, *inter alia*, Art. 157 of the Constitution. Thus, by virtue of Art. 157, there is a strong monitoring system in place for the consideration of Sri Lanka's IIA obligations in the legislative process. Indeed, one of the key aspects of the BOI's campaign to attract FDI to Sri Lanka is the constitutional protection given to Sri Lanka's IIA commitments by Art. 157.[111]

It bears noting, however, that although Art. 157 appears to have a marked effect on internalisation in the legislative process, interviews undertaken for this project demonstrated that the presence of Art. 157 has not resulted in the consideration of IIA obligations within the government machinery more generally.

7.6.1.2   Claims by Foreign Investors

Another reason for the consideration of IIA obligations in the scenarios was the prospect (or existence) of a claim against the government by a foreign investor. This was evident with respect to the Port City project, where

---

110   Constitution, Art. 77.
111   See Board of Investment of Sri Lanka, 'Why Sri Lanka: Investment Protection and Double Taxation', https://web.archive.org/web/20171016140416/www.investsrilanka.com/why_ sri_lanka/investment_protection.

the potential claim by the Chinese investor played a role in the renegotiation and recommencement of the project.[112] With respect to the hedging agreements, the discussion in Parliament only focused on Sri Lanka's IIA obligations once the claims against Sri Lanka were made.[113]

The threat/institution of IIA claims resulted in Sri Lanka's policy makers discussing and considering the impact of Sri Lanka's IIA obligations on their decision making. Nevertheless, it is noteworthy that with respect to the decision to suspend the Port City project in the first place, and the decision by the Central Bank to stop payments under the hedging agreements, that is, the decisions which gave rise to the claims, there is little evidence that Sri Lanka's IIA obligations were considered at that stage. That said, one problem with ascertaining the role played by Sri Lanka's IIA obligations in these decisions is that the minutes of Cabinet Meetings where decisions on these matters are taken as well as any consultation with the Attorney General remain confidential. Only press releases on Cabinet Decisions are publicly available. These press releases do not reflect any consideration of the IIA implications on the government's decision making. Moreover, as noted previously, there seems to be no practice of consulting the Attorney General before decisions to suspend contracts are taken.[114]

7.6.1.3 Opposing the Measures Taken by the Government

Another common theme in the scenarios is that the relevance of IIAs to the government's decisions has often been raised first by opposition MPs in opposing the government. Different parties at different times have used Sri Lanka's IIAs to criticise the decisions of the government of the day. This was true of certain United National Party MPs in opposing the RUEUA Act[115] and of some Sri Lanka Freedom Party MPs in opposing the suspension of the Port City project.[116] Without seeming cynical, the manner of these invocations render it difficult, in the author's view, to see

---

[112] 'Decisions Taken by the Cabinet of Ministers at its Meeting held on 01-08-2016', News. lk, 2 August 2016, www.news.lk/cabinet-decusions/item/14044-decisions-taken-by-the-cabinet-of-ministers-at-its-.

[113] See for example *Parliamentary Debates (Hansard)*, 30 June 2010, vol. 190(2), 249 (Hon. M. A. Sumanthiran).

[114] See Section 7.4.

[115] *Parliamentary Debates (Hansard)*, 9 November 2011, vol. 203(7), 988 (Hon. Wijeyadasa Rajapakshe).

[116] *Parliamentary Debates (Hansard)*, 20 March 2015, vol. 233(5), 541 (Hon. Lakshman Yapa Abeywardena).

them as driven by principle. Rather, the evidence suggests that IIA obligations have been invoked when they serve the broader goals of the party concerned.

7.6.2 Inferences from the Manner in Which IIA Obligations Were Considered

7.6.2.1 Awareness of the Existence but Not of the Content of IIA Obligations

Based on the material surveyed with respect to the scenarios, it can be surmised that the Supreme Court, Parliament, and the Central Bank were aware of Sri Lanka's IIA obligations. However, apart from the Supreme Court, where the Chief Justice's comments following the hedging deal evince an understanding of the content of IIA obligations,[117] the awareness seems to be of the existence of IIA obligations, not of their precise content and scope.[118]

7.6.2.2 Influence of IIA Obligations on Decision Making

Despite evidence of a level of awareness of Sri Lanka's IIA obligations at higher levels of government, the scenarios considered do not show that these obligations have had a consistent influence on the decision making of state organs. Thus, this study demonstrates that even when there is internalisation in government decision making, that is, the existence of IIA obligations are taken into account, such internalisation does not ensure that the government's decision making will steer towards compliance with IIA obligations.

The dispute involving Deutsche Bank provides an illustration. In that scenario, Sri Lanka made the decision to withhold payments under hedging agreements with a number of different banks, including Deutsche Bank. On one explanation of Sri Lanka's action in that scenario, the Sri Lankan state organs truly believed that non-payment was defensible on the international plane because the hedging agreements were illegal. And,

---

[117] Namini Wijedasa, 'Why Mahinda Rajapakse and Sarath Silva Became Enemies'.

[118] See for example *Parliamentary Debates (Hansard)*, 26 November 2012, vol. 213(7), 1360–61 (Hon. Ravi Karunanayake) where the Minister states that if the Supreme Court's injunctions on payments to the foreign banks under the hedging deals remained in place, Sri Lanka would not have had to face claims by the foreign banks concerned.

indeed, this argument succeeded in an arbitration brought against Sri Lanka by one of the banks, Citibank,[119] although it did not succeed in the ICSID arbitration with Deutsche Bank nor in a litigation brought in the English courts by Standard Chartered Bank.[120]

Another plausible explanation, however, is that even though Sri Lanka understood that non-payment under the hedging agreements would be problematic *vis-à-vis* its international obligations, it decided to risk breaching those obligations due to politically expedient domestic considerations. This view seems particularly plausible when one considers (a) the statements of the Petroleum Minister to Parliament that the agreements had been properly concluded; (b) the CPC Chairman's statement that defaulting on the agreements was not an option for Sri Lanka; and (c) the former Chief Justice's statement that Sri Lanka had no valid defence internationally at the time it stopped payments under the agreements. This alternative explanation is further supported by the majority award of the ICSID Tribunal in *Deutsche Bank*, which was particularly harsh in its assessment of the Central Bank's actions, stating that the decision to suspend payments had been motivated principally by public criticism and media pressure.[121]

With respect to the RUEUA Act, it is noteworthy that the relevant state organs considered Sri Lanka's investment treaty obligations through the application of Art. 157 of the Constitution and then decided to enact the Bill into law, taking pains to emphasise publicly that the law was did not expropriate or nationalise private assets. On the one hand, this could be seen as an attempt by Sri Lanka to justify its conduct with respect to the legal content of its international obligations. On the other hand, it may also have been the case that the justifications were offered for fear of losing investor confidence and foreign investment rather than any fear about the legal consequences of breaching Sri Lanka's obligations.[122]

---

[119] *Citibank N.A.* v. *Ceylon Petroleum Corporation*, LCIA Arbitration No. 81215, Award (31 July 2011).

[120] *Standard Chartered Bank* v. *Ceylon Petroleum Corporation* [2012] WLR(D) 232, [2012] EWCA Civ 1049 (England and Wales Court of Appeal); see Finance Training Course, 'Ceylon Petroleum Corporation (CPC) Oil Hedging 2007 – Case study', https://financetrainingcourse.com/education/2014/04/ceylon-petroleum-corporation-cpc-oil-hedging-2007-casestudy

[121] *Deutsche Bank* v. *Sri Lanka*, para. 482.

[122] See in particular, Central Bank of Sri Lanka, 'Revival of Underperforming Enterprises and Underutilized Assets Act', 17 November 2011, Press Release.

Finally, with respect to the Port City project, the decision to suspend the project could potentially be explained by the view that there were failures by the Project Company to perform its obligations under the contract.[123] On the other hand, the timing of the decision following the general election lends currency to the view that the government may have taken a calculated decision to risk violating the state's obligations under the contract with the project company and potentially Sri Lanka's BIT with China due to the political benefits it would gain by suspending the project. Similarly, the decision to renegotiate the contract and recommence the project may plausibly have been influenced by the pressure imposed by the Chinese Government and Sri Lanka's reliance on Chinese investment. But the claim for compensation for losses arising from the suspension of the project was also undoubtedly a factor in this decision.[124]

7.6.2.3   The Impact of Arbitral Awards

As noted above, the scenarios illustrate how it has often only been the institution of claims (or the threat of claims) against Sri Lanka that has brought about consideration of IIA obligations by government officials. Unlike other states that have faced major claims and had arbitration awards issued against them,[125] however, the interviews undertaken for this chapter reveal that Sri Lanka's claims experience has resulted in few, if any, formal measures of internalisation, particularly at the level of line ministries and bodies such as licensing authorities that deal with investors on a day-to-day basis.[126]

The reasons for this may be hypothesised as follows. Many of Sri Lanka's state-owned corporations face claims regularly due to factors such as the lack of proper internal processes and the discontinuity of management upon political change.[127] The case studies also reveal that, at least at higher

---

[123] The interviewee of Interview B1 stated that the AG's Department was preparing a defence based on the failure of the Project Company to obtain environmental clearance.

[124] 'Decisions Taken by the Cabinet of Ministers at its Meeting held on 01-08-2016', News.lk, 2 August 2016.

[125] Dilini Pathirana, 'An Overview of Sri Lanka's Bilateral Investment Treaties', 298 (raising the examples of Venezuela, Bolivia, and Ecuador as states which have denounced the ICSID).

[126] In particular, Interview B2.

[127] This is based on the author's personal knowledge from handling disputes of this nature for the government.

levels of government, the reasons that IIA obligations were overlooked had more to do with political expediency than the lack of processes to consider the same. Thus, it may well be that in addition to shortcomings in regulatory capacity, the nature of the factors which result in claims against Sri Lanka do not trigger the need to formulate processes to internalise Sri Lanka's IIA obligations.

Whilst Sri Lanka has not denounced or attempted to renegotiate its BITs after the *Deutsche Bank* decision,[128] it will be recalled that the provisions in the new Singapore–Sri Lanka FTA were attributed by some interviewees to the impact of adverse arbitral awards.[129] It was also revealed in the interviews that work was afoot to develop a new model BIT along the lines of the investment chapter in the Singapore–Sri Lanka FTA. The reason provided for the interest in developing a new BIT was the regularity with which Sri Lanka was being presented with claims under its existing IIAs by foreign investors.[130] Thus, Sri Lanka does seem to have been pushed by the claims it has faced to attempt to reformulate its treaty-making strategy, along the lines of India following the *White Industries* case.[131] How far the process will go and whether it will culminate in the renegotiation of Sri Lanka's BITs is yet to be seen.

7.6.2.4   The Impact of Interest Groups and Corruption

Another factor of note is the role that interest groups have played in the internalisation of IIA obligations. The material considered indicates that with respect to the hedging agreements, the petitioners before the Supreme Court claimed that there would be no violation of Sri Lanka's IIA obligations if payments were stopped. As examined above, the thrust of the debates in Parliament, which reflected the public sentiment at the time, as well as that of civil society activists before the Supreme Court, was that the agreements were entered into illegally and that the benefit of reduced oil prices should be passed on to the consumer.

---

[128] See also Dilini Pathirana, 'An Overview of Sri Lanka's Bilateral Investment Treaties', 298 (stating that '[Sri Lanka] did not constructively reconsider its conventional approach towards the IIAs, as the North American countries did after defending a number of investment arbitration cases brought under the North American Free Trade Agreement (NAFTA)').

[129] Interview B2.

[130] *Ibid.*

[131] Prabhash Ranjan and Pushkar Anand, 'The 2016 Model Indian Bilateral Investment Treaty: A Critical Deconstruction' (2017) 38 *Northwestern Journal of International Law and Business*, 1, 13.

The RUEUA Act generated a lot of concern from local and foreign investment bodies. The press statement of the Central Bank demonstrates that these concerns influenced the government. Moreover, there was severe pressure from environmental groups advocating for the suspension of the Port City project.[132] Environmental factors were one of the reasons the government cited when suspending the project.

Thus, it appears that the activism of certain interest groups influenced the consideration of IIA obligations in government decision making. With respect to the RUEUA Act, the impact of investors certainly seems to have impacted the consideration of Sri Lanka's IIA obligations. With respect to the two other scenarios however, though different interest groups were vociferously advocating certain positions, it is the author's view that it was the impact on the government's political standing in the national context and not the influence of particular interest groups alone that led to the suspension of payments under the hedging agreement and the suspension of the Port City project, respectively.[133]

7.7   Conclusions: Internalisation and Possible Spillover Effects

Unlike most other countries, IIA obligations are internalised into the Sri Lankan legal order by virtue of the Constitution. As a consequence, there seems to be a general awareness of the existence of IIA obligations within higher-level state organs. Nevertheless, that general awareness does not translate into knowledge of the specifics of these obligations and, as shown, there are few informational or monitoring procedures in place for the systematic consideration of IIA obligations at all levels of government (let alone any remedial mechanisms as defined by Calamita

---

[132] See for example Vositha Wijenayake, 'Colombo Port City Project: A Threat to Sustainable Development?', *Daily Mirror*, 6 March 2015; Fr. Sarath Iddamalgoda, 'Justification of Colombo Port City Project', *Colombo Telegraph*, 13 March 2015.

[133] Corruption may be another factor which influences the manner in which and the extent to which Sri Lanka's IIA obligations are considered in decision making. There were allegations of corruption with respect to entering into the hedging agreements and the Port City project, see for example 'Hedging Deal Consigned to the Dustbin?' *Daily FT*, 23 August 2017; 'Yahapalanaya Govt. Must Answer Previous Allegations against Port City, CHEC', *Daily FT*, 30 May 2017. These allegations, however, have not been tested before courts of law or other enforcement bodies. Corruption was also not an issue that the interviewees, perhaps for obvious reasons, were inclined to mention. Therefore, no conclusions are made on the impact of corruption on the internalisation of IIA obligations.

and Berman).[134] The legislative process, where Art. 157 becomes directly relevant, and essentially serves as a monitoring mechanism, is the one notable exception.

Moreover, the impact of IIA obligations on decision making appears to be limited. Though there are some processes in place for monitoring legislative decisions for their alignment with IIA obligations (such as the Attorney General's role with respect to Bills), and evidence that higher-level state organs consider these obligations in some non-legislative situations (such as the recommencement of the Port City project) the impact of such obligations are often overridden by other factors. Either due to its belief that it can justify its conduct with respect to its obligations or the political expediency of taking decisions in spite of such obligations, the state organs in the situations considered have made decisions which could potentially be in violation of Sri Lanka's IIA obligations, despite showing awareness of them.

On the question of whether the internalisation of IIA obligations has resulted in positive spillover effects on the rule of law and good governance in Sri Lanka, the conclusions one may reach are clear. The interviews and the material considered with respect to the scenarios indicate that IIAs have had little positive impact on the rule of law in general. This is due to the limited internalisation of IIA obligations in the first place and secondly, the questionable positive correlation between IIA obligations on the one hand and the rule of law and good governance on the other.[135]

Only one area of 'positive' spillover may be noted. During the introduction of the RUEUA Act, it appears that the inclusion of a provision for 'prompt, adequate, and effective compensation' under the Act stemmed from Sri Lanka's obligations under its IIAs. As mentioned in the Supreme Court's Special Determination, however, the

---

[134] See Chapter 1. However, see the discussion above on the mechanisms under the Singapore–Sri Lanka FTA (2018).

[135] Moreover, in the scenarios described, it could be argued that Sri Lanka's IIA obligations have hampered the rule of law, as these international obligations (which are incorporated into domestic law by virtue of Art. 157) may conflict with the rights of citizens and other domestic laws, including those promulgated for the protection of the environment. Thus, with respect to the hedging agreements, the state was held internationally responsible for a contract that was arguably *ultra vires* the powers of the government body that had entered into it. Similarly, in the Port City case, it may well have been that the state's commitments under its IIAs to continue with the project stood opposed to its domestic laws

requirement to include a provision on compensation in any legislation concerning takings is mandated by the right to equality before the law and equal protection of the law guaranteed under Art. 12(1) of the Constitution.[136] Nonetheless, it seems clear that the phrase 'prompt, adequate and effective compensation' derives from the parlance used in investment treaties, and this may be considered a substantive spillover of the state's IIA obligation standards to legislation which applies generally. As evinced from the foregoing, however, such examples are few and far in between.

and regulations for the protection of the environment. Though in these cases there would technically be no inconsistency within domestic law by virtue of the supremacy accorded to Sri Lanka's IIA obligations by Art. 157 of the Constitution, the substantive impact of such obligations on the rights of citizens cannot be ignored in an assessment of the impact of IIA obligations on good governance.

[136] See Supreme Court Special Determination No. 3/2003, cited in Supreme Court Special Determination No. 2/2011.

The Impact of Investment Treaties on the Rule of Law in Thailand

TEERAWAT WONGKAEW[*]

8.1 Introduction

Thailand has concluded forty-two bilateral investment treaties (BITs),[1] a regional treaty on investment protection,[2] as well as free trade agreements (FTAs) which contain investment chapters[3] (collectively 'investment treaties'). Thailand is also a party to the Regional Comprehensive Economic Partnership (RCEP).[4] Thailand has lost one investment treaty dispute, namely the *Walter Bau* v. *Thailand* case,[5] and is currently facing a second treaty claim.[6]

Foreign direct investment (FDI) has been an important catalyst for Thailand's economic development. The country is one of the major FDI destinations in the ASEAN region due to its modern legal framework and investment-friendly governmental policies, such as the government's 'Thailand 4.0' policy[7] and the Eastern Economic Corridor Development

---

[*] The views expressed herein are the author's personal views and do not represent the views of the Ministry or the Government of Thailand.

[1] Out of these forty-two BITs, thirty-eight have been entered into force. See Investment Policy Hub, 'Thailand', https://investmentpolicy.unctad.org/international-investment-agreements/countries/207/thailand.

[2] ASEAN Comprehensive Investment Agreement (ACIA) (2009).

[3] Examples include the ASEAN–China Investment Agreement (2009), ASEAN–Korea Investment Agreement (2009), and ASEAN–Australia–New Zealand FTA (2009).

[4] Regional Comprehensive Economic Partnership (RCEP) (2020).

[5] *Walter Bau AG (in liquidation)* v. *The Kingdom of Thailand*, UNCITRAL, Award (1 July 2009).

[6] Kingsgate Consolidated Limited, an Australian investor, sued the Thai government under Australia–Thailand FTA (2004) for the suspension of its gold mining operation. See 'A Second Gold Mine Investor Puts Thailand on Notice of Arbitration Claim – This Time Under Australian Free Trade Agreement', *Investment Arbitration Reporter*, 3 April 2017.

[7] Thailand 4.0 is an economic policy that aims to create a value-based economy driven by innovation, technology, and creativity. This policy will enable Thailand to overcome several economic challenges such as a middle-income trap, an inequality trap, and an imbalanced trap.

Project.[8] Investment treaties have arguably contributed to the creation of favourable conditions and legal stability for foreign investors.[9]

However, the impact of investment treaties on the rule of law – the subject of this volume – within Thailand has received little attention.[10] Yet from both a theoretical and practical perspective, such an inquiry is important. At the theoretical level, there is little, if any, empirical evidence on the impact of investment treaties on the rule of law.[11] At the practical level, the outcome of such an inquiry could assist Thai policymakers and government agencies in adopting appropriate policies to address gaps.

The purpose of this chapter is to examine how, if at all, Thailand internalises its investment treaty obligations. In the process, it will seek to understand the factors that affect internalisation. In doing so, the chapter applies the analytical framework set out in Calamita and Berman's framing introduction chapter.[12] As noted by Calamita and Berman, 'internalisation is a foundational assumption to the claim of the rule of law thesis that investment treaties will improve domestic governance'.[13] The absence of evidence of internalisation, therefore, would be a strong indicator that Thailand's investment treaties have not had the spill-over effects promised by their proponents.

---

[8]   The Eastern Economic Corridor (EEC) is a special economic zone which will be an important centre for trade, investment, regional transportation, and a strategic gateway to Asia. The EEC covers the Rayong, Chonburi, and Chachoengsao provinces, with a total area of 13,000 square kilometres.

[9]   Whilst there is no empirical study which definitively confirms the effect of investment treaties on investment levels, there is one study which suggests that there is no correlation between Thailand's FDI levels and its investment treaty program. See Jason W. Yackee, 'Do Investment Treaties Work – In the Land of Smiles?', in Julien Chaisse and Luke Nottage (eds.), *International Investment Treaties and Arbitration Across Asia* (Brill Nijhoff, 2018), 83.

[10] The lack of reflection on this subject is due to the perception that investment treaties are economic tools rather than 'governance instruments'. Interview Official, 2018. The official interviewed was from the Department of Treaties and Legal Affairs.

[11] See N. Jansen Calamita, 'The Rule of Law, Investment Treaties, and Economic Growth: Mapping Normative and Empirical Questions', in Jeffrey Jowell, J. Christopher Thomas and Jan van Zyl Smit (eds.), *The Importance of the Rule of Law in Promoting Development* (Singapore Academy of Law, 2015), 103; Mavluda Sattorova, 'The Impact of Investment Treaty Law on Host State Behavior: Some Doctrinal, Empirical, and Interdisciplinary Insights', in Shaheeza Lalani and Rodrigo P. Lazo (eds.), *The Role of the State in Investor-State Arbitration* (Brill Nijhoff, 2014), 162. For an example of the kinds of claims made without empirical foundation, see Rudolf Dolzer, 'The Impact of International Investment Treaties on Domestic Administrative Law' (2005) 37 *NYU Journal of International Law and Politics* 953, 953–4.

[12] See Chapter 1.

[13] *Ibid.*

The methodology used is qualitative, taking a process tracing approach. In the preparation of this chapter, I have carried out structured interviews with high- and mid-level government officials responsible for treaty negotiations or the handling of investment treaty disputes.[14] I have also analysed primary sources, official documents, and secondary literature, including media articles.

I have interviewed government officials from several government ministries and departments, including the Department of International Economic Affairs and the Department of Treaties and Legal Affairs at the Ministry of Foreign Affairs (MFA); the Ministry of Commerce; the Bank of Thailand; the Office of the Attorney General; and the Ministry of Justice. My possible (or perceived) bias should be disclosed: I served for several years in the MFA, notably in the Department of International Economic Affairs, which is the lead negotiator for investment treaties, and in the Department of Treaties and Legal Affairs, which provides legal advice on negotiation of investment treaties and investment treaty disputes.

This chapter's main findings are that while the rule of law thesis (as described in Calamita's and Berman's introduction)[15] predicts that investment treaties will lead to improvements in the rule of law, the evidence suggests that for many years, internalisation in Thailand has been quite meagre. Up until the *Walter Bau* case in 2009, there was little awareness within the government as to the risks that could arise from violations of investment treaties. Further, while some training workshops and seminars for government officials had been carried out from time to time, these were ad hoc and untargeted.

The *Walter Bau* award against Thailand in 2009 had the effect of raising awareness within the government about the risks posed by investment treaties. Yet such increased awareness has not translated into more or 'better' internalisation measures at the informational or monitoring level, and it has taken about a decade for it to translate into improved remedial mechanisms.

Calamita and Berman identify three types of internalization measures: informational, monitoring, and remedial.[16] In the Thai case, informational measures, such as government workshops, remain ad hoc, inconsistent, and limited in reach. On the monitoring side, it appears that, with few exceptions, new laws or policies are not being monitored for their

---

[14] I carried out the interviews in 2017 and 2018.
[15] See Chapter 1.
[16] *Ibid.*

compliance with Thailand's investment treaty commitments before they are adopted. This seems to be so even with respect to the enactment of laws on potentially 'risky' topics such as regulating tobacco or introducing sugar taxes. Additionally, with the enactment of the new Constitution of Thailand in 2017, parliamentary and public oversight over the adoption of investment treaties, particularly BITs, has significantly decreased, with potentially detrimental effects on internalisation.

Nonetheless, there have been recent improvements in remedial internalisation, most notably the establishment in 2019 of the Committee on the Protection of International Investment. The Committee is a permanent institutional mechanism for preventing disputes and managing disputes when they arise. It also steers government policy on investment treaty matters.

Moreover, although the *Walter Bau* case has had a minimal effect on processes for internalising Thailand's treaty obligations in government decision making, it does seem to have contributed to a change in the approach that Thailand takes in the negotiation of investment treaties. Following the *Walter Bau* award, Thailand now seeks to include provisions that provide more protection for governmental autonomy in the enactment of public policies. The pending *Kingsgate* case[17] has also contributed to the increasing awareness of investment treaty obligations, which results in more scrutiny of the compliance of government measures with the treaty obligations.

This chapter is organised as follows. Section 8.2 describes Thailand's treaty-making process. Section 8.3 describes the *Walter Bau* case. Section 8.4 examines and analyses internalisation measures in the Thai context. Section 8.5 addresses changes in Thailand's investment treaty policy. Section 8.6 concludes.

8.2   The Investment Treaty-Making Process

Identifying the actors or 'nodes' within government that connect the international treaty-making sphere with domestic governance is the starting point for any investigation into the internalisation of investment treaties. Tracing the process of internalisation begins with identifying such nodes as it is within these nodes that processes of internalisation are most likely

---

[17] *Kingsgate Consolidated Ltd* v. *The Kingdom of Thailand*, UNCITRAL Rules. See also Kingsgate Consolidated Limited, 'Update on Legal Proceedings re Chatree Gold Mine, Thailand', Press Release, 10 November 2017.

to begin. The purpose of this section is, accordingly, to describe the processes and actors through and by which investment treaties get adopted.

8.2.1 Government Entities Involved in the Treaty-Making Process

Two main government entities are in charge of negotiation of investment treaties. The Ministry of Commerce advances the liberalisation of investment, through the conclusion of FTAs and admission of foreign investments pursuant to the Foreign Business Act.[18] The MFA is the lead agency for the conclusion of bilateral or regional investment treaties, including investment protection chapters in FTAs. A third entity – the Board of Investment of Thailand – is responsible for Thailand's investment promotion policy.[19]

The MFA leads the negotiation of investment treaties. During this process, and with a view towards developing an internal agreement on Thailand's negotiation position, the MFA convenes intra-government meetings to consult other ministries or entities on draft treaty texts. The Director General of the MFA's Department of International Economic Affairs Division chairs these intra-government consultation meetings. In such meetings, the MFA secretariat provides background information on the draft treaty and briefs on the relations between Thailand and the prospective treaty party. It also explains the legal consequences of different treaty provision formulations.

The responsibilities of the respective government entities are listed in Table 8.1.

These diverse entities each contribute to different issues. For instance, the Board of Investment is focused on promotion provisions, the Ministry of Finance on expropriation provisions, the Bank of Thailand on free transfer of fund provisions, and the Office of the Attorney General on investor–state dispute settlement (ISDS) provisions. Moreover, the Office of the Council of State considers the compliance and implementation of treaty obligations from a Thai law perspective. Where necessary, the

---

[18] Foreign Business Act, B.E. 2542 (1999). For the provisions in the Foreign Business Act, see Investment Policy Hub, 'Foreign Business Act', https://investmentpolicy.unctad.org/investment-laws/laws/40/thailand-foreign-business-act.

[19] Once a foreign investor seeks to make an investment, other entities get involved too. Notably, for investments in specific sectors, the relevant ministries are responsible for issuing the relevant permits and licences. Also, where investment contracts need to be entered into between government entities and investors, the Office of the Attorney General gets involved. See also Office of the Attorney General Law: Office of the Attorney General Act B.E. 2553 (2010).

Table 8.1 *Responsibilities of respective government entities in the treaty-making process*

Specific issues/clauses	Relevant government entities
Investment promotion	Board of Investment
Definitions of investments/investors	MFA
Expropriation	Ministry of Finance
Post-establishment national treatment and most-favoured-nation protection	All agencies are involved
Fair and equitable treatment	All agencies are involved
Free transfer	Bank of Thailand
Subrogation	Export-Import Bank of Thailand
Compensation for losses	Ministry of Defence
Investor–state dispute settlement	Attorney General's Office
State–state dispute settlement	MFA
Entry of key personnel	Immigration Bureau

MFA also consults other ministries, such as the Ministry of Commerce, Ministry of Industry, Ministry of Agriculture, and Ministry of Education.

In practice – and as one would expect under the public policy theory on complexity of joint action in bureaucratic institutions[20] – the bureaucracy is not a unified unit. Rather, there exists a tension between the interests represented by different government entities and these conflicts ultimately pose challenges to finding an agreed intra-government position. For example, the Board of Investment, being in charge of drawing foreign investors to Thailand and advancing the interests of Thai investors oversees, is inclined to promote a more investor-friendly approach.[21] In contrast, other ministries are concerned with protecting their regulatory space and take a more defensive approach.[22] Ultimately, the MFA, as the

---

[20] See Chapter 1.

[21] Section 13 of the Investment Promotion Act, B.E. 2520 (1977) sets out the duties of the Office of the Board of Investment in promoting foreign direct investment. It can be noted that other agencies that are inclined to adopt an investment-friendly approach include the Ministry of Foreign Affairs and the Ministry of Commerce.

[22] Some examples of these other ministries or parties are the Bank of Thailand (cautious about legal implication) (Interview Officer, 2017); Securities and Exchange Commission, Thailand (potential threats); and Office of the Attorney General, which is responsible for defending states both in domestic and international disputes, wounded from losing a series of arbitration cases in domestic contract-related disputes. Interview Lawyer, 2017.

lead agency, takes all of these positions into account and determines the appropriate negotiating position.[23]

The final word rests with the government cabinet (Council of Ministers), which approves the final draft treaty.[24] Before signing and ratifying the treaty, the Council of Ministers circulates the draft treaty for a final round of comment by all relevant government entities. All government ministries have a designated unit (either the international affairs or the legal unit) with some understanding of and awareness about investment treaty obligations.[25]

8.2.2 Decline in Parliamentary and Public Oversight of Investment Treaties

In 2017, Thailand adopted a new constitution, which replaced the 2007 Constitution of Thailand. While both constitutions contain provisions with respect to the conclusion of international treaties, the 2017 Constitution removed some aspects of parliamentary (National Assembly) and public oversight, in particular with respect to BITs.[26] This change has resulted in reduced parliamentary and public oversight over investment treaties, which will most likely have a negative impact on the internalisation of BITs within Thailand. Here, I describe the legal status before and after the 2017 Constitution.

8.2.2.1 The 2007 Constitution

Section 190 of the 2007 Constitution listed three types of treaties that require the National Assembly's approval (as opposed to treaties which only require cabinet approval) as well as the procedure for their adoption. Essentially, such approval was required with respect to treaties which changed Thai territory, treaties which required domestic legal adoption,

---

[23] Interview Officer, 2018. The officer was from the Ministry of Foreign Affairs.

[24] The approval of the Council of Ministries is required by the Cabinet Resolution dated 7 July 2015 regarding the Thai delegation's capacity to attend international conferences and submit negotiation frameworks. The Resolution stipulates that the relevant agency has to submit the negotiation framework and Thailand's position in the negotiation if it concerns a matter which affects international relations and has a long-term policy commitment.

[25] Interview Official, 2018. The official was from the Department of International Economic Affairs.

[26] Patthara Limsira, 'Thailand – The Section 190 of Constitution of the Kingdom of Thailand' (2009) 2 *Journal of East Asia & International Law* 545 (describing the constitutional situation prior to the 2017 Constitution).

and treaties which had significant impact on the country's economic
and social stability, or which created significant commitments on trade,
investment, or the national budget. Due to their economic impact, FTAs
and BITs were considered to fall under Section 190 and required parliamentary approval.[27] Moreover, before their adoption by the National
Assembly, the Council of Ministers was required to publish relevant information and carry out a public hearing as well as provide clarifications to
the legislature.[28] Once the treaty has been signed, the Council of Ministers
published the details with the public. Where the implementation of the
treaty would affect people or small and medium sized enterprises, the
Constitution required that correcting or helping actions be undertaken
towards affected individuals in a timely, suitable, and fair manner.[29]

While this process advanced democratic accountability, it came
under criticism for being too burdensome and for prolonging the treaty
conclusion process,[30] posing obstacles to the government's treaty-making
abilities. This led to the adoption of a much less burdensome procedure
under the 2017 Constitution.

8.2.2.2   The 2017 Constitution

Section 178 of the 2017 Constitution lists three types of treaties that require
the National Assembly's approval for ratification (as opposed to only
cabinet approval). Parliamentary approval is required for treaties which
change Thai territory, treaties which require domestic legal adoption, and
treaties which may have wide-scale effects on the security of economy,
society, trade, or investment of the country.[31] Although the third type is in
many ways similar to the provision under the 2007 Constitution, Section
178 then goes on to clarify that this third type includes treaties pertaining to free trade, common customs union, or the authorisation of natural resources utilisation, or treaties which cause the country to lose rights
over natural resources.

In practice, BITs have not been understood as falling under this third
category. As such, since 2017, BITs have stopped undergoing parliamentary approval as had previously been the case. They are also no longer

---

[27] Legal Opinion by the Department of Treaties and Legal Affairs, which stated that investment treaties fell within Section 190(2) of the 2007 Constitution.
[28] Constitution of the Kingdom of Thailand, B.E. 2550 (2007), s. 190.
[29] Ibid.
[30] Between 2007 and 2009, all negotiations of investment treaties were put on hold pending
the approval of Thailand's negotiation framework.
[31] Constitution of the Kingdom of Thailand, B.E. 2560 (2017), s. 178.

being publicised for comment by the public.[32] That said, FTAs (containing investment chapters) continue to be subject to parliamentary approval.[33]

To conclude, the MFA and the Ministry of Commerce are the main ministries in charge of investment treaties within the Thai government. They are, thus, the main 'nodes' of government from which we would expect information about investment treaties to flow to other ministries, agencies, and departments – a matter I address further below. Further, the recent amendment to the Constitution reduces the National Assembly's and the public's involvement and oversight over the BIT approval process. This decreased involvement lowers awareness of investment treaty obligations within the domestic system (and among the public) and is ultimately detrimental to internalisation.

8.3 The *Walter Bau* Case

The purpose of this section is to lay out Thailand's experience with the *Walter Bau* case, which was the first investment treaty claim brought against Thailand and which Thailand lost after a long legal battle. This case ultimately served as a trigger for changes in Thailand's remedial internalisation measures as well as a change in its investment treaty-making policy.

The *Walter Bau* case concerned a claim by a German investor against the Thai government. A German investor held shares in a Thai company, Don Muang Tollway (DMT), to which the Thai government had granted a concession contract for a tollway project. The concession agreement had been signed in August 1989, with subsequent amendments. Under the first amendment in 1995, DMT agreed not to request a toll adjustment under the agreement. Under the second amendment in 1996 (MoA2), the parties agreed that, given the government's inability to comply with the agreement's terms, there would be an increase of the toll rates and increased shareholding of Thailand in DMT. Furthermore, MoA2 contained a waiver of claims against the Thai government, and a waiver that allowed changes in the use of the Bangkok airport, and the construction

---

[32] That being said, in view of the financial implications of investment and investor–State disputes, this current interpretation is arguably questionable. Time will tell how this will be interpreted in the future.

[33] Section 178, para. 3 of the 2017 Constitution stipulates that other treaties which may have wide scale effects on the security of economy, society, or trade or investment of the country under para. 2 are *treaties pertaining to free trade*, common customs union, or the authorisation of natural resources utilisation, or which cause the country to lose rights over natural resources, in whole or in part, or on any other treaties provided by law.

of U-turns on the Viphavadi-Rangsit road. It was also agreed that the government's management of traffic would not harm the economic benefits of the concessionaire.

In 2004, DMT was asked to reduce the toll fees for the original tollway from 30 THB to 20 THB and not to impose a toll at all on the northern extension. Eight directors (four of them appointed by the government) voted for the reduction. Later, the Prime Minister and the Minister of Transport announced the toll reduction to the media. In 2007, the third amendment (MoA3) extended the concession period by twelve years to 2034 and provided a new schedule of agreed toll rates which authorised DMT to increase the tolls unilaterally in accordance with the toll schedule.

The claimant commenced arbitration against the Thai government, alleging violations of the Thailand–Germany BIT (2002) provisions on expropriation and fair and equitable treatment. On 1 July 2009, the arbitral tribunal, finding there had been no substantive deprivation of the investor's control of the investment, rejected the expropriation claim.[34] However, it did find that the investor's legitimate expectations had been frustrated and that, consequently, the fair and equitable treatment provision had been violated. It based its findings on three factors: (1) the lengthy refusal to raise tolls as required by the concession agreement; (2) the changes to the road network beyond traffic management; and (3) the temporary total closure of Don Muang Airport.[35] The tribunal ordered Thailand to pay to the claimant €29 million plus interest.[36] Thailand, however, resisted the enforcement of the award,[37] with the cabinet approving the Ministry of Transport's request to litigate the dispute until its final conclusion.[38]

The Office of the Attorney General led Thailand's efforts to resist the award's enforcement. Initially, rather than submitting a request for the setting aside of the enforcement of the award before a court in Switzerland, which had been the seat of the arbitration, they submitted it in 2009 before

---

[34] *Walter Bau* v. *Thailand*, Award, para. 10.18.

[35] *Ibid.*, para. 12.44.

[36] *Ibid.*, para. 17.1.

[37] Space does not permit a full analysis of the procedural manoeuvrings. For an overview, see Roland Kläger, 'Werner Schneider (liquidator of Walter Bau AG) v Kingdom of Thailand: Sovereign Immunity in Recognition and Enforcement Proceedings under German Law' (2014) 29 *ICSID Review – Foreign Investment Law Journal* 142.

[38] The cabinet granted a waiver from complying with the Regulation of the Office of the Prime Minister on the compliance with arbitral award. See B.E. 2544 (2011).

the Bangkok Central Administrative Court.[39] In 2010, the Bangkok court rejected the case. Then, the Thai government's objections to the confirmation of the award were rejected by a New York court.[40] Finally, the Thai government unsuccessfully resisted enforcement proceedings in Germany.[41] Moreover, the German courts accepted the claimant's request and ordered the impounding of the plane of the then Thai crown prince which had been based at Munich airport.[42] The plane was later released after the Thai government posted a bond of €38 million.

8.4   Internalisation of Investment Treaties

The purpose of this section is to survey the informational, monitoring, and remedial internalisation mechanisms – as defined by Calamita and Berman[43] – that are found in Thailand. It will also seek to assess what impact, if any, the *Walter Bau* case has had on internalisation. As we shall see, internalisation measures in Thailand have been historically meagre and inconsistent, albeit with some attempts at improvement in recent years. In the first three to four decades of Thailand's involvement in the investment treaty regime (from the 1960s to the early 2000s), there was little awareness as to possible consequences of a breach of investment treaty obligations,[44] and there were no internalisation measures. Even after the

---

[39] The Supreme Administrative Court affirmed the Central Administrative Court's dismissal of the application to set aside the award on 17 October 2013, see Vanina Sucharitkul, 'From Walter Bau to Hopewell: Pathways to Bangkok Don Muang Airport' (2015) 1 *Asia-Pacific Arbitration Reporter* 309. Thailand did subsequently attack the award in Switzerland in 2011, seeking a revision based upon allegedly newly discovered evidence. That petition was rejected by the Swiss Federal Tribunal as untimely. See Tribunal fédérale [Federal Supreme Court of Switzerland], 23 July 2012, 4A_507/2011.

[40] *Schneider* v. *Kingdom of Thailand*, 2011 WL 12871599 (US S.D.N.Y), *affirmed by* 688 F.3d 68 (US 2nd Cir. 2012).

[41] Bundesgerichtshof [Federal Court of Justice of Germany], 6 October 2016, I ZB 13/15; KG Berlin (lexetius.com/2016, 3669).

[42] Charlotte Chelsom-Pill, 'Germany Releases Thai Prince's Impounded Plane', *Deutsche Welle*, 10 August 2011.

[43] See Chapter 1.

[44] Interview Officer, 2017. The officer was from the Department of Treaties and Legal Affairs. Moreover, another interviewee shared that when there is no dispute, government agencies would not be pressed to do research to follow recent developments in the jurisprudence or review treaty provisions. Interview Official, 2018. The official was from the Department of International Economic Affairs. A former negotiating officer from the Ministry of Commerce also pointed out that negotiations of regional investment treaties did not take note of the current jurisprudence. Interview Officer, 2017. However, negotiation of some BITs, in which the author participated, took note of interpretations by domestic jurisprudence.

Walter Bau case in 2009, which heightened awareness within the government and the public of the potentially dire consequences of violating investment treaty obligations, the case did not translate into the adoption of informational or monitoring internalisation measures which would ensure better dissemination of information of investment treaties or better compliance with investment treaty obligations. Only around a decade after *Walter Bau*, in 2019, were certain remedial mechanisms introduced.

8.4.1 Informational Processes

Despite the intra-government consultation processes in the treaty negotiation process (mentioned in Section 8.2.1), once a treaty is concluded, not much importance is accorded to the dissemination of information within the government regarding obligations arising under investment treaties. The MFA, being the lead ministry in investment treaty negotiation, is the first 'node' in the internalisation process. And indeed, in the past, the MFA and other agencies organised workshops, seminars, and training courses,[45] in which government as well as private entities took part.[46] Such workshops addressed trends and developments in ISDS and treaty obligations. However, given the diversity of the departments within each ministry, dissemination of specialised information relating to treaty obligations has been challenging.

It is telling, for example, that in the *Walter Bau* case, the Ministry of Transport had not been aware of the possible application of investment treaty obligations and had proceeded on the basis of the domestic law framework alone.[47] The fact that a foreign shareholder, who was not a party to the concession contract, could bring a claim for damages against the Thai government was not well understood by the relevant ministries at the time.

Even after *Walter Bau*, informational measures for internalising investment treaty obligations have been lacking. For example, although the Thailand–United Arab Emirates BIT (2015)[48] contained new features

---

[45] Interview Officer, 2017. The legal officer was from the Department of International Economic Affairs.

[46] Government of Thailand, Ministry of Foreign Affairs, Workshop on 'International Investment Agreements (IIAs) towards Global Sustainability' (25 June 2015).

[47] Interview Officer, 2017. The officer was from the Department of Highways, Ministry of Transport.

[48] United Arab Emirates–Thailand BIT (2015).

that arguably merited communication to relevant ministries, this did not take place.[49] The BIT introduced new definitions of key terms, including 'investment', 'fair and equitable treatment', 'national treatment', and 'most favoured nation', and also included features, not included in earlier BITs, such as a provision on the 'right to regulate', the free transfer of funds, and a 'denial of benefits' clause.[50] While it would have made good sense to communicate these changes with other ministries, the MFA and involved ministries did not do so.

It warrants noting that some entities have actively sought to inform themselves about investment treaty obligations, even in the absence of centrally coordinated informational measures. The Bank of Thailand, for example, has organised seminars and hired external experts to address particular issues within the Bank's scope of responsibilities. These external consultants have prepared a report on the legal implications of international investment treaties on the Bank's ability to implement various monetary measures in times of economic crisis.[51] This type of initiative, however, is ad hoc in nature, initiated by the organisation's management when a perceived need arises.

More consistent informational measures going forward would be useful. For one, the MFA and other ministries could be encouraged to disseminate knowledge of investment treaty obligations after negotiations are concluded, especially by explaining the consequences of each provision to the relevant agencies.[52] Further, there could be regular and more focused seminars for government ministries.[53] At present, however, informational measures for internalisation remain ad hoc and inconsistent.

---

[49] Interview Officer, 2017. The officer was from the Department of International Economic Affairs, Ministry of Foreign Affairs.

[50] Article 13, para. 1 of the United Arab Emirates–Thailand BIT states that 'Benefits of this Agreement shall not be available to an investor of a Contracting Party, if the main purpose of the acquisition of the nationality of that Contracting Party was to obtain benefits under this Agreement that would not otherwise be available to the investor'.

[51] The author was involved in the preparation of this report as well as the briefing session of the report.

[52] Interview Officer, 2017. The officer was from the Department of International Economic Policy. Limited human resources are the main reason why there has not been much effort on the part of the agency.

[53] While the seminars carried out in the past raised general awareness, the training during these seminars should also focus on treaty-drafting skills, the consequences of different provision formulations, and relevant case law. For instance, the Ministry of Justice and the Office of the Attorney General would benefit from sessions on drafting ISDS provisions, arbitration procedures, 'fork in the road' provisions, and issues of prior consent.

8.4.2   Monitoring Processes

This section addresses whether and how new laws are monitored for their compliance with international investment treaties before their adoption. In other words, are international investment treaty obligations considered when developing laws or other policies?

It should be noted that there is no legal requirement for new legislation to be checked for compliance with international obligations and there is consequently no specific mechanism dedicated to ensuring that government measures comply with investment treaty obligations. That said, there are several general procedures whereby these potential measures can be reviewed against Thailand's international legal obligations, including those in investment treaties.

Under the normal legislation process, before the Council of Ministers considers a draft law, it is reviewed by all relevant agencies, in particular the MFA and the Council of State, a department under the Prime Minister's office. Within the context of these processes, compliance with investment treaties could be potentially reviewed under three main scenarios.

First, in the context of the drafting process, the government entity in charge of drafting the law may seek the legal opinion of the Department of Treaties and Legal Affairs within the MFA. This department is the leading authority on international law within the Thai government. Second, certain policies or measures may require approval from a national committee, in which the MFA or the Council of State are members.[54] Third, when measures require the cabinet's approval, all relevant ministries are consulted, and it is during this consultation when the MFA or the Council of State could raise investment treaty-related risks.

In practice and – as I lay out in the examples below – although investment treaties were considered in depth during discussions about the possible amendment of Thailand's arbitration law, they appear to have been considered far less deeply, if at all, in the context of other legislative processes. In contrast, there have been significant legal opinions concerning the compliance of measures with international trade obligations (such as WTO agreements and other regional FTAs),[55] as well as human rights[56] and anti-corruption treaties.[57]

---

[54] The Office of the Council of State also reviews compliance of regulatory measures or legislative acts with international obligations. Interview Officer, 2017. The interview was with a legal officer from the Council of State.

[55] Interview Officer, 2017. The legal officer was from International Law Development Division, Ministry of Foreign Affairs.

[56] Interview Officer, 2017. The legal officer was from Treaty Division, Ministry of Foreign Affairs.

[57] The National Anti-Corruption Commission.

8.4.2.1   The 2010 Proposed Amendment of the Arbitration Act

A notable exception to what appears to be the rule of not considering investment treaty commitments was the debate surrounding the 2010 proposed amendment of the Arbitration Act. In the governmental discussions concerning the 2010 amendment, investment treaty considerations were raised and were among the factors which ultimately led to the amendment's rejection.

The background to those discussions were as follows. In 2004, a series of government losses in several commercial arbitration cases[58] gave rise to negative sentiments towards arbitration, both generally[59] and in certain government circles.[60] This culminated in the Council of Ministers issuing a resolution which declared the government's decision to limit the use of arbitration clauses in certain agreements between the state and the private sector ('the 2004 Resolution'). This resolution stated that:

> [C]oncession contracts under the current law are administrative contracts, which should be submitted to administrative courts or courts of justice for dispute resolution. Therefore, the contract that the state enters into with private persons in Thailand or overseas should not include binding arbitration clause. But if there is a problem or necessity or an inevitable request, the cabinet shall approve on a case-by-case basis.[61]

Notably, at the same time as the 2004 Resolution declared an adjustment of the Thai government's policy towards the arbitration of state contracts, Section 15 of the Thai Arbitration Act continued to provide that 'in any contract made between a government agency and a private enterprise,

---

[58] Such as the Thai Office of Arbitration ruling in favour of the BBCD joint venture ordering the Expressway and Transit Authority of Thailand to pay US$150 million compensation regarding the construction of the Bangna-Bangphli-Bangpakong expressway project, on 27 January 2004. The award was subsequently annulled by the Thai Supreme Court in 2006 on the ground of corruption. Supreme Court of Thailand, Decision No. 7277/2549 (2006). For a discussion of the subsequent litigation in the Thai courts, in which the Thai government was also successful, see Bangkok Post, 'Construction firm giant loses legal battle', *Bangkok Post*, 29 June 2017.

[59] See generally Vanina Sucharitkul, 'Thai Administrative Court Overturns an Arbitration Award against the Government', Kluwer Arbitration Blog, 9 October 2014.

[60] Interview Officer, 2017. The interviewed officers consisted of a senior legal officer from the Department of Treaties and Legal Affairs and a legal officer from the Ministry of Justice.

[61] The 2004 Resolution is available at www.cabinet.soc.go.th/soc/Program2-1.jsp?menu=1 (in Thai). The Cabinet Resolution on 4 May 2004 confirms that the resolution on 27 January 2004 only applies to a 'concession contract'. Concession contracts are generally understood to be agreements granting the private sector a right to operate public services for a limited period of time at their own risk using their own funds.

regardless of whether it is an administrative contract or not, the parties may agree to settle any dispute by arbitration. Such arbitration agreement shall bind the parties'.[62]

The filing of the *Walter Bau* case, and Thailand's subsequent loss, aggravated the sense of hostility towards the use of arbitration, leading the Council of Ministers to announce further restrictions and prohibitions on the use of arbitration in State contracts. On 28 July 2009 – four weeks after the *Walter Bau* award – the Council of Ministers issued a resolution ('the 2009 Resolution') to amend the 2004 Resolution and expand the arbitration prohibition, determining that:

> *[E]very type of contract* that the government agency enters into with a private person, in Thailand and overseas, administrative or non-administrative in nature, should not contain a binding arbitration clause. But if there is a problem or necessity or an inevitable request from the other party, the cabinet will grant an approval on a case by case basis.[63]

Again, this was notwithstanding the language of the Arbitration Act stipulating the arbitrability of disputes arising out of government contracts.

In August 2009, the Ministry of Justice proposed to the Council of Ministers an amendment to extend the 2009 Resolution into statutory law by amending the Arbitration Act to include a *total* prohibition of the use of arbitration in State contracts in statutory law.[64] On this occasion, the Council of Ministers tasked the Council of State and other relevant government entities to advise on the proposal.[65]

---

[62] Arbitration Act, B.E. 2545 (2002), s. 15.

[63] Cabinet Resolution dated 27 January 2004 (emphasis added). This prohibition was later loosened on 14 July 2015, when it was amended and the arbitration prohibition was limited to contracts made under joint ventures or concession agreements, as opposed to all contracts entered into by private entities with the public sector. The essential part of the 2015 modification stipulates that 'any contract that government agencies enter into with private persons in Thailand or overseas, whether it be administrative contract or not, if it is one of the following cases: (1) contract that is to be carried out under the Joint Venture Act 2013; [or] (2) concession contract that government agencies grant a concessionary right should not include binding arbitration clause. But if there is a problem or necessity or an inevitable request, the cabinet shall approve on a case-by-case basis'.

[64] This would entail an amendment of s. 15 of the Arbitration Act 2002. The section reads: 'In a contract between a government agency and private party, whether administrative contract or not, the parties thereto may agree to settle their disputes by arbitration. The parties to the contract shall be bound by such arbitration agreement'.

[65] Office of the Council of State, *Memo on the draft amendment to the Arbitration Act 2002*, 3.

The prospect of enshrining the prohibition of arbitration in state contracts into statutory law alarmed foreign investors and raised concerns about compliance with international obligations (especially with respect to existing state contracts). For instance, at a 2009 Asia-Pacific Economic Cooperation (APEC) meeting, Prime Minister Abhisit Vejjajiva met with representatives of the US-APEC Business Coalition who expressed deep concerns over the proposed arbitration prohibition and considered that this might make Thailand less attractive to FDI. Consequently, on 18 November 2009, the Joint Public and Private Sector Consultative Committee (JPPSCC) stated that relevant government entities should clarify to investors that the 2009 Resolution was not a blanket prohibition, but that arbitration would be permitted on a case-by-case basis.[66]

The Council of State objected to the amendment of the Arbitration Act. Reflecting upon the background to the proposed amendment, the Council of State took the view that the Thai government had lost cases not because of the arbitration process *per se*, but rather because of a lack of expertise in contract making, contract management, and dispute management. The arbitration process remained, in the Council of State's view, more efficient and more suitable than judicial proceedings.[67] Moreover, the Council of State took note in their discussions of the BITs and other investment agreements signed by Thailand.[68] There was general consensus among participating government entities that the proposed amendment to the Arbitration Act would jeopardise the pending negotiation of investment treaties,[69] undermine foreign investors' confidence,[70] and potentially breach investment treaty obligations.[71]

---

[66] *Ibid.*

[67] Office of the Council of State, *Memo on the Draft Amendment to the Arbitration Act 2002*, 37.

[68] The Cabinet Resolution on 16 March 2004 authorises the use of arbitration in cases of bilateral investment treaties as well as investment chapters in free trade agreements proposed by the MFA.

[69] It was suggested that Thailand had pending negotiations with fifty-two countries.

[70] This sentiment was gleaned from a summary of discussions from two important seminars organised by Thailand Arbitration Center, namely a seminar on 'Obstacles and challenges in the use of arbitration in state contract' held on 11 November 2014 and another seminar on 'Various Approaches for Amending the 28th July 2009 cabinet Resolution' held on 31 March 2015.

[71] Government of Thailand, Ministry of Foreign Affairs, *Memo on the summary of the meeting on investor-State dispute settlement on 4th December 2009 at meeting room 3*. The memo took note of the outcome of the arbitration experts' meeting organised by the Ministry of Foreign Affairs.

Finally, upon the advice of the Council of State and other government entities, the Council of Ministers decided to reject the proposed amendment to the Arbitration Act, finding that 'the use of arbitration reduces the number of cases adjudicated in courts, especially international commercial disputes, which is a generally accepted practice'.[72] The Council of Ministers also found that prohibiting the use of arbitration in state contracts would 'negatively affect the image and favourable investment conditions in Thailand as well as undermine investors' confidence *as well as international obligations observed by Thailand in various treaties and conventions*'.[73] Notably, although the Council of Ministers ultimately rejected the proposal to amend the Arbitration Act, it left the 2009 Resolution in place until 2015, when the policy was amended and the arbitration prohibition was limited to contracts made under joint ventures or concession agreements, as opposed to all contracts entered into by private entities with the public sector.[74]

Following the rejection of the amendment, the Council of Ministers instructed the Ministry of Justice to introduce measures that would better prevent and resolve problems arising from arbitration disputes between the state and private persons.[75] Further, based on a consultation held among governmental, private sector, and academic stakeholders on 14 October 2010, the National Economic and Social Development Board submitted a report to the Council of Ministers. The report recommended making arbitration available for disputes between the state and private actors, except for certain types of contracts which may require cabinet approval.[76] The proposal also stressed preventive measures, including capacity building measures for government officials and measures to improve their contract management expertise.[77]

To conclude, investment treaties were considered and raised as reasons for the rejection of the proposed amendment of the Arbitration Act.

---

[72] Office of the Council of State, *Memo on the draft amendment to the Arbitration Act 2002*.

[73] *Ibid.* (emphasis added).

[74] The essential part of the 2015 modification stipulates that 'any contract that government agencies enter into with private persons in Thailand or overseas, whether it be administrative contract or not, if it is one of the following cases: (1) contract that is to be carried out under the Joint Venture Act 2013; [or] (2) concession contract that government agencies grant a concessionary right should not include binding arbitration clause. But if there is a problem or necessity or an inevitable request, the cabinet shall approve on a case-by-case basis'.

[75] Cabinet Resolution dated 31 August 2010 and Cabinet Resolution dated 7 December 2010.

[76] Cabinet Resolution dated 7 December 2010. As noted above, this was the policy ultimately adopted in the 2015 revision of the 2009 Resolution.

[77] In this regard, the cabinet designated the Office of the Civil Commission to work with the Ministry of Justice and other agencies.

Moreover, while the proposal was rejected, the remaining concerns over the state's domestic and international arbitration with private actors led the Cabinet to instruct the Ministry of Justice to develop measures which would prevent disputes before they develop into arbitration. Ultimately, this may be seen an example of effective investment treaty internalisation in government decision making through the monitoring of the potential application of treaty obligations to new government measures. As noted, however, although there appears to have been ad hoc internalisation in this situation, it proves to be an outlier to the general absence of internalisation in government decision making.

8.4.2.2 The 2017 Tobacco Control Law

In 2017, Thailand enacted the Tobacco Products Control Act (TPCA).[78] Although the enactment of this law came on the heels of high-profile awards in the claims brought by Philip Morris against Australia and Uruguay, investment treaty considerations did not feature prominently in the discussions on the enactment of the law.

The TPCA replaced the Tobacco Products Control Act (1992) and the Non-Smoker's Health Protection Act (1992), which had regulated the display, purchase, and use of tobacco. The new TPCA introduced broad restrictions on the advertising, marketing, and sale of tobacco products. It prohibits the display of tobacco brand names or logos on tobacco products, in any printed material, video, television, motion picture, electronic media, and advertising signs. It also requires larger warning labels on all cigarette packages. All branding – colours, imagery, corporate logos, and trademarks – must be removed, and the brand name may only appear in small print.[79] The TPCA might also serve as a framework for enacting plain-packaging measures, but as of now, such a process has not been initiated.[80]

---

[78] 'New Tobacco Control Law Passed', *Bangkok Post*, 3 March 2017.

[79] Achara Deboonme, 'Thailand Faces Tough Fight on Plain Packaging', *The Nation*, 16 August 2016.

[80] 'Plain Packs "May Deter Smokers"', *Bangkok Post*, 25 July 2018. It is suggested that the 2017 Tobacco Control Act could provide a framework for issuing plain-packaging measures. Article 38 of the Act states:

> Article 38. Manufacturers or importers of tobacco products for sale in the Kingdom must ensure that the size, color, symbols, and labeling of packaging materials for tobacco and tobacco products, as well as the appearance of trademarks, symbols, formatting, and statements placed on such packaging materials, comply with rules, procedures, and conditions set out by the Minister, upon the advice of the Board. Compliance must be verified before such articles are moved from the place of manufacture or before importation into the Kingdom, as the case may be.

The absence of prominent consideration of the potential investment treaty implications of the TPCA may seem surprising. However, at the time of the MFA's advice in 2015, the *Philip Morris* cases remained pending. The MFA's opinion, therefore, focused on the situation as it was then understood, but did not go further in offering analysis. Thus, even though investment treaty obligations were raised by some agencies, notably the Ministry of Commerce and the MFA, as potential sources for international liability, the level of opinion provided remained at a superficial level. Instead, the emphasis of government advice on the TPCA focused on WTO obligations, notably the TRIPS Agreement, which were seen as being more pertinent to the government's interests.[81]

8.4.2.3   New Alcohol Labelling Requirements

In recent years, Thailand has enacted a series of laws and policies, which establish labelling requirements for alcohol. These policies require large graphic health warnings on all alcoholic beverages and impose other restrictions on the right of manufacturers to use their trademarks. The Alcoholic Beverage Control Act was enacted in 2008 and was followed by Ministerial regulations in 2010. Collectively, they prohibit any advertisement which boasts of efficacies, benefits or qualities of alcoholic drinks or induces one to drink. In 2015, the Ministry of Public Health published the Notification on Alcoholic Beverages,[82] which was notified to the WTO Committee on Sanitary and Phytosanitary Measures.[83] The notification would prohibit the use of various types of messages on alcoholic beverage labels and packages, including any message which misleads consumers as to the product's content, and any message using cartoon images, except images which are trademarks of alcoholic beverages which had been legitimately registered.

---

[81] Interview Official, 2018. The interviewed officials were from the Ministry of Public Health as well as the Ministry of Commerce. The latter official shared that it is unclear whether the discussions on compliance with international obligations concerning intellectual property included investment treaties. These concerns are shared by some WTO Member Countries such as Mexico, Honduras, the European Union, China, the United States of America, and Brazil which raised a series of questions to the Thai representatives during the last WTO's Trade Policy Review in November 2015.

[82] Notification of the Alcohol Beverage Control Committee Re: Criteria, Procedures, and Conditions for Labels of Alcoholic Beverages, B.E. 2558 (2015).

[83] Alan Adcock and Aaron Le Marquer, 'Thailand's New Alcohol Labelling and Message Requirements', *Bangkok Post*, 18 September 2015. See also WTO notification: G/TBT/N/THA/437, 28 March 2014; WTO notification: G/TBT/N/THA/437/Add.1, 27 April 2015.

Although these alcohol labelling requirements have potentially significant, and negative, economic impacts on investors in the beverage sector, there is no evidence to suggest that investment treaties featured in the discussions on the enactment of the regulation. Under the circumstances, it may be that the Ministry of Public Health acted without seeking an opinion on the grounds that the measure was one that it believed to be within its rulemaking competence. At the same time, it is similarly possible that no legal advice was sought due to a lack of awareness within the ministry. Either way, the scenario is reflective of the generally limited scope of internalisation in the development and enactment of government measures.

8.4.2.4 Sugar Taxes

To counter rising obesity, the government raised taxes on soft drinks with high sugar content in 2017.[84] Effective from 16 September 2017, the Thai Excise Department implemented a sugar tax on certain beverages to reduce consumption of sugar and to increase health consciousness,[85] in compliance with the World Health Organization's recommendations. The second phase of the excise tax on sugary drinks came into force on 1 October 2019.[86] These sugar taxes have had an impact on business operations in the beverage sector. It has been reported, for example, that many beverage manufacturers have been adjusting to this healthy trend and creating more healthy product options.[87]

---

[84] Tan Hui Tee, 'War on Sugar: Can Taxman Extract Asia's Sweet Tooth?', *The Straits Times*, 8 May 2016. See also Marimi Kishimoto, 'Thailand's "War on Sugar" Aims to Slim People and Fatten Coffers', *Nikkei*, 11 December 2017; Wichit Chantanusornsiri, 'Six-Year Plan for Sugary Drink Taxes', *Bangkok Post*, 24 July 2017.

[85] See U.S. Department of Agriculture, *Thai Excise Department Implements New Sugar Tax on Beverages* (20 October 2017). Prior to the enactment of the new Excise Tax, imported beverages were taxed at a rate of 20 per cent ex-factory prices or Cost, Insurance and Freight (CIF) values. With the new excise tax, drinks are taxed based on their sugar content. Beverages with over 6 grams of sugar per 100 ml are subject to the new specific sugar tax with beverages containing higher sugar levels carrying a larger tax burden. Beverages subject to the new excise sugar tax are: (1) artificial mineral water, soda water, and carbonated soft drinks without sugar or other sweeteners and without flavour; (2) mineral water and carbonated soft drinks with added sugar or other sweeteners or flavours, and other non-alcoholic beverages; (3) fruit and vegetable juices; (4) coffee and tea; (5) energy drinks; and (6) beverage concentrates to be used with beverage vending machines for distribution at retail areas. See *ibid*.

[86] Pitsinee Jitpleecheep and Phusadee Arunmas, 'Sugary Drink Tax Pushes Innovation', *Bangkok Post*, 29 July 2019.

[87] *Ibid.*

Despite the significant economic impact of such taxes, there is no evidence that investment treaty obligations have featured in the discussions concerning the enactment of this tax. Again, it may be that the relevant authority acted without seeking an opinion on the matter on the grounds that the measure was one within its exclusive competence.[88] At the same time, another possibility is that there may not be a strong awareness within the tax authority of the possible investment treaty implications of tax measures. In any event, the scenario again reflects the limited scope of internalisation in the development and enactment of government measures.

8.4.3   Remedial Processes

8.4.3.1   Dispute Prevention

Although the *Walter Bau* award was issued in 2009, it was only in 2019 that Thailand established an institutional mechanism for *preventing disputes*. Until that point, most dispute prevention measures arose in an ad hoc manner. Two examples may be noted.

First, amidst the 2010 political turmoil in Thailand, the 'red shirt'[89] protests and riots[90] caused damage to property in central Bangkok, including damage to shopping malls owned by foreign investors. Discussions within the MFA raised the possibility that such damage could give rise to disputes under investment treaties, with investors raising claims under the full protection and security provision and demanding compensation for losses.[91]

A memorandum produced by the MFA at the time addressed two main issues: (1) whether the 'due diligence' standard applicable to the full protection and security provision applied to a situation of riot and civil unrest; and (2) whether the government would be required to compensate for losses on a non-discriminatory basis to all investors.[92] The memorandum concluded that there was only an obligation to make prompt,

---

[88] See Excise Tax Act, B.E 2560 (2017).
[89] An apolitical pressure group formally known as the United Front for Democracy against Dictatorship (UDD) and allied to Mr Thaksin's Pheu Thai party.
[90] Human Rights Watch, *Descent into Chaos: Thailand's 2010 Red Shirt Protests and the Government Crackdown* (3 May 2011).
[91] The author, as an officer at the Ministry of Foreign Affairs, was privy to the discussions and drafting of the memo on these issues.
[92] Internal memo prepared by the MFA, which was then circulated to relevant agencies.

adequate, and effective compensation to the investor where the requisition of property or damage had been caused by Thailand's own security forces and where such damage was not justified by necessity. There was no obligation to do so where the damage was a result of riots and civil unrest. Nevertheless, Thailand eventually set up a compensation fund for those harmed by the riots, although there is no evidence to suggest that investment treaty obligations were among the considerations for establishing the fund.[93]

A second case arose in 2009, when local villagers filed a complaint with the Central Administrative Court demanding the suspension of projects at the Map Ta Phut industrial estate in the province of Rayong. They argued that the projects had failed to fulfil the environmental and health impact assessments requirements under Section 67 of the 2007 Constitution,[94] and were thus operating illegally. The Court ordered the suspension of seventy-six projects. Following an appeal to the Highest Administrative Court, eleven of these projects were reinstated, yet the remaining sixty-five projects remained suspended. The combined value of these projects was an estimated US$8 billion.[95]

There was no formal assessment of the potential risk of claims that could result from this judicial ruling (as such an assessment could have been perceived as interference with court proceedings). Yet, there were internal discussions within the MFA on the possibility that affected

---

[93] 'Thailand Compensation for Protest Victims Approved', *BBC News*, 11 January 2012.

[94] See Constitution of the Kingdom of Thailand, B.E. 2550 (2007), s. 67. Section 67(1) of the 2007 Constitution seeks to protect the right of a person 'in the conservation, preservation and exploitation of natural resources and biological diversity and in the protection, promotion and preservation of the quality of environment for normal and sustained survival in the environment which causes no harm to his or her health, well-being or quality of life'. Section 67(2) determines that: 'Any project or activity which may seriously affect the community in the quality of environment, natural resource, and health shall not be permitted, unless its impact on the quality of environment and people's health in the community have been studied and evaluated and the public hearing process to obtain the opinion of people and interested parties has been held, including to allow independent organization, consisting of representatives from private environmental and health organizations and representatives from higher education institutions providing education in environmental, natural resource or health to express their contributory opinions prior to the operation of such a project or activity'. Section 67(3) provides that the 'right of a community to sue a government agency, State agency, State enterprise, local government organisation or other State authority which is a juristic person to perform the duties under this section shall be protected'.

[95] Kochakorn Boonlai and Pisit Changplayngam, 'Thai Court Halts Many New Plants in Big Industrial Zone', *Reuters*, 2 December 2009.

foreign investors might challenge the ruling.[96] There was little awareness amongst the judiciary about the investment treaty implication of judicial decisions.[97]

In 2019, the Thai government moved toward a more institutional and consistent approach to dispute prevention. Following the lessons learned from the *Walter Bau* case, it established the Committee on the Protection of International Investment pursuant to the Regulation of the Office of Prime Minister.[98] The Committee is chaired by the Deputy Prime Minister[99] and is comprised of high-level representatives from the government's most central ministries and departments, including the MFA, Ministry of Finance, Ministry of Agriculture, Ministry of Transport, Ministry of Justice, Ministry of Health, Ministry of Industry, the Council of State, the Board of Investment, the Office of Courts of Justice, the Attorney General, the Department of International Trade Negotiation, the Department of Business Development, the Department of Treaties and Legal Affairs, the Securities and Exchange Commission, the Bank of Thailand, and the Export and Import Bank of Thailand.

The Committee has three main functions: dispute prevention, policy coherence, and dispute management.[100] In its dispute prevention function, it serves as a 'permanent advisory body for line agencies on potential investment disputes and opportunities for settlement or compromise'.[101] For example, the Committee is authorised to recommend measures or mechanisms to prevent an investment dispute.

The Committee is a new, albeit promising, mechanism, which seems to have the potential to address some of the challenges that Thailand has faced with respect to informational and remedial internalisation in particular. That said, as of this writing, it is too early to tell how effective it will be.

---

[96] Such internal discussions took place within the Ministry of Foreign Affairs between the Department of Treaties and Legal Affairs and the Department of International Economic Affairs. The author participated in these discussions.

[97] Interview Official, 2018. The official was from the Office of the Judiciary.

[98] See Regulation of the Office of the Prime Minister on Work Relating to the Protection of International Investments B.E. 2562 (2019). This regulation was published in the Royal Gazette on 28 February 2018.

[99] Designated by the Prime Minister.

[100] OECD, 'Investment Treaty Policy in Thailand', in *Investment Policy Reviews: Thailand* (OECD Publishing, 2021), 211, 227.

[101] *Ibid.*

8.4.3.2   Dispute Management

Until the *Walter Bau* case, and for a decade afterwards, little thought, if any, had been dedicated to the internal management of investor–State disputes.[102] As a result, at least through 2019, the government's intra-governmental management of its investor–State disputes was largely reactive – beginning after the commencement of a suit – and organised in an ad hoc fashion.

The reactive, ad hoc approach is demonstrated by the management of the disputes in *Walter Bau* and *Kingsgate*. In *Walter Bau*, the cabinet established an ad hoc advisory working group to handle the dispute.[103] The working group was chaired by the Permanent Secretary of the Ministry of Transport, because the alleged breach in question was committed by the Department of Land Transport. Other agencies involved included the Office of the Attorney General, which is in charge of defending the state in legal disputes.[104] The Office of the Council of State provided legal advice on internal law aspects. The MFA (Department of International Economic Affairs and Department of Treaties and Legal Affairs) provided expertise on treaty interpretation and international law issues. The Budget Bureau and the Ministry of Finance were in charge of budgetary issues, especially payments of fees and awards. Finally, the Ministry of Transport reported to the Council of Ministers. For the award enforcement proceedings, the Council of Ministers designated the Office of the Attorney General to take the lead in defending the state.

A similar approach has been taken in managing the *Kingsgate* v. *Thailand*[105] case, which commenced in 2017 and is still ongoing as of the date of this writing. As in *Walter Bau*, an ad hoc working group was placed in charge of defending Thailand, comprising the MFA, Ministry of Commerce, Office of Attorney General, and other entities. The Ministry of Industry, whose measure triggered the dispute, was designated as the lead agency.

---

[102] Interview Officer, 2017. The legal officer was from the International Law Division, Ministry of Foreign Affairs.

[103] The Office of the Prime Minister Order No. 41/2549 dated 2 February B.E. 2549 (2006) (mentioned in the Letter from the Ministry of Transport to the Secretary of the cabinet). For the Letter, see https://resolution.soc.go.th/PDF_UPLOAD/2551/21656011.pdf.

[104] The Office of Attorney's General Office Act B.E. 2553.

[105] See 'A Second Gold Mine Investor Puts Thailand on Notice of Arbitration Claim – This Time under Australian Free Trade Agreement', *Investment Arbitration Reporter*, 3 April 2017.

As the government has come to realise following the *Walter Bau* and *Kingsgate* cases, there are several problems with the ad hoc working group approach. Placing the ministry responsible for the contested measure in charge of managing the state's defence on a case-by-case basis, means that ministries with little understanding and expertise of investment treaty arbitration may nevertheless be tasked with the lead role in gathering evidence, hiring legal counsel, and handling the claim. Thus, while other ministries and agencies are available to support the ad hoc working group – and may well have more expertise and experience with investment treaty arbitration – the lead ministry sets the direction and strategy for handling the dispute, subject to the cabinet's approval. Further, given that the lead ministry is the ministry responsible for taking the contested measure, there is a risk that the lead ministry may be reluctant to disclose all relevant (and potentially uncomfortable) facts to the working group, making it difficult to assess the legal situation and prepare the Thai government's defence.[106] Moreover, the lead ministry's decision to negotiate and settle a claim can be a contentious issue. While an early settlement might be a viable option, it may also carry a political cost as the government may face criticism for inadequately defending national interests.[107] Finally, the disputes could give rise to potential liability of the lead ministry as well as the inter-ministerial body.

As noted above, the Thai government in 2019 moved toward a more consistent and institutionalised approach to dispute management by establishing the Committee on the Protection of International Investments. As mentioned, the Committee has several important functions, including dispute management. In this capacity, it 'supervis[es] the government's defence of investor–state arbitrations that might arise in the future, including through establishing a dedicated Taskforce to report to the Committee and make proposals for the Council of Ministers regarding the handling of individual cases'.[108] For example, the Committee is authorised to provide advice and make recommendations in the settlement of disputes, including conciliation, mediation, and arbitration.

---

[106] UNCTAD, *Investor–State Disputes: Prevention and Alternatives to Arbitration* (UNCTAD Series on International Investment Policies for Development, 2010), 85–6: 'Officials in charge of the case will often face reluctance if not dissimulation of facts and documents on the part of the implicated government agency or entity. A lack of cooperation will create tensions and make it impossible to have a clear assessment of the case that would then lead to an amicable settlement or negotiation with the investor'.

[107] *Ibid.*, 83.

[108] OECD, 'Investment Treaty Policy in Thailand', in *Investment Policy Reviews: Thailand*, 227.

Further, in the case of a dispute, the Committee or the responsible ministry will propose to the Prime Minister to set up a taskforce concerning the investment dispute. It will also designate a government entity for handling the administrative aspects of dispute settlement. The taskforce will keep the Committee informed of progress or obstacles in the management of the investment dispute.[109]

To conclude, while intra-government dispute management had previously been ad hoc, an attempt has been made to establish an organised and regular dispute prevention mechanism. As noted, it indicates an attempt to regularise the government's treatment of disputes regarding its investment treaty commitments, although it remains to be seen how effectively the Committee will function.

8.5 Thailand's Changing Approach to Investment Treaties

As laid out above, while the *Walter Bau* case generated reflection and discussion of Thailand's investment treaty policies, these discussions did not translate into a comprehensive reform of Thailand's internalisation measures. Rather, a consensus seems to have emerged as to the need to revise Thailand's investment treaties. Thus, while the treaties concluded in the 1960s and 1970s with countries such as Germany, the Netherlands, and the United Kingdom[110] were mainly sought to attract foreign investment and contained little to no protection of the public interest,[111] this approach starkly changed after *Walter Bau*. The award crystallised the problems inherent in the old treaties with vague terms and underscored the importance of better protection of Thailand's public interests. Having experienced the limitations of its previous approach, the Thai government has now (to some extent) sought new methods to better balance investor rights and public interests.[112]

This renewed approach was not only based on Thailand's isolated experience but also builds on the experience of other countries and

---

[109] Regulation of the Office of the Prime Minister on Work Relating to the Protection of International Investments B.E. 2562 (2019), s. 8.

[110] Germany–Thailand BIT (1961), Netherlands–Thailand BIT (1972), United Kingdom–Thailand BIT (1978).

[111] The official preparatory works on the negotiation of Germany–Thailand BIT. Interview Officer, 2017. The officer was from the Department of International Economic Affairs, Ministry of Foreign Affairs.

[112] UNCTAD, *Phase 2 of IIA Reform: Modernizing the Existing Stock of Old-Generation Treaties* (IIA Issues Note, June 2017).

the consequent emerging global investment treaty practice, which has evolved towards increased protection of the host states' regulatory space.[113] A greater focus on the implications of investment treaty obligations is already evident from Thailand's most recent investment treaties, namely its BIT with the United Arab Emirates[114] and the RCEP investment chapter.[115] Against this background, future negotiations will likely continue to seek to strike a balance between protecting Thai investors overseas and safeguarding regulatory interests.[116]

8.6 Conclusion

Until the *Walter Bau* case, there was little awareness within the Thai government as to its investment treaty obligations and, with the exception of ad hoc seminars or workshops, there were no internalisation processes.

The *Walter Bau* case has increased awareness within the government, yet such increased awareness has not translated into more robust or consistent internalisation measures at the informational or monitoring level. However, it has had some impact on remedial internalisation measures.

Most informational measures – seminars and reports – remain ad hoc and are applied when a need arises (and resources are available). While investment treaty obligations were considered in the development of the new arbitration law, it appears that investment treaty obligations do not receive particular attention in the enactment of laws, including on matters which are known to raise risks of breaching investment treaty obligations, such as regulations involving tobacco, alcohol, and sugar. In this respect, it is interesting to compare the treatment of investment treaties with that of international trade agreements, where monitoring for compliance appears to be more robust. Moreover, the adoption of the 2017 Constitution, with its reduced parliamentary and public oversight over the adoption of BITs, will likely have a negative impact on internalisation.

---

[113] *Ibid.*
[114] United Arab Emirates–Thailand BIT (2015), Art. 8 (exceptions to free transfer obligation), Art. 13 (denial of benefits clause), and Art. 14 (Joint Committee on Investment Treaty).
[115] Interview Official, 2018. The official was from the Department of Trade Negotiation, Ministry of Commerce.
[116] The latest Draft Model BIT, which is not yet publicly available, may include corporate social responsibility provisions. Interview Officer, 2017. The officer was from the Department of Treaties and Legal Affairs.

That said, the lessons learned from *Walter Bau* have translated into the enactment of remedial internalisation measures. Most notably, it has resulted in, first, the government's decision to develop measures that would prevent disputes between the state and private actors before they develop into full blown disputes and arbitration proceedings; and second, the recent establishment of an institutional mechanism – the Committee on the Protection of International Investments – for the prevention of disputes and for the management of ISDS claims if and when they arise.

To conclude, investment treaties as such, as predicted by the rule of law thesis, have not led to improvements in the rule of law. It was only after the *Walter Bau* case that Thailand started reassessing its approach to investment treaties, but then too, reforms have been restricted to remedial mechanisms. Moreover, the lessons from the *Walter Bau* case have not so much resulted in changes to Thailand's internal governance (as the rule of law thesis would have predicted), but rather resulted in a change of approach to its international relations and negotiations.

The Impact of Investment Treaties
on the Rule of Law in Viet Nam

TRAN VIET DUNG

9.1 Introduction

The purpose of this chapter is to lay out Viet Nam's policy and governance with respect to international investment treaties and to examine whether and how international investment obligations are internalised and considered in domestic law or rulemaking. It follows Calamita and Berman's analytical framework and examines whether and how investment treaties are considered in governmental decision making through informational, monitoring, or remedial mechanisms.[1]

After years of instability, a command economy, and communist rule, Viet Nam's *Doi Moi* [Renovation] reform was launched in 1986 to boost the country's underperforming economy and signal an eagerness to restore international ties. Based on these reforms, the Vietnamese government began promoting the development of a market economy and created opportunities for private sector competition. Whereas previously there had been a disdain for foreign investment, the reform introduced foreign direct investment (FDI) as a key element of the country's economic policy, and investment treaties were viewed as significant tools for this transition.

Since the 1990s, the Vietnamese government has signed numerous bilateral investment treaties (BITs) with the hope that they would help to attract foreign investments. At the same time, the government has viewed international treaties as key for developing better diplomatic relations and breaking free from Viet Nam's international isolation.[2] To date, Viet Nam has entered into more than sixty-one BITs and twenty-three other treaties

---

[1] See Chapter 1.
[2] Beth Castelli, 'The Lifting of the Trade Embargo between the United States and Viet Nam: The Loss of a Potential Bargaining Tool or a Means of Fostering Cooperation?' (1995) 13 *Penn State International Law Review* 297.

with investment protection provisions, including standalone invest-
ment agreements (e.g., ASEAN Comprehensive Investment Agreement
(ACIA)) and free trade agreements (FTAs) with investment chapters (e.g.,
Comprehensive and Progressive Agreement for Trans-Pacific Partnership
(CPTPP); Regional Comprehensive Economic Partnership (RCEP)).[3]
Viet Nam has also developed a regulatory framework for investment,
which provides a spectrum of incentives to attract FDI.

Yet in as much as Viet Nam has pursued an active foreign investment
policy, the results of this study suggest that Viet Nam still falls short in
internalising its investment treaty obligations in a number of ways. This
gap has led to an increase in investor–state disputes in recent years.

The chapter is organised as follows: Section 9.2 lays out the research
methodology. Section 9.3 describes Viet Nam's evolving foreign investment policy. Section 9.4 discusses the evolution of Viet Nam's investment
treaties and investor–state dispute settlement (ISDS). Section 9.5 lays
out the governmental processes of negotiating and entering into investment treaties. Sections 9.6 to 9.9 address the extent of internalisation in
Viet Nam and the measures it has adopted to promote internalisation:
Section 9.6 examines monitoring mechanisms in the law-making process;
Section 9.7 examines informational and monitoring mechanisms targeted
at the local government; Section 9.8 examines the internalisation (or lack
of it) in the courts; and Section 9.9 addresses remedial internalisation
measures which have been put in place. Section 9.10 concludes.

9.2 Research Methodology

Carrying out an empirical study into the internalisation of investment
treaties in Viet Nam poses challenges. Not only are there few publicly
available official reports or data on this topic, but information on investor–
state disputes filed against Viet Nam is considered a national secret and,
consequently, is kept confidential. The present study thus mainly draws
upon evidence collected through archival research and semi-structured
interviews.

Archival desk research included examining primary documents that
provide information on the ongoing politico-economic situation and
policy-making process in Viet Nam, such as the Communist Party's documents, speeches, and talks of high-ranking officials, reports by government

---

[3] Investment Policy Hub, 'Viet Nam', https://investmentpolicy.unctad.org/international-
investment-agreements/countries/229/viet-nam.

agencies, and information available on the government's official websites. It also included examining information available in the media.

Semi-structured interviews were based on questions which had been prepared in advance but were sufficiently open to allow for necessary adjustments in the course of each interview. The names of the interviewees have been withheld to enhance the neutrality and objectivity of their views.

Interviewees were selected from groups of people with a sound understanding of the FDI regulatory environment in Viet Nam and/or with direct or indirect involvement in FDI-related issues. These groups included: (1) government officials of central agencies in charge of negotiating and implementing investment treaties; (2) provincial government officials in charge of designing FDI policy and dealing with FDI issues in the localities; (3) lawyers who assist businesses in investing in Viet Nam and/or are involved in investor–state disputes; and (4) experts who have extensive knowledge of the economic regulations and investment treaties of Viet Nam.

I carried out twenty-six interviews during 2018 and 2020 in four provinces: Hanoi, Ho Chi Minh City, Binh Duong, and Quang Ninh. These locations were selected because they are the most relevant regions for foreign investment in Viet Nam. Hanoi is the seat of the Vietnamese central government, where the principal offices and agencies related to FDI are based, including the Ministry of Planning and Investment (MPI), the Ministry of Justice (MOJ), the Central Institute of Economic Management (CIEM),[4] and the Viet Nam Chamber of Commerce and Industry (VCCI).[5] Ho Chi Minh City is Viet Nam's largest city and economic centre, hosting a large number of FDI businesses and law firms, but is also the region that has given rise to most of the investor–state dispute cases against Viet Nam. Quang Ninh (in North Viet Nam) and Binh Duong (in South Viet Nam) have also been successful in attracting FDI. In the areas outside of Hanoi, I carried out interviews with local government officials, including from the Department of Planning and Investment (DPI), the Department of Justice (DOJ), and the Department of Industry and Trade. I also interviewed judges of the High Court (based in Ho Chi Minh City) and the Ho Chi Minh City People's Court.

---

[4] CIEM is a think tank under MPI. It has for many years conducted research on economic regulation in Viet Nam and has played an important role in drafting and implementing some of the business-related laws of Viet Nam, in particular the Enterprise Law and Law on Investment.

[5] VCCI is a national association officially representing the private sector in Viet Nam. In recent years, VCCI has actively participated in economic policy formulation and evaluation.

Arranging and conducting these interviews was a challenging task. As mentioned, information on investor–state disputes is considered a state secret and central government officials were reluctant to share or discuss details. Most high-ranking government officials only agreed to talk about Viet Nam's general policy framework and dispute management mechanism. By contrast, local officials were more open and accessible, although most of them possessed limited knowledge and expertise in international law. The lawyers and experts interviewed were open and cooperative.

9.3 From Disdain to Embrace: The Evolution of Viet Nam's Investment Policy

9.3.1 1945–1985: Disdain for Foreign Investment

In 1945, Viet Nam gained independence from French colonial rule. In the following years and until around 1975, Viet Nam's approach to foreign investors was unwelcoming, with the ruling Communist Party of Viet Nam (CPV) viewing foreign investors as unwanted capitalists and colonialists. In 1975, with the end of the Indochina war, and the unification of the north and the south, the entire country followed a communist economic system[6] – rejecting the notions of private property and individual economic initiative. While there had been some foreign investments in South Viet Nam, these were gradually confiscated and nationalised. The country also continued shielding itself against western influence, with economic relations limited to socialist countries linked to the Soviet Union.[7]

Viet Nam was further of the view that it had absolute sovereign control over its economic and natural resources, denying any substantial protection to foreign investors under international law.[8] Thus, Viet Nam's 1977 policy on foreign investment[9] strongly emphasised state authority, determining, for example, that only the state could enter into a joint venture with

---

[6] United Nations Development Programme Hanoi, *Briefing Note on the Socialist Republic of Viet Nam* (1994), 2: '[T]he Government of the Socialist Republic of Viet Nam attempted to organize the country's political and economic system along orthodox Soviet lines'; see also Luke A. McGrath, 'Viet Nam's Struggle to Balance Sovereignty, Centralization, and Foreign Investment under Doi Moi' (1995) 18 *Fordham International Law Journal* 2095, 2095.

[7] Vu Tuan Anh, *Viet Nam's Economic Reform: Results and Problems* (Social Science Publishing House, 1994), 20–1.

[8] McGrath, 'Viet Nam's Struggle to Balance Sovereignty, Centralization, and Foreign Investment under Doi Moi'.

[9] Decree 115/CP of the Government promulgating the Rules on Foreign Investments, 18 April 1977 ('Decree 115/CP').

a foreign party and that the foreign party's holdings would be limited to 49 per cent.[10] Moreover, it considered the right to nationalise and expropriate foreign property as an inherent and fundamental attribute of sovereignty, which could not be subjected to any pre-conditions, including the 'public purpose, due process and compensation' standard under customary international law.[11] Because of this approach, Viet Nam attracted very little foreign investment, with only one investment licence issued to a French pharmaceutical company,[12] and some investment from socialist countries.

9.3.2 After 1986: The Doi Moi Policy

In 1986, with the adoption of the Doi Moi policy by the CPV, Viet Nam's policy towards international economic cooperation radically changed. The Doi Moi policy moved away from communist ideals and adopted the development of a 'socialist-oriented market economy'.[13] Recognising the significance of foreign investment in fostering the country's industrialisation,[14] attracting foreign investment became central to Viet Nam's economic policy,[15] resulting in the adoption, in 1987, of a new Law on Investment.[16]

---

[10] Decree 115/CP, Art. 7.3.

[11] Decree 115/CP, Arts. 10.1 and 10.2.

[12] Tang Than Trai Le, 'The Legal Aspects of Foreign Investment in Viet Nam' (1995) 1 International Trade and Business Law Journal 45.

[13] Pursuant to the Political Report of the Vietnamese Communist Party Central Committee at Party Congress XII, Viet Nam's 'socialist-oriented market economy' is an economy operating fully and synchronously according to the rules of a market economy while ensuring the socialist orientation suitable to each period of national development. It comprises a modern and internationally integrated market economy which is administered by a law-ruled socialist state and led by the Communist Party of Viet Nam towards the goal of a rich people and a developed, democratic, equal, and civilised country. The term was first used in the 1992 Constitution to characterise the new model of economic structure during the Doi Moi era.

[14] Tran Viet Dung, Anti-Dumping Policy and Law of Viet Nam: A Critical Analysis from Integration and Competition Policy Perspectives (Lambert Academic Publisher, 2011), 55; see also Nghị quyết Đại hội Đảng lần thứ VII [Resolution of the VII Communist Party Congress], 27 June 1991; Nghị quyết của Quốc hội về nhiệm vụ phát triển kinh tế – xã hội 5 năm (1991–1995) và năm 1992 [Resolution of the National Assembly on the tasks of socio-economic development for five years (1991–1995) and 1992], 26 December 1991; Nghị quyết của kỳ họp thứ 9 Quốc hội Khóa IX về đẩy mạnh việc thực hiện nhiệm vụ và ngân sách nhà nước năm 1996 [Resolution of the Ninth Session of the Ninth National Assembly on the promoting the implementation of the state's function and budget of 1996], 30 March 1996.

[15] Đỗ Quốc Sasm (Minister of Planning and Investment), Tờ trình của chính phủ về luật đầu tư nước ngoài (sửa đổi) [Government Statement on Foreign Investment Law (amended)], Ninth National Assembly, 24 October 1996.

[16] Law No. 4-LCT/HĐNN8 on Foreign Investment, 29 December 1987 (amended in 1990, 1992, 1996, and 2000). The Law on Foreign Investment 1987 was replaced by Law No.

Based on the ideas of a market economy, the new Law on Investment encouraged regional and international integration, incentivised foreign investments, and provided them with strong protections, including compensation in cases of expropriation and free repatriation of profits and capital.[17]

Viet Nam came to view foreign investment as so central for the country's economic, social, and technological progress,[18] that it embedded its protection, including under international agreements, in the 1992 Constitution. Article 25 of the 1992 Constitution provides that:

> [The] state encourages foreign organisations and individuals to invest capital and technology in Viet Nam in accordance with Vietnamese law and with international law and practice; ensures the legal ownership of capital and assets as well as other interests of foreign organisations and individuals. Enterprises with foreign invested capital shall not be nationalised.[19]

The reference to 'international law and practice' expressly sought to anchor Viet Nam's treatment of foreign investors with the protections established under international law.

9.4 The Evolution of Viet Nam's Investment Treaties

9.4.1 Viet Nam's Investment Treaties

The *Doi Moi* policy brought about a radical change in approach regarding foreign investors and, with it, a desire to conclude international investment treaties. The government viewed investment treaties as a means for attracting foreign investment as well as a diplomatic instrument for normalising relations with the West after years of isolation and a US trade embargo.[20]

59/2005/QH11 on Investment, 29 November 2005 ('Law on Investment 2005'), which unified the provisions of the Law on Foreign Investment and the Law on Promotion of Domestic Investment to provide for equal treatment between foreign-invested and domestic-invested enterprises in most sectors in Viet Nam.

[17] These standard FDI protection provisions have been provided in the Law on Foreign Investment in 1987 (as amended and supplemented in 1990, 1992, 1996, and 2000) and their presence was continued in the Law on Investment in 2005 (as amended and supplemented in 2014). See also Pham Van Thuyet, 'Viet Nam's Legal Framework for Foreign Investment' (1999) 33 *The International Lawyer* 765; Tang, 'The Legal Aspects of Foreign Investment in Viet Nam'.

[18] Resolution of the VII Communist Party Congress, 27 June 1991; Resolution of the National Assembly on the tasks of socio-economic development for five years (1991–1995) and 1992, 26 December 1991.

[19] Constitution of the Socialist Republic of Viet Nam 1992, Art. 25.

[20] Beth Castelli, 'The Lifting of the Trade Embargo between the United States and Viet Nam'.

After concluding its first BIT with Italy in 1990,[21] Viet Nam concluded BITs with other major capital-exporting countries in Asia and the West, including Germany, Japan, France, the United Kingdom, the Netherlands, Australia, Malaysia, France, Hong Kong, Singapore, Taiwan, and Korea. By 1996, Viet Nam had signed a total of thirty-three BITs with countries in Asia, Africa, Eastern Europe, and South America.[22] These BITs followed the typical format of most BITs concluded at that time and included broadly worded provisions on most-favoured-nation treatment, national treatment (NT), fair and equitable treatment (FET), expropriation, repatriation of capital and profits, and compulsory ISDS processes.

Following Viet Nam's decision to begin entering into BITs with capital-exporting countries, the Vietnamese government also began pursuing further regional and international economic integration beginning around 1995/96, a policy which continues to this day.[23] Viet Nam joined the Association of Southeast Asian Nations (ASEAN) in 1995, and thereafter concluded regional agreements for the protection of foreign investment such as the Framework Agreement for ASEAN Investment Area[24] and the ASEAN Investment Guarantee Agreement,[25] which were replaced in 2009 with ACIA.[26]

Following Viet Nam's accession to the WTO in 2007, the conclusion of FTAs was identified as the country's main strategy to deepen its participation in the global value chain and production network.[27]

---

[21] Italy–Viet Nam BIT (1990).

[22] A list of Viet Nam's BITs is available at the Investment Policy Hub, 'Viet Nam', https://investmentpolicy.unctad.org/international-investment-agreements/countries/229/viet-nam.

[23] The Resolution of VIII CPV Congress on the Strategy on Socio-Economic Development 1996–2000 specified that Viet Nam's reform policy should 'further promote [a] process of integration into the regional and world economy' based on 'the principles of active and constructive penetration of [the] international market'. See Communist Party of Vietnam, *Văn kiện Đại hội Đảng thời kỳ đổi mới và hội nhập [Protocols of the Party Congress in the period of Doi Moi and Integration]* (Chính Trị Quốc Gia [National Political Publication House], 2013), 671–2; see also Nghị quyết số 49-NQ/TW ngày 02/6/2005 của Bộ Chính trị về Chiến lược cải cách tư pháp đến năm 2020 [Resolution 49-NQ/TW of the Politburo on the Strategy of Judicial Reform to 2020], 2 June 2005.

[24] ASEAN Investment Area Framework Agreement (1998).

[25] ASEAN Investment Guarantee Agreement (1987) (as amended).

[26] ASEAN Comprehensive Investment Agreement (ACIA) (2009).

[27] See Nghị quyết số 08-NQ/TW, ngày 05/2/2007 của Ban Chấp hành Trung ương Đảng khóa X về một số chủ trương, chính sách lớn để nền kinh tế phát triển nhanh và bền vững khi Việt Nam là thành viên của Tổ chức Thương mại thế giới [Resolution No. 08-NQ/TW of the CPV Central Committee X on a number of major policies for rapid and sustainable

Accordingly, in the years since WTO accession, Viet Nam has negotiated many regional trade agreements, which include investment protection chapters.[28] As of 2020, Viet Nam had signed fifteen FTAs (of which fourteen are in effect) and was negotiating two other FTAs.[29] Among the most noteworthy treaties concluded during this period are the FTA and separate Investment Protection Agreement with the European Union (respectively, EVFTA and EVIPA)[30] and CPTPP.[31] RCEP is Viet Nam's most recent treaty.[32] Viet Nam is also a party to six 'ASEAN-Plus' FTAs between ASEAN member states and major ASEAN trading partners.[33]

Among other things, the FTAs require the Vietnamese government to simplify and open administrative procedures pertaining to investment

economic growth under the context of Viet Nam being a Member of the World Trade Organization], 5 February 2007; Nghị quyết số 22-NQ/TW của Bộ Chính trị về hội nhập quốc tế [Resolution No. 22-NQ/TW of Politburo on international economic integration], 10 April 2013; Nghị quyết số 06-NQ/TW của Ban Chấp hành Trung ương Đảng khóa XII về thực hiện có hiệu quả tiến trình hội nhập kinh tế quốc tế, giữ vững ổn định chính trị – xã hội trong bối cảnh nước ta tham gia các hiệp định thương mại tự do thế hệ mới [Resolution No. 06-NQ/TW of the CPV Central Committee on implementing effectively international economic integration while maintaining socio-political stability under the context of Viet Nam's engagement in new-generation FTAs], 5 November 2016; see also WTO, *Trade Policy Review: Report by Viet Nam*, WT/TPR/G/410 (2 March 2021), 5–6.

[28] Trinh Hai Yen, *Giáo trình Luật đầu tư quốc tế [Textbook of International Investment Law]* (Nhà xuất bản Chính trị quốc gia – Sự thật [National Political Publishing House – Truth], 2017), 239.

[29] WTO, *Trade Policy Review: Report by Viet Nam*, 6.

[30] On 26 June 2018, the EVFTA was split into two separate agreements, one on trade and one on investment. In August 2018, EU and Viet Nam completed the legal review of the EVFTA and the EVIPA. The parties officially signed the EVFTA and EVIPA in Hanoi in June 2019. Having been ratified by both Viet Nam and the EU (the EU Council and EU Parliament), the EVFTA came into effect on 1 August 2020. The EVIPA, however, has not yet come into force, as it requires additional ratification by each of the parliaments of the EU member states. As and when the EVIPA comes into force, it will replace the existing twenty-one BITs between Viet Nam and various EU member states.

[31] Comprehensive and Progressive Agreement for Trans-Pacific Partnership (CPTPP) (2018). CPTPP is an FTA between eleven countries of the Asia-Pacific Region and was officially signed in March 2018. Viet Nam was one of the key negotiators of this agreement, which it considered as an important platform for its economic development.

[32] RCEP is an FTA between ASEAN member states and five of ASEAN's FTA partners (Australia, China, Japan, New Zealand, and Republic of Korea), signed on 15 November 2020. India, also an ASEAN FTA partner, participated in the RCEP negotiations for more than five years but did not sign the agreement. See 'India decides to opt out of RCEP, says key concerns not addressed', *The Economic Times*, 4 November 2019.

[33] ASEAN–Japan EPA (2008); ASEAN–Australia–New Zealand FTA (2009); ASEAN–Korea Investment Agreement (2009); ASEAN–China Investment Agreement (2009); ASEAN–India Investment Agreement (2014); ASEAN–Hong Kong Investment Agreement (2017).

and business. The implementation of the FTAs is expected, therefore, to bring about reforms in Viet Nam's administration and laws. Moreover, the investment chapters in the FTAs are less vague than Viet Nam's earlier BITs, clarifying, for example, the scope of the terms 'investor' and 'investment', and containing express exceptions to the treaties' substantive guarantees, which protect the host state's autonomy to regulate in the public interest.[34] Further, in some of Viet Nam's most recent FTAs, there has been a move away from traditional ISDS through arbitration: the EVIPA establishes an investment court[35] and, under CPTPP, Viet Nam, New Zealand, and Australia have entered into side letters which exclude compulsory ISDS.[36] Most recently, RCEP was concluded without any provision for ISDS, although the parties agreed that following RCEP's coming into force they would consider whether to add provisions on ISDS.[37]

To conclude, the *Doi Moi* policy generated a radical change in Viet Nam's approach to foreign investors and investment treaties. As of 2021, Viet Nam was a party to more than eighty investment treaties, including BITs and regional FTAs,[38] and ranked third among Asian countries (after China and Korea) in the number of investment treaties concluded.[39] With the Vietnamese government continuing to pursue an open and attractive investment environment, there is every indication that the government will continue to engage actively in the international investment treaty regime.

---

[34] Interviews Officials from MPI, 2018 and 2020 ('MPI Interviews').

[35] Tran Viet Dung, 'Cơ chế giải quyết tranh chấp giữa nhà đầu tư và nhà nước của EVFTA – Sự hình thành tòa án đầu tư quốc tế? [Investor-State Dispute Settlement Mechanism of the EVFTA – Formation of an International Investment Court?]', in Tran Viet Dung and Nguyen Thi Lan Huong (eds.), *Giải quyết tranh chấp đầu tư quốc tế: Một số vấn đề pháp lý và thực tiễn trong bối cảnh hội nhập [International Investment Dispute Settlement: Legal and practical issues in the light of integration]* (Hong Duc Publication House, 2018), 59, 59–60.

[36] The side letters constitute bilateral agreements between the relevant states aiming to prevent the institution of investor–state claims by foreign investors unless the host state specifically consents to a dispute with a particular investor of the other state being submitted against it. The letters were signed and came into force together with CPTPP.

[37] See RCEP, Art. 10.18.

[38] Ministry of Planning and Development, 'Danh mục Hiệp định Việt Nam – Các nước [List of (Investment, Double Taxation) Treaties between Viet Nam and other Countries]', www.mpi.gov.vn/Pages/qhsp.aspx; Center for WTO and International Trade and Viet Nam Chamber of Commerce and Industry, 'Other trade agreements', https://wtocenter.vn/hiep-dinh-khac.

[39] Statistics on the number of investment treaties entered into by countries are available at the International Investment Agreements Navigator managed by the UNCTAD Investment Policy Hub.

9.4.2   From Host State to Home State

Viet Nam's negotiating position with respect to investment treaties has changed over time. In its early BIT days during the 1990s, Viet Nam was a 'rule-taker' and largely accepted the proposals made by its counterparties. At the time, Viet Nam lacked substantial knowledge and expertise on international investment law. In desperate need of inflows of foreign capital and international recognition, it also lacked bargaining leverage.

Over the years, as Viet Nam's economy has grown and matured, Vietnamese enterprises have started to invest abroad. As of 2020, Vietnamese enterprises had invested in seventy-eight countries and territories with total investment capital of USD $20.6 billion.[40] Among the countries receiving investment from Vietnamese enterprises, Laos PDR and Cambodia are the largest recipients with total registered investment capital of over USD $8.5 billion, followed by Russia, Myanmar, Australia, the United States, Germany, and some African and South American countries.[41]

In the negotiation of investment treaties, Viet Nam has, therefore, started to advance its interests as a capital-exporting country,[42] seeking to protect the investments made by Vietnamese companies overseas.[43] For example, in its investment treaty negotiations with Mozambique (2007), Venezuela (2008), Slovakia (2009), Kazakhstan (2009), and the Eurasian Economic Union (2015)[44] – countries which are Vietnamese investment targets[45] – MPI, which is the state agency in charge of negotiating investment treaties, was mandated to maximise investment protection standards.[46] Thus, these investment treaties contain broad protections for foreign investors and their investments, as reflected in the definition of investment and the inclusion of guarantees of full compensation for

---

[40] MPI, Foreign Investment Agency, *Báo cáo tình hình đầu tư ra nước ngoài năm 2020* [*Report on Outward Investment of Vietnamese Enterprises in 2020*] (28 December 2020), 18–21.

[41] *Ibid.*

[42] MPI Interviews; this is also confirmed in the interviews and discussions with representatives of the CIEM (conducted in April 2019) ('CIEM Interviews') and with representatives of the VCCI (conducted in June 2019) ('VCCI Interviews').

[43] Vu Van Chung, 'Tổng quan về đầu tư nước ngoài và đánh giá tình hình quản lý đầu tư nước ngoài tại Việt Nam [Overview of the outward investment and evaluation of status of management of outward investment activities in Viet Nam]', presented at 'The Policy on Outward Investment for Central, Local Investment Agencies and Enterprises in The North', Bac Giang Province (2015), 8–17.

[44] The Eurasian Economic Union comprises the Republic of Armenia, the Republic of Belarus, the Republic of Kazakhstan, the Kyrgyz Republic, and the Russian Federation.

[45] MPI Interviews.

[46] *Ibid.*

expropriation, FET, full security protection of investors' assets, and the free transfer of investment capital.

At the same time, however, Viet Nam has sought to strike a balance between investment protection and regulatory freedom, seeking the inclusion of provisions which safeguard the state's autonomy to regulate in the public interest. Indeed, government officials interviewed for this study indicated that the Vietnamese delegation, in its negotiations over the ACIA, EVFTA/EVIPA, and others, pressed for the inclusion of exceptions for protecting the public interest and public order and raised the issue of corporate social responsibility of foreign investors.[47]

9.4.3   Investor–State Disputes

With the growth of foreign investment activities in Viet Nam since 2010, the number of disputes between investors and national agencies has increased significantly. According to MOJ's Judicial Institute, from 2010 to 2017, there were fourteen cases where foreign investors notified their intention to initiate a claim against Viet Nam or sent a request to national agencies, or to the Prime Minister, to resolve a dispute between them and national agencies.[48]

In addition, Viet Nam has faced eight ISDS arbitration cases.[49] Out of these eight cases, the government settled two – *Cockrell* v. *Viet Nam* and *Trinh* v. *Viet Nam (I)*. In the remaining cases, Viet Nam decided to pursue arbitral proceedings until their resolution. The Vietnamese government is currently involved in two pending ISDS cases, namely *ConocoPhillips* v. *Viet Nam* and *Shin Dong Baig* v. *Viet Nam*.

---

[47] *Ibid*. This is also confirmed in interviews and discussions with the officials of the Department of International Legislation and the Department of Civil-Economic Laws of MOJ, which were conducted in May 2018, April 2019, and November 2020 ('MOJ Interviews').

[48] MOJ, 'ISDS involving the Government of Viet Nam and recommendation for prevention measures', Ministerial Level Research Project (2017).

[49] *Trinh Vinh Binh and Binh Chau Joint Stock Company* v. *Socialist Republic of Viet Nam (I)*, UNICITRAL Rules, Award (14 March 2007); *Michael McKenzie* v. *Socialist Republic of Viet Nam*, UNCITRAL Rules, Final Award (11 December 2013); *Dialasie SAS* v. *Socialist Republic of Viet Nam*, UNCITRAL Rules, Award (17 November 2014); *RECOFI S.A.* v. *Socialist Republic of Viet Nam*, UNCITRAL Rules, Final Award (28 September 2015); *Trinh Vinh Binh and Binh Chau Joint Stock Company* v. Socialist Republic of Viet Nam *(II)*, PCA Case No. 2015-23, Award (10 April 2019); *Bryan Cockrell* v. *Socialist Republic of Viet Nam*, PCA Case No. 2015-03; *ConocoPhillips and Perenco* v. *Socialist Republic of Viet Nam*, UNCITRAL Rules (2017); *Shin Dong Baig* v. *Socialist Republic of Viet Nam*, ICSID Case No. ARB(AF)/18/2.

Most of Viet Nam's investment disputes have arisen out of actions taken by local governments, usually related to land allocation.[50] By way of example, two of the largest recent investment arbitration cases against Viet Nam have involved the government of Ho Chi Minh City, arising out of Ho Chi Minh City's failure to allocate 'clean land' to foreign investors for carrying out an investment project as it had committed to do in a lease agreement.[51]

Another common basis for claims by foreign investors has been incentive schemes offered by local governments. In order to attract FDI, some local governments have offered incentives to foreign investors that go beyond what is permitted under Vietnamese law,[52] resulting in claims and complaints alleging violations of the FET standard when they have been unable to fulfil their undertakings.[53] Taxation matters have also given rise to claims. The *ConocoPhillips* v. *Viet Nam* case, for example, relates to the central government's decision to impose a capital gains tax on a major oil deal between two UK companies (ConocoPhillips and Perenco) over their oil business in Viet Nam.[54] It was reported that the deal raised a profit of USD $896 million for ConocoPhillips.[55] As this transaction was not subject

---

[50] As a matter of background, private ownership of land is not permitted in Viet Nam. The 2013 Land Law (Law No. 45/2013/QH13, 29 November 2013), however, allows land to be leased to foreign-invested firms through annual payment or one-off rental payment to implement projects in agriculture, forestry, aquaculture or salt making, non-agricultural production and business land, construction of public facilities for business purposes, and housing projects for lease. Moreover, the Law authorises the lease of assets associated with provincial People's Committees.

[51] Interviews Officials, 2018 and 2019; the interviewed officials were from the DOJ of Ho Chi Minh City ('HCMC-DOJ Interviews').

[52] Investment projects in Viet Nam do not require contracts or memoranda of understanding (MOUs) between local governments and foreign investors. And, indeed, neither the recent Law on Investment 2020 nor its predecessors in 2014 and 2005 provide authorisation for such contracts or MOUs. Nevertheless, it has been a practice of local governments and foreign investors to sign MOUs on preliminary aspects of investment projects, such as the identification of investors, commitment of capital, location of the project, and local government incentives. Notwithstanding the widespread use of MOUs, there appears to be no consistency among local governments as to their form and content. Some MOUs are sent to MOFA for opinion, since local governments consider them international arrangements. Others apparently receive no review at all, nor is notice of their existence necessarily provided to the central government.

[53] The problem of discretionary decision making with respect to incentives and a lack of coordination between central and provincial authorities was noted by the OECD in its 2018 Investment Policy Review of Viet Nam. See OECD, *Investment Policy Reviews: Viet Nam* (OECD Publishing, 2018), 36.

[54] George Turner, 'Oil Firms Use Secretive Court Hearing in Bid to Stop Viet Nam Taxing Their Profits', *The Guardian*, 15 August 2018.

[55] *Ibid.*

to capital gains tax under UK law, Viet Nam claimed it had the right to levy the tax under the UK–Viet Nam Double Taxation Agreement.[56]

Finally, another common basis for claims has been alleged discriminatory treatment against foreign investors by local governments. In the ongoing *Shin Dong Baig* dispute, for example, a South Korean investor has claimed that in his application for a real estate project licence, he suffered discriminatory treatment by the Ho Chi Minh City authorities and that this was in violation of the NT guarantee in the Korea–Viet Nam BIT.

9.5 Negotiating and Entering into Investment Treaties

9.5.1 Investment Treaty Negotiation Process

The Law on Treaties sets out the rules for the negotiation and conclusion of treaties. Under the law, the Prime Minister is empowered to authorise a government agency to propose a plan for a treaty as well as to negotiate and conclude it.

Although it is not stipulated by the law, MPI is usually appointed by the government to be the lead agency for the negotiation and conclusion of standalone investment treaties.[57] For FTAs, as the state agency in charge of international trade, the Ministry of Industry and Trade (MOIT) is assigned the role of the lead agency for the negotiation, however, MPI still is given primary responsibility for drafting and reviewing the investment chapter therein.[58] In the case of EVIPA, MPI was assigned the role of lead agency in negotiating the investment protection treaty immediately after Viet Nam and the EU decided to separate the investment section from the EVFTA.[59]

In proposing investment treaty negotiations, MPI must perform a number of tasks, including making a preliminary assessment of the political, national defence, security, socio-economic, and other impacts of the investment treaty; reviewing existing laws and other investment treaties to which Viet Nam is a contracting party; and comparing these with the main contents of the treaty expected to be negotiated.[60]

---

[56] *Ibid.*
[57] The Government has started to give this mandate to MPI (and its predecessor, the State Planning Commission) ever since the establishment of the national regime for the adoption and implementation of international treaties in 1989.
[58] MPI Interviews; Interviews Officials, 2019; these officials were from the Government Office ('GO Interviews').
[59] *Ibid.*
[60] Law No. 108/2016/QH13 on Treaties, 9 April 2016 ('Law on Treaties'), Arts. 9.1(a)–(b).

Viet Nam has a confidential model investment treaty, which serves as a basis for negotiations.[61] In addition, in the course of negotiation of investment treaties, MPI consults and coordinates with the Ministry of Foreign Affairs (MOFA) and MOJ[62] to ensure that the draft treaty does not include provisions that would conflict with national law and other international obligations.[63] Although MOFA's and MOJ's review is an essential part of the process, with the existence of the model treaty, their evaluations have become more of a formality. In practice, over the years, MOFA and MOJ have been consistently supportive of investment treaty negotiation proposals, which are seen as advancing the state's policy of expanding its investment treaty network.[64] The ultimate decision of whether to initiate negotiations lies with the Prime Minister, who then also formulates the treaty negotiation and conclusion strategy.

Once approved, MPI coordinates the negotiation and drafting process among the line ministries, such as Ministry of Finance (MOF), the Ministry of Natural Resources and Environment (MONRE), or the State Bank of Viet Nam (SBV), in order to receive their opinions in regard to issues or insights within their respective field of state management.[65] Representatives from these agencies have regularly participated in negotiations on regional agreements, especially when negotiation rounds have been held in Hanoi, and are always invited to comment on draft texts emerging from each negotiating round.[66]

Before submission for official signing, all treaties must still be subject to final review by MOFA, MOJ, and other relevant agencies.[67] Accordingly, MOFA is required to assess specifically the following aspects of the treaty: (1) the necessity and purpose of the conclusion of the proposed investment

---

[61] MPI Interviews; GO Interviews. The text of this 'Model IIA' is confidential and only serves as an internal guidance document for the negotiators.

[62] Law on Treaties, Arts. 9.1(c) and 11.1(b).

[63] GO Interviews. MOJ usually makes an assessment of the bilateral/regional investment treaty *vis-à-vis* the civil code, commercial law, investment law, enterprises law, securities law, foreign exchange law, and law on foreign trade.

[64] GO Interviews; MOJ Interviews; MPI Interviews.

[65] GO Interviews; MPI Interviews.

[66] *Ibid.*

[67] Law on Treaties, Art. 17.2. MOFA must complete the review and provide its written opinion on the draft investment treaty within fifteen days from the date of receipt of the full dossier from MPI, while MOJ is given twenty days to do the same. When a treaty is subject to contentious opinions, the review time can be extended but it still must not exceed a certain prescribed time. Pursuant to the Law on Treaties, MOFA can extend the review no more than thirty days (Art. 18.1) and MOJ can extend the review no more than sixty days (Art. 20.2).

treaty on the basis of an assessment of the relationship between Viet Nam and the counterparty; (2) whether the provisions of the proposed investment treaty conform with fundamental principles of international law as well as with the national interests and diplomatic policies of Viet Nam; (3) the compatibility between provisions of the proposed investment treaty and existing investment treaty obligations of Viet Nam; (4) the treaty-making process itself; and (5) the consistency between the Vietnamese language version of the treaty text and its foreign language version.[68] Meanwhile, MOJ must assess the following aspects of the proposed investment treaty: (1) compliance with the Constitution; (2) compliance with national laws; (3) the possibility of direct application of the whole or part of the treaty; and (4) the requirement for amendment, supplementation, denunciation, or promulgation of domestic legal documents for the implementation of the treaty.[69]

To avoid disagreement at the final stage, the negotiation delegation is always comprised of representatives from MPI, MOJ, and MOFA.[70] Additional meetings with other relevant agencies are organised if there is any divergence of opinion during the course of negotiations,[71] in an attempt to analyse the issue and consolidate the national negotiating position.[72] As a result of this process, the agencies involved in the negotiation process have generally developed a good cooperative relationship and substantial disagreements between them are quite rare.[73] So far, disagreements have mainly related to the detailed definition of certain technical terms, such as 'investment' and 'investor'; the scope of exemptions, FET, and indirect expropriation; or certain non-standard provisions proposed by the counterparty, such as the proposal by the EU for the establishment of the investment court system under the EVIPA.[74]

The investment treaty negotiating and drafting process reveals the role of MPI as a key node for expertise within the Vietnamese government. Moreover, the involvement in this process of MOJ, MOFA, and some line ministries suggests that there is at least some level of awareness as to the existence of investment treaties across the government ministries,

---

[68] Law on Treaties, Art. 18.2.
[69] Law on Treaties, Art. 20.2.
[70] MPI Interviews; GO Interviews.
[71] GO Interviews.
[72] Decree 150/2016/ND-CP of the Government on The Functions, Tasks, Powers and Organizational Structure of the Government Office, 11 November 2016, Art. 2.
[73] MPI Interviews; GO Interviews; MOJ Interviews.
[74] MPI Interviews; CIEM Interviews.

though questions remain as to the spread of the awareness (e.g., whether it is limited to legal departments or extends to diverse departments) and the depth and specificity of such knowledge.

9.5.2   The Treaty Approval Process

There are two different constitutional processes for adopting treaties in Vietnamese law: one which requires legislative[75] approval and one which requires only the agreement of the executive government. The Constitution empowers the National Assembly of Viet Nam (NAV) to make decisions on external relations policy and to ratify or annul certain types of treaties,[76] including those signed by the President,[77] and treaties containing provisions 'inconsistent with statutes and resolutions taken by the National Assembly'.[78] Thus, any draft treaty that contains provisions which are different from existing law, or requires amendments to existing law, the annulment of existing law, or promulgation of a new law, must be submitted to the NAV Standing Committee for approval.[79] Hence, all other treaties that do not fall into these categories need only be adopted by the executive government.[80]

Since investment treaties have not been viewed as requiring changes or amendments to national law, most of Viet Nam's BITs have not required NAV approval and have been adopted by the executive government.[81] In contrast, FTAs such as EVFTA, CPTPP, and RCEP require amendments to existing laws in such fields as competition, financial service, e-commerce, intellectual property, human rights, labour standards, environmental protection, and rules of origin. To that end, these treaties have been subject to NAV approval, even though the investment chapters, like standalone investment treaties, are not considered to affect the existing domestic laws of Viet Nam.

9.5.3   Implementing Investment Treaties

As a matter of general procedure, after a treaty comes into effect, the Prime Minister is responsible for its implementation. The Prime Minister

---

[75] National Assembly of Viet Nam.
[76] Constitution of the Socialist Republic of Viet Nam 2013, Art. 70.14.
[77] Law on Treaties, Art. 29.1(dd).
[78] Law on Treaties, Art. 29.1(d).
[79] Law on Treaties, Art. 29.1.
[80] Constitution of the Socialist Republic of Viet Nam 2013, Art. 96.7.
[81] MPI Interviews; MOJ Interviews.

approves the treaty implementation plan and decides on any directives or measures of implementation. Hence, MPI assists the Prime Minister in preparing the implementation plan.[82] Such plan must set out in detail the implementation schedule, the responsibilities of the various state agencies in organising the treaty's implementation, the proposed amendment, supplementation, annulment, or promulgation of domestic legal documents for the purposes of implementation, as well as any measures of organisation, management, and funding regarding the implementation itself.[83]

MOFA and MOJ are responsible for overseeing the implementation of treaties. Although under the Law on Treaties, other state agencies, including the Supreme People's Court, the Supreme People's Procurator, the State Audit Office, ministerial-level agencies, and the People's Committees of provinces and centrally run cities, are also involved in implementing treaties,[84] their roles are vague and not clearly defined.

Pursuant to its obligations under the Law on Treaties, MOFA must report annually to the Prime Minister, or, as requested, to the NAV, on the implementation of international treaties. It also regularly prepares a report for the Government to submit to the NAV on the conclusion and implementation of treaties. In contrast, MOJ is responsible for all aspects of domestic legal implementation, and oversees any required amendment, supplementation, or annulment of domestic laws and regulations. It also serves in a monitoring function by assessing the conformity of domestic legal documents with that treaty. MOJ may also take initiative or cooperate with MPI in recommending to the Prime Minister interpretations and modes of application of the provisions of an investment treaty in cases where there is a contentious interpretation or application of such provisions.

As noted, investment treaties in Viet Nam have not been considered to require the adoption of new domestic laws. Thus, in practice, the general procedure for implementing treaties in Viet Nam has played a limited role with respect to investment treaties. This situation may be contrasted with the treatment of Viet Nam's international trade commitments, for which the procedure for implementing treaties has been actively used. Accession to the WTO, for example, has required Viet Nam to make major changes to its domestic legal system. It is estimated that to meet the requirements of joining the WTO, around 500 normative documents were either

---

[82] Law on Treaties, Art. 76.2.
[83] GO Interviews; MPI Interviews.
[84] Law on Treaties, Art. 80.1.

created or modified,[85] of which sixty new major laws were adopted by the NAV during 2003–2005.[86] For investment treaties, however, this kind of scrutiny with respect to implementation has not occurred. Instead, the 'implementation' of new investment treaties in Viet Nam has focused principally on efforts by MPI and MOJ to disseminate information about the existence of these treaties within the government.[87]

9.5.4 The Legal Status of Investment Treaties

The *Doi Moi* policy and the consequent embrace of regional and international integration generated a change in perception by the Vietnamese government regarding the relationship between international and national law. Traditionally, Viet Nam had supported the theory of dualism, which considers international law and national law as two different legal systems.[88] International law was considered to be a part of Viet Nam's legal system only once it had been accepted into national law by a domestic legal act.[89] Thus, Vietnamese courts only apply international law, which had been adopted into national law.[90]

Following the adoption of the *Doi Moi* policy, and with Viet Nam's growing participation in regional and international integration, Viet Nam has taken a more flexible approach towards the status of international treaties. The Law on Conclusion, Accession to and Implementation of Treaties 2005 acknowledged for the first time the superiority of international treaties over national law.[91] The 2005 Law stipulated that in the case of a conflict between domestic norms and an international treaty, the treaty shall prevail.[92] Further, it provided that, when deciding to be bound by a treaty, the Government or the NAV (as appropriate) must determine whether

---

[85] OECD, *Investment Policy Reviews*, 27.
[86] Tran Hao Hung, 'Evaluating the Implementation of Investment-related WTO Commitments and Orientations to Improve Legal Framework on Investment', Ministerial Level Research Project, Hanoi (2010); see also WTO, *Report of the Working Party on Viet Nam's Accession to the WTO*, WT/ACC/VNM/48 (17 October 2006).
[87] MPI Interviews; MOJ Interviews.
[88] Tran Thi Thuy Duong and Nguyen Thi Yen, *Giáo trình Công Pháp Quốc tế [Textbook of Public International Law]* (Hong Duc Publication House, 2013), 67–8.
[89] *Ibid.*
[90] Interviews Judges, 2019 and 2020. These judges were from the High People's Court in Ho Chi Minh City and the People's Court of Ho Chi Minh City ('PC Interviews').
[91] Law No. 41/2005/QH11 on Conclusion, Accession to and Implementation of Treaties, 14 June 2005 ('Law on Conclusion, Accession to and Implementation of Treaties').
[92] Law on Conclusion, Accession to and Implementation of Treaties, Art. 6.1.

the treaty's provisions are explicit and specific enough for its direct implementation, in whole or in part, or whether implementing legislation is required.[93] The new Law on Treaties 2016 reconfirmed these principles and the procedures of treaty making, while also clarifying that the Constitution supersedes conflicting provisions in international treaties.[94]

The principle of the superiority of international treaties over national law has had an impact on the internalisation of investment treaty commitments in Viet Nam. The clear statement of superiority clarifies the Vietnamese government's obligations – as a matter of Vietnamese law – to incorporate any investment treaty commitments it has undertaken into its dealings with foreign investors. Thus, based on interviews with officials at both the central and provincial level, it appears that when foreign investors raise investment treaty considerations before the relevant authorities, these authorities routinely will revisit the terms of domestic laws and regulations in order to assess investors' complaints.[95] That said, it is also clear that this approach is not always taken, particularly among some state authorities, including provincial courts,[96] which still have a habit of not applying international treaty norms in their dealings with foreign investors.

9.5.5   Adoption of Investment Laws

Finally, while investment treaties are not adopted as domestic laws into the domestic legal system, Viet Nam has reformed its national investment laws in a manner that generally aligns with investor protections found in investment treaties.[97] To this end, in 2005, Viet Nam merged the Foreign Investment Law and the Domestic Investment Encouragement Law into a unified Law on Investment,[98] which ensured, *inter alia*, the application of

---

[93] Law on Conclusion, Accession to and Implementation of Treaties, Art. 6.3.

[94] Law on Treaties, Art. 6.1.

[95] Interviews Officials, 2018; interviewed officials were from the DPI of Ho Chi Minh ('HCMC-DPI Interviews'); Interviews Officials, 2018; interviewed officials were from the DPI of Hanoi ('HN-DPI Interviews'); HCMC-DOJ Interviews; Interviews Officials, 2019; interviewed officials were from the DOJ of Binh Duong Province ('BD-DOJ interviews').

[96] HCMC-DOJ Interviews; PC Interviews. The judges in Viet Nam often apply international treaties in the recognition and implementation of foreign or international judgements or arbitral awards. Some of these international treaties include the New York Convention on the Recognition and Enforcement of Foreign Arbitral Awards (1958) and bilateral treaties with provisions on mutual judicial assistance.

[97] MPI, 'Tờ trình dự án ban hành Luật đầu tư (sửa đổi) [Proposal for Project of Adoption of the Law on Investment]', www.mpi.gov.vn/Pages/tinbai.aspx?idTin=1391&idcm=308.

[98] Law No. 59/2005/QH11 on Investment, 29 November 2005.

NT; further, in 2014, Viet Nam further revised the Law on Investment[99] to improve market access for foreign investors. The Law on Investment 2014 clarified and differentiated between the concepts of 'foreign investor' and 'foreign-invested economic organisation', liberalised foreign investment in sectors which had previously been prohibited (out of the fifty-one previously prohibited sectors, the Law on Investment 2014 retained only six prohibited sectors), and also facilitated investment by simplifying foreign investment procedures.

In 2020, Viet Nam again amended its Law on Investment to further refine the framework for foreign investment in Viet Nam.[100] Among the issues addressed in the Law on Investment 2020 are the liberalisation of the economy through the adoption for the first time in Viet Nam of a market access 'negative list' for foreign investment;[101] an expansion of business sectors and investment projects eligible for investment incentives; and the refinement of the processes for terminating and suspending investment authorisations, including on the grounds of national security.[102]

Further, Art. 13 of the Law on Investment 2020 provides that where a new law is promulgated that provides less favourable investment incentives than those currently enjoyed by an investor, the investor shall continue to enjoy the current incentives for the period originally set forth prior to the new law. This provision does not apply in the event of regulatory changes for reasons of national defence and security, social order and security, social ethics, public health, or environmental protection. Where the regulations have been changed for the above reasons, certain measures can be adopted to assist the affected investor, such as deducting the loss actually suffered by the investor from their taxable income, adjusting the objectives of the investment project, or assisting the investor in their recovery. However, the investor needs to file a written request within three years from the effective date of the new legal document in order to benefit. Additionally, Art. 15 provides for certain investment incentives, including tax reductions or exemptions, land rental reductions or exemptions, accelerated depreciation and increase in expenses deductible for tax purposes. It is not clear what prompted the inclusion of this provision in

---

[99] Law No. 67/2014/QH13 on Investment, 26 November 2014.
[100] Law No. 61/2020/QH14 on Investment, 17 June 2020 ('Law on Investment 2020').
[101] Under this new approach, foreign investors are afforded national treatment with regard to investment except in those sectors explicitly set out in an accompanying List of Restricted Sectors. See Decree 31/2021/ND-CP, Appendix I, 26 March 2021.
[102] Law on Investment 2020, Arts. 47–8.

the Law, including how its relationship to Viet Nam's investment treaty obligations may (or may not) have been taken into account in its drafting.

9.6   Monitoring Mechanisms in the Legislative Process

Calamita and Berman identify three main types of internalization measures: informational, monitoring, and remedial.[103] In this section, I review the monitoring mechanisms in the legislative process, that is, in the making of binding laws or regulations.

Pursuant to the Law on Promulgation of Legal Documents (LPLD),[104] Vietnamese law establishes mechanisms which facilitate the monitoring of international investment obligations in the law-making process, at least at the level of the central government. Notably, the mechanisms established under the LPLD are mechanisms of general application. They are not designed to address Viet Nam's international investment commitments specifically. Two aspects of the LPLD are worth highlighting in particular: (1) the provisions requiring the legal review of prospective laws and regulations, and (2) the provisions providing an opportunity for public comment in the law and regulation-making process.

9.6.1   *The Legal Review of Prospective Laws and Regulations*

The LPLD introduced a monitoring process for ensuring that new laws and regulations are compatible with Viet Nam's international treaty obligations. Under the LPLD, any proposal for a new law or regulation, whether by the legislature, the executive branch or the People's Supreme Court, must take into account relevant international treaties to which Viet Nam is a party.[105] This mandate is implemented by requiring that the government entity proposing a new law or regulation undertake a formal examination, *inter alia*, of its compatibility with Viet Nam's international agreements.[106] By statute, the responsibility for this assessment

---

[103] See Chapter 1.
[104] The Law on Promulgation of Legal Documents was adopted in 2015 and subsequently amended in 2020. See Law No. 80/2015/QH13 on Promulgation of Legal Documents, 22 May 2015 ('Law on Promulgation of Legal Documents 2015') and Law No. 63/2020/QH14 on Amendments to the Law on Promulgation of Legal Documents, 18 June 2020.
[105] Law on Promulgation of Legal Documents 2015, Arts. 32–3.
[106] Law on Promulgation of Legal Documents 2015, Arts. 34 (legislation), 85 (decrees), and 97 (decisions of the Prime Minister).

falls to MOFA.[107] Thereafter, MOJ is charged with appraising the proposal for a new law or regulation, including appraising its compatibility with Viet Nam's international agreements.[108] Following the Law on Treaties, the LPLD confirms that in the event of a conflict between an international treaty and a provision of Vietnamese law (apart from the Constitution), the international treaty shall apply.[109] Indeed, the LPLD goes further, stating affirmatively that the 'application of Viet Nam's legal normative documents must not obstruct the implementation of the international agreements to which the Socialist Republic of Vietnam is a signatory'.[110]

The use of MOJ expertise as a means to screen legal regulations during the drafting process has brought some immediate positive results whereby the quality of the laws and regulations adopted in the last decade[111] have improved and the number of rules considered to be in conflict with Viet Nam's international treaties has decreased significantly compared to the period before 2010.[112] That said, according to MOJ, although the drafting of laws and regulations has improved, weak drafting skills of agencies remains a significant problem.[113] Moreover, notwithstanding a promising start, MOJ faces immense challenges in ensuring the effectiveness of this screening mechanism because of resource constraints as well as a lack of expertise in certain technical areas.[114] Indeed, legislative errors and loopholes are still found in newly adopted laws and regulations, resulting in the need to amend and supplement them, wasting already limited government resources and causing difficulties in law enforcement.[115]

---

[107] Law on Promulgation of Legal Documents 2015, Arts. 36, 86, and 97. In practice, it is MOFA's Department of Law and International Treaties which undertakes the analysis.

[108] Law on Promulgation of Legal Documents 2015, Arts. 39, 88, and 98.

[109] *Ibid.*, Art. 156.

[110] *Ibid.*

[111] In Viet Nam, the drafting of a normative document – a law or regulation – is usually assigned to the line ministry of the relevant sector. For instance, drafting law on investment areas is assigned to MPI, while environmental law is vested in the hand of the MONRE.

[112] Vo Van Tuyen, 'Evaluation of more than two years of implementation of the LPLD 2015', presented at 'Solutions to improve the quality of the drafting of legal documents', MOJ, Hanoi (19 June 2018).

[113] *Ibid.*; GO Interview; VCCI Interviews.

[114] MOJ Interviews.

[115] One of the clearest examples of the problem is the Criminal Code (Law No. 100/2015/QH13, 27 November 2015), which was adopted by the NAV in 2015, but due to some erroneous provisions it needed to be amended and supplemented in 2017 (Law No. 12/2017/QH14 on Amendments to the Criminal Code, 20 June 2017).

9.6.2   *The Opportunity for Public Comment*

The LPLD also includes provisions designed to increase transparency and public participation in the law drafting process, requiring that draft laws and regulations undergo a public notice and comment process[116] that lasts at least sixty days.[117]

In the area of investment, MPI is the lead agency in developing investment laws and policies. In line with the LPLD, all investment related laws drafted by MPI have been subject to public comment and consultation since 2015. Such public consultation introduces an avenue of monitoring of proposed laws for alignment with international investment obligations.

For example, in 2013, MPI proposed the adoption of a new Law on Enterprises. MPI initiated the adoption of a new Law on Enterprises to improve the legal environment for foreign investors. Its proposal stated that Viet Nam's legal environment – with inconsistencies in the implementation of international treaties, discrimination between foreign and domestic investors, and the absence of a transparent and coherent mechanism for implementing investment protection guarantees – posed risks to foreign investors.[118]

MPI's report on the necessity of the proposed amendment to existing investment laws was made available to the public through the respective governmental and parliamentary electronic platforms.[119] MPI also ran conferences and workshops to collect opinions from interested parties. This information was also distributed directly to business associations for further public dissemination and posted on the VCCI's electronic platform.[120]

MPI's Proposal on Drafting the Law on Enterprises highlighted the comments made by business associations and foreign chambers of commerce – such as the American Chamber of Commerce, the European Chamber of Commerce, and leading law firms.[121] While the degree to which these comments influenced the final outcome is unclear, their direct consideration in the drafting process is noteworthy and provides an example of internalisation.

---

[116] Law on Promulgation of Legal Documents 2015, Arts. 5–6.
[117] See Law on Promulgation of Legal Documents 2015, Arts. 57, 81, 97, 105–8, and 110.
[118] MPI, 'Tờ trình dự án ban hành Luật đầu tư (sửa đổi) [Proposal for Project of Adoption of the Law on Investment]', www.mpi.gov.vn/Pages/tinbai.aspx?idTin=1391&idcm=308.
[119] The electronic platform of the National Assembly of Viet Nam can be accessed at http://duthaoonline.quochoi.vn and MPI's website can be accessed at www.mpi.gov.vn.
[120] The Viet Nam Chamber of Commerce and Industry's electronic platform can be accessed at www.vibonline.com.vn.
[121] GO Interviews; VCCI Interviews.

9.7 Informational and Monitoring Measures for Local Decision Making

As mentioned above, Calamita and Berman identify three main types of internalization measures: informational, monitoring, and remedial.[122] In this section, I lay out the state of informational and monitoring measures in local governmental decision making.

9.7.1 The Absence of Internalisation Measures

The Law on Investment 2020 has given more power to local governments in assessing and approving investment projects. For example, it abolishes the requirement that projects with a capital of USD $215 million or more be 'pre-approved' by the Prime Minister. Instead, the provincial Peoples' Committees are now authorised to approve all investment projects which do not fall under the exclusive jurisdiction of the NAV and the Prime Minister.[123] Despite the increased authority of local governments over foreign investment matters, however, it is also observed that there are very few internalisation efforts targeted at the level of the local government. Further, other than ad hoc events such as hosting trainings organised by MPI and MOJ,[124] local governments themselves do not run any internalisation efforts.

Ho Chi Minh City is somewhat of an exception. Dealing with the highest number of FDI complaints and investment arbitration cases in the country,[125] there is evidence of some informational internalisation measures. In 2010, faced with increasing number of FDI complaints raised by foreign investors based on investment contracts or investment treaties, the People's Committee of Ho Chi Minh City sought to improve informational internalisation and initiated a large capacity-building program for the judicial and licensing authorities of the city in an attempt to improve their knowledge of investment treaties.

---

[122] See Chapter 1.

[123] This includes projects involving the development of nuclear power plants, land reclamation at the borders, construction and operation of international airports and deep seaports, oil and gas processing, telecommunication infrastructure, casinos, etc. The exclusive jurisdictions of the NAV and the Prime Minister are set out in Arts. 30 and 31 of the Law on Investment 2020, respectively.

[124] MOJ Interviews; HCMC-DPI Interviews; BD-DPI Interviews; HN-DPI Interviews; HCMC-DOJ Interviews; BD-DOJ Interviews.

[125] MOJ, *Report of the Workshop Investor-State Dispute Resolutions: Experience for Viet Nam*, 15 February 2018. The Ho Chi Minh City Government has faced nearly 52 per cent of all contract-related investment arbitration cases in Viet Nam.

The People's Committee also requested MOJ to set up monitoring or remedial internalisation measures by establishing a special MOJ division with which the People's Committee and other city departments could consult on matters related to investment treaties, particularly with respect to settling complaints.[126] This division would also have been tasked with improving informational internalisation by disseminating information about Viet Nam's trade and investment treaties to local administrative agencies.[127] While this initiative did not materialise, in practice, the People's Committee of Ho Chi Minh City consults with the DOJ on the international law implications of the City's investment policies and decisions.[128] Thus, an ad hoc informal monitoring mechanism has developed with respect to one locality – Ho Chi Minh City.

In contrast, the People's Committees in the Binh Duong and Quang Ninh provinces do not appear to have been concerned with the country's investment treaty obligations when making policy.[129] While MOJ officers based in these provinces are responsible for advising the local government and agencies on the legality of their measures and have some general understanding of Viet Nam's investment treaty obligations, they tend not to approach the questions addressed to them in a systematic way.[130] Thus, in these provinces, although there are mechanisms which seem capable of providing a monitoring function, they have not been used to this end.

Thus far, it does not appear that the lack of monitoring in these provinces has led to investor grievances. Nevertheless, it is easy to see how it might. The actions taken by the Binh Duong government to assist foreign-owned companies that suffered harm due to a workers' riot in 2014 provides an example.

The riots were set off as an angry reaction to oil drilling by the Chinese government in a part of the South China Sea claimed by Viet Nam. Thousands of Vietnamese workers set fire to foreign factories and rampaged through industrial zones in the Binh Duong and Dong Nai provinces, primarily targeting Chinese companies, but also damaging assets of many Taiwanese companies that were mistakenly thought to be Chinese.[131] The Binh Duong

---

[126] HMC-DOJ Interviews.
[127] *Ibid.*
[128] *Ibid.*
[129] QN-DPI Interviews; QN-DOJ Interviews; BD-DPI Interviews; BD-DOJ Interviews.
[130] QN-DOJ Interviews; BD-DOJ Interviews.
[131] Ho Binh Minh and Manuel Mogato, 'Viet Nam Mobs Set Fire to Foreign Factories in Anti-China Riots', *Reuters*, 14 May 2014.

People's Committee conceded responsibility for not providing adequate and timely protection and security and took the initiative to negotiate measures to fix the damage caused. Based on interviews with Binh Duong officials, it appears that the Binh Duong government made such decisions without analysing the Viet Nam's obligations under the relevant investment treaties.[132] Instead, it appears to have mainly acted out of a concern for discharging the province's policy to create a safe environment for investors.[133]

However, the situation may change in the future when the Vietnamese government starts to decentralise the authority of handling of investment disputes and holds the local government accountable for the measures taken by them that are complained or sued by foreign investors.[134] This policy is expected to create an impetus for provincial authorities to learn about international law as well as improve their legal expertise in the field of state management of foreign investment.

9.7.2 Training and Workshops

To tackle low levels of internalisation among local officials in provincial governments, MPI and MOJ have begun encouraging informational internalisation in recent years by organising workshops and training courses on investment treaties for provincial government officials, especially for legal officers in local government.[135]

The internalising effect of these informational measures, however, has been limited for two main reasons. First, due to limited budget and human resources, training sessions and workshops have been relatively short (usually lasting two days), ad hoc, and dependant on the financial support of international donors (i.e., the US Agency for International Development (USAID), Multilateral Trade Assistance Project (MUTRAP), which is funded by the EU, the UK Prosperity Fund, and the UN Development Programme (UNDP)). As a consequence, these events have usually addressed general investment treaty trends and overall developments in ISDS but have not gotten into detailed technical discussions. Yet, an

---

[132] See for example Taiwan Province of China–Viet Nam BIT (1993); China–Viet Nam BIT (1992).

[133] BD-DPI Interviews; BD-DOJ Interviews.

[134] Decision 14/2020/QD-TTg of the Prime Minister on Promulgation of Regulation on Coordination in Settlement of International Investment Disputes, 08 April 2020 ('Decision 14').

[135] MPI Interviews, MOJ Interviews.

awareness of the technical details (e.g., how FET is interpreted) is actually highly significant to ensure compliance with these obligations. Second, the participants in these training sessions have come from different departments and agencies and, in practice, have tended to pay attention to issues they are already familiar with, without concentrating on the full implications that international treaty obligations may have in their day-to-day activities and functions.[136]

More recently, MPI has initiated a project to develop a handbook for government officials designed to provide them with a concise, practical explanation of the operation of Viet Nam's investment treaty obligations and how those obligations apply to day-to-day government decision making. The project relies upon international and domestic experts to draft the handbook[137] and is financed by the ASEAN–Australia–New Zealand Free Trade Area (AANZFTA) Economic Cooperation Support Programme (AECSP) and the Australian Department of Foreign Affairs and Trade.[138] At the launch of the project in 2021, which involved a consultation in Hanoi with officials from across Viet Nam, the Deputy Director General of the Department of Legislation at MPI explained the internalising rationale for the handbook: 'The implementation of investment treaty commitments poses significant challenges for government officials. Therefore, we would like to develop a handbook to assist our officials in managing and implementing those commitments'.[139] While it is not clear at the time of writing how effective the handbook will be in achieving its aims – especially at the provincial level – the project is noteworthy as an example of the Vietnamese government's continuing efforts to promote the internalisation of its investment treaty obligations.

9.8 Internalisation in the Courts

The Vietnamese courts have made little effort to assess and disseminate international treaties in general and investment treaties in particular.[140] Even the courts in Ho Chi Minh City, the largest economic centre of Viet

---

[136] HCMC-DOJ Interviews; BD-DOJ Interviews; HN-DPI Interviews; QN-DP Interviews.
[137] The principal author of the handbook is Professor N. Jansen Calamita, one of the editors of the present volume. See ASEAN–Australia–New Zealand FTA Economic Cooperation Support Programme (AECSP), 'Viet Nam Coordinates Efforts to Prevent and Tackle Investor-State Disputes', Press Release, 15 January 2021.
[138] *Ibid.*
[139] *Ibid.*
[140] The Vietnamese courts' implementation of the New York Convention has been a source of grievance among investors. Vietnamese courts tend to interpret extensively their power to

Nam with extensive international business relations, also rarely consider the issues from the perspective of international treaties, but primarily mainly make decisions based on analysis of national law.[141]

Indeed, the lack of awareness regarding Viet Nam's investment treaty obligations by the Ba Ria-Vung Tau Province Court and Procurator's office was the main reason for the ISDS proceedings in *Trinh v. Viet Nam (I)* in 2004.[142] Trinh, a Dutch national, was prosecuted under the Criminal Code of Viet Nam for 'breaching regulations on land management and protection' and 'offering bribes'. In 1998, the court of the Ba Ria-Vung Tau Province sentenced Trinh to thirteen years in prison and confiscated all of his assets in Viet Nam.[143] After returning to the Netherlands, Trinh brought a claim under the Netherlands–Viet Nam BIT (1994) before the Stockholm Chamber of Commerce. The case was eventually settled for an undisclosed amount.[144] Notably, Viet Nam's experience in the case does not appear to have brought about changes in the perceptions of the Vietnamese courts regarding the obligations contained in investment treaties.[145]

9.9 Remedial Internalisation Measures

As mentioned above, Calamita and Berman highlight the role of remedial internalization measures.[146] In this section, I provide an overview of the remedial measures which the Vietnamese government has introduced in the past decade – mechanisms which are geared towards preventing or settling disputes with foreign investors.

---

refuse recognition and enforcement to arbitral awards on the ground that they are in violation of fundamental principles of Viet Nam's legal system. As a result, and despite Viet Nam's obligations under the New York Convention, it is often difficult to obtain enforcement of an arbitral award obtained in a foreign jurisdiction. See OECD, *Investment Policy Reviews: Viet Nam*, 41 and 157.

[141] PC Interviews.

[142] Luke E. Peterson, 'U.S. Investor Pursues UNCITRAL Arbitration Claim Against Viet Nam; Tribunal Empaneled to Hear Allegations of Treaty Breach', Investment Arbitration Reporter, 1 December 2011; see also Quoc Thang, 'Vì sao ông Trịnh Vĩnh Bình kiện Chính phủ đòi 1,25 tỷ USD? [Why Mr. Trinh Vinh Binh requested the Government to Compensate 1.25 billion USD?]', VN Express Online, 1 September 2011.

[143] *Ibid.*

[144] *Trinh Vinh Binh v. Viet Nam (I)*, UNICITRAL Rules, Award (14 March 2007); MOJ Interviews.

[145] PC Interviews.

[146] See Chapter 1.

As Viet Nam has become more integrated into the global economy, the government has been attentive to the need to address disputes with foreign investors, fearing that if these disputes are not properly handled it may have a negative impact on the image of Viet Nam as an attractive target for foreign investment.[147] As discussed below, however, until recently the government had not adopted procedures designed to consider the investment treaty implications of investor grievances. Instead, Viet Nam relied on administrative law procedures of a general character, which were not especially effective at considering the international aspects of investor–state disputes. In 2014, however, the government established a new regulatory framework for addressing disputes with foreign investors. Following on that initiative, the government has more recently begun working with the World Bank to develop a pilot programme of an 'early warning' system, designed to address the early resolution of investor grievances. This section examines these remedial internalisation measures.

9.9.1   Administrative Reconsideration and Judicial Review

In 2011, Viet Nam adopted the Law on Complaints.[148] The Law on Complaints replaced earlier legislation, originally adopted in 1998,[149] which, together with the 1996 Ordinance on Procedures for Settlement of Administrative Cases,[150] had marked the beginning of Viet Nam's development of a body of administrative law, providing legal bases for citizens (and foreigners) to exercise rights of complaint with regards to decisions of the state's administrative agencies.[151]

Under the 2011 Law on Complaints, whenever a dispute arises between a citizen or foreigner and a state body (whether at the national or the local level), the individual (whether a corporate body or a real person) may resort to a process of administrative reconsideration. Through this process, the individual may make a complaint and request administrative

---

147 MOJ Interviews.
148 Law No. 02/2011/QH13 on Complaints, 11 November 2011 ('Law on Complaints 2011').
149 See Law No. 09/1998/QH10 on Complaints and Denunciations, 2 December 1998, as amended by Law No. 26/2004/QH11, 15 June 2004 and Law No. 58/2005/QH11, 29 November 2005.
150 Ordinance on Procedures for Settlement of Administrative Cases, 3 June 1996.
151 For a broad survey of the history of administrative law in Viet Nam, see Nguyen Thi Minh Ha and Ha Thi Han, 'Judicial Review of Administrative Actions in Vietnam Since Independence 1945' (2019) 2 Asian Constitutional Law: Recent Development and Trends 101.

reconsideration if they believe that an administrative decision infringes upon their lawful rights or interests or that a state body has exceeded its lawful decision-making power, such as illegally imposing duties on them or failing to protect their property rights.[152]

The complainant may submit their request for administrative reconsideration to the entity which adopted the challenged administrative decision, whether at the local or central government level.[153] Remedies available include the restoration of the individual's rights and administrative compensation.[154] Individuals who are not satisfied with the decision of administrative reconsideration may initiate an administrative lawsuit against the relevant state agency in accordance with the Law on Administrative Procedures.[155] The Law on Administrative Procedures was originally adopted in 2010,[156] replacing the 1996 Ordinance on Procedures for Settlement of Administrative Cases.[157] The 2010 Law was itself replaced by a newer version in 2015.[158]

In broad brush, the Law on Administrative Procedures sets forth fundamental principles for administrative procedures; tasks, powers, and responsibilities of agencies managing administrative procedures; rights and obligations of individuals involving in administrative proceedings; and procedures for instituting lawsuits, settling administrative cases, and enforcing administrative judgments. Taken together, the Law on Complaints and the Law on Administrative Procedures establish a legal framework for the challenge of administrative decisions in Viet Nam, available to citizens and foreigners alike.

There are a number of points to be made about the Vietnamese administrative law regime from the perspective of internalisation. First, as stated, both the Law on Complaints and the Law on Administrative Procedures are laws of general application. The rights and procedures established by these laws are available to domestic as well as foreign investors.

Second, neither law (nor their predecessors) was established as a response to Viet Nam's investment treaty commitments, but instead was

---

[152] Law on Complaints 2011, Art. 7.
[153] See Law on Complaints 2011, Arts. 17–26 (delineating the competences of different government entities).
[154] Law on Complaints 2011, Art. 12.
[155] Law on Complaints 2011, Art. 7.
[156] Law No. 64/2010/QH12 on Administrative Procedures, 24 November 2010.
[157] Ordinance on Procedures for Settlement of Administrative Cases, 3 June 1996, as amended on 25 December 1998 and on 5 April 2006.
[158] Law No. 93/2015/QH13 on Administrative Procedures, 25 November 2015.

part of the more general process of public law reform following Viet Nam's adoption of the *Doi Moi* policy, and subsequently accelerated by its accession to different trade agreements. As noted by Nguyen Van Quang,[159] the development of Viet Nam's administrative laws was addressed to provisions such as Art. 7 of Chapter VI 'Transparency-related Provisions and Right to Appeal' of the United States–Viet Nam Trade Relations Agreement, which requires the establishment of procedures for administrative challenge:

> The Parties will maintain administrative and judicial tribunals and procedures for the purpose, inter alia, of the prompt review and correction (upon the request of an affected person) of administrative action relating to matters covered by this Agreement. These procedures shall include the opportunity for appeal, without penalty, by persons affected by the relevant decision. If the initial right of appeal is to an administrative body, there shall also be the opportunity for appeal of the decision to a judicial body. Notice of the decision on appeal shall be given to the appellant and the reasons for such decision shall be provided in writing. The appellant shall also be informed of the right to any further appeal.[160]

Others have noted the importance of Viet Nam's membership in ASEAN in shaping Viet Nam's administrative law,[161] as well its accession to the WTO.[162] It is not possible, therefore, to characterise the Law on Complaints, the Law on Administrative Procedures, or any of their predecessors, as a rule of law spill-over effect resulting from Viet Nam's investment treaty commitments.

Finally, although Viet Nam's law has developed to establish mechanisms for challenging administrative action in Viet Nam, and potentially resolving investor grievances at an early stage, it is noteworthy that there was a consensus among lawyers for foreign investors in Viet Nam interviewed for this project that these mechanisms have failed to create an effective process for resolving investor–state disputes.[163]

---

[159] Nguyen Van Quang, 'Judicially Reviewable Administrative Actions: The Development of Vietnamese Administrative Justice' (2013) *Law and Politics in Africa, Asia and Latin America* 367, 379.

[160] United States–Viet Nam Trade Relations Agreement (2000).

[161] Hao Duy Phan, 'The Effects of ASEAN Treaties in Domestic Legal Orders: Evidence from Vietnam' (2019) 17 *International Journal of Constitutional Law* 205, 211.

[162] Dinh Van Minh, 'Administrative Law and Judicial Review', Vietnam Law & Legal Forum, 1 September 2010.

[163] Interviews Lawyers, 2019; these lawyers had acted for FDI businesses in ISDS claims ('Lawyer Interviews').

9.9.2 Investor–State Dispute Prevention and Management

In the aftermath of the ISDS claims faced by Viet Nam from 2010 to 2013, the government noticed that the state agencies involved in these cases had been uncoordinated in their responses. Of particular concern, the agencies involved were not exchanging information or consulting internally to properly respond to and manage the claims.[164]

To address this issue, in 2014, the Prime Minister adopted special Decision 04/2014/QD-TTg ('Decision 04'), which set out uniform guidelines for state bodies in the settlement of international investment disputes.[165] Decision 04 defined 'international investment disputes' broadly, comprising not only disputes arising under international investment agreements (IIAs), but also those arising under commercial contracts where provision is made for arbitration or other international form of dispute resolution.[166]

With respect to claims arising under IIAs, Decision 04 designated MOJ as the 'presiding authority' for settling all investor–state disputes.[167] MOJ was tasked with, *inter alia*, receiving and handling information and documents related claims by foreign investors; acting as the focal point of contact with the investor and the arbitral tribunal; coordinating among government agencies with respect to developing strategies to resolve the dispute; managing Viet Nam's retention of outside counsel and experts and its appointment of arbitrators; and reporting about IIA disputes to the Prime Minister.[168] Under Decision 04, where a state agency received a complaint or requests for consultations from a foreign investor involving the possibility of an IIA claim, that agency was required to notify MOJ of the situation and to direct the foreign investor to send its complaint to or request for consultations with MOJ.[169]

---

[164] GO Interviews; VCCI Interviews; Lawyer Interviews.

[165] Decision No. 04/2014/QD-TTg of the Prime Minister on Promulgation of Regulation on Coordination in Settlement of International Investment Disputes, 14 January 2014 ('Decision 04').

[166] *Ibid.*, Art. 2.

[167] *Ibid.*, Art. 5. For other kinds of disputes, the lead agency varies. See Art. 5.3 (providing that the lead agency in an international investment dispute arising out of a contract is to be state agency that concluded the contract with the foreign investor); Art. 5.4 (designating the Ministry of Finance as the lead agency for disputes involving loans, government debts, etc.).

[168] *Ibid.*, Art. 6.

[169] Decision 04 provides generally that state agencies that receive complaints or requests for consultations from foreign investors, but do not have competence to resolve the complaint, are required to direct foreign investors to send their complaints or request for consultations to the competent agency and to notify the competent agency directly. *Ibid.*, Art. 9.2.

Decision 04 was replaced in 2020 by Decision No. 14/2020/QD-TTg ('Decision 14').[170] Unlike Decision 04, Decision 14 does not make MOJ the default presiding authority in situations involving IIAs. Instead, the presiding authority for the settlement of an investment dispute is the ministry, ministerial-level agency, or provincial People's Committee that has enacted a measure about which a foreign investor makes a complaint or claim.[171] The presiding authority is given the power to 'preside over' matters concerning, *inter alia*, the 'formulation of strategies, roadmaps and procedures' to resolve the dispute and Viet Nam's retention of outside counsel and experts and its appointment of arbitrators.[172] Decision 14 makes clear, however, that the presiding authority must do so in cooperation with MOJ, as 'the Government's legal representative body'.[173] Decision 14 also gives MOJ general responsibility to act 'a contact point that assists the Government and Prime Minister to unify the resolution of international investment disputes'.[174]

Decision 14 establishes special procedures in the event that an investment dispute is submitted to arbitration. In such cases, a 'cross-sectoral working group' (CSWG) must be established.[175] The CSWG includes representatives of the presiding authority, MOJ, and other 'relevant organizations and individuals', such as MPI.[176] The presiding authority retains primary responsibility for managing the resolution of the dispute; however, the CSWG is empowered to work with the presiding authority to formulate a strategy for resolving the dispute, which is then subject to final approval by the Prime Minister.[177] In addition, the CSWG is tasked with assisting and advising the presiding authority and MOJ throughout the dispute settlement process.[178] Decision 14 also contains provisions addressed to funding the expenses incurred in dispute resolution, for example, the retention of outside counsel, experts, etc.[179] Upon final

---

[170] Decision 14/2020/QD-TTg of the Prime Minister on Promulgation of Regulation on Coordination in Settlement of International Investment Disputes, 8 April 2020 ('Decision 14').
[171] *Ibid.*, Art. 5.1.
[172] *Ibid.*, Art. 6.
[173] *Ibid.*, Arts. 6.4–6.7.
[174] *Ibid.*, Art. 7.
[175] *Ibid.*, Art. 14.
[176] *Ibid.*, Art. 15.
[177] *Ibid.*, Art. 14.
[178] *Ibid.*, Arts. 14 and 16.
[179] *Ibid.*, Art. 28.3. See also Ministry of Finance, Circular 85/2018/TT-BTC, 3 September 2018 (providing guidelines for costs estimation, management, use and settlement of state budget for prevention and settlement of international investment disputes).

settlement of the dispute, the presiding authority, in cooperation with MOJ, is required to submit a report to the Prime Minister reviewing and assessing the resolution of the dispute.[180]

In addition to working on the development of processes for resolving and managing investment disputes, the government has also continued to work on dispute prevention. In 2018–2019, the government began a project with the World Bank, supported by the EU, to launch a pilot programme of the World Bank's so-called Systemic Investment Response Mechanism (SIRM).[181] As described by the World Bank, the SIRM is:

> an early warning and tracking mechanism to identify complaints and issues that arise from government conduct. It collects data and identifies patterns in the sources of government generated political risks affecting investments and quantifies investments that are retained, expanded, or lost as a consequence of addressing or not those political risks.[182]

While few details about the progress and implementation of the project are available, on the basis of what is known, the SIRM appears capable of complimenting the processes implemented by the Vietnamese government through Decision 14.

The establishment of mechanisms to coordinate Viet Nam's response to formal investment treaty claims and to address investor grievances short of formal claims evidences the Vietnamese government's continuing efforts to internalise its treaty obligations as a matter of policy priority. As noted above, however, significant gaps remain in informational and monitoring internalisation measures, especially as between the central and provincial levels of government, hindering the government's ability to prevent investor–state disputes in the first place.

9.10   Conclusion

Over the course of the last thirty years, Viet Nam has gradually accepted the international practice on promotion and protection of foreign investment and has become a contracting party to over eighty investment

---

[180] *Ibid.*, Art. 23.
[181] Nguyen Hung Quang, Roberto Echandi and Priyanka Kher, 'Systemic Investment Response Mechanism: Key Elements and Diagnostics for Vietnam', presented at 'Workshop on Preventing and Minimizing International Investor Grievances and Disputes', MPI and MOJ, Ho Chi Minh City (22 June 2018), https://vnlawfind.com.vn/wp-content/uploads/2019/10/Systemic-Investment-Response-Mechanism_NHQ_22Jun18_EN.pdf.
[182] World Bank Group, *Retention and Expansion of Foreign Direct Investment: Political Risk and Policy Responses* (2019), 43.

treaties. The Vietnamese government has also demonstrated its commitment to fulfilling its obligations under investment treaties by enacting a national investment framework in compliance with its investment treaty obligations.

In the past decade, Viet Nam has been subject to a rising number of investor claims and complaints. Many ISDS claims have arisen from the conduct of local governments. While the central government law-making process appears to be subject to a monitoring mechanism, there have been few informational and monitoring mechanisms targeting the local government where most of the relevant conduct is undertaken. More recently, however, Viet Nam has undertaken a number of initiatives designed to increase informational diffusion of investment treaty obligations and to establish processes for remedial internalisation, aimed at preventing and managing investment claims. Challenges remain, however, especially with respect to local government, but the evidence suggests continuing efforts in this regard.

Finally, there seems little evidence to support the claim that Viet Nam's investment treaty commitments have had a spillover effect on general rule of law conditions in the country. Although there has been much reform of the Vietnamese state since the adoption of the *Doi Moi* policy, the changes witnessed appear to have been driven by forces other than concerns about investment treaty commitments. As discussed, legislative reforms embodied in instruments like the Law on Complaints, the Law on Administrative Procedures, or any of their predecessors – laws which apply to foreign *and* domestic actors – seem to have been driven by concerns arising out of Viet Nam's commitments under its trade agreements and its participation in ASEAN. While it may be that there has been a spillover from these treaties, the evidence does not show such spillover effects from Viet Nam's investment treaties.

Assessing the Rule of Law Promise

The Impact of Investment Treaties on National Governance

N. JANSEN CALAMITA AND AYELET BERMAN

10.1 Introduction

The investment treaty regime rests on the premise that committing to investment treaties will bring about substantial economic and governance benefits for developing states. By providing special legal protections to foreign investors, it has been supposed that investment treaties will encourage foreign investment and promote economic growth. Moreover, proponents have suggested that, once states enter into these treaties, they will make improvements to their domestic governance in order to minimise the likelihood that they will face claims by foreign investors. These improvements of domestic governance – the logic goes – will ultimately have a positive spill-over effect with regards to governance and the rule of law in the state generally as new practices become embedded in the administration of government as a whole.[1]

This 'rule of law thesis' reflects what has been the prevailing academic and policy wisdom on investment treaties for decades. To date, however, most empirical research on the investment treaty regime has focused on assessing the impact of investment treaties and investment treaty claims on foreign investment flows. Empirical studies examining the impact of investment treaties on domestic governance have been few and far between. The purpose of this study therefore has been to contribute to developing a detailed empirical understanding of the impact of investment treaties on domestic governance in a select group of Asian states. In so doing, we have attempted also to develop a framework for analysing the internalisation of investment treaty commitments in government decision making more generally.

---

[1] See Chapter 1.

A number of assumptions underlie the rule of law thesis. The first assumption is that states make policy choices to seek to comply with their international treaty obligations. The second is that states internalise their treaty obligations, and that these obligations are taken into account in governmental decision making. The third is that taking steps to internalise investment treaty obligations ultimately will lead to improved governance practices becoming operationalised in the state's dealings with all addressees its legal system, not only foreign investors.

There are reasons to be sceptical of the rule of law thesis and its underlying assumptions about state behaviour. As laid out in Chapter 1, low regulatory capacity, disorganised bureaucracies, and fragmented governmental structures are common in many low- and middle-income countries, and these factors pose significant challenges to the state's ability to internalise its international legal obligations. These challenges have already been suggested by Mavluda Sattorova's empirical work in Central Asia, in which she observed anecdotally that government officials were often unaware their state's investment treaty obligations, and took decisions, admittedly, without taking the state's international legal obligations into account.

It is against this background that we have sought to understand in greater depth and in a systematic and academically rigorous way what role investment treaties have in governmental decision making across different states. In other words, are the state's investment treaty obligations taken into account, or 'internalised', within governmental decision-making processes? And if so, how?

The empirical investigation of our research question has consisted of eight detailed case studies of countries located in Asia. These case studies have served as a foundation for testing our analytical framework by examining whether and to what extent these governments take investment treaty obligations into account in their governmental decision-making processes, and whether such internalisation has had observable spillover effects on governance in the state more generally. They include three lower-middle income countries: India, Myanmar, and Sri Lanka; three upper-middle income countries: Indonesia, Thailand, and Viet Nam; and two high-income countries: Singapore and the Republic of Korea.[2] The case studies have been developed by locally based authors with knowledge of the languages, laws and government structures of the subject countries,

---

[2] Country income classifications are based upon the 2019 World Bank country income data.

and with an ability to gain access to government officials and other stake-holders for the purpose of developing evidence through interviews and other sources.

In this chapter, we present our analysis of the case studies against the analytical framework we set out in Chapter 1. Before proceeding, however, we recap briefly the main features of our analytical framework.

First, our analytical framework provides a typology of three main institutional processes of internalisation: 'informational', 'monitoring', and 'remedial'. *Informational processes* diffuse information and communicate the state's international legal obligations to relevant domestic actors. *Monitoring processes* refer to processes by which proposed polices or decisions are screened *ex ante* for consistency with international obligations. *Remedial processes* are designed to correct or defend the state's compliance with its international obligations in situations in which there is concern that investment obligations have not been met in the first instance.

Second, within the typology of measures that we have identified, we highlight four main cross-cutting characteristics of internalisation processes: (i) *specific* versus *adapted*: processes may have been designed specifically for investment treaty obligations or they may have been adapted for use with investment treaties from a different original purpose; (ii) *ad hoc* versus *consistent*: processes may be developed and used ad hoc or they may have a consistent and institutional character; (iii) *formal* versus *informal*: processes may be reflected through informal (non-binding) or formal (binding) rules, norms, and practices; and (iv) *principle* versus *practice*: processes may be established in principle but may not be followed in practice.

Third, we organise our thinking about the factors that may affect internalisation into three main categories: the *public administration context* (covering matters such as bureaucratic culture or regulatory capacity), the *national context* (covering matters such as politics or regime type), and the *international context* (covering matters such as investment claims and investment treaty conclusion).

Finally, we note again the limitations of our study. We recall that the focus of this project has been on decision making in the executive branch and its bureaucracy, as well as in the legislature. Decision making in the judiciary has not specifically been within its scope. Moreover, it has not been the purpose of this study to develop evidence to make general claims about the internalisation of investment treaty obligations in Asia writ large or more broadly. Rather, the more modest ambition of this study has been to address questions about the functioning of the investment treaty regime in eight specific Asian countries, examining whether and how these governments take investment treaty obligations into account in their decision making, and whether there are observable spillover effects of changes in general governance.

With these points in mind, we lay out our main findings.

10.2   Observable Evidence of Internalisation

The eight countries covered in the case studies have concluded significant numbers of BITs and/or other types of treaties, such as free trade agreements (FTAs), which include provisions on investment: from the Republic of Korea with 130 such treaties to Myanmar with 29. Moreover, with the exception of Singapore, all of the countries studied have faced publicly known claims under their investment treaties: from India with twenty-six known claims to Myanmar with one known claim. The numbers for each country at the time of writing are set out in Table 10.1.

Table 10.1 *Number of Investment Treaties and Known ISDS Claims in Case Study States*

Country	Number of treaties (BITs and treaties incl. investment provisions)[a]	Country	Number of known ISDS claims[b]
Republic of Korea	130	India	26
Indonesia	95	Viet Nam	14
Viet Nam	94	Republic of Korea	13
India	93	Indonesia	7
Singapore	92	Sri Lanka	5
Thailand	68	Thailand	2
Sri Lanka	35	Myanmar	1
Myanmar	29	Singapore	0

[a] Gross number of treaties signed in aggregate not accounting for entry into force or subsequent termination. Source: UNCTAD, Investment Policy Hub, International Investment Agreements Navigator, https://investmentpolicy.unctad.org/international-investment-agreements.

[b] UNCTAD, Investment Policy Hub, Investment Dispute Navigator, https://investmentpolicy.unctad.org/investment-dispute-settlement, supplemented by information provided in the case studies in this book.

On the assumptions of the rule of law theory, such widespread adoption of investment treaties and/or experience with investment treaty claims would be expected to bring about the internalisation of investment treaty obligations into government decision making and, even further, to lead to general improvements in governance throughout the state. The evidence provided by these case studies, however, suggests that the impact of investment treaties on governmental decision making has been minimal. The conclusion of investment treaties has led generally to little or no internalisation in the countries covered. Moreover, while experience with investor-state dispute settlement (ISDS) appears to have triggered at least some internalisation, even following ISDS the level of internalisation has remained generally low and largely limited to ad hoc, informal informational measures. We find in these case studies, therefore, as set out in detail below, no evidence to support the systemic claims of the rule of law theory.[3]

Below we set out our main findings, distinguishing between internalisation in the period after investment treaty adoption but prior to ISDS, and internalisation in the period after a host state has been subjected to an ISDS claim.

10.2.1   Internalisation after Treaty Adoption but Prior to ISDS

As outlined above, all the studied countries have concluded a significant number of investment treaties. The case studies of the low- and middle-income countries (Indonesia, India, Myanmar, Thailand, and Viet Nam), however, do not find significant evidence of the adoption or existence of informational, monitoring, or remedial internalisation processes following the conclusion of investment treaties (but prior to ISDS claims). Thus, internalisation processes appear to have been absent in executive and bureaucratic decision making as well as in legislative law making.

Knowledge pertaining to investment treaties appears to have remained centralised within the executive, in particular the ministries charged with negotiating investment treaties. Depending on the country, this would be

---

[3] It seems at least possible that the absence of internalisation processes led to governmental decision making which did not take investment treaty obligations into account and which, in turn, resulted in decisions that led to disputes, if not ISDS claims. Understanding whether the lack of internalisation measures actually contributed to a particular ISDS claim is beyond the scope of this project but is an interesting and important area for further research, and of practical relevance for the prevention of ISDS disputes.

typically the Ministry of Justice, Ministry of Foreign Affairs or Ministry of Industry or Trade. Notwithstanding the existence of knowledge about investment treaty commitments within these nodes of government, the case studies observe no mechanisms for the diffusion of that knowledge from the 'negotiating' ministry to other parts of government, or mechanisms for monitoring governmental decision making for consistency with the obligations containing within the state's investment treaties

In contrast to the low- and middle-income countries studied, in the high-income countries, the case studies reveal evidence of a greater degree of internalisation upon treaty conclusion but prior to ISDS. Thus, the government in Korea in 2010, in advance of the entry into force of the United States–Korea Free Trade Agreement, adopted a number of informational internalisation processes, such as creating the *Easy Understandable ISDS Guide* and establishing a nationwide training program administered by the Ministry of Justice.[4] In Singapore, the processes adopted for internalisation appear to have been even more robust, especially following Singapore's conclusion of its FTA with the United States in 2003. The Singapore case study describes a government in which informational and monitoring internalisation appears to be quite strong. In some respects, the measures are informal; it does not appear that formal, black letter procedures are spelled out. There is, however, a strong administrative culture of coordination and consultation within the government and it is in this context that information is shared, and decisions are reviewed. Moreover, the bureaucracy is highly skilled and cohesive, and there is a high-level political commitment to international law. These factors appear to combine to produce a high level of internalisation.[5]

Finally, Sri Lanka presents an interesting anomaly among the case studies. In contrast to Singapore and Korea which are high-income countries and where higher internalisation might be somewhat expected,[6] Sri Lanka is a lower-middle income country with low regulatory capacity and other bureaucratic and political challenges. Nevertheless, in contrast to the other low- and middle-income countries surveyed, Sri Lanka developed a monitoring mechanism prior to facing any ISDS claims. Under Art. 157

---

[4] See Chapter 4.
[5] The high level of internalisation of investment treaty commitments may explain why Singapore has not faced any known ISDS claims. As mentioned above, however, the question as to the relationship between internalisation and claims is beyond the scope of this project. See Chapter 6.
[6] See Chapter 1.

of the Sri Lanka Constitution, investment treaties are given direct and express force of law in Sri Lanka and may not be contravened by executive, administrative, or legislative act, except on grounds of national security. Because this is a constitutional guarantee, it falls within the scope of the general monitoring process in place to ensure that governmental acts are consistent with the constitution. Operationally, this means that the attorney general is charged with reviewing governmental acts to ensure that they are consistent with the constitution, including Art. 157 and Sri Lanka's investment treaty obligations.

Nevertheless, despite this monitoring mechanism, Sri Lanka has found itself several times in breach of its investment treaty obligations. As indicated in the case study, in these cases it appears that there was an awareness of Sri Lanka's investment treaty obligations in the decision-making process, but that domestic political considerations ultimately carried the day.[7] Sri Lanka, thus, provides an illustration of the distinction we noted in Chapter 1 between internalisation and compliance. While a country may have internalisation measures in place and take its international obligations into account in its decision making, in the 'battle of the norms' between those obligations and other interests, the government may ultimately prefer the latter over the former.

10.2.2 Internalisation after ISDS

Except for Singapore, all of the countries studied have faced publicly known claims under their investment treaties: from India with twenty-six known claims to Myanmar with one known claim. Looking across all of the case studies we find evidence that in middle- and high-income countries, ISDS claims have generated increased saliency as to the existence and risks of investment treaties within ministries and the legislature. For example, there is clear evidence of discussions within the legislature and in the executive concerning investment treaties in the Indian parliament in the aftermath of the 2011 *White Industries* award.[8] Similarly, in Korea there is evidence of a strong increase in the political salience of investment treaties in the National Assembly following the commencement of the *Lone Star* case.[9] Likewise, interviews carried out with government officials

---

[7] See Chapter 7.
[8] See Chapter 2.
[9] See Chapter 4.

in Indonesia and Thailand suggest that within the central government there has been a heightened awareness of investment treaty obligations since the *Churchill Mining*[10] and *Walter Bau*[11] cases, respectively. It warrants noting, however, that although these case studies found evidence of increased saliency at the level of the central government, for example, in government ministries and national legislatures, the saliency in regional or local governments appears to remain low.

The rule of law thesis predicts that such claims will not only increase general awareness but will actually trigger internalisation and an overhaul of domestic governance. In what follows below, we set out our main findings as to the informational, monitoring, and remedial mechanisms established by host states after being sued for investment treaty violations.

10.2.2.1   Informational Mechanisms

Our findings suggest that following ISDS claims, most countries have adopted *informational* measures to varying degrees. That is, they have adopted processes designed to diffuse information about the state's investment treaty commitments within government. For example, India's Ministry of External Affairs and Ministry of Finance,[12] Indonesia's Ministry of Foreign Affairs and Investment Coordinating Board (BKPM),[13] and Viet Nam's Ministry of Planning and Industry[14] all started running periodic training workshops for government officials. In Korea, the Ministry of Trade supports the Center for International Investment Arbitration which runs capacity-building events. Moreover, following its first ISDS claims, Korea revised its original handbook on investment obligations, adding a second handbook (*Easy Understandable ISDS Cases by Policy Type*), and devoting additional resources to its training program.[15] Viet Nam has done the same.[16] Most recently, Korea established a Dispute Response Team which is intended to issue guidelines to educate public officials and prevent investment disputes.

While these informational measures suggest some level of internalisation following ISDS claims, none of these informational measures

---

[10] See Chapter 3.
[11] See Chapter 8.
[12] Chapter 2.
[13] Chapter 3.
[14] Chapter 9.
[15] Chapter 4.
[16] Chapter 9.

effectuate consistent and formal or institutional reform. With the exception of Korea's Handbook and Dispute Response Team, these informational measures tend to be ad hoc, informal, and sporadically run.[17] Moreover, they tend to remain targeted at high-level government and rarely educate government officials in line ministries or regional governments, that is, the officials who make most of the decisions – such as cancelling licenses – which affect foreign investors.[18] Moreover, it bears noting that in most of the low- and middle-income countries, the financial resources for instituting these measures tend to be dependent on support from international organisations – such as UNCTAD, UNDP, the World Bank, donor states, or international law firms.[19]

10.2.2.2   Monitoring Mechanisms

Although ISDS appears to have heightened the saliency of investment treaties at the central government level in a number of case studies, we find little evidence that this has translated into the establishment of *monitoring* measures. While most countries have some kind of general monitoring mechanisms for reviewing the general legality of new laws (such as legal review by the Attorney General), we find little to no evidence that these have been applied to review for consistency with international investment obligations.

In India, for example, which has had five known ISDS cases, there appear to have been some efforts to establish monitoring mechanisms for reviewing government measures for consistency with international investment obligations. There was a government proposal to adopt a 'Centre State Investment Agreement' – which would have tried to overcome the coordination and information gap between central and regional governments as well as appointing an international law advisor to bolster institutional expertise. Political and bureaucratic objections, however, led to the shelving of the proposal and no such monitoring mechanism has been created.[20]

Exceptions are potentially found in Korea and Viet Nam.[21] In Korea, there is an anecdotal example of a proposed rule being reviewed under a

---

[17] Whether Viet Nam's handbook initiative will be consistently maintained is not yet clear. *Ibid.*
[18] The Korean and Vietnamese handbooks are an exception in this regard.
[19] Chapter 9; Chapter 3.
[20] Chapter 2.
[21] Chapter 4; Chapter 9.

general notice and comment procedure for consistency with the KORUS-FTA. More significantly, however, under the recently enacted Regulation on International Investment Dispute Prevention and Response, the Dispute Response Team has a duty to monitor whether governmental measures may give rise to potential investment treaty disputes, though it remains to be seen how this will function in practice. In Viet Nam, similar monitoring may take place as a result of the recently enacted Decision No. 14/2020/QD-TTg and through the Systemic Investment Response Mechanism pilot programme.

10.2.2.3   Remedial Mechanisms

Although ISDS has heightened the saliency of investment treaties at the central government level, the responses in terms of establishing remedial measures for preventing investment disputes have been mixed.

First, most of the countries surveyed remain without remedial measures for preventing international investment disputes. Second, some countries have attempted to establish remedial measures yet failed due to political or bureaucratic hurdles. For example, in Indonesia, following the *Cemex*, *al-Warraq*, and *Churchill Mining* cases, there was a government proposal to establish a lead agency to head a system for coordinating Indonesia's response to investor complaints to address, in part, the possibility of resolving those complaints short of arbitration, that is, a process of remedial internalisation.[22] However, political and bureaucratic objections led to the shelving of the proposal and no such process for internalisation was created.

Third, some of the case studies find evidence of remedial mechanisms which were not adopted in response to investment treaties but could, nevertheless, potentially have a role in investment treaty internalisation. Thus, there is evidence of mechanisms which were installed as part of other domestic administrative reforms, such as investment facilitation and promotion reforms. In our analytical framework, we considered that it might be possible that mechanisms or processes designed for one purpose could be 'adapted' for use in internalising investment treaty obligations. What is notable in these case studies, however, is that even though we find mechanisms which seem readily capable of helping to internalise investment treaty commitments, there is limited evidence that the states involved have begun to do this, that is, that they have begun to adapt these processes to investment treaty internalisation.

---

[22] Chapter 3.

For example, Korea and Myanmar have adopted measures to allow for the adjustment of investor complaints at an early stage. In Korea, it is the Foreign Investment Ombudsman, established under the Korea Trade-Investment Promotion Agency.[23] In Myanmar, it is the Myanmar Investment Grievance Mechanism.[24] Notably, these are not mechanisms that were adopted to internalise investment treaty obligations. Rather, they are mechanisms that were adopted as part of domestic investment facilitation reforms, that is, reforms designed to improve the transparency and efficiency of the domestic regulatory and legal investment framework. Moreover, although these are mechanisms through which investment treaties could possibly be considered (and thereby internalised), historically this has not been the case. Indeed, in the office of the Korea Ombudsman, for example, until recently there has been a distinct lack of knowledge about investment treaties. It is only within the last several years, following the spate of cases it has faced, that Korea has begun to consider how the Ombudsman might be connected to Korea's other internalisation efforts, namely the informational work of the Ministry of Justice.[25]

Finally, only two of the countries studied have established remedial measures for preventing investment treaty disputes: Viet Nam and Korea.

Viet Nam, having had fourteen known ISDS cases, appears to be an exception among the low- and middle-income countries studied. Over the past decade, Viet Nam has introduced a number of laws and policies that can be characterised as monitoring and remedial internalisation measures, for example, the 2011 Law of Complaints, the 2019 introduction of a Systemic Investment Response Mechanism, and new Ministry of Justice guidelines for settlement of investment disputes. These measures both monitor the alignment of govern decisions with investment treaty obligations and notably provide investors with dedicated tools to seek the adjustment of complaints and grievances before they rise to the level of a formal treaty claim. Notably, however, these remedial processes apply to decision making within the central government and have not been extended to regional or local governments (an issue we address later in this chapter).[26]

---

[23] Chapter 4.
[24] Chapter 5.
[25] Chapter 4.
[26] Chapter 9.

For its part, Korea has adopted the Regulation on International Investment Dispute Prevention and Response which establishes a standing International Investment Dispute Response Team and procedures which institutionalise and centralise the responsibility for the prevention of disputes. As noted, the relation between the Response Team and the Ombudsman remains to be explored.

10.2.2.4 'External' Investment Treaty Reforms

The rule of law theory assumes that in order to minimise the risk of investment treaty liability, states will undertake domestic regulatory adjustments. As we have seen above, however, this is simply not an observable process in most of the low- and middle-income countries studied. Indeed, rather than influencing countries to undertake 'internal' reforms and improve internalisation process at home, some countries have opted to focus on 'external' reforms to their investment treaty relations. In other words, rather than improving internalisation processes, they have opted to adjust their international obligations to reduce the risk of international claims for their conduct. Some have sought to renegotiate investment treaties to allow for more regulatory leeway, while others have sought to exit the system altogether.

Thailand's case provides an example whereby the political tensions caused by the *Walter Bau* case have not so much led to internalisation improvements but have led to changes in the Thai's government position in its investment treaty negotiations. Under this current approach, the government negotiates treaties which provide more regulatory autonomy to the host state, and it is also working on several initiatives for renegotiating and/or jointly reinterpreting existing treaties to provide greater protection to host states.

More extreme responses are illustrated by the Indian and Indonesian case studies. In both countries, we find a response to investment treaties for which the rule of law thesis seems not to account. Both states have faced a significant number of ISDS claims. India has faced twenty-five known claims and Indonesia has faced seven. Nevertheless, not only have India and Indonesia not adopted significant internalisation measures (as described above), but they have responded by either (i) terminating their investment treaties altogether; or (ii) renegotiating their treaties in a manner which attempts to reduce the scope of their obligations and, thereby – potentially – obviates the need for deep domestic government adjustments.

Thus, for example, following the *White Industries* case, India sought to conclude sweeping joint interpretative statements with the counterparties of twenty-five of its BITs, and in 2016 adopted a new model BIT, sharply narrowing the scope of coverage and protection afforded to foreign investors.[27] At the same time, India also issued notices of termination for nearly sixty other BITs. In Indonesia, similarly, the government announced in 2014 that it would terminate Indonesia's BIT with the Netherlands and further declared its intention to terminate its sixty-seven other BITs. At the same time, Indonesia finalised a new model BIT also sharply narrowing the scope of coverage and protection afforded to foreign investors.[28] This followed the government's 2012 Presidential Decree which sought to limit the jurisdiction of investor–state arbitral tribunals. Notably, having declared its intention to withdraw from existing bilateral commitments in 2014, Indonesia entered into a new BIT with Singapore in 2018 and an FTA (with an investment chapter) with Australia in 2019.[29]

10.3 Explaining Levels of Internalisation

The rule of law theory assumes that investment treaties will bring about reforms in state governance by virtue of the disciplines they impose upon the regulatory process in host states. Yet as our findings suggest, notwithstanding extensive state experience with investment treaty making and growing experience with ISDS, most of the low- and middle-income countries in our study have not significantly internalised their investment treaties. In this respect, Viet Nam represents an exception with regards to the systemic way in which it has approached internalisation, particularly after ISDS. Sri Lanka likewise represents something of an anomaly with its unique constitutionalising of investment treaty commitments, although, as that case study shows, the constitutionally elevated position of investment treaties seems more honoured in the breach than in practice.[30] At the same time, the evidence suggests that in the higher income countries in our study – Singapore and Korea – there has been more extensive internalisation both before and, in the case of Korea, after ISDS.[31]

What then explains these varying levels of internalisation across the states covered in this study? Is it possible to hypothesise the cause(s) of the

---

[27] Chapter 2.
[28] Chapter 3.
[29] *Ibid.*
[30] Chapter 7.
[31] Chapter 4; Chapter 6.

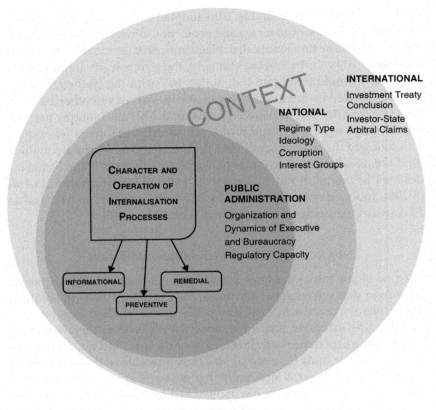

Figure 10.1   Model of factors impacting internalisation

low levels of internalisation found in most of the low- and middle-income countries? Conversely, is it possible to explain the relatively high degree of internalisation found in some of the cases and not others?

In Chapter 1, building upon a diverse literature in public policy, law and development and international relations, we theorised that there would be general categories of factors at three different levels which might impact internalisation: *international* (e.g., ISDS claims, treaty conclusion), *national* (e.g., regime type, interest groups) and *public administration* (e.g., bureaucratic organisation, capacity, and resources). Figure 10.1 illustrates this framework.

Out of the eight case studies contained in this volume, we identify eight factors which appear to have significantly impacted internalisation.

Notably, they are found at all levels of our framework. On the international level, the presence of ISDS claims appears to be of singular importance for triggering attempts to develop at least some internalisation processes within government. Also, on the international level, while we do not find that the conclusion of investment treaties has generally led to the development of internalisation measures, we do note evidence suggesting that FTAs concluded with certain states – particularly the United States – may have a greater internalisation impact, at least in high-income states.

On the national level, we find evidence that levels, and perhaps kinds, of internalisation, can be affected by the structure of government. Decentralisation of decision-making authority can have a significant impact on internalisation, whether the decentralisation is from the central government to the regional and local levels or within the central government to line ministries and statutory bodies. Also, on the national level, the case studies present evidence of the effect of politics and interest groups on internalisation.

Lastly, on the level of the public administration, we observe evidence of the impact of bureaucratic organisation on internalisation, for example, through the loss of institutional knowledge as the result of policies requiring the rotation of officials with specialist knowledge of investment treaties. Moreover, within the public administration we see evidence of the impact of regulatory capacity and resources on both increased and decreased levels of internalisation. We address these factors more fully below.[32]

10.4   International Level

10.4.1   ISDS Claims

As noted above, the most important observable indicator of the likelihood of internalisation measures being adopted (at least to some degree) in these case studies is the presence of ISDS claims against the state. Whereas the evidence suggests that the simple conclusion of investment treaties has led generally to little or no internalisation, ISDS has increased awareness

---

[32] It is important to note that we address here only those factors which been observed in these case studies. We do not exclude the possibility that other factors, which have been unobserved, may have played a role as well. Moreover, we do not exclude the possibility that examinations of different states might reveal different factors affecting internalisation, although we believe that our broad framework with its typology and categorisation should be generally applicable.

of investment treaties within the central governments of all of the countries surveyed. At the same time, however, while ISDS claims appear to have triggered at least some efforts towards internalisation in most of the states under study, such internalisation has not been deep or substantive. The internalisation measures observed have been organisationally ad hoc, sporadically implemented, and largely limited to informational measures such as running periodic workshops. Thus, following ISDS claims, the low- and middle-income countries in this study – with the exception of Viet Nam – appear not to have adopted monitoring or remedial internalisation processes, although, again, there is evidence of the ad hoc adoption of informational measures. With respect to Korea – the only high-income state in the study to have faced ISDS claims – the evidence shows the establishment of informational internalisation processes prior to ISDS, and a revision of those measures, together with the development and adaptation of the Ombudsman remedial process and Dispute Response Team, following Korea's receipt of its first and consequent ISDS claims.

10.4.2   *The Identity of the Counterparty to the International Agreement*

The identity of the party with which an international agreement is concluded may also play a role in the internalisation of investment treaties. The case studies of the two high-income, high-capacity states, Korea and Singapore, provide examples. In Korea's case, the negotiation of the United States–Korea FTA in 2006–2007, and the subsequent process of its ratification (2007–2011), generated widespread public debate and brought about significant public consultations in a way in which Korea's previous FTA negotiations had not.[33] These debates and consultations appear to have heightened awareness within the National Assembly and within government more broadly. Indeed, it appears that it was as a consequence of the conclusion of the United States–Korea FTA that the Korean Ministry of Justice undertook its first informational internalisation measures – the development of a handbook for government officials and programmes of training.[34]

The Singapore case study similarly suggests that the negotiation and conclusion of the United States–Singapore FTA from 2000 to 2003 may

---

[33] See, for example, Chile–Korea FTA (2003), Singapore–Korea FTA (2005), India–Korea CEPA (2009), EU–Korea FTA (2010), and Peru–Korea FTA (2011).
[34] Chapter 4.

also have had a triggering effect on internalisation with respect to investment treaty obligations. Although Singapore had already signed three FTAs with investment chapters by the time it entered into the FTA with the United States,[35] the US FTA was seen as a 'game changer' within the Singaporean government due to its complexity and the size of the US economy.[36] Not only was Singapore required to make numerous changes to its law as a result of the FTA's substantive chapters, for example, intellectual property, competition, etc., the Singaporean government also recognised the need to take steps to internalise the commitments of the investment treaty chapter. This appears to have been less to do with the content of the investment chapter's commitments – in many respects the investment chapter reflected commitments that Singapore had undertaken in its prior investment treaties – and more to do with the fact that the counterparty was the United States.

10.5   National Level

10.5.1   Central Government Fragmentation

Public international law rests upon a fiction that states function as unitary entities. Thus, the state is responsible for the acts of all its organs, in all its branches, across all its levels. At the central government level, this entails treating the different ministries, agencies, and departments of central government as unitary, coordinated entities. Yet, as public policy and the development literature reveal, and as the findings of these case studies support, state decision making is complex and often uncoordinated or, at least, it may be coordinated in ways which do not present themselves upon a superficial examination.

All of the case studies in this volume indicate that institutional knowledge about investment treaties is centralised in specialised nodes within central government, usually the ministry in charge of negotiating investment treaties for the state and, perhaps, the ministry charged with representing the state in ISDS, if one has been designated. Thus, in all of the case studies there is evidence that the ministries in charge of negotiating investment treaties function as nodes of institutional knowledge

---

[35] New Zealand–Singapore EPA (2000), Japan–Singapore EPA (2002), and Australia–Singapore FTA (2003).
[36] Chapter 6.

about the state's investment treaty commitments, for example, the Indian Ministry of Finance, the Indonesian Ministry of Foreign Affairs and the National Investment Coordination Board (BKMP), the Singaporean Ministry of Trade and Industry, etc. Likewise, in the case studies in which the state has appointed a lead ministry to handle the defence of the state in ISDS, the evidence shows that the ministries charged with defending the state similarly represent nodes of specialised knowledge about the state's treaty obligations, for example, the Korean Ministry of Justice, the Singaporean Attorney General's Chambers.

The internalisation challenge which states face, however, is the effective diffusion of this specialised knowledge to government actors outside of these specialised nodes. In the alternative, as we have suggested in our introductory framework, governments might seek to address the lack of diffusion through the establishment of processes for the monitoring or remediation of decision making to assess its adherence to the state's international obligations. The case studies here bear out this identified challenge, reflecting a general disconnect between those specialised nodes of central government which negotiate the state's treaties and defend its interests and the other parts of the government – line ministries, statutory boards – which are often in direct contact with investors and are charged with carrying out the day-to-day business of government.

As noted, many of the states studied do appear to have adopted informational measures (mostly occasional and ad hoc) addressed, *inter alia*, to central government line ministries. Some, like Viet Nam and Korea, have adopted monitoring or remedial internalisation processes as well. Singapore stands as a true outlier in the group: internalisation across government is high, largely because of the informal – yet reliable and persistent – coordination and communication among the different ministries, including its specialised nodes.[37] For the others, however, there is scant evidence of internalisation mechanisms designed to coordinate among the central government units or informal practices which serve this function. Given the relative size of these governments compared to the government of Singapore, the relatively limited resources at their disposal (compared, for example, to the government of Korea), and their limitations of regulatory capacity (compared, for example, to the government of Viet Nam), these findings do not appear to us surprising. From them, we venture to suggest that the greater the fragmentation and complexity

[37] Chapter 6.

of central government decision making the greater the challenges that are posed to the internalisation of investment treaty commitments.

10.5.2 Decentralised National, State, and Local Governance

The case studies further suggest that decentralised national, regional, and local governance may add a further level of complexity and challenge to internalisation. Two of the states studied in this volume are federal states: India and Indonesia. Both case studies reveal the difficulties that shared decision-making competence between federal and state authorities have presented with respect to the internalisation of investment treaty obligations. Absent formal communication and coordination channels between central and regional governments, decentralised decision making creates the risk that officials at the regional or local level will take decisions without taking the state's international obligations into account. In Indonesia, for example, provincial governments remain unaware of Indonesia's investment treaty obligations, and there are no remedial or monitoring processes in place that would address provincial decisions. This internal coordination weakness can create problems which lead to disputes, as reflected in the ISDS claims Indonesia has faced involving the issuance of conflicting mining licenses.[38] In India, attempts to bridge this gap by enacting the Centre State Investment Agreement have failed.[39]

In other case studies, we see states recognising the challenges posed by local actors taking decisions or making representations without approval or formal review from central authorities. Thus, in Viet Nam, which is a unitary state, notwithstanding the internalisation processes which have been adopted, there remains a problem with local authorities acting on their own to enter into memoranda of understanding (MOUs) with investors. These MOUs do not appear to be subject to a consistent process of review or notification, thus reflecting a gap in informational and monitoring internalisation.[40]

Singapore, again, represents an outlier among the countries in the case studies. Singapore is a small, unitary state and both its size and its lack of decentralisation appear to have been conducive to the internalisation of investment treaty commitments in government decision making. With a unitary government and unicameral, parliamentary system

[38] Chapter 3.
[39] Chapter 2.
[40] Chapter 9.

of government (discussed further below), decision making is highly centralised, thus facilitating informational, monitoring, and remedial internalisation processes.[41]

10.5.3   The Role of the Legislature

Although our preliminary analytical framework had not identified legislative involvement in the adoption of investment treaties as a factor impacting upon internalisation, the findings from the case studies suggest that the legislature's exclusion from the BIT adoption process – a characteristic found in all of the case studies – may negatively affect internalisation.

There is a commonality across the case studies whereby the legislature is disconnected from the investment treaty adoption process at two critical stages. First, in all of the countries surveyed, BITs are adopted by the executive and need not be ratified by the legislature. Second, as BITs do not generally contain obligations requiring positive legislative action, they have not required or been subject to transposition into the domestic law of any of the surveyed countries. As a result, most of the BIT obligations of the states studied here appear to have essentially come into force 'under the radar' of the legislature. This is in contrast to FTAs which, in all of the case studies, are characterised by heavy legislative involvement, at both the ratification and domestic law transposition stages.[42]

The consequences of legislative exclusion emerges, for example, in the India case study, where the Indian Parliament had essentially never addressed investment treaties before the first ISDS case was brought against India.[43] Because India's investment treaties had been concluded in the form of BITs, India's constitution had not required parliamentary involvement. Once India began receiving claims, however, and especially following its loss in *White Industries*, the Indian Parliament became actively involved and the political salience of investment treaties rose. This in turn appears to have led directly to India's decision to change its law regarding commercial arbitration so as to address the matter at issue in the *White Industries* case, as well as contributing towards India's revision

---

[41] Chapter 6.
[42] Like BITs, the investment chapters of FTA do not generally require transposition into domestic law. It is the other chapters of FTAs that generally necessitate legislative enactments.
[43] Chapter 2.

of its model BIT to limit the scope of its international obligations; its issuance of notices of termination for nearly sixty BITs; and its invitations to
the counterparties of twenty-five of its BITs to conclude sweeping joint
interpretative statements of the commitments thereunder.[44]

10.5.4   Political Commitment to International Law

In Chapter 1, we noted the possibility that regime type and characteristics
may impact the way in which a state internalises its international treaty
obligations. Drawing on literature looking at compliance with international law, we noted the possibility that regimes with fewer veto players
might see less internalisation as there may be fewer institutional checks
and balances already present within the system.[45] Similarly, we also
observed that ideology may be a factor affecting internalisation, given
research suggesting that the ideology of certain governments correlates
with compliance with investment treaty obligations.[46]

Based on the case studies, we find some examples in which the political system and the government's ideology appear to have influenced its
approach to international law, and, consequently, the extent of the government's efforts to internalise the state's investment treaty obligations.
For example, during Indonesia's military regime, there appears to have
been weakening of concern with compliance with international legal
obligations.[47] In Myanmar too, the military regime – whose actions were
responsible for the only ISDS claim against Myanmar to date – had not
been subject to oversight.[48] Further, even being no longer under military regime, nationalistic sentiments in Indonesia have proved a powerful force in the 'battle of norms' as compared to international investment
obligations.[49] In Sri Lanka too, political considerations appear to have
consistently trumped international treaty considerations.[50]

---

[44] *Ibid.*
[45] See Chapter 1.
[46] See, for example, Abram Chayes, Antonia Chayes and Ronald B. Mitchell, 'Managing
Compliance: A Comparative Perspective', in Edith Brown-Weiss and Harold Jacobson
(eds.), *Engaging Countries: Strengthening Compliance with International Environmental
Accords* (MIT Press, 1998) 39–62; Quan Li, 'Democracy, Autocracy, and Expropriation of
Foreign Direct Investment' (2009) 42 *Comparative Political Studies* 1098.
[47] Chapter 3.
[48] Chapter 5.
[49] Chapter 3.
[50] Chapter 7.

In contrast, Singapore's strong commitment to the international rule of law helps to explain why internalisation has been so robust within Singapore. Being a small country with limited physical power, promoting the international rule of law has been a central component of Singapore's foreign policy strategy.[51] Government decisions are, therefore, reviewed for consistency with international legal obligations as a matter of course.

Sri Lanka is also unique in the development of its legal approach to investment treaties, which as mentioned above are protected under Art. 157 of the Constitution, conferring supremacy over conflicting national laws or regulations. After its devastating civil war, Sri Lanka became focused on liberalising its economy and improving its international reputation as a safe place to invest. In that context, decision makers concluded that a constitutional guarantee of foreign investor rights was the strongest possible signal it could give,[52] explaining the relative anomaly of the constitutional protection of investment treaties.

10.6   Public Administration Level

10.6.1   Bureaucratic Organisation and Culture

Finally, we note two conditions with respect to the public administration that appear to influence internalisation in a number of case studies. The first concerns the organisation of the bureaucracy and the second is regulatory capacity.

Aspects of the dynamics of organisational and inter-organisational processes have already been noted above in connection with central government fragmentation and the difficulty of coordinating action and decision making across government. Similar dynamics have also been addressed in connection with the decentralisation of decision making found in federal systems and in circumstances in which local authorities undertake decision making outside of the oversight of agencies with specialised knowledge of investment treaty obligations. Here, however, we draw attention to a more granular aspect of bureaucratic organisation which appears to affect internalisation: personnel policy.

---

[51] Chapter 6.

[52] Chapter 7. See Dilini Pathirana, 'An Overview of Sri Lanka's Bilateral Investment Treaties: Status Quo and Some Insights into Future Modifications' (2017) 7 *Asian Journal of International Law* 287.

In many of the states in our study, such as India, Indonesia, Korea, and Myanmar, we see that officials who work within one of the nodes of specialised investment treaty expertise do so only for a limited period of time before they are rotated to other positions within the bureaucracy.[53] Moreover, the positions to which they are rotated appear not to bear any relation to their former work on investment treaties, nor to leverage that specialised knowledge in a new context. Rather, simply in accordance with general government personnel policy, officials working both on investment treaty negotiations as well as ISDS defence are apt to find themselves removed from those positions after a set period of time and reassigned to work on some other matter altogether.

In principle, the rotation of government bureaucrats is designed to produce well-rounded officials with an appreciation of a range of subjects. The risk of such a system, however, is that rotation undermines the development of institutional knowledge and continuity. While the rotation of officials could theoretically act to diffuse knowledge about investment treaty commitments informally throughout government as those officials are transferred to different posts, in practice this does not seem to occur. As noted, the reassignment of officials seems to take place without consideration of any possible diffusion-value of the new appointment. Rather, the evidence suggests that the reassignments simply result in a loss of institutional expertise, which requires the bureaucracy to make a new 'investment' to develop expertise in new personnel, until they too are reassigned.

10.6.2   Resource and Regulatory Capacity

As noted in Chapter 1, the importance of regulatory capacity to implement and comply with international treaties is widely recognised in the public policy literature, as well as the international legal literature. The public administrations in developing countries in particular often lack scientific, technical, financial, and other capacities, which in turn can impact their ability to effectively internalise the state's international obligations.[54]

---

[53] Chapters 2, 3, 4, and 5.
[54] See, for example, Beth A Simmons, 'Treaty Compliance and Violation' (2010) 13 *Annual Review of Political Science* 273, 286; Wade M. Cole, 'Mind the Gap: State Capacity and the Implementation of Human Rights Treaties' (2015) 69 *International Organisation* 405, 405–6.

Moreover, we noted research by Williams, finding a positive link between regulatory capacity and investment disputes, where the lower the income level (taken as a proxy for low state capacity), the higher the likelihood for disputes.[55]

The case studies in this volume demonstrate that resource and capacity constraints add an additional level of complexity and challenge for internalisation in all the low- and middle-income countries surveyed. In India, perhaps most clearly, a lack of capacity in the bureaucracy and the judicial system resulted in the systemic judicial delays which led to the *White Industries* case.[56] In Myanmar, an absence of technical expertise and resources, and a chaotic, overstretched and uncoordinated bureaucracy, serve as an ongoing obstacle to internalisation.[57] Similarly, in Indonesia and Viet Nam, efforts to institute informational internalisation measures through workshops and the training of government officials have been curtailed by an absence of sufficient resources, leaving those countries to rely upon support from international donors and organisations.[58] In contrast, the high-income states examined do not face such constraints. Singapore has been able to build a financially robust and highly skilled public administration which has been crucial for its deep internalisation of its treaty obligations.[59] Likewise, in Korea, although there are gaps in the internalisation of its investment treaty commitments, Korea has been able to dedicate considerable resources within a professional bureaucracy to conduct an institutionalised, nationwide programme of informational internalisation and to produce numerous editions of high-quality training materials.[60]

In sum, the evidence suggests that resource and regulatory capacity limitations play a real role in making all types of internalisation more difficult for the developing states in this study. At the same time, however, the evidence also suggests that the presence of resources is not a guarantee of internalisation. As discussed above, a wide variety of factors appear at play in these case studies and we would be hesitant to identify any one of them as indispensable for internalisation.

---

[55] Zoe P. Williams, 'Risky Business or Risky Politics: What Explains Investor State Disputes?', unpublished dissertation, Hertie School of Governance (2016).

[56] Chapter 2.

[57] Chapter 5.

[58] Chapter 3; Chapter 9.

[59] Chapter 6.

[60] Chapter 4.

10.7 Rule of Law Spill Over?

In Chapter 1, we noted that the rule of law thesis posits that the internalisation of obligations owed to foreign investors will lead to improvements in domestic administrative practices more generally, that is, that improvements to the rule of law will be felt by all within the host state, not only covered foreign investors.[61] Now, with the benefit of detailed case studies looking at internalisation in eight different countries in Asia, we return to this proposition to ask whether there is evidence that investment treaties or investment treaty arbitration has brought about these spill-over effects.

Our approach to assessing the presence of spill-over effects is largely inferential. We proceed from the position that for investment treaties to improve governmental administration, the obligations contained within them must be internalised into the decision-making processes of government. Axiomatically, investment treaties cannot serve as the trigger for changes in governance unless those treaties are taken into account in the government's decision making. Internalisation is thus a prerequisite for any 'rule of law' spill-over effects. That said, however, internalisation by itself is not sufficient to ensure that there will be a broad governance spill-over. As discussed in Chapter 1, it is entirely possible for a state to adopt internalisation measures that remain limited to the treatment of foreign investors and, therefore, have no evident effect on governance within the state generally.

As discussed above, and as detailed in the case studies, we have found little evidence in most of the low- and middle-income countries surveyed, that investment treaties and/or ISDS have brought about sustained or systemic internalisation of investment treaty disciplines. Rather, the evidence from the case studies suggests that in general the conclusion of investment treaties has led to little or no internalisation, while ISDS seems at most to have triggered some ad hoc, sporadically implemented informational measures of internalisation. Thus, as noted, even following ISDS claims, the low- and middle-income countries in this study – with the exception of Viet Nam – have not adopted the monitoring or remedial internalisation processes that would seem most likely to bring about changes in governance that have a general application to all of the addressees of the state's legal system, and not just foreign investors. Given the limited evidence of internalisation that we find in these case studies, we conclude

[61] See Chapter 1.

that there is insufficient evidence to support the central predicate of the rule of law theory's spill-over claim.

We do not, however, go so far as to say that there is no evidence that investment treaty disciplines – as enforced through ISDS – have triggered governance reforms in discrete cases. Our observations suggest, however, that rather than (as the rule of law theory would predict) strengthening the governance system for the addressees of the state's legal system as a whole, these reforms have been limited to creating private dispute settlement systems for investors and otherwise facilitating investment transactions. It appears, therefore, that rather than strengthening domestic courts, the existence of investment treaties has prompted the establishment of substitute dispute settlement mechanisms.

For example, the *White Industries* case played an important role in triggering a change in India's arbitration and conciliation law. Aiming to ensure that arbitration involving foreign parties would be dealt with expeditiously going forward, the Indian Parliament amended the 1996 Arbitration and Conciliation Act in 2015 with the aim of reducing judicial intervention in arbitration, thereby avoiding delays in the process.[62] Although the amendment was driven by India's ISDS experience and the desire to avoid similar claims in the future, the change was one of general application and benefit to arbitration users throughout India. Similarly, in Myanmar, investment treaties indirectly influenced the decision to adopt an Investor Assistance Committee and Investor Grievance Mechanism.[63] Again, although these mechanisms appear to have been driven by concerns about Myanmar's investment treaty commitments, the mechanisms are available to both foreign and domestic investors. Lastly, in Indonesia, following the *Churchill Mining* case, changes were made to the process for issuing mining licenses, whereby regional governments were stripped of their authority in order to centralise licensing with the government in Jakarta.[64] As in India and Myanmar, although this change was triggered by Indonesia's investment treaty obligations, the change itself was general, applicable to all mining licensees, foreign and domestic. These examples represent the most visible and direct impacts found in the case studies of investment treaty commitments or ISDS on domestic governance.

[62] Chapter 2.
[63] Chapter 5.
[64] Chapter 3.

10.8 Conclusion

The common assumption underlying the rule of law theory is that in order to avoid international investment claims, governments will consider their state's international investment treaty obligations. The purpose of this study has been to carry out an empirical investigation into this assumption. To this end we have carried out, with our partners, qualitative case studies of eight lower-middle, upper-middle and high-income countries in Asia.

The findings of our study suggest that the simple conclusion of investment treaties has not triggered the adoption of informational, monitoring, or remedial measures in low- and middle-income countries. Thus, internalisation processes appear absent in executive and bureaucratic decision making as well as in legislative law making. Notwithstanding the existence of knowledge about investment treaty commitments within specialised nodes of government, the case studies observe no mechanisms for the diffusion of that knowledge to other parts of government, or mechanisms for monitoring governmental decision making for consistency with the obligations containing within the state's investment treaties.

In contrast to the low- and middle-income countries studied, in the high-income countries, the case studies reveal evidence of a greater degree of internalisation upon treaty conclusion but prior to ISDS. In both Singapore and Korea there is evidence of the development of varying internalisation processes upon conclusion of FTAs with the United States (and prior to any ISDS). For Korea, these processes appear to have been limited to informational internalisation processes, while in Singapore the processes adopted for internalisation appear to have been more robust, including both informational and monitoring processes. As noted, Sri Lanka presents an interesting anomaly with respect to its constitutional internalisation of investment treaty commitments, although despite this monitoring mechanism, Sri Lanka has found itself several times in breach of its investment treaty obligations.

Further, although the rule of law theory predicts that ISDS claims will trigger internalisation and an overhaul of domestic governance, the evidence from the case studies suggests that the effect of ISDS claims on internalisation has not nearly been so striking. Our findings suggest that while ISDS may increase saliency as to the existence and risks of investment treaties within central government ministries and the legislature, the dearth of internalisation processes in low- and middle-income countries has remained persistent. Most notably, we find little evidence of *monitoring* or *remedial* measures, with the exception of Viet Nam, which has introduced a number of laws and policies that can be characterised as monitoring and remedial internalisation measures, and Korea, which has adopted a new framework for investment dispute prevention and has begun to consider how existing processes can be adapted to promote the internalisation of investment commitments.

Even though most of the states considered in this study have not adopted monitoring or remedial processes following ISDS, it appears that most countries have adopted *informational* measures. That is, they have adopted processes designed to diffuse information about the state's investment treaty commitments within government. While these informational measures suggest some level of internalisation following ISDS claims, one would be hard pressed to consider this a significant change as none of these informational measures effectuate consistent and formal or institutional reform. Except for Korea, and, possibly, Viet Nam, these informational measures tend to be ad hoc, informal and sporadically run, often dependent on support from international organisations.

A further aspect of the complexity of real-world state responses to investment treaties and ISDS is suggested by the Indian and Indonesian case studies. In both countries, we find a response to investment treaties for which the rule of law thesis seems not to account. Both states have faced a significant number of ISDS claims, yet neither have adopted significant internalisation measures. Rather than working on 'internal' reform, they have responded by seeking 'external' reform that would reduce their risk of liability under the international investment regime. They have been either terminating their investment treaties altogether or renegotiating their treaties in a manner which significantly reduces the scope of their obligations and, thereby – potentially – obviates the need for deep domestic government adjustments. Thailand, likewise, has given its focus to negotiating or jointly reinterpreting existing treaties in a manner that would increase host state autonomy and reduce potential exposure to liability.

What explains these varying levels of internalisation across the states covered in this study? In Chapter 1, we theorised that there would be factors at three different levels which might impact internalisation: *international* (e.g., ISDS claims, treaty conclusion), *national* (e.g., regime type, interest groups), and *public administration* (e.g., bureaucratic organisation, capacity and resources). Through the case studies we have identified eight main factors across these three levels which appear to have affected internalisation.

10.8.1   *International Level*

First, as noted above, the most important observable factor affecting the likelihood of internalisation in these case studies is the presence of ISDS claims against the state. Whereas the evidence suggests that the simple conclusion of investment treaties has led generally to little or no internalisation, ISDS appears to have triggered at least some efforts towards internalisation in the states under study. That said, we conclude that the observable internalisation in these case studies has generally not been deep. Instead, it has generally been organisationally ad hoc, sporadically implemented, and largely limited to informational measures.

Second, the identity of the country with which an international agreement has been concluded may also play a role in heightening attention to commitments prior to ISDS. In the case studies of the two high-income countries included in this book, Korea and Singapore, there is evidence that FTA negotiations with the United States in particular acted as a catalyst for the development of informational internalisation measures.

10.8.2   National Level

Third, in all of the countries studied, fragmentation within the central government has proved to be a serious challenge. (Singapore is the exception.). There often appears to be an institutional and informational disconnect between those specialised nodes of central government which negotiate the state's treaties and defend its interests and the other parts of the government – line ministries, statutory boards – that are often in direct contact with investors and are charged with carrying out the day-to-day business of government.

Fourth, decentralised national, regional, and local governance adds a further level of complexity and challenge to internalisation. In federal states like India and Indonesia, we observe that the lack of communication and coordination channels between central and regional governments and decentralised decision making creates the risk that officials at the regional or local level will take decisions without taking the state's international obligations into account. Similarly, in other case studies involving non-federal states, such as Viet Nam, there is evidence of the challenges posed by local actors taking decisions or making representations without approval or formal review from central authorities.

Fifth, the case studies suggest that the inclusion or exclusion of the legislature from domestic treaty ratification may have an impact on internalisation. In all the countries surveyed, whereas BITs are adopted by the executive and need not be ratified by the legislature, FTAs, including FTAs which include investment provisions, require legislative approval. As a result, most of the investment treaty obligations of the states studied here have essentially come into force 'under the radar' of parliament. One consequence of this seems to be that investment treaty commitments have generally lacked salience within the legislature until the state has faced a high-profile claim (although a high profile claim is not a guarantee of political salience or legislative attention).

Sixth, national politics are often in conflict with international obligations, and whether or the extent to which governments consider international law depends on political attitudes towards international law. Thus, the case studies show examples in which political attitudes towards international law have affected the extent of the government's efforts, if at all, to internalise the state's investment treaty obligations. In Sri Lanka, for example, political attitudes towards international law appear to have affected its development of a process of monitoring internalisation, while domestic political considerations have consistently trumped consideration of investment treaty commitments. While in Indonesia and India, nationalistic sentiments appear to have led to decisions to avoid investment treaty commitments altogether through a rejection of those commitments. Finally, in contrast, a strong political commitment to the international rule of law helps to explain the robustness of internalisation within Singapore.

10.8.3 Public Administration Level

Seventh, the organisation of the bureaucracy plays a role in internalisation. Bureaucratic fragmentation and the difficulty of coordinating action and decision making across government emerge in almost all the case studies. In some cases, this is evident within central government. In other cases, it may also be a by-product of decentralised decision making in federal systems. Further, it may also arise in circumstances in which local authorities make decisions outside of the oversight of agencies with specialised knowledge of investment treaty obligations.

Bureaucratic organisation also affects internalisation on a more granular level, namely at the level of personnel policy. Many of the case studies reveal policies by which officials who work within one of the nodes of specialised investment treaty expertise do so only for a limited period of time before they are rotated to other positions within the bureaucracy. While the rotation of officials could theoretically act to diffuse knowledge about investment treaties informally throughout government, in practice this does not seem to occur. Rather, the evidence suggests that the reassignments simply result in a loss of institutional expertise.

Eighth, and lastly, the case studies confirm the importance of regulatory capacity to the effective internalisation of the state's international obligations. The case studies demonstrate that resource and capacity constraints add an additional level of complexity and challenge for internalisation in all the low- and middle-income countries surveyed. At the same time, however, the evidence also suggests that the presence of resources is not a guarantee of internalisation.

Our study set out to examine the claim that the internalisation of obligations owed to foreign investors will lead to improvements in domestic administrative practices that will be felt by all within the host state, not only covered foreign investors – 'rule of law spill-over'. We have attempted to do so inferentially, proceeding from the position that in order for investment treaties to improve governmental administration, the obligations contained within them must be internalised into the decision-making processes of government. In other words, internalisation is a prerequisite for any 'rule of law' spill-over effects; investment treaties cannot serve as the trigger for changes in governance unless those treaties are taken into account in the government's decision making.

On the basis of the case studies contained in this volume, we have found little evidence in most of the low- and middle-income countries surveyed, that investment treaties and/or ISDS have brought about sustained or systemic internalisation of investment treaty disciplines. Rather, the evidence from the case studies suggests that in general the conclusion of investment treaties has led to little or no internalisation, while ISDS seems at most to have triggered some ad hoc, sporadically implemented informational measures of internalisation. Given the limited evidence of internalisation that we find in these case studies, we conclude that there is insufficient evidence to support the central predicate of the rule of law theory's spill-over claim.[65]

Finally, our study has focused on eight Asian countries, and our conclusions are limited to the observations made in these countries. Nevertheless, given that the underlying factors which we have identified as presenting challenges to internalisation tend to be shared by many low- or middle-income countries as well as some high-income countries, we venture to suggest that there is good reason to suspect that there has been limited internalisation of investment treaties in other countries not covered by this study.

---

[65] As noted above, we do not go so far as to say that there is no evidence that investment treaty disciplines – as enforced through ISDS – have triggered governance reforms in discrete cases. Our observations suggest, however, that rather than (as the rule of law theory predicts) strengthening the governance system for the addressees of the state's legal system as a whole, these reforms have been limited to creating private dispute settlement systems for investors and otherwise facilitating investment transactions.

Printed by Printforce, United Kingdom